Empowerment State, Governance and Beyond

EMPOWERMENT STATE, GOVERNANCE AND BEYOND

V. RAVINDRA SASTRY AND
G. RAM REDDY

RESEARCH INDIA PRESS
New Delhi (INDIA)

ISBN : 978-81-89131-58-6

Price 1195/-

First Edition: 2014

Published by :
RESEARCH INDIA PRESS
E-6/34, Sangam Vihar
New Delhi-110062
Phone: 011-26047013, (M) 9818085794
E-mail: researchindiapress@gmail.com

Typesetting by
G. R. Sharma
9968281826

CONTENTS

ACKNOW LEDGEMENT

The Centre for Advanced Study(Phase-I), Department of Political Science, Osmania University, Hyderabad, sincerely extends it's thanks to UGC, New Delhi, for enabling to bring out this Volume

Also, the team members of the program express it's unreserved gratitude towards the teaching and nonteaching staff members of the Depatment of Political Science, Osmania University, for facilitating the publication of this volume.

Editors

FOREWORD

The department of political science of Osmania University established its reputation not only for its good teaching but long research tradition starting from early seventies. Prof G. Ram Reddy who headed the department during this period laid very strong foundations on which the department stands today and by the present generation of scholars continue the legacy, some of whose works are known at national and international levels. In keeping these strong academic traditions they have been conducting seminars on contemporary socially relevant issues and raising certain questions for further probing. The present volume is one of these initiatives on empowerment.

Empowerment is a concept that needs both conceptual clarity and empirical evidence so as to assess the democratic deficit of a society struggling to evolve from formal democracy into a substantive democracy. In formal democracy, power is posited in institutions in such a manner that it is dispersed so that centralization of power is contained. Power unchecked has an intrinsic propensity to become despotic. This raises another question that in a democracy where sovereign power theoretically rests with the people, the issue of empowerment of the people is problematic. In fact, it is contradiction in terms. Therefore, a debate on empowerment seeks to look at the sections which are powerless and see the causes for not only disempowerment but various attempts for their empowerment.

In this volume almost all the powerless sections- dalits, tribals, muslims, women and children are covered. These sections together would constitute in sheer numbers an overwhelming majority. The papers suggest the helplessness of these sections and analyze some of the policy initiatives to empower them. It is always the limitation of such a debate that while it looks at these sections in isolation as the other side of the spectrum- the powerful- escape the attention. It is necessary that the discipline of political science probes into the dialectical relation between the centres of power in the society and strategies of shift of power from these centres to those which are marginalized in sharing of the power.

This volume is important because its concerns are around the weak. As long as the debate on these sections is alive, the discipline continues to be relevant and in one form or the other contributes to the debate on deepening of Indian democracy. Editors deserve compliments for their sensitivity and concern.

Prof. G. Haragopal
Centre for Human Rights
University of Hyderabad

INTRODUCTION

Michel Foucault has characterized the modern world in which power relations operate almost at every level through the construction and legitimation of a knowledge that speaks the language of the powerful in a society. This for him is the power/knowledge nexus that lies hidden in layers and layers of a certain kind of articulation which favours some against others. The realization that society is a sphere of operation of power relations has led to the investigation of the concept of power and along with it the notions of disempowerment and empowerment. The last few years have witnessed greater emphasis on a discourse of integration of groups into social wholes through empowerment and the product of this empowerment which is inclusion into the social whole with a view to ensure a better and more egalitarian distribution of social goods. This emphasis has led to greater research into what constitutes empowerment and the benefits that accrue with it. Disempowerment and empowerment are seen at various levels – the micro or the individual and –the macro which is the whole in which this individual operates. The macro changes contextually, sometimes it is the society in general or sometimes it is a workplace or an aggregation of certain group of people. In order to understand how empowerment has to be brought about it is necessary to start with an operable definition of what constitutes empowerment. When seen in this way, empowerment is "process by which individuals and groups gain power, access to resources and control over their own lives. In doing so, they gain the ability to achieve their highest personal and collective aspirations and goals".

In order to understand empowerment sometimes it is necessary to also look into its opposite which is disempowerment. Hegel had astutely suggested that sometimes it pays to look at what something is not, in order to understand what something is. Disempowerment of people who belong to a particular population group produces powerlessness that influences the lives and futures of the individuals and the fate of the entire community. Powerless people, as already noted, expect a lack of connection between their behavior and desirable outcomes, and defend themselves by means of extreme fatalism, self-contempt, and indifference to their deplorable situation. As a consequence of the negative valuation that is part of the disempowering processes directed towards a social group, this group is systematically denied identities and roles possessing social value, and important resources. These two – roles and resources – are the basis for the exertion of interpersonal influence and for effective social functioning. Hence, inability to exert interpersonal influence and inability to function effectively in society, which various theories identify as personal problems, are structural manifestations of powerlessness. Now this is a clear case for arguing that any civilized society should have people who are empowered and not disempowered.

It is no surprise therefore that Empowerment Theory wants to make a place for itself among those new social theories that are attempting to connect the personal and the social, the individual and society, the micro and the macro. Connecting the individual and the collective in a way which is not organic-biological or systemic-mechanical is the great challenge of sociology in recent years. For the individual – the micro level – the empowerment process is a process of increasing control and transition from a state of powerlessness. Community empowerment – the macro level

– is a collective social process of creating a community, achieving better control over the environment, and decision making in which groups, organizations or communities participate. Beside these two there is a necessity to develop the theoretical meaning of empowering professional practice, through which an abstract theory is translated into a practical tool of intervention. An empowerment theory requires a convincing integration of the micro and macro levels in order to make clear the interrelations among individual, community, and professional empowerment. In the search for this integration, we will see three theories which have taken on the challenge of connecting the individual and his/her behavior with the society and its processes.

The first of these three is the Structuration Theory proposed by Anthony Giddens. Giddens' structuration theory – which is also called the theory of duality of structure, after its central principle – is the most developed among those sociological theories that integrate micro and macro levels of analysis. In this theory, the social structure has neither primacy nor preference over the human agency, and vice versa. Social structure is the outcome of human action, and this action is made possible within the boundaries of the social structure in which it takes place. Giddens makes use of the term "system" to describe the overt pattern of social structures. The social outcomes – both the intentional and the unexpected – are an embodiment of the actions of human agencies. Social systems are reproduced social practices that are embedded in time and space.

Rules and resources are drawn upon in the production and reproduction of social action. At the same time they are the means of system reproduction (the duality of structure). Human agency is enabled by means of social rules and resources. The rules guide and inform the action, and the resources provide it with energy: purpose, power, and efficacy.

The three concepts that are central to an understanding of human agency and the social structure are communication, power, and sanction. These represent human actions as well as structures of meaning (communication), systems of rule and authority (power) and systems of morality and legitimation (sanctions).

Giddens breaks the mechanical character of social structure, in that he sees it as a cluster of rules and resources, and hence a fundamental part of human activity, and not as an obstacle to activity. Structure is always both constraining and enabling.

Communication: In order to communicate, people draw interpretative schemes from symbolic structures of signification.

Power: A system of domination is made possible due to the existence of social structures of rule and authority.

Sanctions: In order to impose sanctions, people rely on norms which are part of a social structure of morality and of a system of legitimation.

The concepts of structure and action are produced and reproduced on the human agency level, and exist as concepts of meaning on the social structure level. I have chosen the structuration theory as a basis for empowerment theory because it is critical, self-critical, holistic, relates directly to the concept of power, and binds micro and macro phenomena in the one explanation. The principle of duality of structure is suitable as an explanation for the various levels of empowerment, as it is for analysis of any social process. Individual empowerment is human agency whose structural outcomes are not intentional; it may have structural consequences but these are not the essence of the process. Community empowerment is human activity that has structural and organizational aspects, which are aimed at changing social systems and creating structural alternatives. Professional practice is another form of human agency, one that is made possible through existing social systems. When its outcomes are oriented to producing the two kinds of empowerment, it is called empowering.

The next important theory of empowerment is The Transactional Theory in environmental psychology. It may be appropriate to see this in the context of the environment about which there is a great deal of discussion. The transactional theory in environmental psychology proposes a bridge between the micro level – the person – and the macro level—the environment. In the transactional approach, which is influenced by both phenomenology and ethnomethodology, the unit of analysis is a holistic entity – an event, generally – in which people, psychological processes, and environments are involved. The transactional whole is not composed of separate parts (like the whole in systems theory), but is a compound of inseparable factors that are dependent upon one another for their very meaning and definition. The whole – person-environment – is a happening that is changing all the time. Various aspects of the event accord mutual meaning to one another, for in a different setting, or with different actors, a particular person would have acted differently. The observer (the researcher), too, is part of the event, since she defines the event and its boundaries, and her approach and behavior dictate part of the phenomenon. Understanding the observer during the event, his/her point of view, his/her role and his/her position, is part of the interpretation of the event. The transactional theory is pragmatic, eclectic, and relativistic. Despite its ambition to be able to predict, it recognizes that the events are liable to be idiosyncratic and non-recurrent.

Several Principles Stem from this Theory

1. Change is a property of the whole entity—of the event itself. Change is expected since processes are temporary by their very definition. An understanding of the change – of how it comes about and of its form – is required in order to understand the phenomenon, and not, as in other approaches, in order to understand the change and its

reasons. The description and analysis of the event focus on the study of process and change.

2. Since the basic research unit is an event involving psychological, temporal, environmental, and social aspects, any focus of the research on one of these aspects turns the others into a context. For example, if the focus of the study is the psychological aspects of an event, then the physical environment is its context.
3. The perceptions and perspectives of the participants in an event are important for an understanding of the event. The analysis is not done solely from the perspective of the researcher who, as already noted, is one aspect of the event. The transactional approach studies the ways different observers interpret the same event.
4. Methodological eclecticism: Research methods are produced out of the event not imposed upon it. The theory and the structure of assumptions are constants, while the strategies of study may vary. A study is designed according to the problem and the question being studied. Hence, even when it is not possible to do the research empirically, it is important to report and acknowledge this, so that even without empirical research it will be possible to understand the entire picture theoretically. From transactional theory, empowerment theory has taken the place of the professional as an inseparable part of the social situation itself, the emphasis on the process, and the freedom to move between focus and context that this theory permits the researcher.

The next important theory is Feminist Theory. The declaration that the personal is political is the feminist rationale for removing the separating fence between the micro as a personal domain and the macro as a public domain. The split between the personal and the public domains is essentially a social means of isolating women and separating them from communities which could validate their views about life and society. The recognition of the existence of mutual influence between private activity and social structures demands a connection between the personal world and what happens in political and public life. The change in the values and beliefs of the individual woman, in the goals that she sets herself, in the life-style she chooses and in the understanding of her existential problems is a political declaration that is aimed at a change of the social structures that influence her life. The concept social individuality makes the feminist dialectics explicit. The woman is an individual within the social reality in which she grows up and develops with the contradictions between her and society. According to this holistic view, the separation between self, others, and community, is artificial, because these three create one another within a single complex whole. The powerlessness of one woman, which changes by means of her activism in collaboration with others in her situation, is a process that empowers the entire community of women. Feminist thought attacks the illusion of objectivity. Since knowledge about the social world is always created from a social position, no comprehensive and uniform social outlook really exists. People positioned in different places in the social structure know different things about the world. Hence, when a social view is presented as objective and exclusively valid, it is only an expression of the excessive rights that a certain group has appropriated for itself in the social order

Several important ideas follows from this thinking: The work of production and maintenance in society is done by subordinates whose work is in most cases invisible, and because of a dominant social ideology is not appreciated either by the society or by those who actually do the work. As a consequence, the understanding of the real components of production in society is distorted. A senior manager in a large company can devote all his time to his job thanks to his wife, who takes care of him, their children, his elderly parents, and their home. For the firm, and for the society as well, the invisible work of this woman is of no economic value. It is women, irrespective of their status, who do most of this invisible work, not only in the domestic domain, cleaning, cooking, maintenance, and providing emotional and sexual services. In paid work too they do most of the activities of coordinating, such as waiting, arranging meetings, mediating, being interrupted, which are also considered unimportant. Another part of women's work, which is more obvious in its contribution to social production – motherhood – receives social glorification and idealization, which convert it into an unrealistic experience. As a consequence of this women walk on a line of fault that separates the dominant ideology about their role in social life from their actual experience as they understand it. The incompatibility between the private reality and the social generalizations creates a constant dissonance with reality, and women navigate their lives according to this sense of separation between them and the society. On this line of fault, women navigate in different ways: some by repression, some by acquiescence, some by rebellion, and some by an attempt to organize social change.

Theorists must engage in dialectical analysis of the knowledge process, and be conscious of the constant tension that exists between the subject and the object—each affecting and changing the other. The knower (the subject, the theorist) has to admit his interaction with the knowledge (the object), for knowledge about the social world is always created from a social position. The connection between the personal and the political, which characterizes the feminist approach, has been warmly adopted into the theory of empowerment, as has the premise that feminism is valid not only for women, but also for everyone whose world is characterized by oppression and marginality. Empowerment wants to turn public attention to the distress of groups that are in need of social change.

All that has been said here about women may be applied analogously, although not in a totally identical form, to all powerless people who are subordinate to others. These people cannot express themselves as individuals, and silently accept other people's interpretations of their actions and failures. This is the source of the culture of silence that characterizes life in conditions of inequality. The conclusion of feminist theory is to question accepted categorizations that were developed by disciplines that are basically dominated by men (such as sociology, for example). The aim is to create alternative concepts which can help to explain the world as it appears to its invisible and disadvantaged subordinate subjects.

So far we have seen the relationship between the micro and the macro in three different theoretical constructs. All the three constructs, the feminist to the least extent, seem to deal with the macro as the bigger whole that is encountered on a daily basis in various ways. However, this seems to not take into consideration the Super Macro or the Meta Macro which is the State. Nothing can be farther from the truth. The State through the process of governance is constantly interacting with the individual or the micro and this interaction is not significantly different from the other interactions between the disempowered micro and the various macros which in more ways than one reinforce the nature of disempowerment. As a Super Macro or a Meta Macro the State gains more significance than any other macro because it has the ability to empower those individuals or groups that have been rendered insignificant by disempowerment. The re-empowerment or sometimes first time empowerment lead to the inclusion of more and more individuals and disempowered groups into the discourse of governance as significant actors with significant roles.

The seminar of which I have been the director and the papers that were presented there and which are now being published in this volume, deal with the various theories and narratives of disempowerment, empowerment and re-empowerment of specific subjects. The idea behind the seminar was to arrive at tenable explanations for the disempowerment of some and how they could be included into the social process significantly through empowerment. I must say the seminar did reach its goal in generating a healthy and vibrant discussion around the concepts of empowerment and inclusion. Various paper presenters have chosen different dimensions of empowerment. Some have been State centric; others have talked about a more diffuse concept of governance while others have gone beyond the usual frameworks and generated new ones which brought out newer dimensions of the question of empowerment. I am sure that you as the reader will find enough fodder in this volume to reflect upon and I would say that our job is more or less successful if this volume makes you think about things which till now you have simply not bothered to interrogate.

Prof. V. Ravindra Sastry
Coordinator, Centre for Advanced Study, and
Head, Dept of Political Science,

Dr. G. Ram Reddy
Deputy Coordinator, Centre for Advanced Study
Dept. of Political Science, Osmania University
Hyderabad, India

LIST OF CONTRIBUTORS

1. Prof. S. Palekar, Faculty Member, Department of Post Graduation studies and Research in Political Science, Gulbarga University, Gulbarga, Karnataka.
2. Dr.Ajay Gudavarthy, Faculty member, Centre for Political studies, Jawaharlal University, New Delhi.
3. Prof. Bishnu Charan Chowdhary, Faculty Member, Department of Political Science, Berhampur University, Berhampur, Odisha.
4. Prof. Satyanarayana Sangitha, Head, Centre for Political Institutions, Governance and Development, Instititute of Social and Economic Change, Bengaluru, Karnataka.
5. Prof. A. V. Satish Chandra, Chairperson, Centre for Policy and Governance, Tata Institute of Social Sciences, Hyderabad, Andhra Pradesh.
6. Prof. M. Hussain (Retd), Department of Politics and Public Administration, SriVenkateshwara University, Tirupati, Andhra Pradesh.
7. Prof. G. Ram Reddy, Faculty Member, Department of Political Science, Osmania University, Hyderabad, Andhra Pradesh.
8. Prof. G. Lalaiah, Faculty, Department of Political Science, Osmania University, Hyderabad, Andhra Pradesh.
9. Dr. P. Arjun Rao, Reader in Public Administration (Retd), A.V. College, Hyderabad, Andhra Pradesh.
10. Dr. D. Dwarakanath, Reader in Political Science (Retd), A. P. S. Degree College, Vikarabad, Andhra Pradesh.

11. Dr. K. Vidyasagar Reddy, Associate Professor, Department of Political Science, Mizoram University. Aizwal, Mizoram.

12. Dr. K. Saibaba, Reader in Political Science (Retd), V. V. College, Hyderabad, Andhra Pradesh.

13. Dr. Yasmin, Assistant Professor (Senior Scale), Department of Political Science, Osmania University, Hyderabad, Andhra Pradesh.

14. Dr. Kaneez Zehra, Assistant Professor, Department of Political Science and Public Administration, Maulana Azad National Urdu University, Hyderabad, Andhra Pradesh.

15. Dr. Shyam Singh, Research Coordinator, Oxfam India, New Delhi.

16. Dr. Gunti Ravinder, Assistant Professor, Department of Political Science, Dr. B. R. Ambedkar University, Hyderabad, Andhra Pradesh.

17. Dr. V. Bhumaiah, Assistant Professor (contract), Department of Political Science, Palamuru University, Andhra Pradesh.

18. K. Damodar Reddy and C. Narasimha Reddy are Ph.D Scholars in The Department of Politics and Public Administration, S. K. University, Ananthapur, Andhra Pradesh.

19. P. Venkateswar, Research Scholar, CPS, JNU, New Delhi.

20. P. Manjula, Research Scholar, Department of Political Science, Osmania University, Hyderabad, Andhra Pradesh.

21. S. K. Mahaboob Bakshe, Research Scholar, Department of Political Science, Osmania University, Hyderabad, Andhra Pradesh.

CITIZENSHIP, IDENTITY AND EMPOWERMENT

AJAY GUDAVARTHY

The liberal idea of citizenship as a transformative identity available to empower the hitherto excluded and marginalized social groups, raises serious questions about not only the relation between citizenship and the emerging identity politics (Dalit, women, etc) and social movements (class, environmental, human rights, peace, etc) but also the very concept of social and political empowerment driving the political discourse. The issue becomes even more complex when raised in the context of plural and developing societies such as India.

A typical liberal democratic way of looking at the relation between citizenship, identity politics and social movements would be – 'how does a concept which has at its core the principles of universality and of equality of status accommodate the politics of particularity and differences associated with the new wave of identity politics? ' (Hunt and Purvis, 1999: 458). In other words, it is assumed that while the liberal idea of citizenship implies a singular identity with universalistic aspirations, identity politics necessarily entail particularism and fragmentation. The identity of a citizen becomes the quintessentially 'political' and all other identities and politics are relegated to an 'extra-political' or even pre-political status. To critically intervene in this debate, it is insufficient to look for better ways of reconciling citizenship and politics of identity; instead we need to question the underlying liberal assumptions and claims to universality on the one hand and look for alternative principles that can take us beyond liberal ethos, on the other. This paper would argue that the liberal idea of citizenship is inherently incompatible with the aspirations for substantive democratization, empowerment and preservation of co-operative practices for solidarity, emerging from the contemporary identity politics and social movements. *It is imperative in the process of democratization and empowerment to undermine, and not reconcile, the project of citizenship as against the radical political articulations*.

Citizenship is the identity that operationalises liberal principles to achieve and sustain formal democracy. It is grounded in four basic overlapping liberal principles – free choice/individualism; autonomy/atomization; critical self-reflection/self-interest-private property; universalism/abstract and formal. The continuity and harmony between these principles delineates the contours within which citizenship and the democratization it purports to achieve limit themselves.

The idea of free choice gains its substantive content in the way the individual is conceived in Liberalism. Extension of free choice is possible only with the growth of individualism. "Liberalism defines the individual in austere and minimalist terms. It abstracts the person from all his or her `contingent` and `external` relations with other people and nature, and defines the person as an essentially self-contained and solitary being, encapsulated in and unambiguously marked off from the `outside` world by his or her body"[1]. Citizenship conceived as a `matrix of rights and obligations governing the members of a political community` entrenches free choice or liberty, in the individual's separation and assertion against the collective. He individual is unassmilable, lest his or her individuality gets blurred. "In one form or another, the idea of self-enclosure, of a bounded self, accessible and available to others only to a severely limited degree, is an integral part of the liberal view"[2]. Neither is the self expected to open up nor enter a free and close dialogue with others.

Any limits on free choice would be construed as a compromise of the individual's autonomy. In the substantive sense, the extension of such an idea of autonomy would only be protected and sustained at the cost of atomization of individuals. It is therefore understandable as to why any other form of social organisation is considered either primordial or pre-political under the liberal imagination. Caste, for instance, does not only signify rigid hierarchies but also the strong intra-caste bonds (it is otherwise very difficult to explain contemporary caste struggles around 'consolidation' rather than 'annihilation' of caste identities). They have shared notions of mobility, honor and dignity. Individuals outside this have very little ontological presence and therefore liberalism cannot comprehend or conceptualize the positive ethos around the horizontal intra-caste bonds. Instead, citizenship institutes rights by glorifying conflict of interests as inevitable and indispensable and gravely undermines the history of common struggles and development of rights as a result of collective efforts. It is therefore that liberals like Kymlicka perceive it as unproblematic to argue against the rights of the community to expel individuals who wish to follow modern liberal ideas as against its core norms and beliefs (Kymlicka, 1995: 153). For him, it is simply an unjust measure. While individual autonomy is an important value, the community's right to self-preservation is completely undermined. It under no circumstances becomes a worthwhile goal to pursue. It is in these underlying processes of atomization and assertion of rights in and through conflicts that feminists perceive as masculinity, as it "involves an arbitrary boundary creation and an assertion of hyper-separateness to reinforce a lack of security in a person's sense of their self as a separate person"[3].

The ideal of critical self-reflection becomes meaningful in preserving self-interest, instrumental rationality, and a strong sense of private ownership. Apart from individuals having a strong sense of 'owning his or her body and having proprietary rights over its constituents', the protection of private property is conceived as a source of dignity (ala Locke) and motivation to grow. Any idea of radical redistribution and collective ownership of resources is considered inimical to the basic construction of a liberal society. Any argument highlighting 'the sickness of affluence' and undermining higher incomes and sustained economic growth as the way to a better future (Clive Hamilton, 2003) are either not taken seriously or are quickly declared as the votaries of totalitarian (planned) societies. Citizenship, which emanates from the conception of a nation state, is rooted in the emergence of the market and market relations. 'Relations in the market society are guided by functional solidarity i.e. solidarity that guarantees the successful execution of transactions in a market society. Citizenship is the condensed form of functional solidarity in a formal democracy` (G. Ajay and G. Vijay, 2000: 1036). Citizenship identity would therefore exist in perpetual tension with all ideals of a 'post-growth' society.

Finally, citizenship as representing universalistic aspirations comes at the cost of abstracting individuals from their concrete socio-economic structural positions and extending formal notions of equality, participation, representation and consent, around procedurally neutral institutional arrangements. Abstract identity of citizenship and formal democracy are very closely linked. It is because in the state, citizenship is blind to concrete socio-economic differences, that it can afford pretentious claims to universality. It presumes the birth of the state and functioning of the civil society is based on free choice and consent of citizens who are inherently, naturally and equally free. They have voluntarily and willingly entered into a contract and thereby what comes into operation is 'self-assumed obligation'. Those who entered this contract are faceless and abstract entities, otherwise it is important to answer as to 'when did a society exist for free consent to be exercised' (Hirschman, 1989: 1228; Carole Pateman, 1967). Concomitant ideas such as a neutral public sphere (or for that matter secularism) expect individuals to interact as citizens i.e. bearers of formal and state derived rights and obligations. 'The abstract state and the abstract citizen complement and entail each other'. Individuals are expected to lead bifurcated lives with inner duality. The continuity between the 'public' and the 'private' is broken and the former emerges undermining the latter. The recent rise of right-wing fundamentalist politics in India, for instance, is largely an outcome of the previous Nehruvian attempts to build an artificial public sphere that exists by suffocating the identity in the so-called 'private' sphere (be it gender or religious identities). Right-wing politics therefore build on striking continuity between the public and the private. It, for instance, in their women's' organisations such as the Durga Vahini politicizes the women's identity around the traditional symbols such as Durga or Seetha. These organic linkages are any day stronger than the weak hegemonising and homogenising identity of citizenship.

Universality of citizenship is coterminous with the neutrality of a formal democracy. A government is only expected to lay down a framework of formal and general rules. Guaranteeing of right to equality, adequate representation, substantive participation and consent is structured around procedural neutrality of the liberal democratic institutions. "Democracy as method of government is not whatever the people at a given moment may happen to decide but a set of arrangements for securing their control over the public decision-making process on an on-going basis"[4]. Institutions such as the parliament, independent executive and judiciary are seeking to realise formal equality and participation i.e. increasing opportunities and providing equal access to all. Contemporary social movements view social relations in terms of a process and structural constraints and perceive transformation not as segregated and incremental but interconnected and quantum. It is only in such a context that one can explain as to why the state resorts to coercive mechanisms, evident in fake encounter killings, Dalit massacres, communal riots, or for that matter, advanced capitalist liberal democracies such as the US resort to highest death penalties (and most of them being Blacks is more than a coincidence- G.Ajay and G.Vijay, 2000: 1036). The state cannot accommodate all demands within its limited, incremental and formal process of democratization and therefore its falsely presumed that the state and civil society are complimentary in a liberal society. Complimentarity at best hides and at worst justifies state coercion.

Thus, abstract and universal aspirations of citizenship are invariably linked to formal democracy. As long as this link is perceived as given, limits and constraints on democratization will also be considered necessary. Some of the defenders of liberal democracy have argued that liberal democracies are in a 'paradoxical conjunction' where institutions characteristic of liberalism are indispensable to maintain and sustain democracy but this entails a liberal constraint on democratisation in terms of extending popular control and equalizing the conditions for its exercise for one and all. In other words, securing individual rights are necessary to guarantee popular control over the process of collective decision-making; separation of powers necessary for rule of law and the possibility of legal redress; epistemological premise that there is no final truth about what is good for society are all necessary to maintain democracy. They might limit substantive democracy but they are necessary limits. For instance, the principle of representation allows for a highly specialized/professional decision-making but might keep people at arms length from the political process and result in a depoliticised and privatized citizenry. But with space/time constraints, formal representation is the best option available (D. Beetham, 1993: 61). When democracy is grounded in liberal tenets, constraints look reasonable and imperative. What we are instead looking for is the signposts that take us comprehensively beyond such 'paradoxical conjunctions' based on liberal assumptions and propositions.

II

The process of social transformation and empowerment becomes even more symbolic, formal and crisis-ridden, when it is perceived around the identity of citizenship in plural and developing societies such as India. The crisis of social transformation persists not due to proliferation of identities and assertion of multiple interests, as it is often projected by liberals, but in attempts to dovetail them into neat and homogenizing and neutral conceptions of citizenship. It is the basic premise that 'this tension (between citizenship, identity politics and social movements) is a uniquely productive one, working a crucial condition of possibility for sustaining democratic politics', emulated in the Indian political discourse and practice that is primarily responsible for the crisis in social transformation in terms of its inability to establish an egalitarian and democratic social order, as it necessarily perceives change merely in symbolic accommodation of diverse demands. In fact some scholars have suggested that 'democracy' sustains itself in India due to its multi-layered and culturally plural communities outside the hegemonic realm of the modern liberal state. 'Democracy' is realised in the struggle against the modern compulsion on society 'in every instance, to adjust to the state'. There is a need to indegenise democracy, preserving social plurality and taking up social transformation as a 'live political agenda' (A. Nandy, 1989: 5). In other words, substantive democratization is possible not in reconciling citizenship based on liberal tenets, but undermining it as against the emerging identity politics and social movements of various kinds, including women, Dalit, environmental, etc. citizenship project puts strict limits on how far these movements are allowed to articulate themselves and fails to (rather incapable of) recognize alternative political principles and precepts hidden in them, essential for substantive democratization. Political discourse needs to continuously experiment *beginning with* the basic cooperative assumptions and goals of these movements rather than judge, co-opt and coerce them into the 'universalistic' project of citizenship.

It is evident that the post-colonial state through its liberal institutional arrangements is repeatedly and progressively failing to match up to the demands of various social groups. It needs a more diverse and graded approach to address the complex polity made of 'both an association of individuals and a community of communities, recognizing both the individuals and communities as bearers of rights' (B. Parekh, 1993: 170). A democratic government working around liberal principles institutionalizes change through 'short-term particularistic compromise' (referred to otherwise in the everyday lingo as 'populism'). It would continue to be responsible for political and administrative mismanagement of public capital and erosion of institutional insulation of the decision-making process (P. Bardhan, 2001). Civil society (including identity politics and social movements) itself will respond through consolidation of segmentation (Rajputs and Jats demanding to be included as the OBCs), strengthening parochialism ('Sons of the soil' kind of demands by the Shiv Sena, AGP, etc), politics of patronage (symbolic gestures of instituting Ambedkar statues and parks). *Civil society and social movements representative of it are not immune and insulate from the responses from the state. They too begin to articulate issues in the language and discourse more easily comprehendible by the modern liberal democratic state.* The crisis is, not due to the improper reconciliation between the citizenship identity and plural identities and social movements but precisely in these very attempts to do so. Therefore we need to look for political principles and norms that have not emerged in course of these attempts to reconcile citizenship and identity politics and social movements and essentially lie outside the liberal ethos.

III

Civil society is no unproblematic domain (Neera Chandoke, 2002: M.W.Foley and Bob Edwards, 1996). It needs to be transformed, governed and strengthened through the principles that challenge the basic liberal tenets. To begin with the emphasis should shift from the vertical interaction between the state and civil society mediated through the identity of citizenship, to mechanisms that could possibly strengthen mutual horizontal obligation between social groups and individuals. A strong sense of 'fair play' needs to be encouraged where "anyone who takes part in and enjoys the benefits of a co-operative practice must contribute to the production of these benefits, even when his or her contribution is not necessary to their production"[5]. In other words, 'the body politic' needs to be regarded as a 'cooperative enterprise' and groups and individuals owe obligation 'not to some impersonal force- usually called the state – but to the co-operating members of the political society' (R. Dagger, 1997: 69). In such a co-operative effort the classical Simmons-type distinctions between 'receipt' (involuntary) and 'acceptance' (voluntary) of benefits does not stand good. It is pertinent and relevant more in the context of a vertical obligation to an impersonal (and imposed) state and where individuals consider themselves externally 'dropped into' a co-operative scheme. Individuals instead 'grow into' social and political communities where we personally identify and expand our agency in forming and reforming the community around us. Recognising and operationalisation of the ideal of 'fair play' is plausible only by fostering 'civic virtues' - acting for the common good even when it proves personally painful (R. Dagger, 1997: 79). 'Civic Virtues' invariably require us to go beyond the 'self' as the only reference point, and thereby cannot be fostered around the liberal identity of citizenship. Some citizens of the modern states do think this way but only when a 'war or natural disaster leads to recognize that we're all in the same boat' and thereby the limits of 'civic virtues' are set either in conditions of crisis, or in terms of a quid pro quo rationality or benevolent charity with a top down approach. While the need is to naturalise these reactions to unnatural conditions, appeals to inculcate 'civic virtues' in modern liberal citizens is limited by the logic of immediate 'mutual benefit', represented by and popularized currently through the idea of 'social capital'. It refers to 'civic engagement' as forming associations *through* and *for* 'mutually beneficial collective action' (R. Putnam, 1995). It necessarily depoliticises co-operative relations and activity by limiting it to creation of 'user groups', stakeholder groups', and beneficiary groups such as 'water-users associations', 'self-help groups', etc. 'Trust, networks and norms' are only made sense of through the instrumental value they hold. ' Social capital can be transmuted, so to speak, into financial capital: In novelist Amy Tam's *Joy Luck Club*, a group of mah-jong-playing friends evolves into a joint investment association' (R.Putnam, 1993: 29). Further, when modern liberal citizens are *implanted* into co-operative relations they encourage (politically) clientelism. What constitutes the nature of social capital is "not what you know, its who you know. It is wisdom born of our experience that gaining membership to exclusive clubs requires inside contacts that close competitions for jobs and contracts are usually won by those with 'friends in high places"[6]. It is this type of neo-clientalism that is the basis for the fund-bank sponsored concepts of 'good governance' and 'decentralization'. These are more than evident, for instance, in the trends emerging in Andhra Pradesh with its 'Vision 2020'. Through programmes such as Janmabhoomi and formation of self-help groups (SHGs) new forms of political patronage is created, which in turn helps to undermine traditional democratic (Panchayat) institutions (Seetharamam, 2004). The distinction between the party and the Government is nearly collapsed, to disempower the people and help vested interests.

'Civic Virtue'- bearing with personal pain- is beyond the modern liberal citizenship ethics. It is possible only when ideals of liberty are recasted, not around a 'reactive autonomy' but 'relational autonomy', where the self- derives its strength from its context of relations (Hirschman, 1989: 1231; refer 1992). For this, mutual obligation between individuals and groups has to become 'given' and relative autonomy and freedom from it needs to be reasoned and justified within the context of the co-operative living. However, the ideals of making obligations 'given' and pursuing them at the cost of personal pain could be at times disempowering. For instance, when applied to the tribal displaced by the Narmada Dam. In fact, they could be (mis) used by the state (language of nationalism/patriotism) to draw absolute obligation from its citizens. Therefore it needs to be further qualified by making obligation not only 'given' but also 'graded', rather than standardized. Obligation would be unevenly distributed and would be co-terminous with the cultural status, political power and economic resources accessed by groups and individuals, and rights would be inversely proportionate. Instead of a liberal idea of a culturally neutral, universally valid, equal obligation on a common basis for all citizens, alternative political discourse would forge obligations and rights unequally around structural inequalities. The better-off sections have a higher obligation to 'nurture and help improve the quality of collective life including to highlight and help alleviate the material distress, inequalities, injustices and various forms of repression' (B. Parekh, 1993: 241). Digression from such obligation would be nothing short of breaking down the cooperative practices on which the polity is based and political communities are forged. Co-operative practices are constitutive of both the principles of obligation being 'given' and 'graded'.

For this edifice around the scheme of political obligation as civic virtue, being 'given' and 'graded', identity politics and social movements and individuals working *in* and *thorough* them are the bearers and best representatives. Both these principles are alien to the liberal ethos. Identity politics and social movements do not face the conventional liberal dilemmas, as they articulate transformative politics, neither solely at the level of enclosed and exclusivist communities nor at the atomized individual level. They, in fact, sustain themselves by continuously experimenting with an open-ended relation between the individual and the community. It can therefore be argued that their politics acknowledge the valid fear that 'if individual rights are said to produce atomized, disinterested individuals, valuing... cultural diversity is not likely to generate the politics of 'common good' (Gurpreet Mahajan, 2001: 178). Similarly they protect certain universal values, however informed by concrete socio-economic conditions. It is precisely for this reason that while caste/Dalit politics struggle against the hierarchies within the caste system, they also preserve the intra-caste solidarity and the sense of mutuality between individuals; the women's movement fights against a patriarchal family system but glorifies values such as sharing, caring, selflessness as feminine; human rights movement preserves 'universal' aspirations for rule of law, peace and harmony but contexulises militant and violent ethnic, nationality or naxalite movements in concrete socio-economic conditions and therefore pleads to understand 'violence' in a broader context (rather than as a 'law and order' trouble, which to my mind, is an extension of liberal understanding). However, to make these struggles sustainable and operationalise the principles emerging from them, we need to avoid 'essentialising' them. Instead, struggles 'within' and 'outside' these movements need to be protected by institutionalising the 'right to struggle' or 'right to intolerance'(H. Marcuse, 1965) and these rights exist within the contours of the idea of co-operative relations and not outside or in conflict with them. Co-operative relations as 'civic virtues' inform the purpose of 'right to struggle/ intolerance'. Such a right is again beyond liberal ethos as M. Walzer rightly observes, 'the idea that men can be obligated to disobey has not played much part in liberal political theory' (M Walzer, 1967). Going beyond the civil society, identity struggles and social movements working for mutuality to become 'graded' and internally built around the 'obligation to disobey', grounds the transformative politics for substantive democratization and is capable of raising and addressing issues beyond liberal democracy and its project of citizenship.

Notes

1. Bikhu Parekh, 'Cultural Particularity of Liberal Democracy' in David Held (ed) Prospects for Democracy, Polity Press, Cambridge, 1993, p. 158.
2. *ibid.*
3. Nancy J.Hirschmann, 'Freedom, Recognition, and Obligation: A Feminist Approach to Political Theory' in American Political Science Review, Vol. 83, No. 4, Dec 1989, p. 1236.
4. David Beetham, 'Liberal Democracy and the Limits of Democratisation' in David Held (ed) *op.cit*, p. 58.
5. Richard Dagger, Civic Virtues, Oxford University Press, Oxford, 1997, p. 68.
6. Michael Woolcock, 'Social Capital in Theory and Practice", in Social Capital and Poverty Reduction, UNESCO, Paris, 2002, p. 28.

References

Ajay, G. and Vijay, G., (2000), 'Civil Society, State and Social Movements' *Economic and Political Weekly.*

Bardhan, Pranab, (2001), 'Sharing the Spoils: Group Equity, Development and Democracy' in Atul Kohli (ed) The Success of India's Democracy, Cambridge University Press, Cambridge

Beetham, David, (1993), 'Liberal Democracy and the Limits of Democratisation' in David Held (ed) Prospects for Democracy, Polity Press, Cambridge.

Chandoke, Neera (2003), The Conceits of Civil Society, Oxford University Press, New Delhi.

Dagger, Richard (1997), Civic Virtues, Oxford University Press, Oxford.

Foley, Michael and Edwards, Bob, 'The Paradox of Civil Society' *Journal of Democracy*, 7 1996.

Hamilton, Clive (2003), Growth Fetish, Allen and Unwin, London.

Hirschmann, J. (1989), 'Freedom, Recognition, and Obligation: A Feminist Approach to Political Theory' in *American Political Science Review*, Vol. 83, No. 4.

Hirschmann, J., 'Political Obligation, Freedom and Feminism' *American Political Science Review*, 179, 1992.

Kymlicka, Will, Multicultural Citizenship: A Liberal Theory of Minority Rights, Oxford University Press, Oxford, 1995.

Mahajan, Gurpreet (2001), Identities and Rights, Oxford University Press, New Delhi.

Marcuse, Herbert (1965), 'Repressive Tolerance' in R.P.Wollf, Herbert Marcuse and B.Moore, Critique of Pure Tolerance, Beacon Press, Boston.

Nandy, Ashis (1989), 'The Political Culture of the Indian State' Daedalus, 118, 4 Fall.

Parekh, Bikhu (1993), 'Cultural Particularity of Liberal Democracy' in David Held (ed) *Prospects for Democracy*, Polity Press, Cambridge.

Parekh, Bikhu (1997), 'Dilemmas of a Multicultural Theory of Citizenship' Constellations, Vol 4(1).

Parekh, Bikhu, (1993), 'A Misconceived Discourse on Political Obligation' Political Studies.

Pateman, Carole (1986), The Problem of Political Obligation: A Critique of Liberal Theory, University of California Press, California.

Purvis, T. and Hunt, A. (1999), 'Identity versus Citizenship: Transformations in the Discourses and Practices of Citizenship' Social and Legal Studies (457).

Putnam, Robert (1993), The Prosperous Community- Social capital and Public Life' *The American Prospect*, Spring.

Putnam, Robert (1995), 'Bowling Alone: America's Declining Social Capital' Journal of Democracy, Vol. 6.

Seetharamam, Kakarala (2004), The Challenge of Democratic Empowerment, Hivos, Bangalore.

Walzer, Michael (1967), 'Obligation to Disobey' in Political Theory and Social Change, Aldine, New York.

Woolcock, Michael (2002), 'Social Capital in Theory and Practice", in Social Capital and Poverty Reduction, UNESCO, Paris.

BACKWARD CLASSES EMPOWERMENT THROUGH EDUCATION:
Problems and Perspectives of BC welfare hostels in Telangana

CHALAMALLA VENKATESHWARLU

INTRODUCTION

The development of any Nation depends on its educational system. It has been proved that education is the key to human progress and social change. Education is a powerful tool for empowerment of an individual. The principal objective of education has been the development of the whole individual. It is intrinsic to human personality. It carries both intrinsic as well as instrumental values. It develops confidence both in the individual and the community regarding their own capacities to creatively shape their lives and enhance their strengths intellectual, political, social and economic against oppression, exclusion and discrimination. Thus, Backward Classes/Caste (BC) or Other Backward Classes (OBC) empowerment undoubtedly depends on education, rather than other things. Since the ages, these sections of the people were denied educational opportunities. Despite the fact that scholars, activists and other agencies fought for marginalized educational rights.

Mahatma Joti Rao Phule saw education as a potent weapon in the struggle for revolutionary social transformation. For him, the purpose and content of education were radically different from both hegemonic and colonial models of education. His ideal was an education that would bring an awareness among lower castes of oppressive social relations and their hegemonic moral and belief systems that pervaded their consciousness... an education that would instill western secular values, encourage critical thought and bring about mental emancipation. It would fulfill practical needs but would be broad-based enough to inspire a social and cultural revolution from below[1]. After Phule, Dr.B.R.Ambedkar's agenda of radical social transformation was inseparable from the project that India's freedom movement embraced to build a modern, open, equal, inclusive and just society – free not just from foreign domination, but from all forms of prejudice, superstition, hierarchy, discrimination and subjugation which constitute social exclusion[2].

BAHUJANS (ADIVASI DALIT BAHUJANS) AND EDUCATION

The Indian constitution recognizes marginalized communities on the basis of caste such as Scheduled Caste (SC), Scheduled Tribes (ST) Other Backward Classes (OBC) and Minorities. These communities are also backward in the field of education. According to the census of India 2001[3], the total population of SCs is 16.2% and ST's is 8.1% out of the total Indian population. Though there is no official head count for OBCs, the National Sample Survey says that the population of OBC tends to be 41% of the total population. As per the NSS, 2001 the literacy rate of SCs in rural India is 46.6% and 66.2% in urban India, the literacy rate of STs is 42.2% in rural areas, and 70% in urban areas and the literacy rate of other Backward class (OBC) is 54.8% in rural India and 75.3% in urban India[4]. The enrollment of SCs up to class 8th is 19.87%, for STs it is 10.69% and among OBCs it is 42% in the primary classes and 41.23% in the upper primary level[5].

Among the thinkers, Gramsci and Paulo Freire considered education as the primary tool for emancipation of the oppressed. The contributions of these thinkers gave new directions to understand the concept of education. According to them education is an important agent for social transformation and empowerment of the masses. According to Gramsci, education and cultural formations play a key role in evading counter-hegemonic action[6]. He also indicated the forms in which these actions could be built. He promoted the spirit of equality in adult education spaces in the form of discussion circles, clubs, trade unions, political parties, cultural reviews etc. Paulo Freier in his classic, *'Pedagogy of the Oppressed'* brought out a revolutionary theory of education. He wanted education to be made a liberating exercise rather than a domestication one. He introduced several new concepts like banking system of education, dialogic etc, to elaborate his Pedagory of the oppressed. He wanted the educator to be on the side of the oppressed and promote learning through dialogue on the basis of the learner's experience with praxis[7]. He insisted that the educator should always be conscious of the culture, class gender, race etc, of the subject. Writing based on their respective backgrounds, Gramsci as a political analyst and Paulo Freire as an educationalist, both argued for the emancipation of the oppressed using education, particularly adult education as an agency.

Mahatma Jotirao Phule has a remarkable influence in fields like education, agriculture, caste system, women and widow upliftment and removal of untouchability[8]. He is most known for his efforts to educate women and the lower castes as well as the masses. He, after educating his wife, opened the first school for girls in India in 1848. In September, 1873, Jotirao, along with his followers, formed the Satya Shodhak Samaj(Society of Seekers of Truth) with the main objective to liberate the Bahujans, Shudras and Ati-Shudras and also to prevent them from exploitation and atrocities done by the Brahmins. His fight to attain equal rights for peasants and the lower caste and his contribution to the field of education has recognized him as one of the important personalities in the Social Reform Movement in Maharashtra. Dhananjay Keer, his biographer, rightly notes him as "the father of Indian social revolution".

If we look back into the history of India, we find that education was never within the reach of its entire population. Like many other resources education too was inequitably distributed across the country. Discriminatory practices due to a rigid caste system have been instrumental in perpetuating this scenario. A look at early education movements, right from the times of Jotirao Phule and Narayan Guru[9] to the present day reveals that education campaigns were intrinsically non-Brahmin in origin. These movements strongly believed that 'education is enlightenment and enlightenment is empowerment'. It helps to make for a better future society. Ambedkar recognized the importance of education in shaping the future and cautioned the under privileged not to lose any opportunity to get that right. He said, 'we may forego material benefits, but we cannot forego out right extent'. He put all his efforts to guarantee the education to the fullest without any discrimination to all the citizens of independent India. But after 60 years of its implementation, political order and the ruling elite of this country could not succeed in providing access to the "Right to Education" to its people. A prolonged movement now, the government has in the parliament of India has recently passed ***Right to Education*** Act (RTE), 1st April, 2010, through which education has become fundamental right of all children of age group 6-14[10].

After independence, when India launched the task of nation building, it chose the path of planned development[11]. This was flagged off with the launching of five year plans. Since economic development was conspicuously poor, planners focused more on economic development defined mainly as the growth of GNP, which was symbolized by new factories, dams, mega projects, mining, educational institutions etc. The special facilities provided to Backward Classes (Other Backward Classes), Scheduled Castes (SCs), and Scheduled Tribes (STs) and—to promote their educational advancement, the provision of hostels is an important one. The role of hostels in the educational advancement of the Backward Classes (BCs) is critical. The children of Backward Classes, whose economic and social situations at home are highly unfavorable, often perform poorly in schools. The significance of a good hostel in the promotion of education among these groups is thus obvious. The Committee on Untouchability pointed out that a good hostel is a real home for the students. Thus hostels are not merely feeding institutions. Consequently, the Government of India has stressed the needs for sufficient hostel facilities for Backward Classes students in all the four Five-Year Plans, In the Third Plan, the Government of India provided special grants to state governments for construction of hostels for Backward Classes. Among the special facilities provided by the government to promote the educational advancement of the BCs is the scheme of Ministry of Social Justice & Empowerment. Several committees have, however, pointed out that the working of the social welfare hostels in the various states has been far from satisfactory. As a result the students are deprived from the basic facilities like delay in scholarship payment, no proper infrastructure to read, such as table lamps, books etc especially at the time of examinations and are deprived from writing the examinations.

Education in general and primary education in particular is the foundation upon which the edifice of education and thereby human development is built. The benefits of school education are relatively more significant to society than to the individual persons – education is thus a socially profitable investment. Regrettably, the situation in Andhra Pradesh is far from satisfactory. Educationally, Andhra Pradesh is backward among the states in South India.

State Interventions

The problem of SC/ST and Backward community peoples' education has remained crucial for the educational planners and policy makers[12]. Several studies were conducted in this direction and innovation approaches were also adopted. However, the impact of the progress was not much on the overall development of the backward communities. This has resulted in a widening distance between OBCs and others, giving rise to various forms of inequalities. Moreover, the OBCs in India are heterogeneous with varied culture[13]and economy which indents for a local need-based effort by the government, both at state and central levels.

There are various development activities which are planned and implemented for the OBCs. Education is one among such activities. It is perceived that by educating the disadvantaged groups it will enable them to have other avenues of occupations and also facilitate in the overall socio economic development as well as mobility in these communities[14]. Besides, a number of residential schools for BC girl students have been set up under Kasturba Gandhi Balika Vidyalaya Scheme of Sarva Siksha Abiyaan (SSA). Several such institutions have been established in educationally backward blocks of the state. Additionally SSA has established another four residential schools targeting these girls. About 2 lakh BC students were being accommodated in Andhra Pradesh, 1,742 hostels and another 14,000 students in 45 residential schools exist from 3rd class to Degree level. In Telangana around 500 BC hostels are operational. In Hyderabad 22 hostels are located in the capital city from third class to degree level[15]. High priority is given for educational development by allocating about 70% of the annual budget of the social welfare department to this sector.

The following institutions are being run exclusively for BC students:

1. Residential schools
2. Ashram schools
3. Hostels
4. Post metric scholarships
5. Single-teacher schools(GVVK) Hostels

The role of these hostels in their education advancement is considerable. To achieve this objective, the government of Andhra Pradesh has started a large number of social welfare hostels and at present there are 1,742 hostels functioning in the state with BC children comprising 70% of the hostel inmates.

Andhra Pradesh Chief Minister K. Rosaiah recently announced setting up of 300 hostels for backward class college students with at least one in each Assembly constituency[16]. An equal number of hostels for girls were already sanctioned by the government in 2008-09. Mr. Rosaiah, speaking at the 184 birth anniversary celebrations of Jyothirao Phule organised by the Backward Classes Welfare Department, assured allocation of more funds for backward classes' welfare, with an additional budget of Rs.1,521 crores for 2010-11, while renewing his government's commitment to uplift the downtrodden sections. But, he has not mentioned the problems of the existing BC hostels in sustaining themselves before planning for another 300 new hostels in Andhra Pradesh.

BACKWARD CLASSES WELFARE DEPARTMENT

The goal of the Backward Classes Welfare department is to ensure better opportunities for the poor BCs to utilize educational facilities, to eradicate poverty, and eliminate current inequalities that prevent the Backward Classes form realizing their full potential thus establishing a just and egalitarian society.

OBJECTIVES

- To increase access to education to persons belonging to BC communities.
- To provide quality education to meritorious BC Students pursuing studies at pre-matriculation level.
- To promote higher education and impart quality education on par with general students.
- To reimburse tuition fees.
- To provide coaching facilities to eligible BC Students.

SERVICES

Hostel Facilities for BC (Pre-matriculation) Students

This department provides free boarding and lodging facilities for Backward Class children, with a total of 1,429 hostels, out of which 1,104 are for BC Boys and 325 are for BC Girls. Among the total hostels 1,415 are for BC hostels and 14 hostels for de- notified tribes. Generally, the sanctioned strength is 100. Admission of boarders' percentage of caste composition: BCs - 76%, (A-21%, B-31%, C-3%, D-21%). SCs-10%, STs-5%, Minorities -3% others - 6%. In the above hostels 1,72,786 boarders are provided with free boarding and lodging. There is a uniform schedule in all these hostels for day-to-day academic and other routine activities.

Also there is a uniform menu for all the hostels at the rate of Rs. 338/- per month for 3rd to 7th class boarders and Rs 412/- per month to 10th class boarders. The department also bears the expenditure for soap and oil @ Rs. 20/- per boy p.m. and Rs.25/- per girl per month as cosmetic charges. 2 pairs of clothes along with bedding material, trunk boxes, plates & glasses are also given to the hostel boarders as per the existing budget facilities[17].

Residential Schools

There are 30 Residential Schools for Backward Classes (19 Boys & 11 Girls) under the administrative control of AP

Residential Educational Institutions Society, Hyderabad, funded by the Department of Backward Classes Welfare.

Post-matriculation Scholarships

In order to promote higher education and impart quality education on par with general students, this department awards residential & non-residential post matriculation scholarships to students belonging to Backward Classes at all levels of post matriculation Courses in Cases where the parents' annual income does not exceed Rs.1,00,000/- per annum.

Vide G.O.Ms.No.18 the government has issued certain guidelines for sanction of post-matric scholarships and reimbursement of tuition fees. In the G.O., the government has agreed for sanction of post-matric scholarships and reimbursement of tuition fee and special fees to the eligible category "A" (convenor quota) BC students on saturation basis on par with the Social Welfare Department from the year 2008-09.

BC STUDY CIRCLES

To provide coaching facilities to eligible BC students to improve their performance in competitive examinations viz., Civil Services, SSC, RRB, State Service, EAMCET, DSC for teachers, etc.

LOCATION OF STUDY CIRCLES

1. Hyderabad
2. Warangal
3. Mahabubnagar
4. Kurnool
5. Ananthapur
6. Guntur
7. Visakhapatnam
8. Rajahmundry

PROBLEM OF THE STUDY

In this context, the present study was taken up among children residing in social welfare hostels for OBCs in Telangana Region. The study focuses on problems and perspectives of OBC students in Social Welfare Hostels. There is vast literature, focusing on SCs and STs on the status of education, influence of students' access to education, stratification within the educational system and the resulting inequalities of educational opportunities, differential utilization of educational facilities, drop-out rates, aspirations and achievements. However less attention was paid to the Backward Caste Communities especially to Chakali, Mangali, and Kumari etc. There are no studies worth mentioning specifically on the Backward Caste Communities with regards to elementary education in rural areas. The BCs are facing numerous problems socially, economically, politically and more specifically backward in education.

PROBLEMS AND ISSUES OF SOCIAL WELFARE HOSTELS

The government has initiated the above for the benefit of backward section people through the education. Despite this, BC students are facing a lot of problems at social welfare hostels in general and tribal welfare hostels in particular. The government is provides low mess charges, non-availability of breakfast, water and sanitation problems and students live in poorly maintained facility buildings which are cracked. SC, ST and BC student hostels and residential schools in a number of districts in Telangana brought to light the pathetic and unhygienic conditions prevailing and the serious problems faced by the students in the state. The inadequate allocation of funds by the state government has resulted in the improper maintenance of the hostels and residential schools. The healthcare of these hostel children is of utmost importance as they are in a period of growth and development and need an optimum health and nutrition care. The majority of the children is in the age group of 10-14 years

– the study revealed that the boys and girls in the hostels are suffering from major diseases like skin infections, diarrhea and eye infections etc.

'The Prajashakthi' Telugu daily covered the issue in the main page on the status of children in BC, SC and ST hostels covering Telangana districts namely (1) in Telangana recently, in Karimnagar-Mahadevpur BC hostel situations, (2) In Mahabubnagar-Balanagar, BC girls hostel, (3) Khammam-Devaragonda mandal Mudikonda ST hostel, (4) Medak-Narsapur ST hostel and (5) Ranga Reddy-Pudur mandal SC hostel[18]. *Eenadu* has also covered this problem in the editorial *Endamavi Sankshemam*[19]. CNBC as part of its Budget 2008 tour visited the Manchara village in Ranga Reddy to see the state of affairs in the region. As expected their observations are that the facilities in the hostel are very poor. The report says that the Government spends about Rs. 11 to 20 per day per girl child to provide facilities which include three square meals, books, clothes and a box to store her belongings, plus accommodation. Most of the students featured in the report said that the facilities are too congested for them and that their classes are getting disturbed because the classrooms are too close to each other. Hence these girls are neither getting a good education nor good living conditions. For this purpose the study is taken in two districts, namely Nizamabad and Warangal districts.

PROBLEMS OF SOCIAL WELFARE HOSTELS IN NIZAMABAD AND WARANGAL DISTRICT

Nizamabad Social Welfare Hostels

Nizamabad district is in Telangana region of Andhra Pradesh state in India. The total population of Nizamabad district is 20,37,621 as per 1991 census, while the BC. Population in the district is 8,30,549 which constitute 40.78% of the total population.

The Department of School Education has the major objective of achieving Universalisation of Elementary

Education. Under Universalisation of Elementary Education all children in the 5 to 15 age group have to be progressively brought to school. Keeping this in mind the department has been making efforts to improve enrolment and retention of all school-age children in schools. The district gross enrolment ratio for the age group of 6-10 years being 10.09 and the drop out rate for the same age group is 12.05. Nizamabad district authorities have taken several steps towards education particularly in social welfare hostels.

Appointment of Special Vidya Volunteers in SC, ST & BC Hostels: It has been decided to provide special tutors for the children of SC, ST and BC hostels in the district during the year 2007-08. The special tutors provide academic guidance and support to the children in the morning session from 6 A.M. to 8 A.M. and in the evening session from 5 P.M. to 8 P.M. It is planned to provide special tutors @1:40 according to admitted strength, up to maximum of 3 tutors per hostel.

Kasturba Gandhi Balika Vidyalayas (KGBVS): The government of India under the central sector has introduced the scheme of KGBVS. The schools are residential in nature and are aimed at creating residential schooling facilities for girls belonging to SCs, STs and OBCs. Under it, 94 KGBVs are sanctioned in 19 Districts. For Nizamabad District, 15 Schools are allotted in the following mandals under Model - I (with 100 capacity in all 3 classes VI, VII & VIII for the present year). In these 15 schools, 7 schools are already functioning from 2005-06 and preparatory arrangements are made to start. The remaining 8 schools will start in the month of November 2007.

Government - Social Welfare Hostels

67 Hostels (52) Boys including (2) Anandanilayams 15 Girls Hostels including (1) Anandanilayams) are functioning in this District. (6084) boarders are admitted during the year 2006-07. Out of (67) Hostels (17) are special hostels for 8th to

10th class students. In these special hostels, tutors for coaching 10th class students in (4) subjects i.e., English, Maths, Science & Hindi appointed with a monthly remuneration of Rs.500/- to each tutor to improve educational standards and achieve good results in 10th class during 2006-2007. In addition to this Patashala monthly magazines are supplied every month. Work books, question banks, and "all-in-one" are also being supplied to all 10th class students well in advance. Unit tests, slip tests etc. are being conducted to achieve good results. Out of (67) Hostels (52) Hostels are functioning in government buildings, out of which (46) government buildings require minor/major repairs. Some of the hostels are functioning in private buildings

Integrated Hostel Buildings

- The government has sanctioned (5) integrated hostel buildings to Nizamabad district, out of them (2) for SCs, (2) for BCs and (1) for STs. Proposals have been submitted to the Govt. for finalization of location.

S.C. College Hostels

(2) Boys and (3) Girls College Hostels are functioning at the following places.

With total strengths of (450) students:

1. College boys' hostel at Nizamabad
2. College girls' hostel at Nizamabad
3. College boys' hostel at Kamareddy
4. College girls' hostel at Kamareddy
5. College girls' hostel at Nizamabad (Newly sanctioned during the year 2006-2007[20]

Maintenance of BC Welfare Hostels

For educational development of Backward Classes, boy and girl boarders (43) B.C. hostels of which (33) for boys and (10) for girls are functioning in this district. (4102) boarders were given admission during the current year. Out of (43) BC hostels (32) BC hostels are functioning in government buildings and (11) BC hostels are functioning in private buildings. Out of (11) hostels in private buildings follow (3) BC hostel buildings are in finishing stages.

1. Girls, Jukkal
2. Boys, Morthad
3. Boys, Gandhari.

As mentioned above, construction of (3) BC hostel buildings, will also be taken up shortly. (08) Hostel buildings are functioning in private buildings, in which the government has sanctioned for construction of (5) government buildings as shown below.

1. Boys, Makloor
2. Boys, Mopal
3. Boys, Nizamsagar
4. Boys,Birkur
5. Girls, Kamareddy

(1) The sanctioned strength of (43) BC hostels	6. :: 7. 4102
(2) Renewal boarders (Boys)	8. :: 9. 1883
(3) Renewal boarders (Girls)	10.:: 11. 619
(4) Fresh boarders (Boys)	12.:: 13. 1279
(5) Fresh boarders (Girls)	14.:: 15. 321
Total ==>	16.:: 17. 4102
Total Boys	18.:: 19. 3162
Total Girls	20.:: 21. 940
Total ==>	22.:: 23. 4102 [21]

With these minimum facilities provided by the government, the BC students showed talent in the year of 2005-2006 in 10th class results. For the year 2005-06 (601) BC hostel boarders appeared for SSC examination out of which (359) passed in 1st division, (140) passed in 2nd division and (35) passed in 3rd division. With a total pass (534) and a percentage of 88.85%, the district percentage is 83.30%. Out of (601) boarders (30) boarders got 500 and above marks.

During the year 2006-07 an amount of Rs.272.81 lakhs has been released by the Director, BC. Welfare, A.P., Hyderabad. Out of this, an amount of Rs.226.05 lakhs was incurred in the hostels. The boarder will be provided food and other facilities free of cost as shown below:

1. Note books
2. Bed sheets and carpets
3. Plates, glasses and trunk boxes.
4. 2 pairs of dresses.
5. Cosmetic charges paid: Rs.20/- for boys and Rs.25/- for girl boarders. In English, Maths, Science and Hindi subjects, remuneration of Rs.500/- per month per subject will be paid to the tutor.
6. Tutors will be appointed in the hostel for SSC. Boarders.
7. Maabadi, Patashala, "all-in-one" books and work books will also be supplied to the hostel boarders.

Warangal Social Welfare Hostels

In Warangal district there are social welfare hostels for boys and girls SC, ST and BC hostels located in mandal and division level. SC hostels are 103 and students 15843, ST hostels 42 and 4000 above students are studying in these hostels[22]. In each room they are 20 to 30 students living together. The divisions are in Jangoan, Narsampet, and Mahabubabad and especially in ITDA Eurunagaram division like kannayagudem, Mangapet, Chunchupalli. The survey brought to the notice the lack of even basic amenities like drinking water, toilets, bathrooms and own buildings. For example, 136 girls in the ST hostel at Eturunagarm in

Warangal were forced to take mass bathing in one single bathroom. The students had to walk more than two kilometers for attending nature calls in open areas due to lack of toilets and bathrooms. The students suffer from contagious diseases and viral fever regularly because of the unhygienic conditions in the hostels. Though there are directions that doctors should visit the hostels regularly, no medical check up is arranged for the students even once in a year. Only when the hostel students are admitted to hospitals or only when they die, the officers concerned wake up. Medical kits are not provided to the hostels though a sum of one thousand rupees was allocated for this purpose. The survey revealed that the 10 hostel students in Jangoan, Narsampet, and Mahabubabad and especially in ITDA Eurunagaram in Warangal districts died, with no preventive and curative medicare was provided to them.

ST, SC and OBC students who are studying 3rd to 10th classes in the schools run by different managements both government and quasi-government, are being admitted into tribal welfare hostels, ex-primary schools, upper primary schools, high schools, AGHS, pre-matric scholarships (BAS), residential schools (English medium), colleges of excellence, mini gurukulams – these hostels are managed by a Hostel Welfare Officer.

In Warangal district,[23] about 200 girl students staying at Hanamkonda are paying the price for being poor. These students are entitled to receive tri-monthly supply of free provisions but they receive provisions once in a year. Some students, who are conscious of their hygiene, use dry brick powder or neem tree branches brush their teeth. The children bathe without bathing soap.

When we interviewed some students, they shared that they were given 300 gm Colgate toothpaste in the month of June along with other essential provisions. Said S. Krishna Kumar (name changed), a Class IX student from Tadawai mandal, they received their provisions only once, since the start of the academic year. According to the rule every month the hostel student should be provided three washing bars, two bath soaps, talcum powder, oil and shampoo but they are deprived of their regular supply of cosmetics. The students also complained that they are not even provided the benefit of a haircut. "Those who can afford go to a private saloon or have to wait till they visit their native places," said another student.

As regards to food, the only occasion they have a non-vegetarian treat in the entire year is on Republic Day and Independence Day. "Mutton and chicken are served on these two days," said the students, pointing out that on all evenings they get to eat only plain dal-rice.

The *Deccan Chronicle* reported in August 28th and 29th 2009 that at least 34 students of the AP Social Welfare Residential School at Eturnagaram have taken ill with viral fever over two days. The downpour which lasted for a week resulted in unhygienic conditions and had contaminated the water at the school resulting in the outbreak of viral fever. A total of 400 students study in the school located in the Agency area of the district[24].

The analysis of the BC hostels reveals that the facilities provided by government are poor. The quality of assets created and maintained are very poor. These children suffer from many disadvantages like illiterate parents, absence of educational atmosphere, irregularity and dropouts, lack of nutritional food and lack of resources.

It is therefore very pertinent that teachers should be properly trained and asked to be patient towards these children. The right type of teacher training and education can play a significant role in helping us to achieve the goal of literacy among the BC students/ children.

CONCLUSIONS

At district level, social welfare institutions need to be strengthened and given more autonomous powers to conceptualize, formulate and execute programmes with necessary independence. Education should be given a priority. The kind of education that is to be given to the BC students should be capable of equipping them with necessary skills so that their productivity is enhanced. Accent should be given to non formal education so that children show interest for the formal systems of education. Special programmes should be taken up to enhance awareness among BC students about social welfare schemes and development programmes. It is clear from the above analysis that the state has not taken this major problem seriously.

The study revealed that the welfare departments who have started with the objective of empowering the marginalized children through education are playing the role of civil society in providing freedom to educate children. Such a programmed approach is unlikely to yield desired results. The policies for empowerment of the marginalized are limited to white papers only. Education should generate an aesthetic sense in the community so as to enable them to live with self respect and be self dependent.

Kofi Annan, former United Nations Secretary-General rightly pointed out, *"Literacy unlocks the door to learning throughout life, is essential to the development and health, and opens the way for democratic participation and active citizenship."* We need to take this into account and provide minimum educational facilities for social welfare hostels particularly BC welfare hostels. There is a need to understand and analyze the dynamics between the politics and development of Backward Classes identities.

RECOMMENDATIONS

Having examined the issues relating to development and the reasons for the emergence of various movements in Telangana and India, there is a need to explore what possible interventions can be made. Unless right interventions are made with utmost commitment and sessions, the issues that we have mentioned above will continue to escape attention. Some of the possible areas of intervention are as follows.

- Deliberate and conscious efforts should be made to encourage the participation of BCs in the conceptualization, formulation and execution of development programmes. There is an urgent need for the institutions, of their participation in social development programmes at different levels.
- In spite of all the efforts, the education of BCs has not shown any marked improvement. There is a need for strategies to lessen dropout rate, abstentism etc.
- Existing schemes/programmes on education in different departments sponsored by central and state governments need to be pooled under one department for transparency and avoiding of duplication and overlapping of schemes and programmes in different departments.

Acknowledgement

I would like to thank Prof.Kancha Ilaiah, a Thinker, Social Activist and Professor at the Dept. of Political Science, Osmania University, and Hyderabad-India for his suggestions and guidance. I would like to thank Prof.V.Ravindra Sastry, Head & Coordinator (CAS), Dept. of Political Science, Osmania University, Hyderabad, Andhra Pradesh-India.

Notes and References

1. Omvedt, Gail, "Dalits and the Democratic Revolution", Dr. Ambedkar and the Dalit movement in Colonial India,: Sage. New Delhi, 1994.
2. *Ibid*, pp. 55-67.
3. Census of India 2001 registrar General & Census commissioner, New Delhi, India.
4. National sample survey organization, 55the round (2000).
5. National sample survey organization, New Delhi, India.

6. Gramsci, A., Prison Notes Books, Lawrence and Wishart International Publishers, London, 1971.
7. Friere, P., Pedagogy of the Oppressed, Translated by M. B. Ramoś, New York, Seabury press, 1970.
8. Mahatma Jotirao Phule, Collected Works of Mahatma Jotirao Phule, Vol.II, Educational Dept. of Government of Maharashtra, Bombay, 1991.(Mahatma Jotiba Govindrao Phule (April 11, 1827 — November 28, 1890), also known as Mahatma Jotiba Phule was an activist, thinker, social reformer, writer, philosopher, theologist, scholar, editor and revolutionary from Maharashtra,India in the nineteenth century. Jotiba Phule and his wife Savitribai Phule were the pioneer of women's education in India).
9. C. R. Mitra, Sree Narayana Guru and social revolution, Archana, Kottayam, 1979.
10. Right to education act.
11. Bishwaranjan, Mohanty, Displacement and Rehabilitation of Tribals, Economic and Political Weekly, March 26, 2005, p. 1318.
12. Yadappanavar, A.V., Tribal education in India, Discovery Publishing House, New Delhi, 2003.
13. Mazumdar, D.N, Races and cultures of India, 4th edi, Asia Publishing House, New Delhi, 1973.
14. Chalamalla Venkateshwarlu, Englishlo chaduvukonivvara, surya, 25-6-2008.
15. Interview with, Jajula Srinivas Goud, State General Secretary, BC Sakshema Sangham in Hyderabad, 2010.
16. The Hindu, Apr 12, 2010.
17. Data from Andhra Pradesh Government of Social Welfare Department - Residential School for Scheduled Castes/ Scheduled Tribes, 2009.
18. Prajashakthi, Nithyam akali nakanakalu, Hyderabad, 18-07-2006, p. 5.
19. Eenadu, Endamavi Sankshemam, Hyderabad, 17th February, 2010.
20. Data collected from the social welfare dept. of Collector office in Nizamabad district in Telangana, 2009.

21. *Ibid.*
22. Surya, Sankshamam, district special,Warangal, 19th February, 2010.
23. Deccan Chronicle, Nov. 20, 2009.
24. Deccan Chronicle, Aug 29, 2009.

STRATEGIC REFORMS FOR DALIT EMPOWERMENT

K. DAMODARA REDDY AND G. NARASIMHA REDDY

INTRODUCTION-DALITS IN INDIA

Dalits, termed as God's children (Harijans) by M.K.Gandhi, in actual don't seem to be so. The Hindu Manudharma actually says that Dalits, the most vulnerable community forms almost 1/3rd of the District's population. The term 'Dalit' has its roots in Sanskrit (dal) which means broken, cracked, trodden down, crouched or destroyed. It is interesting to note that the prophet Isaiah uses this word having the root in Hebrew language 'DAL', meaning broken or crushed or the poor of the land and the frail one, which denotes the poor or the lowly of the society. It is the self-designation of those who are astride of the fowl Hindu caste called in the Indian constitution as 'Scheduled Castes'. They are not even treated as human beings and are neglected in society. They are deliberately made poor and outcast and their work is exploited. They are shoved to the corners of society by the landlords and upper castes, who call themselves aristocrats.

EMPOWERMENT OF DALITS

In India the word "Dalit" means "oppressed people". They are defined as "untouchables" by the caste system and occupy the lowest level of society. The Dalit peoples' use of water wells is limited. They face restrictions on entering temples or residences of higher-caste people, their ability to own land is limited, and their residences are frequently isolated and scattered from the rest of the population. In addition to this social discrimination, Dalit people also face physical violence and murder. Dalits live in abject poverty and are forced into jobs such as street cleaning, disposal of excrement and animal carcasses, and leather tanning; sometimes they are also forced to work as indentured servants.

Within the group, Dalit women occupy the lowest caste, class, and gender position, and have long since been the object of oppression and violence in all parts of their daily lives. The atrocities against Dalit women are the primary issue which in turn results in an evil kind of situation in society. Due to lack of literacy and sufficient knowledge, they are being assaulted by the upper-caste people. As per the bad economic conditions in the state Dalit children are treated as servants in the houses with good economic conditions. They are harassed mentally and physically tortured. Due to the poor background they have to perform their tasks facing ill treatment.

CONSTITUTIONAL PROVISIONS FOR DALITS

The Constitution of India formally abolished "untouchability" when it went into effect in 1950 and there have been subsequent laws prohibiting brutality and protecting civil rights, which were to function as a Dalit protection law. However, due to resistance on the part of upper-castes, these laws do not function as they were intended to.

The phenomena of atrocities against the Dalits is generally understood by the people in terms of physical violence such as rape, murder, hurt, arson, looting and other offences as defined in the Indian Penal Code (IPC). Such a meaning of atrocities is partial as it does not include cognizance of other aspects and like abusing, humiliating, taunting and making remarks by a person or group against others or socio economic oppression to them.

Caste atrocities are an integral feature of Dalit life. The government machinery keeps on collecting their statistics year after year and issues them in a report by the Commissioner for SCs and STs (now the National Commission for SCs and STs). There are at least three Articles (15, 17 and 23) in the Constitution of India which seeks to mitigate this evil. To give effect to these Constitutional provisions the following acts also have been in operation:

1. The Untouchability (Offences) Act, 1955, later amended and re-titled as the Protection of Civil Rights Act, 1955.
2. The Scheduled Castes and Scheduled Tribes (Prevention of Atrocities Act) 1989 and the Bonded Labour System (Abolition) Act, 1976.

Coupled with the weakness of Dalits, their growing assertiveness and refusal to submit to the casteist dictates of the village lords, rebellion ethos assimilated through the Ambedkarian struggle and process of general awareness also causes atrocities to increase.

GOVERNMENT POLICES AND PROGRAMMES TO DALITS TOWARDS EMPOWERMENT

The social disadvantage suffered by Dalits in India was taken note of in the Constitution of India which was drafted under the chairmanship of Dr. Ambedkar - a person who had spearheaded the most momentous anti-caste movement of the depressed classes. It provided Dalits with many safeguards, viz.,

1. Social, educational, cultural and religious safeguards,
2. Economic safeguards,
3. Political safeguards and

4. Safeguards for employment.

The free-market ethos of the Reforms, conceptually can neither confirm to the democratic spirit of the Indian Constitution of 'one vote, one value', nor can it coexist with the system of positive discrimination embodied in these safeguards. For the market grants a moneyed person more value, and overtly believes in the jungle law of 'might is right'. To a large extent, the primary motivation behind these Constitutional provisions was liberal, democratic aspirations that characterized the freedom movement. However, these aspirations and the initial ideological zeal of the founding fathers withered away in no time and what survived was its utilitarian dimension for the electoral politics. The sorry state of the executive compliance with these Constitutional provisions amply bears the fangs of the Indian society. The reforms will bring a kind of legitimacy to this attitudinal resistance. These safeguards will stand eroded as the reforms gain in momentum. The influence of the reforms is bound to be all-pervasive. However, only a few issues of importance to the Dalit masses have been picked up for discussion here.

PRESENT POSITION OF DALITS IN INDIA:

Dalits who have played an imperative role in social transformation do not cultivate the fruits of the reforms due to the following reasons-

'Lack of Awareness an Impediment for Dalit Empowerment'

Lack of awareness has become an impediment for Dalits and tribals (Scheduled Castes. SCs and Scheduled Tribes, STs) in availing various schemes being implemented for their empowerment by the Government of Andhra Pradesh.

The state government is extending financial assistance from Rs. 5 lakh to Rs. 1 crore under credit guarantee for micro and small enterprises schemes. Under the industrial investment promotion policy of 2005, known as the Tata-

Birla scheme, the entrepreneurs could avail loan up to Rs. 5 crore without any collateral security. But the bankers are not sanctioning loans for lack of collateral security. Many applications were submitted for availing different schemes, but to no avail.

The Practice of Untouchability

Untouchability means the avoidance of physical contact with persons and things because of beliefs relating to pollution or infection. It is widely prevalent in regard to cultural matters such as temple entry and the domestic sphere such as marriage, place of shelter, inter-dining and social get-togethers.

Agrarian Dependence

Most of the Dalits are landless agricultural labourers. Low wages for more work, under employment and unemployment are the part and parcel of the occupational life of the Dalit people. They depend on moneylenders and rich farmers for their unforeseen expenses. They borrow money from them and most of the income goes for paying the interest. Rural indebtedness is very common in these villages. As a result, bonded labour is prevalent in a disguised manner. Literally speaking Dalits, the manual labourers are the legal holders of this civilized world.

Housing Pattern

A major portion of the Dalits lives in huts built with mud walls and thatched roofing. Their huts become easy prey when there are natural as well as man-made calamities. Dalits even now reside in adverse areas like the outskirts of the village. They do not have an equal opportunity to share even water near the hand pumps. Due to improper power facilities, they are far away from the awareness and the fruits that lavish them with development through the electronic media.

Denial of Self-Dignity & Opportunity

The real problem of Dalits is not just economic. It is primarily social & psychological. It is not a color problem. The sense of inferiority and other negative attitudes of the Dalits have remained the same for generations. Fundamentally every Dalit is a victim who is in urgent need of restoring his or her human dignity and human rights.

STEPS TO BE TAKEN FOR DALIT EMPOWERMENT:

In order to attain an efficient empowerment system, certain strict strategies should be put in practice like:

- Rights regarding to the provision of housing, health and property
- Providing food security with an efficient distribution system
- Rules of reservation policy should be adopted by the private sector
- Reservation and financial assistance in education institutions
- Policy of eliminating caste discrimination and ensuring that all public authorities and institutions – do not engage in caste-based discrimination which has been traditionally followed
- Freedom to choose religion
- Eradication of social interaction between Dalits and non-Dalits
- Distribution of land to the landless agricultural labourers

CONCLUSION

The Dalits in India, being the poorest of the poor have been hit the hardest. Their social disabilities, largely reinforced by and sustained on economic deprivation, are bound to get accentuated with these policies. The Indian reforms were essentially 'crisis driven' and not 'strategy driven' when they were adopted. There have since been changes in the formation and key persona. The broad Indian reality is that India has too many poor. No statistics, moreover, can adequately capture the heinous socio-cultural inequality that is an abiding part of Indian reality. It has acute inequalities not only in economic but in also in socio-cultural terms.

The reform strategy thus should embody sustainable economic empowerment of rural masses; investments to enhance their capability and effective measures for accelerated development of the disadvantaged sections like Dalits. The pre-requisite to reforms therefore could be radical land reforms, massive investments in rural areas into agriculture-related infrastructural projects, universalisation of primary education, primary health care system and reinforcement of positive discrimination in favour of Dalits. The devil of casteism can be tamed only by freeing the general masses of people from the anxieties and uncertainties about basic survival. The general conditions of deprivation have rendered them vulnerable to be the preys of the frequent machinations of the vested interests that make them see the enemy within their own class. The relative equality thus can be the bedrock for launching the socio-cultural offensive in the form of mass-education programmes. But this all may still not be enough. The policy of positive discrimination in favour of Dalits will have to be reinforced much more vigorously in all the sectors of the economy, than ever before. They need to be reframed and simplified for effective implementation.

References

Centre for Monitoring the Indian Economy (1996): *Public Finance in India*, June 1996, p. 32.

Gaiha, R. (1994), *Impact of Structural Adjustment of State Level - A Comparative Analysis of Andhra Pradesh, Maharashtra and Karnataka*, Faculty of Management Studies, University of Delhi, August, Mimeo.

Bandyopadhyay, D. (1995), "Impact of SAP: Hunger and Jobless Growth", *Mainstream*; May 13, 1995, p. 12.

United Nations Conference on Trade and Development (1995), *UNCTAD Statistical Pocket Book*, p. 69.

Mukherjee, Amitava (1994), Quoted in Bandyopadhyay D., *op. cit.* (3), p. 13.

EPW Research Foundation (1995), 'Myth of Inflation Control'; *Economic and Political Weekly*, January 7, 1995, p. 21.

Kurien, C. T. (1996), 'The Real Impact ', *Frontline*, February 9, 1996, p. 97.

SOCIAL EMPOWERMENT: A Case of Reservations in the Private Sector

K. VIDYASAGAR REDDY

CASTEISM AND SOCIAL EXCLUSION

The hierarchical caste system is deeply rooted into the Indian society, whether it is North or South, Tamils or Bengalis and cities or villages. The chaturvarna system of four castes was legitimised in the name of Hindu social order. Traditionally, of all the three upper castes viz. Brahmins, Kshatriyas and Vaishyas, the Brahmins were custodians of dharma, the Kshatriyas vested with political power and the Vaishyas were the traders and ran the economy. Whereas, the fourth group, the so-called lower castes, described as the Shudras were engaged in manual labour. But then, Hindu chauvinists preached and practised the Manu code of social exclusion (Manu Smritis) whereby a vast majority of Shudras were deprived of their basic human rights. Out of the Shudra community, Atishudras were created so as to be treated as social untouchables and to remain as slaves.

Thanks to social reformers like Buddha, Kabir, Jyotiba Phule, Sant Ravidas, Sahuji Maharaj, Periyar, Narayan Guru and Dr. B.R.Ambedkar, the cruel social evil of untouchability was questioned over a period of time. Dr. Ambedkar was more forthright in his struggle against casteism at home and abroad. Owing to his serious efforts of educating and organising the untouchable communities, the process of social liberation was initiated long before India attained Independence. Due to his efforts, the British government conceded to several demands. All those excluded communities, who were treated as untouchables for centuries, were recognised as those who deserve special support in the development.

Social empowerment of these communities was the main idea behind the demand of reservations in different sectors. Seeking fair share for them in the development was justified. Not only that they should develop educationally and employment-wise, but also contribute to the development of the nation. Deprived of any other means of life, it is humanitarian if they are provided with certain means of livelihood. For instance, education empowers, as it enables them get employment. These are essential for not only economic upliftment, but also to elevate themselves in the social hierarchy. Like all other human beings, these marginalised communities are also expected to lead a just human life, a dignified one, if not a luxurious life!

GENESIS OF RESERVATIONS

In fact Dr. B. R. Ambedkar is on record of having raised this issue long before it was incorporated in the Indian Constitution. Initially, he was inspired by Chatrapathi Sahuji Maharaj of Kolhapur[1]. For, he implemented the concept of reservations for non-Brahmins in the early part of 1900. Dr.Ambedkar continued his fight for implementation of reservations through his appeals to the British authorities,[2] way back in 1919. Further, during the period of the Simon Commission[3] too, he voiced the need of granting reservation facilities for those marginalised communities who had been deprived of even a few human rights for centuries. At the time of the three Round Table Conferences during the period of 1930-31, held at London, Dr. Ambedkar focussed his attention on the question of special treatment to these communities in education and employment. He raised the issue singlehandedly and influenced the Constituent Assembly in 1947.

Owing to Dr. Ambedkar's leading role in the Constitution making[4], reservations were included therein, whereby the government was bound to implement them on the basis of principle of positive discrimination and reimbursement for past disadvantages. But, the policy was restricted only to the public sector that was aided by the state and government. Although the state offered variety of concessions to the private sector, it was left free from social and legal obligations as it was hardly under the control of the government. The private sector was free to run the business the way it wanted. Ultimately, the states were entrusted with the task of supporting all those marginalised communities that were disempowered so far. Of course, the policy of reservation was not to be implemented with a retrospective effect, and also not beyond the share of population in the country.

Thus, the government has formally documented castes and sub-castes, belonging to the SCs and STs, primarily to settle on reservation policy in education and jobs through census in the post-independence period. The Indian reservation system relies entirely on quotas for scheduled castes and scheduled tribes, as per their population figures. The main objective of the reservation policy in India was to guarantee social empowerment of these communities like Dalits and Adivasis[5], which constitute around 16 and 8 percent respectively in the total population of India, whereas, 15 per cent and 7.5 per cent of them (SCs and STs respectively) are assured of reservations. Thus, the reservation policy per se is just an inclusive policy that ensures social representation and economic justice, as it merely seeks its representation in certain fields of governance. As part of securing their share of social empowerment, these excluded communities were justified in demanding their legitimate share in all fields including that of political power.

SABOTAGE FROM 'WITHIN'

This concept of 'Reservations' aimed at ensuring the betterment of underprivileged and deprived sections of society was sabotaged from 'within' in the initial days. There were bureaucrats and employees that belonged to the upper strata of society who were unenthusiastic with regard to implementation of reservations. Except in the category of manual work and sanitation and other menial jobs, these reservations were not implemented beyond 10 percent in the higher category of posts. Since the positions (IAS, IPS etc.,) that were recruited by the UPSC[6] were mandatory, these were implemented as per the notification.

In other words, except in the top-level central services, the jobs in other categories are still unoccupied by the Dalit candidates. Thousands of such posts were kept vacant year after year for want of able candidates passing the concerned qualifying tests. The fact that several governments both at the centre and in states and public sector units were found to be advertising, the 'backlog vacancies' in the name of special-drives, so as to recruit members from these reserved categories vindicate the above proposition. As backlog posts were seldom recruited periodically, large masses of unemployed candidates remain jobless.

Thus, these reservations[7] were being renewed decade after decade. Even though constitutional obligations are binding upon all the government departments, none bothered to adhere to them seriously. It is only in the last few years, owing to the efforts of some Dalit leaders and their movements that there was some improvement in this direction. Even then, none of the state government departments could ever claim that the required vacancies were duly filled up. More than the case of lack of availability of suitable candidates in these communities for the prescribed positions, it is the employers' biased attitude against such candidates that is largely responsible for the prevailing situation. Of course, some court cases[8] in the Supreme Court a couple of years ago could help the community in securing some justice in terms of revising the orders of promotion among other benefits.

CONSTITUTIONAL OBLIGATIONS

Thanks to democracy, numbers matter more than anything else. Since political power is vested in those who command majority votes, during the course of periodic elections, the marginalised communities deserve their fair share. As a matter of fact, Dr.Ambedkar has implemented the principle of political equality in the Constitution of India. Thus, political power is supposed to be distributed among all voters equally. Obviously, the SCs and STs who constitute around one-fourth of the country's population are those who are entitled to enjoy political power accordingly. It is very fair and constitutional.

But, what has happened over the period of the last six decades in the country is well known to everyone. Never were they allowed to enjoy the benefits of reservations, as per the stipulated percentage. Their share of opportunities was grabbed by those who were seldom entitled. More so was in the case of education and employment. Yet, the upper castes devised methods of sabotaging these political reservations too. For instance, those spineless and selfish representatives belonging to these lower castes would be so selected and picked up as to get them elected as 'reserved' legislators! As Kanshiram[9] termed them as stooges in the hands of upper castes, such legislators merely dance to the tunes of their upper caste masters. Even such little gesture or tokenism as reservation policy was implemented only in the public sector.

In all other sectors, less said the better, as reservations are not applicable to them at all! Be it land, real estate, industry or any natural resource for that matter, their share of involvement is not traceable in any of them. As if these are all privatised, or privately owned (as right to property was a fundamental right for long) by those few top Indians, otherwise known as, Upper caste men, the SCs and STs were barred from their access. Thanks to the Nehruvian policy of mixed economy[10], the private sector was given a partisan treatment. Incidentally, the Industrial Act of 1948 reserved a mere 18 sectors into public domain, leaving the rest to the private sectors. Over a period of time, the public sector was restricted with just half a dozen sectors, whereby the private sector became so potent that it dictated terms to the government.

PRIVATE RESERVATIONS

In any case, the vast majority of private institutions were never asked to provide jobs to the candidates of the marginalised communities. Obviously, the private sector that employs around 90 percent of the work force in the country was under no obligation to fulfil the constitutional requirements. Meanwhile, several studies[11] on the Labour Market reveal that insignificant percentage of these communities was employed, while excluding a large majority of them by way of social discrimination. Whereas those near and dear or kith and kin (Thanks to Bhai-Bhatijavad type of nepotism) of the private managements were given more jobs, beyond their population proportion!

Thus the reservation policy was devised to undo the prevailing/age-old reservations to the upper-castes from time immemorial. In a way, it can be described as a measure of 'reverse reservation'. These Constitutional reservations are anti-discriminatory in nature, indeed! In the absence of these, equal opportunities in education and employment can never be given to the marginalised communities, as is the practice in private institutions so far! It is sufficient to cite the case of OBCs in education and employment, or in Political institutions, where their representation is disproportionate to their population figures. In comparison, SCs and STs are better represented than the OBCs in public sector, a fact that none can contest

The half-hearted approach on behalf of the upper-caste biased bureaucracy was responsible for the partial implementation of reservations. In a way, this policy helps to realize the goal of empowerment of the Dalits and tribals in the long run. It can address certain social inequalities that encompass Indian society from time immemorial. For, these social inequalities leave the so-called lower-castes deprived in everything from education to economy. Thus, the policy of reservations intends to bring about proportional representation, as it is a mode of distributing benefits based on the ratio of their population.

Meanwhile, the government of India having recognised the severity of the problem, made some attempts to solve it by offering reservation facilities in the private sector in 1965, at a time when the American President Kennedy implemented the Civil Rights Act of 1964 in favour of those discriminated Negroes and other minorities for centuries! It is interesting to quote the Executive Order (10925) in that context: Such public policies are intended 'To overcome the present effects of past racial discrimination'. Such an affirmative action was introduced only to set right the deformities of the then American system, and thus tantamount to 'reverse discrimination'.

But then, more than the private sector, the bureaucracy was reluctant to implement the same. Thus, the concept received a setback as the government retreated on the issue. Further, the Indira Gandhi-led government tried to proceed on the issue in 1972, but in vain. That was also the time when the first ever Private Reservation Act was implemented in Northern Ireland[12]. Similar acts were made by the Malaysian government with regard to protecting the local-Malays (sons of the soil) from the 'control by outsiders' during the same time.

Incidentally, the public sector that had been retreating itself for over several decades has not been able to offer ample career-prospects, be it in education or in employment. At a time when the number of educated among these unprivileged classes is increasing in geometrical progression, their share of jobs in the public sector is dwindling. This is more so since the last two decades all in the name of the so-called free market and phenomenon of globalisation. Obviously, these economic reforms envisage the withdrawal of the state from its social obligations once and for all. Thus, each country should decide about the nature and extent of globalization that can be constructively introduced in their socio-economic and educational systems. Thus there is a serious need of private reservations in the country.

GLOBALISATION AND AFTER

Meanwhile, in the wake of decade-long globalisation[13], the state pursued the policies of liberalisation, privatisation and globalisation, whereby the public sector became sick. Still, the private sector was persuaded to take over and own such, the so-called sick units that were under public sector, at a throw away prices! Meanwhile, the winds of change in the name of 'Economic Reforms' have slowly shaken the very foundations of the Dalits and Adivasis. In consequence, more than anyone else it is these who would be the first ones to be affected very adversely in the event of the 'no reservation in private sector'. Unlike others, who had some land, assets, education and employment, with the help of which they could manage for some time, the marginalised could not face the ground realities. Their survival and growth depends upon the state support. However, if the state withdraws such support and removes certain employees, then one can imagine the fate of marginalised communities. According to a Report of Working Groups[14] on Empowering of SCs, due to the LPG policies in 1992-97 itself, 1,13, 450 SCs lost jobs in the central government (public sector) alone. What about those SC employees working in the state governments' public sector units in the country? In a way, the state has clearly abdicated its constitutional obligation.

Whereas, the private sector was strengthened in such a way that it absorbed more work force. While the private sector enjoys the support of the state in establishment and management of the business ventures, it demonstrates its unwillingness to oblige the constitutional regulations on the issue of providing employment opportunities to marginalised and underprivileged communities. Meanwhile, there are also some voices raised against the phenomena of globalisation and its aftermath. While the upper strata of society is in a position to survive the pressures of the globalisation, as it has grabbed some job-opportunities in the private sector, marginalised communities that are dependent on the state support have been left orphaned.

More than anybody else, it is Dalits and Adivasis who were entrapped in the vicious circle of globalisation. The globalisation phenomenon elevated those who could afford access to quality education in corporate institutions[15]. The marginalised students ended up studying in government-aided schools and colleges with poor facilities. That was a time when the issue of caste discrimination was taken up, on par with the racial discrimination, at the World Conference in 2001[16]. Although government representatives led by the Indian External Affairs Ministers that represent the upper caste bias were reluctant to equate caste with race, the people's groups and dalit representatives like Uditraj, Paul Diwakar and others put forward the argument quite forcefully. They had substantiated their argument on the basis of statistics that delineate the attacks against the marginalised in the country. For instance, even after passage of the SC/ST (Prevention of Atrocities) Act in 1989, the safety and protection of Dalits is left to their fate, as there is rise in crime rate against them.

Further, the National Human Rights Commission (NHRC) noted in its 2002 report: "Under-reporting (atrocities) is a common phenomenon and the police resort to various machinations to discourage SC/ST (persons) from registering their cases, to dilute the seriousness of the violence to shield the accused persons from arrests and prosecution". Besides, the judiciary should also be made accountable for the lapses, as most of the accused under the IPC Act, have been acquitted under the SC/ST Act. Suffice it to cite a case of notorious Khairlanji (Maharashtra) where the criminals now serving the death penalty were acquitted under the SC/ ST Act. According to the National Bureau of Crime Report (2006), 27,070 crimes were committed against Dalits, though many more go unreported.

Similar attempts were made at other global fora thereafter. At the national level too, there were some attempts to raise the issue of reservations in the private sector at Bhopal[17] and other places. In consequence, the congress government in Madhya Pradesh and other states was ready to comply with the Bhopal declaration that aimed at offering better facilities at all levels, including the private sector. Other states and political parties were compelled to concede the demand of private reservations, gradually. For instance, the Maharashtra government, under S K Shinde tried to implement the same but failed, due to protest from the business lobbies.

NOT A CHARITY, BUT A SOCIAL INCLUSION

In any case, this concept of private reservation cannot be considered as charity[18], but a right from a government that has exposed its insincerity. Further, it is a social inclusive policy as the government has failed to create jobs to its qualified aspirants. Whereas on the other hand, the government has permitted private educational institutions of a corporate nature to establish themselves in the country. But what about social obligations? Thanks to Dr.Ambedkar, the government policy of reservations in education and employment spheres has played a remarkable role for Dalits and Adivasis. The constitutional provision that merely envisages a proportionate representation of them as to their population, not beyond that, is subjected to a half-hearted approach.

Whatever be the criticism, the reservation facilities have given certain economic means of livelihood to over 1.5 million Dalits, for instance. Besides, over 50,000 Dalits have been able to enter the field of government authority so far. Adivasis too have entered the service sector accordingly. Obviously, over a period of time these physical benefits have instilled some confidence in the Dalit and Adivasi communities. Besides economic benefits, political reservations have also helped significant number of them to occupy the positions of power at all levels. Obviously, these changes have empowered them socially, and thus many more are yet to be empowered gradually.

UPA GOVERNMENT

Ever since the previous[19] United Progressive Alliance (UPA) government at the centre promised to introduce job reservations in the private sector, there were a few discordant reactions from some elite and non-political quarters. In fact, as part of its Common Minimum Programme (CMP), the Congress-led political coalition provided this measure in the election manifesto way back in 2003. Since the given laws are not so specific as to ensure reservations in the private sector compulsorily, there is a need for formulating a new set of such laws. Of course, there was an attempt made by the UPA regime in 2005 and also in 2009 to bring about a law in this regard. But the so-called consensus was not arrived at on the subject.

Besides, the executive organ of the government has to be motivated to enforce the laws concerning private reservations. Unless its attitude is not changed the bureaucracy will not implement the policy effectively. Further, the government should create such an atmosphere wherein the judicial interference should promote, rather than preclude implementation of the reservation policy. At last, there emerged some political consensus, following apparent attempts from several quarters like, Ambedkar organizations and Dalit-based parties. The Congress-led UPA government was already under the obligation to implement the job reservations in the private sector too. However, thanks to vote-bank politics, the political parties of all hues were compelled to consider the serious nature of this demand and thereby echoed with the aspirations of the hard-up classes.

Meanwhile, the UPA promise[20] has created many a controversy on the subject. That in turn has been responsible in raising certain related questions. For instance, whether Private sector is bound by the law of the land? Is it not a beneficiary of state support while establishing business ventures and industries? Whether the qualified Dalits and Adivasis are to be excluded in the private employment? Is it not possible for the private sector to train these disadvantaged communities before being employed? These are some solemn questions that deserve serious consideration.

RESERVATION CRITICS

Incidentally, there surfaced some reservation critics from different quarters. Their arguments were so ridiculous and humiliating that the marginalised communities retaliated at once. Besides the business houses, the so-called experts who seldom supported job reservations in the public sector for so long were also the ones who raised serious objections in the name of 'merit' and 'meritocracy'! Although undeclared reservations to certain privileged communities[21] were never done away with, the defenders of merit were making hue and cry on the concept of reservations in the private sector.

In any case, the argument of a score sheet in a qualifying examination deciding the appointment of a candidate does not hold good. For, merely a degree or two does not equip anybody with the needed skills to do a job. There is a serious need of imparting training to any job aspirant for the period of a certain time frame, so that he would be practically fit to underta0ke the job. Once that exercise is undertaken, then there does not exist any such problem of appointing an ill-equipped candidate in any post, be it reserved or otherwise.

As usual, a section of the media has persistently been prejudiced against the downtrodden and Dalit communities in this country. Preoccupied with elite notions and prejudices in favour of the creamy layer in the country, the media has undermined the significance of reservations in private sector. Thus, Manyasri Kanshiramji (BSP Founder) was on record for criticising the media, money and mafia as those institutions that strengthen the status-quo!

ALTERNATIVE STRATEGIES

Ever since the Bahujan Samaj Party[22] was formed, there surfaced an alternative path of struggle that promised capturing state power for marginalised communities. Within a decade of its existence, the party became a recognised national party, having its strong base in the state of Uttar Pradesh. By the year 2007, despite the death of Kanshiramji, Mayawatiji alone led the BSP in the Assembly elections successfully and became the chief minister (fourth time) on her own! More than what she achieved as the power centre, Mayawatiji created confidence among the marginalised communities in the state and outside. Not only did she emerge as the alternative to both the Congress and BJP, but also initiated several policies and schemes that brought about social empowerment in the state.

Of course, she had not only promised reservations in the private sector, but also implemented them in a big way. Besides the SCs, BCs, open category persons that belonged to the economically backward communities were also promised private reservations[23] in the state. Further, she had requested the centre to implement the same in the central government positions too. For the first time such positive steps have been taken by the BSP regime in the state of Uttar

Pradesh in the country. Certainly, it marks the beginning of a new era in the history of marginalised communities in India.

Her alternative strategy towards the private sector was that it should provide reservations to the marginalised communities, as the private sector was getting the benefit of government concessions in the establishing of industries and ventures. Failure to do so would deprive the private sector from enjoying such government concessions. Unlike other state governments, she did not seek any kickbacks or bribes for her party or for herself, from these private sector agencies! Rather, she enforced private reservations with the use of a disincentive policy.

To conclude, due to prevailing age-old suppression and oppression, these communities have been discriminated by those who were at the helm of affairs. They were denied land, property, assets and even education. For years together, they were enslaved and kept as bonded labourers by the dominant communities. Obviously, they were given no representation in the governance of the nation. It is only after India became a Republic that all these communities were treated equally by the constitution. Certain political rights were given to them. It is only after a couple of decades of independence, that they were encouraged to use their constitutional rights. Similarly, given a chance, these communities could utilise the opportunities available in the private sector. This inclusive policy seems to be the most appropriate strategy that can empower those marginalised communities that have been excluded from the governance of a representative democracy such as India. More than before, the concept of private reservations has attracted a vast mass of population, as the process of globalisation has adversely affected the marginalised communities in a big way, today.

Notes and References

1. A Small Princely State in India.

2. British government appointed Sougthborough Committee on Franchise.
3. Visiting India in 1922.
4. Chairman of the Drafting Committee.
5. Otherwise described as the Scheduled Castes and Scheduled Tribes in the constitution.
6. Union Public Service Commission, New Delhi.
7. Contemplated for first ten years only.
8. Filed by the of All India Confederation SC &ST Organizations, that was led by Udit Raj of the India Justice party.
9. Kanshiram's book, 'The Chamcha Age: An era of stooges'.
10. Which promised the so-called socialistic pattern of society.
11. Sukhdev Thorat and others (ed), 'Reservation and Private Sector', Rawat Pub., New Delhi.
12. The Report of the Working Party on Discrimination in the Private Sector of Employment, 1973.
13. 1990-2000.
14. 10th Five year Plan, Planning Commission, Govt. Of India, New Delhi, (2001).
15. See an Article 'Globalisation of Education' by K V Sagar, in *www.Countercurrents.Org*.
16. At Durban, South Africa.
17. During the regime of Digivijay singh of the Congress party.
18. See An Article 'Reservations in Private Sector...', by K V Sagar in the www.Countercurrents.org.
19. 2004-09.
20. Reservations in Private Sector.
21. That own the business, partially or otherwise.
22. Founded by Manyasri Kanshiram in 1984.
23. One-third of the 30% was meant for the SCs.

DR. B. R. AMBEDKAR: HIS VIEWS ON DEMOCRACY

G. LALAIAH

Dr. Babasaheb Bhimrao Ambedkar was one of the illustrious sons of India, who struggled to restructure the Indian society on the most egalitarian and humanitarian principles. He was not only a great national leader but also a distinguished scholar of international repute. He was the first Indian political thinker who realized the inapplicability of the western pattern of democracy to India. For him, it was not enough to make a distinction between the state and society, state and government and state and nation. But he went to the roots of these institutions and pointed out, the importance of taking into account the elements constituting these institutions, which are the people. Western writers like Harold Laski and MacIver did not go further than suggesting a distinction between the state and society and so on. They made only superficial references to the social and economic status of the various classes of people, who constitute the society and the state.

Dr. Ambedkar criticized western writers, in his book "What Congress and Gandhi have dome to the Untouchables." To him, western writers failed to recognize the social and economic contradictions.

The definitions of democracy given by Walter Bagehot or Abraham Lincoln did not satisfy Dr. Ambedkar. Bagehot defines democracy as "Government by discussion", Lincoln as – the Government of the People, by the people and for the people[2].

Thus according to Dr. Ambedkar a mere façade of democracy would not achieve the purpose of democracy, which should be the welfare of the whole people.

MEANING OF DEMOCRACY

According to Dr. Ambedkar, Democracy means a form and method of government where revolutionary changes in the economic and social life of the people, are brought about without bloodshed[3]. To him, if democracy can enable, those who attempt to bring about fundamental changes in the social and economic life of the people, and the people accept those changes without resorting to bloodshed, such democracy is the real test. It is perhaps the severest test. To him, democracy is a mode of associated living. He considered that the roots of democracy were to be found in social relationships in terms of the associated life between the people who formed the society. Poverty, illiteracy and caste discriminations were the positive dangerous to the democracy[4].

Dr. Ambedkar sought to remove the contradictions generated by social and economic inequalities. He wanted to establish the principle of one man, one vote and one value, not only in the political life of India but also in social and economic life. In other words, he wanted political democracy to be accompanied by social democracy.

To Dr. Ambedkar, Social democracy involves three things: an attitude of mind, an attitude of respect and equality towards their fellows and a social organization free from rigid social barriers. To him, democracy was incompatible and inconsistent with isolation and exclusiveness resulting in the discrimination between the privileged and the unprivileged. He wanted high political objectives, but they must keep harmony with social aims. He regarded democracy as both a social ideal and a political method[5].

PARLIAMENTARY DEMOCRACY IN INDIA

During the discussion in the Constituent Assembly, Dr. Ambedkar said, "Personally speaking, I am very greatly attached to the Parliamentary System of Government[6]. We must understand what it means and we must preserve it in the Constitution. To me, parliamentary democracy is unknown to us at present, but we must adopt this institution. India was far more advanced in ancient times. If you go through the "Suktas" of Mahaprinnibban, you will find ample of evidence in support of my point. In these Suktas it is stated that, while Bhagwan Buddha was dying at Kushinagara a message to this effect was sent to the Malla's who were sitting in the session. When they received the message about the Buddha, they decided that they shall not close the session but would carry on with their work and will go to Kushinagar after finishing the business of the parliament.[7]

According to Dr. Ambedkar there are three main things inherent in parliamentary systems of government. They are:

1. Parliamentary government means the negation of hereditary rule. No person can claim to be a hereditary ruler. One must be elected by the people from time to time to become a ruler. He must obtain the approval of the people. Hereditary rule has no sanction in a parliamentary system of government.
2. Laws have to be made for the welfare of the people and with their consent. No single individual can claim that he knows everything to such an extent that he can make the laws and carry on government. The laws are to be made by the representatives of the people in parliament; they are the people who can advise the men in whose name the law is proclaimed. That is the difference between the monarchical system of government and the democratic system of government. In a monarchy, the affairs of the people

are carried on in the name of the monarch and under the authority of the monarch. In a democracy, the affairs of the public are carried on in the name of the Head of the State, but the laws and the executive measures are the authority, on which the government is carried. The Head of the state is titular, he is merely a symbol.

3. Parliamentary system of the government means that, at a stated period those who want to advise the head of the state must have the confidence of the people in themselves renewed.

To him, "this is also not enough parliamentary system of government, but is much more than the government by discussion. There are two pillars, on which the parliamentary systems of government rest. These are the fulcrum on which the mechanism works. Those two pillars are (1) an opposition and (2) free and fair elections[8].

ESSENTIAL CONDITIONS FOR THE SUCCESSFUL WORKING OF DEMOCRACY

Dr. Ambedkar advocated some essential conditions for the successful working of democracy. They are:

1. **No glaring inequalities in the society:** Dr. Ambedkar was conscious of the social and economic inequalities in the Indian society. According to him, for the successful working of democracy there must be no glaring inequalities in the society. There must be statutory provisions to safeguard the interests of the suppressed and the oppressed people. Society must be based on the principles of liberty, equality and fraternity, in order to ensure social conditions. Dr. Ambedkar thought that it was necessary to annihilate the caste system in the Hindu society to bring a revolutionary change in the attitude and the thinking of the Hindus[9].

2. **Existence of the opposition:** The existence of an effective opposition is an important factor in successful working of a democracy. After every five years, those, who are in authority, must be subjected to scrutiny by the people, who will decide their continuance as the party in power.
3. **Equality in law and administration:** There must be equality in law and administration. There must not be a spoils system, as is to be found in the USA, for efficient functioning of democracy. There is a need of permanent civil services implementing the policy of the government without fear of the executive. He further quoted that one need not, at this stage, dilate too much on equality before the law. Although, there might be cases here and there, where there is no equality before the law, what is important is the equality of treatment in administration.
4. **Constitutional morality:** There must be a steady growth of constitutional conventions and the people must be educated in the scrupulous observance of these conventions. The people should not allow their respect and loyalty to the leader to grow into a blind faith of Bhakti Cult. Dr. Ambedkar cited the example of George Washington. When he was requested by the people to stand for the second time for the Presidentship of America, Washington said, "My dear people you have forgotten the purpose for which we made this constitution. We made this constitution because we did not want a hereditary monarchy and did not want a hereditary ruler for a dictator[10].

In the name of democracy, there should be no tyranny of the majority over the minority. The minority must always feel safe. Although the majority is carrying on the government, the minority will not be hurt and the minority will not be imposed upon. Thus, there should be adequate scope for the adjournment motions of the minority to redress their grievances.

Dr. Ambedkar appreciated Harold Laski for his insistence on the moral order as a requirement of democracy. He says that, if there is no moral order, democracy will go to pieces. It requires a public conscience. According to Dr. Ambedkar, public conscience means, conscience which becomes agitated at every wrong, no matter who is the sufferer and it also means that everybody, whether he suffers that particular wrong or not, is prepared to join the aggrieved to secure justice. He cautioned that, with the making of the constitution, the task of building a democratic society is not over. The task has only begun and the people have to make efforts to accomplish it. A political democracy without an economic and social democracy is an invitation to trouble and danger[11]. Social democracy alone can assure the right to liberty equality and fraternity.

Thus democracy is not only a form of government but also a way of life, through which social justice can be established[12], with a deep faith in the parliamentary tradition. Dr. Ambedkar fully agrees with the view that, there should be three necessary functions of government,

1. To make laws.
2. To execute them and
3. To punish those who commit breach of law.

He believes that only by dividing the powers of government, each department can function with the utmost care and effectiveness[13].

LIMITATIONS OF PARLIAMENTARY DEMOCRACY

According to Dr. Ambedkar, there are some limitations which will lead to the failure of parliamentary democracy in a country.

1. In parliamentary democracy, the executive may be held up by the legislature, which may refuse to pass

the laws, which the executive wants. If it is not held up by the legislature, it may be held up by the judiciary, which may declare the laws as illegal. Parliamentary democracy gives no free hand to dictatorship and that is why it became a discredited institution in countries like Italy, Spain and Germany, which readily welcomed dictatorship[14]. Dr. Ambedkar is against dictatorship, there is also a great deal of discontent and dissatisfaction against parliamentary democracy in the countries where people are opposed to dictatorship.

2.

3. There is another wrong ideology, which has vitiated the institution of parliamentary democracy. "All political societies get divided into two classes; the rulers and the ruled. This is an evil. If the evil stopped here, it would not matter much, but the unfortunate part of it is that the division become so stereotyped and stratified that rulers are always drawn from the ruling class. This happens because, generally people do not care to see that they govern themselves. They are content to establish a government and leave it to govern them[16]. Dr. Ambedkar warns the harbingers of democracy that if parliamentary democracy fails in this land, the result will be rebellion, anarchy and communism. He says, "I want you to take note of these eventful certainties, and if you wish that the parliamentary democracy prevails in this country, if you are satisfied that we will be assured of our liberty of thought speech and action, if we should preserve our independence, if we cherish the inherent right of individual liberty then it is your duty as a student, as intelligent community of our country to strive your utmost, to cherish this parliamentary system of government in its true spirit and to work for it." To him a parliamentary democracy can be maintained

under guarantees of freedom of speech and criticism together with political and economic initiative for the individual.

CONCLUSION

Thus, according to Dr. Ambedkar democracy is not only a form of government, but also a way of life through which social justice can be established. Social justice demands that society should provide welfare to all. It is not merely the greatest happiness of the greatest number. Otherwise, the interests of the majority might gain precedence over those of the minorities.

Notes & References

1. G. S. Lokhande "Bhimrao Ramji Ambedkar", Intellectual Publishing House, New Delhi, 1982, p. 22.
2. *Ibid.*, p. 23.
3. Bhagwan Das – "Thus Spoke Ambedkar", Buddhist Publishing House, Jalandhar (Punjab), 1963, p. 61.
4. Dhananjaya Kher – "Ambedkar: Life and Mission", Popular Prakashan, Bombay, 1961, p. 488.
5. W. N. Kuber – "Dr.Ambedkar A critical study", Peoples Publishing House, New Delhi, 1973, p. 207.
6. Bhagwan Das – "Thus Spoke Ambedkar", Buddhist Publishing House Jalandhar (Punjab), 1963, p. 49-50.
7. *Ibid.*, p. 50-51.
8. *Ibid.*, p. 59-60.
9. G. S. Lokhande - "Bhimrao Ramji Ambedkar", Intellectual Publishing House New Delhi, 1982, p. 24-25.
10. G. S. Lokhande – "Bhimrao Ramji Ambedkar", Intellectual Publishing House New Delhi, 1982, p. 28.
11. *Ibid.*, p. 29.
12. *Ibid.*, p. 30.
13. K. S. Bharati – "Foundation of Dr. Ambedkar", Datta Sons Publishing, Nagpur, 1990, p.158.

14.. *Ibid.*, p. 140.
15. *Ibid.*, p. 140-141.
16. Bhagwan Das – "Thus Spoke Ambedkar", Buddhist Publishing House, Jalandhar (Punjab), 1963, p. 31.
17. K. S. Bharati – "Foundation of Dr. Ambedkar", Datta Sons Publishing, Nagpur, 1990, p. 141.

EMPOWERMENT AND EVOLUTION OF WOMEN SELF HELP GROUPS IN ANDHRA PRADESH

H. D. Dwarakanath

INTRODUCTION

The government of Andhra Pradesh has taken up the theme of "women's empowerment and evolution" as one of the strategies to tackle socio economic poverty. Self help groups movement through savings has been taken up as a mass movement by women a path chosen by them to shape their destiny for better development. Vision 2020 of the state agenda in the last few years placing the people especially the usual women in the fore front has enabled the formation of a large number of self help groups (SHGs') through out the state and majority of women are saving one rupee a day. The state government is consciously making an effort to assist the "DWCRA Self Help Groups" by providing revolving fund under various programmes.

Self help groups on DWCRA methodology is the most dominant form of Micro finance in India. Organization of women around thrift and credit has emerged as one of the most effective methods for poverty eradication and women empowerment. In the late 80's the self help DWCRA groups promotion was pioneered by the NGO's across the country continue to be engaged in strengthening the DWCRA group in rural India to generate self employment potentialities. In the late 1990'sgovenrment has become a dominant player in the promotion of self help DWCRA groups in south India.

EVOLUTION OF SELF HELP (DWCRA) GROUPS IN ANDHRA PRADESH

Associate Professor (Retd), SAP Degree & PG College, Vikarabad, RR Dist., AP. Currently associated with Centre for Advanced Studies, Department of Political Science, Osmania University, Hyderabad, A.P.

Self help DWCRA groups as a sub scheme of Integrated Rural Development Programme (IRDP) made a pioneering beginning in Andhra Pradesh in the year 1982-83 with UNICEF co-operation. The primary objective of DWCRA self help groups is that of focusing attention on the women members of rural families living below the poverty line with a view to generate self employment on a sustained basis. The savings and credit movement gathered momentum in 1993 in Nellore district in Andhra Pradesh. The women in the district had been organized into Mahila Mandals during total literacy campaign (TLC is known as Akshara sankranthi in Telugu language). Subsequently these groups sphere headed "Anti-Arrack" (Abolition of country liquor) movement. The movement was successful and wide spread to the neighbouring districts eventually leading to imposition of prohibition in the state. Later the movement was converted into savings and credit groups known as "Podupu Lakshmi" (Thrift groups). Hence there has been a phased expansion of DWCRA self help groups in Nellore district and by the year 1994-95 these groups are extended to all the villages covering 22 districts and 1100 Revenue Mandals in the state of Andhra Pradesh.

The rural women in Andhra Pradesh have taken initiative in improving their socio economic status by participating in all the government sponsored programmes such as Family welfare, Child health, Self employment, Vocational training,

Promoting their nutritional and educational status, Awareness on environment, Public health through sanitation and clean drinking water etc.

Andhra Pradesh leads self help DWCRA groups movement in India with almost 8,50,825 groups covering about 1 crore, 11 lakh, 85 thousand women members. Cumulatively over 3,50,000 groups have been linked to banks under linkage bank programme.

Table I

Growth of DWCRA Self Help Groups in Andhra Pradesh (Period 1995 to 2010)

Year	*No of SHG (DWCRA) Groups*	*Corpus Fund Released (in Crores)*
1995-1996	40514	90.00
1996-1997	73678	122.00
1997-1998	85415	240.00
1998-1999	99243	310.00
1999-2000	200110	520.00
2000-2001	310000	808.00
2001-2002	413366	1201.94
2002-2003	451248	1432.18
2003-2004	475546	1624.95
2004-2005	510506	1875.25
2005-2006	530168	1988.78
2006-2007	625680	2118.00
2007-2008	718920	4328.00
2009-2010	850825	5218.00

Andhra Pradesh alone has about half of self help groups existing in the country. Up to 1994 only 10 thousand groups were functioning and in the last six years, three was a massive scaling in the DWCRA groups are not only resorting to thrift but also are talking small loans out of the corpus fund available with the micro finance groups. The group corpus consists of savings of the members, government assistance and also bank loan. Members used the bank loan out of group corpus for their personal needs initially. However, in the long run loans are utilized for income generating activities. An amount of Rs 1624.95 crores is mobilized as corpus fund and utilized for income generating economic activity.

THE COVERAGE OF RURAL WOMEN

It has been planned by the state government to cover all the rural poor women under self help groups by 2015. It is programmed to cover at least one women from a below poverty line level as a member of DWCRA. At present all the habitations in the state of Andhra Pradesh have at least one self help DWCRA group.

Table II
Progress of DWCRA Groups (SHGs) in Andhra Pradesh as on 31st March, 2010

Number of DWCRA Groups	*Number of Women Members*	*Population covered*	*Amount saved by SHGs (Crores)*	*Loan availed from Banks (Crores)*	*Government Assistance (Crores)*
8,50,825	1,11,00,081	About 4.0 Crores	2864.50	3210.20	5218

With the help of government assistance with the net work of DRDA and support from financial agencies, the women's savings and credit is now wide spread in Andhra, Rayalseema, and Telangana region. The podupu lakshmi movement started (1995) in Nellore district is started with the slogan of "Save a rupee a day" is called by different names, for example, Anantha Mahila Shakthi in Ananthapur, Mahalakshmi in Mahabubnagar, Podupu Jyothi in Ranga Reddy, Sambhavana in Nalgonda, Pragati Lakshimi in Nizamabad, Grama Lakshmi in Chitoor, and Mahila Shakthi in East Godavari districts in Andhra Pradesh.

PARTICIPATION OF WEAKER SECTIONS

It is quite interesting to note that the movement started by the backward class women followed by scheduled castes and minorities to achieve economic sustainability. The DWCRA groups under Micro finance system have attracted mostly the scheduled caste and scheduled tribe women living below the poverty line in rural Andhra Pradesh. The table given below indicates the participation of different categories in this movement.

Table III
Categorywise Classification of Self Help DWCRA Groups in Andhra Pradesh - 2010

S. No.	*Category*	*No of Women Members*	*Percentage*
1	Scheduled Caste	281502	33.33%
2	Scheduled Tribes	122850	15.20%
3	Backward Classes	3748074	41.99%
4	Others	618788	9.64%

The above table reveals that the participation of weaker sections of followed by backward class women played a greater role in mobilizing the thrift deposits and credit movement to achieve economic stability. About 28150 (33%) of SC women and 348074 (41.99%) of backward class women are actively participating in the evolution of Self Help Groups.

COVERAGE OF DWCRA PROGRAMMES IN ANDHRA PRADESH

The progress of SHGs reveals that by 2000 the self help DWCRA groups became flagship programme of Andhra Pradesh to implement poverty eradication programmes.

The state government introduced schemes like Deepam (Subsidized gas connection for DWCRA women) for which state government sanctioned revolving fund. In addition to the central government schemes several thousands of groups are formed instantly to access various government schemes. To give further impetus to Self Help Groups movement the state government established a separate department called "women employment and self employment" under the ministry of Rural Development and panchayati raj to focus on promoting for DWCRA groups to increase bank linkage to promote micro enterprises.

In this task the NABARD played a proactive role in sensitizing NGO's (Non government organizations), government officials and bankers towards bank linkage. The empowerment reveals that a greater co-ordination was witnessed among DRDAS, banks and NGO's during 1999-2002. The NGO's that had internal capacities supported capacity building of DWCRA groups. During 1996-2001 UNDP funded poverty alleviation programme was implemented in Mahabubnagar and Kurnool districts with a total out reach of 1,200 self help DWCRA groups. In 1999 CARE began the implementation of a DFID funded project called "Credit and savings for house hold enterprises" (CASHE) to support the emergence of quality through NGO's and government.

PROMOTION OF SAVINGS AND CREDIT GROUPS

The District Rural Development Agency actively involved in transforming DWCRA (SHGs) into savings and credit groups to generate self employment opportunities. Many district administrative machineries have taken steps towards continuing support and strengthening DWCRA groups. In Srikakulam and Nellore districts the DRDA and NABARD are jointly conducting training programme for group leaders and Bank Managers. It is note worthy that, Ranga Reddy is the second largest district in the state next to Nellore to popularize empowerment of Rural women in generating self employment through economic activity under thrift deposit mobilization scheme. About 12309 Self Help Groups with 1,72,000 women members in Ranga Reddy have deposited Rs. 56.6 crores as corpus fund by 31st March, 2008. The self help groups in Ranga Reddy district had a rare distinction of appreciation of world leaders including Mr.Bill Clinton former President of U.S.A., Mr.Kofi Annen, Secretary General of U.N.O. described the savings and credit system of self help groups as a great revolution in Andhra Pradesh in bringing socio economic transformation among the rural women groups. In Nalgonda district the DRDA has promoted nearly 2,800 groups in just two months. In Cuddapah district the DRDA has planned to promote 100-150 village level MACTS, and enrolled 3000 new groups and provided necessary tool kits to women. The state government has specially established (SAPAP) South Asia Poverty Alleviation Programme operating in three districts of Andhra Pradesh namely Ananthapur, Kurnool and Mahabubnagar. It has promoted over 2700 groups covering over 42000 villages. A village organization has been formed at each village, where all the groups in village have been federated.

The evolution of NGOs as financial intermediaries has been a growing trend over the past few years. Some NGOs have accessed loan from Rashtriya Mahila Bank (RMB) and had advanced loans to women groups. Such NGOs in Andhra Pradesh include Youth Charitable Organization (YCO) and Vishakha Zilla Nava Nirmana Samithi (VZNNS) Gramasiri, CARDS and ASSiST in Guntur, Youth Club, Bejipuram and SVCT in Srikakulam district, RASA and PODA in Chittoor and multi purpose social service society in Cuddpah district. Apart from this SHARE a Grameena Bank is the biggest NGO regularly operating in six districts with an out standing of Rs. 28 crores by September 2009, with 100 percent repayment rate. Its members savings amount is around Rs one crores similarly St Ann's Social Service Society, Vishakhapatnam and Swayamkrushi Sangam in Narayankhed in Medak district are also planning to advance loans to Self Help Groups on the Grameena Bank model.

SHG BANK LINKAGE PROGRAMME

The primary aim of self help DWCRA bank linkage programme is to integrate informal savings and credit groups with main banking system by providing credit facility to groups to enhance their fund base. The expectation is that DWCRA members will be enabled to access frequent and comparatively small loans from savings and revolving released by the government. Once a DWCRA group demonstrates its capability to absorb out side credit, bank loans are extended to those groups. The capacity of self help groups reflected in terms of savings pooled by the members.

The self help DWCRA groups' linkage programme was started in 1992 as a pilot project to link 500 groups with banks and upgrade to regular banking programme. In the year 2003 itself 1,23,548 DWCRA groups, accessed bank finance to the tune of Rs 339.61 crores benefiting around 8,16,536 women beneficiaries to improve their standards of living.

In order to support self help groups at the grass root level, NABARD, Commercial and Regional Rural Banks(RRBs) are providing direct assistance to the DWCRA groups under self help linkage of NABARD.

Table 4
Self Help NABARD Linkage Scheme (1998-2010) in Andhra Pradesh

S. No.	*Year*	*Amount (Rs. in Crores)*	*DWCRA Groups in Lakhs*
1	1998-99	41.90	0.12
2	1999-2000	88.63	0.44
3	2000-2001	173.38	1.03
4	2001-2002	44.00	0.44
5	2002-2003	52.00	0.75
6	2003-2004	56.20	1.20
7	2007-2008	60.20	1.80
8	2008-2009	63.15	2.10
9	2009-2010	66.21	2.60
	TOTAL	645.67	10.48

Ever since the formation of DWCRA self help groups in Andhra Pradesh, non –governmental organizations are funding for the rural women's in income generating activities. Today under economic sustainability more than 200 committed NGO's facilitating formation of DWCRA groups and for their sustenance. The NGOs are working in close collaboration with DRDA's in training capacity, building, and skill development training programmes

TRAINING FOR WOMEN IN ECONOMIC PRODUCTIVITY

Income generation through Economic activity has become an integral part of DWCRA scheme and technical skill oriented training provides an opportunity to learn economic productivity from their own family members. The DWCRA groups in Andhra Pradesh are producing more than one hundred varieties of products. The programme has initiated employment and income generating opportunities for women through traditional and modern occupations such as spinning, weaving, coir industry, carpet and chappal making, domestic and food products, agarbathi making, papad making, khadi, leather items to promote employment opportunities.

LIST OF INCOME GENERATING PRODUCTS OF DWCRA GROUPS

The DWCRA Groups in Andhra Pradesh are fully engaged in economic activity producing some useful items to the customers. These products are sold by the DWCRA groups in the District Sales Exhibition. The products are sold in the market for a remunerative price.

THE LIST OF THE PRODUCTS MADE BY SELF HELP GROUPS/DWCRA GROUPS ARE GIVEN BELOW

The analysis of Table 5 reveals that, a majority of self help women groups are engaged in vegetable growing and marketing them in towns, which is highly remunerative to them. Most of the women groups in Andhra Pradesh are supplying vegetable to the school's mid meal programme in different parts of the state. As a matter of fact, the women groups are also involved in preparing mid meal programme

Table 5

S.No.	*Economic Activity*	*DWCRA Groups involved (%)*	*S.No.*	*Economic Activity*	*DWCRA Groups involved (%)*
1	Leaf plate making	15.0%	11	Sericulture	16.0%
2	Toys making	21.0%	12	Vegetable vendors	32.0%
3	Chalk piece making	81.0%	13	Agarbathi making	12.5%
4	Preparation of colour pencils	26.8%	14	Candle making	25.3%
5	Book binding	32.3%	15	Milk dairy	28.6%
6	Laundry	8.0%	16	Food items/Pickles	32.5%
7	Kiran shops	17.0%	17	Sari business	18.2%
8	Sheep rearing	21.8%	18	Small Tea stalls	8.5%
9	Agriculture labour work	42.3%	19	Ready made food making	21.5%
10	Basket making	22.0%	20	Tailoring	11.5%

to the school going children in Adilabad, Khamma, Warangal, Medak, Nalgonda, Ranga Reddy, Chittoor and Srikakulam districts.

The socio economic survey of Self Help DWCRA Groups conducted by DRDA in different districts in the state has indicated that the economic productivity and income generating activity has really helped the rural women to earn an additional monthly income, ranging from Rs. 250-2000 per month depending on enterprising activity taken up by DWCRA groups in the villages.

OUTSTANDING ACHIEVEMENTS OF SELF HELP GROUPS

In Andhra Pradesh more than 52% of DWCRA Groups were financed by commercial banks under SHG Bank Linkage Programme. This number is more than all India figure, excluding that of Andhra Pradesh. In Andhra Pradesh alone 3,10,488 self help groups were provided repeat finance by grants during 2008-09, which comes to 76% of total SHGs in

Table 6
Self Help Groups Status Achievements Under State Revolving Fund for 2004-05 and Projections for 2005-08

S. No.	*District*	*SHGs*	*Members*	*Savings (in lakhs)*	*Corpus (in lakhs)*	*Groups formed 2004-05*
1	VIZIANAGARAM	26056	374868	6324.57	8134.39	1056
2	VISAKHAPATNAM	20201	292572	3273.68	4465.95	93
3	EASH GODAVARI	29068	311528	3565	7212	8357
4	WEST GODAVARI	54527	708124	8036.62	28622.01	4720
5	KRISHNA	37002	414216	7005	30712	11655
6	GUNTUR	25032	325420	3598.22	10533.37	0
7	PRAKASHAM	30182	342008	9250.76	12153.51	3474
8	NELLORE	22010	288000	3626	5730	0
9	CHITTOOR	17809	266595	3331.2	5167.99	75
10	CUDDAPAH	32339	449715	4875.43	1394.14	0
11	ANANTHAPUR	20214	211649	5528.54	8135.38	1256
12	KURNOOL	25534	331942	2916.81	8062.11	1782
13	MAHABOOBNAGAR	21926	285038	4690.26	22677.06	2162
14	RANGA REDDY	29507	443000	7409	972	0
15	MEDAK	15281	206492	3387.96	16600.74	0
16	NIZAMABAD	19859	258167	4946.35	7578.23	2995
17	ADILABAD	20497	256213	1686.06	3235.22	1804
18	KARIMNAGAR	19324	265787	1470.58	3590365	919
19	WARANGAL	25836	372234	6425	9487	4642
20	KHAMMA	28137	365781	6681.75	8843.87	170
21	NALGONDA	31277	323040	3143.79	6290.3	1377
22	SRIKAKULAM	28130	365690	6777	10200	7153
	TOTAL	579748	7458079	107949.6	3806572	53690

Source: A Report on functioning analysis of self help groups in Andhra Pradesh, Ministry of Rural Development, Government of Andhra Pradesh

the state of Andhra Pradesh. As per the reports of the Bankers the recovery of loans is of 95% against 87% when comparative to other states. The SHGs have taken various economic generating activities by availing themselves of the facility under Bank Linkage Programme and increased their production to the extent that it applies to entire country. Recently, the women SHGs in Andhra Pradesh have got orders for their finished products from other countries, such as, Sri Lanka, Malaysia, Singapore, Bangladesh, etc. The DWCRA women have actively participated to market their products in fares, melas and exhibitions organized at state, national and international level and are able to market their products through Internet facility. Well known companies viz-a-viz, Hindustan Lever Limited, Food World, Apna Bazaar, have come forward to tie up with DWCRA groups to market their products.

The issue of extending loans to DWCRA groups and SHG Bank Linkage Programme since 1998-99 created path of their economic empowerment. The income generating activity taken up by DWCRA Self Help Groups and access to the banks and financial institutions attracted the attention of not only other states but at international level also. Many dignotaries from other states and other countries visited Andhra Pradesh and praised women movement and implementation of economic activity undertaken by self help groups with bank linkage programme in Andhra Pradesh. The women empowerment in economic activity of rural women remains a mile stone in eradicating poverty, illiteracy and unemployment in rural Andhra Pradesh.

SPECIAL PROJECTS BY SHGS IN ANDHRA PRADESH

Economic Generation through Coir production by Women SHGs in East Godavari District: The Government of India have sanctioned special project of economic generation through coir production by women SHGs in East Godavari District with a total cost of Rs. 1452.00 lakhs (Central Rs. 1089.00 lakhs and state Rs. 363.00 lakhs) to shared between centre and state in the ratio of 75:25. Bank component is Rs. 1066.00 lakhs. The GOI has released an amount of Rs. 1034.55 Lakhs and the state government has released their matching share of Rs. 34.85 lakhs so far for implementation of the project. The project so far has benefitted 27900 beneficiaries. So far an amount of Rs. 1474.28 Lakhs has been utilized and

11982 beneficiaries have received training and mobilized bank credit of Rs. 1239.44 lakhs.

Economic Generation through Fashion Designing and Garment Manufacturing in East Godavari District: The Government of India have sanctioned special project on Economic Generation through Fashion Designing and Garment manufacturing by women SHGs in East Godavari District with a total cost of Rs. 1200.00 lakhs (Central Rs. 900.00 lakhs and state Rs. 300.00 lakhs) to be shared between central and state in the ratio of 75:25 and Bank component of Rs. 855.00 lakhs. So far an amount of Rs. 720.00 lakhs has been released by Government of India and State Government has released Rs. 240.00 lakhs. Providing technical training on latest Garment making machinery and establishment of fashion garment manufacturing unit for the benefit of SHGs is the main purpose of the project. The project proposes to benefit 13680 beneficiaries.

Poverty Alleviation through improved Agricultural Technology in Chittoor District: The Government of India has sanctioned special project of poverty alleviation through Agricultural Technology in Chittoor District with a total cost of Rs. 1500.00 lakhs (Central Rs. 1125.00 lakhs and state Rs. 375.00 lakhs) to be shared between central and state in the ratio of 75:25 and bank component of Rs. 3080.00 lakhs. This project is for providing internationally reputed Israel Technology for improved yields. Introduction of irrigation techniques like sprinklers and for providing high yielding/ hybrid varieties. So far an amount of Rs. 1564.60 lakh has been utilized including the interest funds available under the project for installation of Drip and Sprinkler system covering 7560 acres covering 9164 beneficiaries. The mobilization of bank credit is Rs. 1519.13 lakhs. The project is working successfully in the district.

Development of Handicrafts clusters of Kalambari painting at Srikalahasthi in Chittoor District: The Government of India has sanctioned above project under

SGSY and envisages development of the craft through participatory mode of crafts persons for the benefit of 300 beneficiaries. The total Government share is Rs. 298.74.00 lakhs (Central Rs. 224.06 lakhs and state Rs. 74.68 lakhs). The Government of India has released 89.624 lakhs and state government has released its share of Rs. 29.87 Lakhs. Supporting the traditional skill through creation of improved facilities through common facility centre and provide design interventions for improvement in designs in Kalambari paining to be able to reach export makers are the objects of the project. So far an amount of Rs. 9.55 lakhs has been utilized by 300 beneficiaries.

Action plan to create Technologically Qualified Global Workers in Ranga Reddy, Medak, Nalgonda and Warangal Districts of Andhra Pradesh: The Government of India has sanctioned special project of Action Plan to create Technologically Qualified Global Workers in Ranga Reddy, Medak, Nalgonda and Warangal districts with a total cost of Rs. 799.21 lakhs (Central Rs. 599.41.00 lakhs and state Rs. 199.80 lakhs) to be shared between central and state with bank component of Rs. 539.00 lakhs. This project is to technically trained and qualified workers to create a base for garment manufactures to set up export garment units in Andhra Pradesh. This project is for the benefit of 12000 beneficiaries. 10 training centres have been started and 540 sewing machines have been purchased. So far 2649 candidates are trained and 864 trainees got wage employment.

The government of India has sanctioned special project for providing economic assistance to IAY house beneficiaries of Madakasira Block, Ananthapur District with a total cost of Rs. 621.00 lakhs (Central Rs. 465.75 lakhs and state Rs. 155.25 lakhs) to be shared between central and state in the ratio of 75.25, the bank component is Rs. 361.00 Lakhs. An amount of Rs. 186.30 lakhs has been released by Government of India. The state government has also released its matching share of Rs. 62.10 lakhs. The main object of the project is to provide economic upliftment through income generating activities for the incumbents who were assisted in housing scheme under Indira Awas Yojana earlier and also for providing appropriate technologies for value addition for the locally available agro and mineral based activities. The project is for the benefit of 6275 beneficiaries. So far 2611 beneficiaries were assisted with a total expenditure of Rs. 260.63 lakhs and bank credit worth Rs. 286.22 lakhs has been mobilized. Agriculture, Minor Irrigation, Sericulture, Dairy, Sheep rearing are the main activities taken up.

Recently conducted research study by different organizations in Andhra Pradesh reveals the need for innovative technologies for the women have been found to be the very encouraging. There is a growing need to train the rural women in better packaging technology. There is need to improve design in addition to providing of marketing support, training for capacity building of women will be taken up by organizing training for women in Mahila Pranganam (Women Training Centre) and other local institutions in other districts.

Similarly, the District Rural development Agency (DRDA) has identified 6000c luster volunteers to support the groups at the village level. These volunteers are selected by the DWCRA groups in their villages and expenditure is borne by them. The cluster volunteers of DWCRA group leaders Additional Grama Sevikas (AGS) Lady VDOs and other will be trained in the district Training Centre. Thus greater support will be provided to the DWCRA Groups by implementing poverty eradication programmes like IRDP, Food for Work, Drought Relief, etc. It is already planned to provide 50 percent of the IRDP subsidy and credit to the women groups through CMEY, SC Corporation and Minority Corporation by covering them under group loans.

Marketing support is provided to the DWCRA groups set up in all the districts and permanent DWCRA Bazaar is nearing completion at Hyderabad. Products worth more than 100 crores were sold through DWCRA Bazaar in the four last years(2006-10). Training and Technology Development Centre (TTDC) has been established in each district to introduce innovative technology for the qualitative improvement of products made by the Self Help DWCRA Groups.

AN APPRAISAL

With the intermediation of voluntary organizations the rural poor join together to secure better economic growth. This has resulted in the formation of a large number of Self Help Groups in Andhra Pradesh to mobilize savings and recycle the resources generated among members. Most of the Self Help Groups in the state have came up due to dynamic leadership of certain individuals with in a group through the catalytic role played by the NGOs in developing such groups.

It is a paradoxical truth that women led Self Help Groups in districts like Nellore, Vizianagaram, Chittoor, Ranga Reddy, Karimnagar and Nalgonda have achieved success in bringing the women to the main stream of decision making. Self Help Groups have organizational skills, to disburse micro credit to the rural women and encourages them to enter into entrepreneurial activities. The women groups working under DWCRA in Andhra Pradesh have successfully demonstrated how to mobilize and manage thrift, appraise credit needs to maintain linkage with the banks and enforce financial self discipline. This research of participation of Self Help Groups in Andhra Pradesh reveals that women groups in different districts and mandals are continuously striving hard for better future for the rural women by enhancing the status of women as participants in the domestic economic social and cultural spheres of life.

Evolution and progress of DWCRA Self Help Groups has now become a modern economic weapon for the rural urban poor to fight against poverty. Many big and small institutions are taking part in the evolution of Micro Finance vigorously. Many programmes from "Garibi Hatao to Integrated Rural Development" started by the Government enthusiastically through which the DWCRA Self Help Groups have successfully achieved their goal. Andhra Pradesh has been in the forefront of the Self Help movement in India. Alongside women's own savings is a major initiative in providing SHG members with bank credits.

The effective organization of self help groups is a significant development in the process of empowerment. The emerging changes in the values and attitudes of the members of the SHGs are a clear manifestation of socio-economic empowerment yielding relatively quicker results. The socio economic programmes reinforce each other and promote all round development of the children, the women, the households and the communities. It is a process which ultimately leads to self fulfillment of each member of the society. It is in this direction that SHGs are moving towards fulfilling their objectives with meaningful strategic direction.

References

Batra S., and Dangal R. C. (1999), Financial Services – New innovations, Deep and Deep Publishers, New Delhi.

Behro J. H., Elavin (1999), Women and Rural Credit – A Delivery System 'in capturing complexity' Eds, Romy Barooah & K.Cloud, Sage Publication, New Delhi.

Anju Bhatia – Women's Development and NGOs, Rawat Publications, Jaipur and New Delhi.

Gupta R. C. (1998), Self Help Groups – A Guide for Self Help Saving and Loan Management for Groups, Rastriya Mahila Kosh, Ministry of HRD, Government of India, New Delhi.

Karamkar K. G. (1999), Self Help Groups – Micro Finance Need and Concept in India, Sage Publication, New Delhi.

Nagarjan B. S. and Lilitha N. (2000), 'Self Help Groups in Rural Development', Dominant Publishers and Distributors, Jaipur.

Puhazhendhi V. (2000), Evaluation Study of Self Help Groups in Tamil Nadu, NABARD, Madras.

Murthi Desai (1998), Policy Approach to Women and Poverty Eradication, *The Indian Journal of Social Work,* Vol. 59, Issue 4 and 8, New Delhi.

Pankaj Naithani (2001), Micro Financing – The Self Employment Activities, Kurukshetra, Ministry of Rural Development, Vol. 49, July, New Delhi.

Gurumoorthy T. R. (2000), Self Help Groups Empower Rural Women, Kurukshetra.

Agrawal R. C. (1999), Role of Women in Achieving Social Goal of Economic Development - *Indian Journal of Social Research.*

Jain S. D. and Reddy V. K. (1979), Role of Women and Rural Development, 1979, *Indian Journal of Social Work,* Vol. IV(10).

Kochar J., Pandya R. D. (1997), Status of Women in India, Kurukshetra, *Journal of Rural Development,* Vol. 40.

Meenakshi Apte (1979), Rural Women and Development in India, *Indian Journal of Social Work,* Vol. 39.

Nandan S. C. (1982), Role of Women in Rural Development, Vol. 30.

Rama Muzumdar (1998), Poverty Alleviation Programme and Rural Women, Kurukshtetra.

Rao V.K.R.V. (1997), Integrated Rural Development, Southern Economics, Vol. 16, No. 14.

Bhatia B. M. (1976), Rural Development Only Way to Improve the Poor, Statesman.

Agrawal S. M. (1979), New Strategy for Rural Employment, Khadi *Gramodyog,* Vol. 24, No. 8.

Hariprasad R. (1998), Development and Grassroot Democracy, Kurukshetra.

EMPOWERMENT OF CHILDREN THROUGH THE RIGHT TO EDUCATION: FACT OR FICTION

K. Saibaba

There are many areas with which the State endeavours to empower itself. One of the most important areas of the modern State is "to play a vital role in the area of education as a provider, facilitator and regulator of education at all levels.[1] The State has a crucial role in this arena from Elementary Education to Higher Education. However, it has a constitutional obligation to provide education to children below 14 years of age. This obligation, which was entrusted to it by a Directive Principle, has now become compulsory, in as much as, it has become a part of Justifiable Rights under Part III. The objective of this Paper is to critically examine the role of the State in constituting and implementing the recent Act, popularly known the RTE Act and estimate its stand in empowering the children through the Act.

The Indian constitution recognises the right to education in various articles enshrined in the parts III, IV and IVA. The constitution (86th Amendment) Act, has added certain provisions to the constitution which have recognized the importance of right to education to receive primary and secondary education as a "fundamental right." As Praveen

Jha and Pooja Parvati have pointed out, "after much dithering from almost seven years subsequent to 86th Constitutional Amendment, the Union Legislature brought the Act known as THE RIGHT OF CHILDREN TO FREE AND COMPULSORY EDUCATION ACT, 2009 which received the presidential assent on 26th August, 2009 taking foreword to free and universal education."[2] It took seven more months for the act to come into force, in as much as, it was on April 1, 2010 the union government has complied with the necessary requirement of the Gazette of India and issued a notification in this regard.[3] Addressing the journalists on the landmark Right to Education Act in New Delhi on 31st March, 2010, Kapil Sibal, the Union Minister for Human Resource Development, said "It is a historic day as the Right to Education Act comes into effect. For the first time, education will become a constitutional right. It is tryst with destiny in the area of education.[4]

It is pertinent to note that various judgments of the courts have impelled the state to activate itself in bringing the Right to Education Act (RTE Act), the enforcement of which, as Kapil Sibal, says "represents a momentous step forward in our 100 year struggle for universalizing elementary education."[5] The Supreme Court, in many cases, such as Mohini Jain vs. state of Karnataka,[6] J.P. Unni Krishnan vs. state of Andhra Pradesh,[7] TMA Pai Foundation vs. state of Karnataka[8] and Imamdar vs. state of Maharashtra[9] held the opinion that right to education was one of the implied rights of right to life and personal liberty.[10] Even the National Commission to review the working of the Constitution (2000), headed by Justice M.N. Venkatachalaiah made a strong appeal to the government of India to take the responsibility of Universalising elementary education by elevating it as a Fundamental Right through a Constitutional Amendment. All this led to the following changes in the Constitution (86th Amendment) Act, 2002.

Insertion of 21 A (PART – III – Fundamental Rights)[11]

The state shall provide free and compulsory education to all children of the age of six to fourteen years in such a manner as the State may, by law, determine.

Modification of Article 45 (PART IV – Directive Principles of State Policy)[12]

The State shall endeavour to provide early childhood care and education for all children until they complete the age of six years. (Before the modification, Article 45 reads – *"The State shall endeavour to provide, within a period of ten years from the commencement of the Constitution, for free and compulsory education for all children until they complete the age of fourteen years."*)

Insertion of Clause – K in 51 A. (PART IV A – Fundamental Duties)[13]

IT SHALL BE THE DUTY OF EVERY CITIZEN OF INDIA

(K) who is a parent or guardian to provide opportunities for education to his child, or, as the case may be, ward between the age of six and fourteen years.

Thus, the Right to Education has been elevated as a constitutional right. It is duly recognized as a Fundamental right in Para III. It is also enshrined as a positive direction in Part IV. Even the citizens of India have a Fundamental Duty under Part IV – A. In this way, the right of children to free and compulsory education has become a 'shining star' in our Fundamental Law of the Land. As Prof. G.B. Reddy points out, this Amendment ought to be lauded by one and all, provided the right to receive primary education is made effective in its letter and spirit.[14] As Prof. Manohar Rao says, "it (The RTE Act) has to be exercised to achieve not only well being of the citizens in their future intellectual, social and economic life, but also inculcate among them a sense of individual and social consciousness for the contribution of the welfare and prosperity of our secular society, unity and integrity of the nation."[15]

In the context of the evolution of the right to education as a Fundamental Right, this paper focuses its attention on certain aspects like child labour, pathetic conditions of parents to send their wards to schools, problems involved in the implementation of the Act, opposition of private schools and experiences of some countries in regard to their Acts on providing right to education and ongoing debate in regard to the Act.

For clarity and convenience, this Paper deals with the following themes.

1. Child Labour: Need to impart compulsory primary education
2. The Right of Children to Free and Compulsory Education Act, 2009 – A Critical Appraisal
3. An Overview of the experiences of some countries which have recognized right to education to children
4. Conclusion

CHILD LABOUR: NEED TO IMPART COMPULSORY AND PRIMARY EDUCATION

It is gainsaying of the fact that the philosophy of enacting the Right of Children To Free and Compulsory Education Act (RTE ACT) rests mainly on the need of the child for receiving education without being exploited by doing labour which swallows the educational and emotional development. It is said that '**The child is the father of the man.** '[16] and today's children are tomorrow's citizens. Notwithstanding the definitions of child labour,[17] the meaning which could be visualized by common sense – we may emphasize that every child needs to care in his tender infancy by playing and nourishing himself with at least elementary study. This is necessary not only to the child but to the whole nation. No parent really wants their children to be labourers and no nation stands for child labour. But, the facts, prevailing in most of the countries including India show that the "child labour" is an existing reality. Due to a number of social and economic factors,[18] the children are forced to work in many places like match and fireworks industry, stone quarries, fishing, handloom industry, beedi industry, carpet weaving, glass industry and many other places.[19] A substantial proportion of India's poor children are engaged in agriculture labour, or pretty traders, housework and sibling care.[20] There are heart-burning stories of children who were forced to work, while their dream to go to school was shattered.[21] The pathetic condition of children, who are engaged in labour and who have deprived their schooling, losing their charm of tender childhood, is a common phenomenon mostly in the Third World Countries. It is alarming to note that this menace is with its diabolic countenance in a developing country like India. In spite of many laws and constitutional provisions[22] to safeguard the children from exploitation, we do still find that millions of children in India are "left out in the cold."[23] The laws seem to remain only on paper. In fact, as Madhubhasi Sridhar points out, "every non-schooling child is a child labour."[24] To eradicate the child labour, it is necessary to recognize the right to education as a fundamental right. It engages the child in education and keeps him away from the clutches of doing labour. The objective of the Constitution (86th Amendment) Act, 2002 which culminated into the RTE Act, 2009 which came into force on 1st April, 2010 stands on the philosophy of eradicating child labour and providing the right of children to receive free and compulsory education from 6 to 14 years of age.

THE RIGHT OF CHILDREN TO FREE AND COMPULSORY EDUCATION ACT, 2009: A CRITICAL APPRAISAL

The next theme of this Paper is a critical appraisal on the Right of Children to free and Compulsory Education Act,

2009 which came into force from 1st April, 2010. The main objective of this Act is to provide free and compulsory education to all children of six to fourteen years of age. The underlining Philosophy of the Act, as it has already been mentioned, is to free the children from the 'clutches of child labour' which is very inhuman and ignonimous. The Act is the transformation of the objective of providing free and compulsory education to children from the non-Judicial part to the Judicial part of the Constitution.[25] The non-Judicial provisions of the Constitution, though 'fundamental in the governance of the country'[26] are not mandatory on the part of the State to enforce them, whereas it is mandatory on the part of the State to implement the injunctions of the provisions of the Part III of the Constitution which is regarded Judicial and enforceable. In this context, we are directed to have the opinion that the RTE Act is a great milestone, as, it, being under Judicial provisions, could do 'wonders' by providing education to all the children. One may even 'dream' that child labour would disappear soon and each and every one in India would become literate and educated. But, all this is only a fantasy, unless the Act is implemented with letter and spirit. Just by transforming a directive principle into a fundamental right, we cannot fulfil the objective without commitment, responsibility and adequate financial resources. There are many loopholes in the framework of the Act which provide a way to the authorities to be away from the "bounden responsibility of providing education to children." Let us examine the summary of the text and provisions of the Act and appraise them later.

Text of the Act at a Glance[27]

The Right of Children to Free and Compulsory Education Act, 2009 (No. 35 of 2009) received the assent of the President of India on 26th August, 2009. It came into force on April 1, 2010 (in accordance to the provision of the Act of the Gazette of India. Clause 3 of the Section 1 of Chapter 1

(PRELIMINARY) which reads: "It (The Act) shall come into force on such date as the Central Government may, by notification in the Official Gazette, appoint)." The Act has Seven Chapters and one Schedule.

The Chapter 1 is named **PRELIMINARY. Section 1** deals with – short title, extent and commencement. According to it, the Act may be called the Right of Children to Free and Compulsory Education Act, 2009. It shall extend to the whole of India except the State of Jammu and Kashmir. It shall come into force on such date as the Central Government may, by notification in the Official Gazette, appoint. **Section 2** defines some terms of the Act. They are: appropriate government, capitation fee, child, child belonging to disadvantaged group, elementary education, guardian, local authority, National Commission for protection of child rights, notification, parent, prescribed, schedule, school, screening procedure, special category and State Commission for protection of child rights. All these terms have been defined to satisfy legal requirements and they may be subject to interpretation by legal luminaries.

Chapter II is named – **"Right to Free and Compulsory Education."** It deals with certain aspects like – Right of Child to free and compulsory education, special provisions for children not admitted to or who have not completed elementary education and Right of Transfer to other schools. (Sections - 3 to 5)

Chapter III, named as **"Duties of Appropriate Government, Local Authority and Parents,"** has certain aspects like – Duty of appropriate government and local authority to establish school, sharing of financial and other responsibilities, Duties of appropriate government, Duties of local authority, Duty of parents and guardian and Appropriate Government to provide for pre-school education. (Sections - 6 to 11)

Chapter IV, named as **"Responsibilities of Schools and Teachers,"** deals with – Extent of School's responsibility for free and compulsory education, no capitation fees and screening procedure for admission, proof of age for admission, no denial of admission, prohibition of holding back and expansion, prohibition of physical punishment and mental harassment to child, no school to be established without obtaining certificate of recognition, norms and standards for school, power to amend schedule, School Management Committee, School Development Plan, qualification for appointment and terms and conditions of service of teachers, Duties of teachers and redressal of grievances, pupil-teacher ratio, filling up vacancies of teachers, prohibition of deployment of teachers for non-educational purpose and prohibition of private tuition by teachers. (Sections – 12 to 28)

Chapter V is named as **Curriculum and Completion of Elementary Education**. It deals with – curriculum and evaluation procedure and examination and completion certificate. (Sections 29 and 30)

Chapter VI is named as **Protection of Right of Children.** It consists of – monitoring of the child's right to education, redressal of grievances, Constitution of National Advisory Council and Constitution of State Advisory Council. (Sections - 31 to 34).

Chapter VII named **Miscellaneous,** deals with – power to issue directions, previous sanction for prosecution, protection of action taken to good faith and power of appropriate government to make rules. (Sections – 35 to 38)

Finally, **The Schedule** deals with Norms and Standards for a school. It deals with: number of teachers (from first to fifth class and sixth to eighth class), building (how it should be), minimum number of working days/Institutional hours in an academic year, minimum number of working hours per week for a teacher, teaching learning, equipment, library and play material, games and sports equipment.

Above is a glance of the text of the Gazette of India of the RTE Act, 2009. The Gazette was issued by T.K. Viswanatham,

Secretary to the Government of India on 27th August, 2009. The provisions enshrined in the Act could be summarized in brief as follows.

Main Provisions of the RTE Act, 2009[28]

- Children of 6 to 14 years have a right to receive free and compulsory elementary education (1st to 8th Classes) from the neighbourhood schools.
- Responsibility of providing funds for the implementation of the provisions of the Act lies with the Central and State governments equally.
- The appropriate government shall be responsible for the establishment of school and its building and for the provision of infrastructure along with the teaching staff and learning equipment.
- It is the responsibility of the government to ensure compulsory admission, attendance and completion of elementary education.
- Every parent or guardian has fundamental responsibility to join his Ward in the neighourhood school.
- The appropriate government may take necessary arrangement for providing free pre-school education for the children between three to six years, so that the children would be prepared for elementary education.
- All the schools receiving aid or grant from the appropriate government fully or partially shall have to admit the children belonging to the weaker and disadvantaged to the extent of at least twenty five per cent of the strength of the class. The appropriate government shall bear the expenses.
- No school shall collect any capitation fee and shall subject the child to any screening procedure. Any school that violates this provision shall have to pay a fine of Rs. 25,000/- for the first contravention and each 50,000 for each subsequent contravention.

- The age of the child shall be determined on the basis of birth certificate. However, no child shall be denied admission in a school for lack of age proof.
- No child admitted in a school shall be held back in any class or expelled from school till the completion of elementary education.
- No child shall be subjected to physical punishment or mental harassment. Whoever contravenes this provision shall be liable to disciplinary action.
- No school (other than the school of appropriate government or local authority) shall be established without obtaining a certificate of recognition from the appropriate authority. According to the Act, there are certain norms which must take into account by the authority to accord such recognition to the school. If any person establishes or runs a school without obtaining a valid certificate, he shall be liable to fine Rs. 1 lakh.
- If there was any school established before the commencement of the Act and does not fulfill the necessary norms and standards as prescribed, it shall have to take steps to fulfill such norms and standards at its own expenses within a period of three years. If it fails in this, its recognition shall be withdrawn. If the person runs the school even then, he shall be liable to the fine prescribed.
- Save the unaided private schools, a school shall constitute a School Management Committee consisting of the elected representatives of the local authority, parents or guardians of children admitted. The Committee shall consist of at least three fourth of parents or guardians. Half of the members shall be women.
- The School Management Committee shall perform the functions namely monitor the working of school; prepare and recommend school development plans, monitor the utilization of the grants and perform such other functions as may be prescribed.

- Teachers shall be appointed on the basis of minimum qualifications prescribed.
- The teachers shall have to maintain punctuality and teach the students in accordance to the teaching schedule. They have to estimate the level and standard of the children and teach accordingly. If necessary, they have to take extra classes, conduct meeting with parents and provide information to them about the progress of the students. No teachers should take private tuitions or private teaching activity.
- No teacher shall be deployed for any non-educational purpose other than certain assignments of the government such as the duties on population census, election and disaster relief.
- There should not more than ten per cent of vacancies of the total sanctioned strength of the teaching staff.
- The curriculum and the evaluation procedure for elementary education shall maintain certain values such as – conformity with the value enshrined in the Constitution; all-round development of the child; building up the child's knowledge; potentiality and talent; development of physical and mental abilities to the fullest extent; learning through activities; discovery and explanation in a child-friendly and child-centered manner; medium of instruction; as far as practicable; be in child's mother tongue; making the child free from fear, trauma and anxiety and helping the child to express views freely, comprehensive and continuous evaluation of the knowledge and his or her ability to apply the same.
- No child shall be required to pass any Board examination till the completion of elementary education.
- The Schedule of the Act prescribes certain norms and standards. It prescribes the number of teachers for a prescribed strength of students, depending on the class and strength. It gives an account of teachers of various

disciplines. It also emphasis the significance of fine arts, vocational courses, gymnasium etc. It recommends necessary infrastructure to teachers and students like special rooms for teachers, head-teacher's room, water facility, kitchen, separate toilets for boys and girls, playground, library, etc.

A perusal of the text and features of the Act sounds melodious. The objectives of the Act could be appreciable. As Robert Frost says, "The Woods are lovely, dark and deep," (in his Poem "Stopping by Woods on a Snowy Evening) the provisions of the Act are very enchanting. But, at the same time, we cannot forget what Frost has said – "Many Miles to go before I sleep" – from which we have to know that we have to do "many things" to achieve the objectives enshrined in the Act. There are critics who have critically highlighted the Act on different dimensions. Let us discuss the views of critics in this regard.

Critical Appreciation of the RTE Act, 2009

The Right of Children to Free and Compulsory Education Act, 2009 (RTE) has been made enforceable from April 1, 2010. In fact, the ideal of providing compulsory education to children below 14 years is already enshrined in the Constitution in Part – IV (Directive Principles of State Policy Art 45) (before 86th Amendment).[29] According to this provision, the State shall endeavour to provide fair and compulsory education to all the children of below 14 years – "within a period of ten years." But, the State could not implement the provision effectively during the sixty years of the Indian Republic. Does the wrong lie in the incorporation of the ideal in the Directive Principles of State Policy – which, though non-Judicial in nature, is fundamental in the governance of the country? Would the things improve if the ideal is made Judicial, by incorporating it in the Fundamental Rights? Is it possible to bring a dramatic change in the social fabric by just shifting a provision from Non-

Judicial Part to Judicial Part? Does the Act (which is in accordance to Article 21-A) provide guarantee to right to education of children without loopholes? Are there provisions in the Act to fight against the obstacles that come in the way of children to receive education? Does the Act provide quality education which enables them to stand on their own feet or simply leave them to improve a little better than putting thumb impressions on forms? Can the "State" solve financial obstructions to meet the Act properly? Like this, there are many questions which are forwarded by academic circles and critics of the RTE – Act. Let us examine a few of them.

1. The RTE Act, 2009 defines child as a "male or female child of the age of six to fourteen years."[30] However, the Act says that the children below six years may receive pre-school education until they complete the age of six years from an appropriate government which may make necessary arrangements in this regard.[31] But, it may be noted that this comes under present Article 45 of the Constitution which is non Judicial.[32] Critics like Praveen Jha and Pooja Parvati point out that the Act has "no clarity even on the basic understanding of who is a child."[33] According to them, the Act fails to cover all children and does not provide definite timelines for many provisions.[34]

   At the same time, it may be pointed out that a child may complete 8th Class by age 14. There are suggestions from some schools that the child must be entitled to receive education up to the age of the 18 at least, so that he can complete Intermediate which is a basic qualification nowadays. Hence, the Act is to be amended to suit these requirements. One of the suggestions of the Students' Federation of India which issued a press statement reads: "Education of children of 0 to 6 and 14 – 18 has to be brought into the purview of the Act, thereby universalizing both primary and secondary education.[35] Krishna Kumar in his article *"India's Children have a*

Precarious Right" published in *The Hindu* also pointed out that "the law does not cover pre-school education."[36] For this, he had made a suggestion according to which – 'a first step can be recognizing the year before Class 1 as a necessary pre-school year to provide enabling experience for the success of eight years of formal education stipulated by law. This step would require sustainable planning and coordination among the departments of Child Development, Health and Education."[37]

2. Another important criticism in regard to the RTE Act is in regard to the **financial burden** to ensure quality education. To provide free and compulsory education to millions of children in India, the central and state governments have to bear huge expenditures. The National University of Educational Planning and Administration, "Calculates that Implementation Act will cost of Rs. 1, 71,000 crores for five years.[38] But, such a huge funding seems to be burdensome to the central and state governments, in as much as the Finance Commission has given Rs. 25,000 crores to the States and Rs. 15,000 has been approved for Central Government for 2010-11 academic year."[39]
3. Feasibility of providing quality education is also a question among the critics. The Act lists certain norms and standards to which every school needs to adhere. The Act has certain contradictory provisions which may dilute this ideal. Section 19.2 of the Act says, "where a school does not fulfil the norms and standards specified in the Schedule, it shall take steps to fulfill such norms and standards on its own expenses within a period of three years from the date of such commencement." The Act does not stop here. The next Section (Section 20) says that central government may change the Schedule.[40] All this would dilute the ideal of the Act.

The Act has ignored many aspects which are necessary for **quality education**. The Act, though laudably says that the teachers should not be engaged in non-education acts, excludes them from extra duties other than population census, elections and duties pertaining to disaster.[41] It is known however that the academic schedule brings in several extra duties.

The Act has given importance to the enrolment of students, but it seems that there are no provisions to retain them. S. Viswanathan in a feature *"They need schools of joy, not hate,"* says:

> "Enrolment is the relatively easy part. But how will the institutions involved in this gigantic foundational project ensure that all children admitted in the schools are retained until the complete their studies? Apart from a possible respect of large scale dropout of students, there is this widely heard complaint: the education offered in most schools is of poor and substandard quality."[42]

It is heartening to note that Kapil Sibal, the Union Minister for Human Resource Development gave importance to quality education. Let us see how far this will become a reality.

4. The most important problems of concern in regard to the implementation of RTE Act are many – such as child labour, social taboos, poverty of parents etc. Though the ideal of the Act is to encounter these issues, it has not provided sufficient ground work for the achievement of the ideal. Millions of children, due to obvious reasons, are engaged in many petty jobs like rag-picking, agricultural labour, petty trades, housework and so on. Their parents mostly are helpless in this regard as they cannot afford the maintenance of the family without their help. They do not find any purpose or meaning in sending their children to schools, as they feel that the education would provide nothing to them. In addition to these, there are many social taboos which come in the way of the parents to send their wards to school. Many parents

especially of tribal areas and villages do not like to send their daughters to school, even though they somehow send their sons to school. Apart from this, "some recent studies indicate that certain practices in the Indian society like untouchability, the segregation of Dalits in the mid day meal arrangements in schools and the humiliation inflicted on Dalit boys and girls in class rooms in some states keep some children away from studies."[43]

5. According to some critics, the right cannot be Judicial in nature, in as much as a child of six years is too young to claim his right. Krishna Kumar says, "one hardly needs to remember that this right is different from others enshrined in the Constitution, in that the beneficiary – a six-year old child – cannot demand it, nor can he or she fight a legal battle when this right is denied or violated.[44]

6. The Act enjoins private schools to admit at least 25 per cent of children belonging to weaker sections and disadvantaged groups in the classes.[45] Critics point out that it is very difficult to execute.[46] Puspa M. Bharghava comments on this aspect further. The comment is:

> "Why do we have only 25 per cent poor children in private aided schools? Why not 10, 20, 40, 60 or 80 per cent? Would it not create a divide amongst the children of the poor, leave aside a greater divide between the children of the rich and the poor. No method is prescribed for selecting the 25 per cent poor students for admission into Unaided Private Schools. Selection by lottery would be ridiculous. In the absence of viable provision, the Private Unaided Schools can choose the 25 per cent poor children in a way that the choice would benefit the school."[47]

7. The Act (12.2) (Chapter IV) promises the private schools that the state reimburses expenditure incurred by it for the education of poor children. But, the private schools charge the students in their own way. They have separate charges in respect to laboratory, computer education,

sports, uniform, painting and so on. As Puspa M. Bhargava says all these things are not mentioned in the Act.[48]

8. The private schools claim that they provide quality education. Forcing them to implement the Act without sufficient subsidies in against the citizen's right Art. (19.1.g) to 'practice any profession or to carry out any occupation, trade or business.' It is a controversial question whether 'running a school for profit is constitutional or not.[49] The lobbyists in private have gone to the Court, challenging the validity of the Act.[50] According to a news item, "The Supreme Court has admitted the challenge."[51]

9. The RTE Act is opposed and supported by a few Muslim scholars.[52] According to critics, it is 'draconian and anti-Muslim.' According to them, Article 30 of the Constitution allows the minorities 'the right to establish and administer educational institutions of this choice'. The Act, they point out, does not include madrasas Niaz Ahmed Farooqui of the Jamiat Ulama-e-Hind said, "The law says no one can run a school without prior permission. Does that mean madrasas will be prosecuted? How can the civil society accept this? How can you take away rights given to us by the Constitution?"

   However, some Muslim scholars have welcomed the Act. Abdul Khalique said that "the RTE Act is a progressive law and let us not oppose it. Let us find a way to reconcile the Article 30 with the RTE Act."

AN OVERVIEW OF THE EXPERIENCES OF SOME COUNTRIES WHICH HAVE RIGHT TO EDUCATION TO CHILDREN

Providing compulsory and free education to children is recognized almost universally. It is one of the human rights, recognized by the UNO by its Universal Declaration of Human Rights on December 10, 1948. Article 26(1) of the

Declaration says: "Everyone has the right to education. Education shall be free, at least elementary and fundamental stages. Elementary education shall be compulsory. Technical and professional education shall be made generally available and higher education shall be equally accessible to all on the basis of merit."[53] Many countries, following the directions of the UN Declaration of Human Rights, had recognized the right of children to receive free and compulsory education at least in their elementary stage. Let us know a few of them.

Republic of Trinidad and Tobago[54]

Republic of Trinidad and Tobago is a small Country in the continent South America. Peggy Mohan, who has written a detailed article "Right to Education: Lessons from Trinidad and Tobago" in the *Economic and Political Weekly* appreciates the efforts of this country in making primary education free for all children and ensuring quality education to them. The government of Trinidad and Tobago made many efforts to translate its objective into reality. It made negotiations with the existing school boards and the teachers' unions, the private and church schools. The government took responsibility of paying all running expenses and staff salaries of all schools. Thus, the government had become a good investor and stakeholder in the private schools. It has separated primary and secondary schools. Thus, the government has made certain experiments. The author says that there is a need to make a comprehensive study of the experiments of this country in regard to its efforts in making right to education successful. He says: "As India begins to grapple with the issue of implementing the RTE Act, 2009, it would do well to look at examples like that of Trinidad and Tobago."

Australia[55]

Australia is one of the countries which are much concerned with child labour. To eradicate child labour, it has made certain laws to provide free and primary education to children.

Bangladesh[56]

The Government of Bangladesh has many schemes to provide compulsory free primary education. The children are given a monthly stipend, so that they can earn and learn, without troubling their parents. In this way, it may be said that efforts of the Government of Bangladesh are close to social and economic conditions of the people.

Chad[57]

Elementary education is compulsory in Chad. The Government of Chad has collaboration with UNICEF in dealing with child labour.

Colombia[58]

The Government of Colombia ensures basic education to children below 14 years of age. It prohibits child labour.

Ghana[59]

The Education Act of Ghana recognizes free, compulsory, universal and basic education programmes. Education has been compulsory to all children of school age. Child labour is prohibited.

Iran[60]

In Iran, elementary school education is mandatory. The government provides necessary incentives for this.

Namibia[61]

The Government of Namibia has a special Ministry of Basic Education and Culture. This ministry has a compulsory education system and requires the children to attend school until the age of 16. It prohibits child labour.

Oman[62]

In the Sultanate of Oman, there seems to be no problem of child labour. Yet, free education is provided there at all levels. The laws of Sultanate of Oman guarantee the non-employment of children.

Pakistan[63]

In Pakistan also, there are certain Acts like the Employment of Children Act, 1991, which regulate the employment of children.

Uganda[64]

The National Constitution of the Republic of Uganda provides for basic education for children "as a responsibility of the state and the parent to protect the children from social and economic exploitation." There are many Acts in Uganda which prevent employment of children under the age of 12 and regulate employment of children at the age of 18.

Thus, there are many countries in the World which are striving for the eradication of child labour and provide basic education to children. But, due to many social and economic realities, the countries are struggling to achieve this noble objective. In India, there are many Constitutional and Legal provisions to abolish child labour and provide minimum basic education to children. The members of the Constituent Assembly made a provision of Article 45 by enjoining the State to "endeavour to provide free and compulsory education for all children until they complete fourteen years of age. It is not fair to say that the Central and State Governments have not done anything in this regard.[65] Still, the objective has not been fulfilled as to our "Great Expectations." As it has been mentioned earlier, the National Commission of the working of the Constitution, and many Constitutional Cases[66] have highlighted the need of recognizing the right to education as a Fundamental Right. "The State had respected this and recognized the right to education as the Fundamental Right by 86th (Constitutional Amendment) Act, 2002. The Union government brought it in the form of Act which by the government's notification. By the Government notification, it came into force on 1st April, 2010. The Act has noble objectives, though it may face certain obstacles and criticism in the process of implementation.

CONCLUSION

The RTE Act, 2009 is a historic law, making education a Fundamental Right to every child. It is the result of our hundred year's struggle for universalizing elementary education. There are many provisions in the Act, which make the children free from fear, stress and anxiety, in as much as there are provisions which prohibit corporal punishment, detention and expulsion. Many provisions of the Act enrich the relationship between child and teacher, child and parent and parents and teachers. The Act benefits many disadvantaged sections including physically handicapped students. As Prime Minister Manmohan Singh says, "It empowers the individual and enables the nation." Kapil Sibal the HRD Minister called it "A Tryst with Destiny." Providing education to the children strengthens democracy. Though, the RTE Act is very sound in its philosophy, it has certain loopholes, some of which have been presented in this paper. It must be pointed out that every Act has both merits and demerits. It is necessary to overcome the defects of the Act by necessary commitment and with strong determination. The following are some suggestions which may be considered for effective implementation of the ideal of right of children to receive education.

1. Efforts have to be made to enable the parents and wards to comprehend the benefits of educating their children. For this, the press and electronic media have to give a large coverage. Voluntary organizations have to come forward actively in carrying out this mission along with the efforts of government.

2. Steps have to be taken to provide pre-school education for children below six years effectively.
3. The central government must bear all the expenses in regard to the implementation of this Act.
4. Teachers should not be deployed for any non-education purpose including the duties related to elections to the Union and State Legislatures. However, their services may be taken to meet certain conditions of exigency.
5. Effective steps should be taken to ensure that all children complete their studies with joy. For this, the authorities have to give importance to consider a provision which enables the children to have 'food for the belly along with food for thought.'
6. Vocational education has to be imparted along with regular education. At the same time, it is necessary to give importance to moral-based education which could mould the children to become good citizens.
7. Steps have to be taken to eliminate social taboos like: rich and poor children, boys and girls, untouchability, etc.
8. A uniform pattern of norms must be implemented in all schools – government or private. The facilities like laboratory, computer education, sports, etc. should be same in all schools, so that there would be no differences between the students on the basis of haves and have-nots.
9. The government has to give primary importance to enable the children to receive education. It is necessary to provide free and compulsory education to children up to 10th class at least.

By and large, the RTE Act is indeed a great, noble initiative. Every right-thinking citizen should act like a soldier in mobilizing and motivating those who are not eager to get their children educated. It is necessary for all the concerned to activate themselves in translating the spirit of the Act into reality.

It may be pointed out that laws by themselves do not bring dramatic changes in the social fabric of a society, but they undoubtedly contribute greatly to it. The very formulation of the RTE Act and willingness of the government to implement it, no doubt, is a great step and a token of regard for the Indian Constitution which envisages a Welfare State. It is said that "failures are stepping stones to success." This proverb strengthens one to be undaunted in his mission. It may be hoped that our government will carry the spirit of RTE Act effectively with a great commitment. Its success in this endeavour enables it to take the next project of decommercialising of the entire education system at the national level and regard the right to education for higher studies too. The nation's progress depends on the accessibility of education to its people.

Notes

1. G. B. Reddy 2003. *"Right to Education in India-Its Evolution as a Fundamental Right and its Consequences"*. Paper published in "Dimensions of Education under the Indian Constitution Prof. G. Manohar Rao (Ed). Gogia Law Agency, Hyderabad, p. 76.
2. Praveen Jha & Pooja Parvati, 2010. *"Right to Education Act. 2009: Critical Gaps and Challenges."* EPW (Vol. XLV No. 13), March 27, 2010, p. 20.
3. Reported in The Hindu (April 2010), p. 1.
4. *Ibid.*
5. Kapil Sibal, *"Joining hands in the interest of Children."* The Hindu, April 1, 2010, p. 10.
6. AIR 1992 SC 1858.
7. AIR 1993 SC 2178.
8. AIR 2003 SC 3226.
9. AIR 2005 SC 3226.

10. All these cases dealt with different aspects of education. The dictum in these cases was that right to education flowed directly from right to life guaranteed by Art. 21 of the constitution. The citizens, according to *Mohini Jain*, could demand the State to provide adequate number of educational institutions and satisfy their educational needs. According to *Unni Krishnan*, free and compulsory primary education must be provided. The central idea of different interpretations of education is that right to education is the integral part of right to life and personal liberty of Art. 21 and hence it must be regarded as a fundamental right. In the Indian Constitution, Article 45 (before 86th Constitutional Amendment) Act, enjoins the state to provide free and compulsory education to all the children below 14 years. As this was in Part IV of non-Justifiable right, one could estimate how well it could be translated into reality. By interpreting Art. 21 which deals with right to life and personal liberty in a wider sense, the courts have found "right to receive education" as the meaningful right of right to life of Art. 21 A. To establish this, the courts have quoted the verses of ancient Sanskrit books, different provisions of the Indian constitution and other constitutions, UN Declaration of Human Rights etc.

11. The words *"in such manner as the State may, by law, determine"* have certain implications. It underlines the fact that Art. 21 A, would not come into force immediately. The nature and date of its application shall have to be determined by the State. It took seven long years for the enactment of the Bill which, again, took more than seven months to be declared to have come into force. A serious look at the provisions of the Act takes one on Robert Frost's famous Lines *"Many miles to go...*

12. In Art 21 A, a child between ages six to fourteen years shall be provided free and compulsory education. It, otherwise, implies that a child below six years does not come under the benefit of Art. 21. A. The new provision of Art. 45 enjoins the State to provide early childhood care and education for all children until they complete six years. It means that children below six years come under non-Justifiable obligation of the State (as if it were all the children below fourteen years were taken care of in the pre-86th constitutional provision). In other words,

the meaning of "child" of Art. 21, A is different from that of Art. 45.

13. This is a new clause under Art. 51 A. It has made the parent or guardian as the stakeholder to provide opportunities for education to his child.

14. G. B. Reddy. *Op. cit.* p. 76. (Dimensions of Education ....)

15. G. Manohar Rao, 2003. Preface to *"Dimensions of Education under the Indian Constitution"* (As the Editor's remarks). Gogia Law Agency, Hyderabad, p. 1-2.

16. Famous Line of William Words Worth in the poem "MY HEART LEAPS UP".

17. The term 'child' has many definitions which are contradictory to each other. They range from 'o' to 21 years. The RTE Act, 2009 says that 'child' means a male or female child of the age six to fourteen years, Section 2.C (Chapter I).

18. According to Dr. Madabhushi Sridhar: "There are two aspects that drive the child away from school. One – abject Poverty at home and two – corporal punishments or cost of books and notebooks at school". (See: *The Constitution (86th Amendment) Act, 2002: Right to Universal compulsory Free Primary Education with Reference to child Labour", Paper published in Dimensions of Education under the Indian Constitution 2003, Hyderabad, (Gogia Law Agency). Dr. P.S.R. Murthy in his Thesis "Socio Economic Study of Women and Child Labour in Ranga Reddy District of Andhra Pradesh"* points outs some social and economic factors as the causes of child labour. According to him, 'Lack of education of the parents, lack of recreation facilities at home, lack of job security of the parents and impact of cinema, television and peer group are social factors and poverty of the parents, financial crisis of the family, self of reliance etc. are economic factors. (Thesis submitted to the Nagpur University for the award of Doctor of Philosophy in Commerce in 1999 (Guidance of Dr. Madhukar Rode).

19. Refer the Thesis of Dr. PSR (Ibid) for details – p. 54 to 56. He has highlighted the pathetic status of child labourers in Sivakasi in 'match and fire works' (where the children work in dingy and dark sheds handling poisonous chemicals) and the same

status of the unfortunate in stone quarries, fishing, beedi industry, carpet weaving, glass industry etc., in many States. At the same time, the children are paid low remuneration with excess hours of work. They are subject to physical abuse and are under hazardous working conditions.

20. *Making the RTE work* (Editorial, the Hindu dated 3rd April, 2010).
21. Madabhushi Sridhar, *Dimensions of Education under the Indian Constitution*.(op.cit), p.108.
22. Many Constitutional provisions in Fundamental Rights, Directive Principles and Fundamental Duties (Art. 14-17, 19-22, 23-24, 25, 29, 32, 42, 45, 47 51 A) have provided certain safeguards to children and other weaker sections. The Central Government has made many Acts like Guardian and Wards Act, 1980, Child Marriage Act, 1929, Hindu Marriage At, 1956, Orphanage Act, 1960, The Juvenile Justice Act, 1986, Pre-Natal Diagnostic (Regulation and Prevention of Misuse) Act, 1994 etc. have to provide protection to children. Even the UNO in many Resolutions sought in the protection of children. But the problem of Child Labour remains cold ever.
23. Making the RTE WORK (Ed – The Hindu, dated 3rd April, 2010.
24. Madabhushi Sridhar (*op. cit*), p. 108.
25. See the above reference 11 and 12.
26. Art. 37 of part IV reads "The provisions contained in this part shall not be enforceable by any Court, but the principles therein laid down are nevertheless fundamental in the governance of the country and it shall be the duty of the state to apply these principles in making laws"
27. Taken help from THE GAZETTE OF INDIA (No.35 of 2009).
28. Taken help from the "Main points of the RTE Act 2009" (Telugu version) issued by The Secretary of School Education of Andhra Pradesh (dt. 27-03-2010) and also the Gazette of India (No.35 of 2009)."
29. See the above reference No.12.
30. Clause C of Section 2 (Chapter I) of the RTE Act, 2009.

31. Section 11 of (Chapter III) reads: "With a view to prepare children above the age of three years for elementary education and to provide early childhood care and education for all children until they complete the age of six years, the appropriate Government may make necessary arrangements for providing free, Pre-School education for such children".
32. Read Art. 45 after The Constitution (86th Amendment) Act, 2002 – see the reference. No. 12.
33. Praveen Jha & Pooja Parvati, 2010. *Right to Education Art. 2009: Critical Gaps and Challenges*. EPW (Vol) XLV No. 13) March 27, 2010, p. 21.
34 *Ibid.*
35. People's Democracy, April 4, 2010, p. 11.
36. *"India's Children have a precarious right"* (The Hindu, April 3, 2010) Article by Krishna Kumar.
37. *Ibid.*
38. *"Making the RTE work"* (Editorial, The Hindu, April 3, 2010).
39. *Ibid.*
40. "The Central Government may, by notification, amend the Schedule by adding to, or omitting there from, any norms and standards". (Section 20 of the RTE Act).
41. Section 27 (Chapter IV) of Act reads: "No teacher shall be deployed for any non-educational purpose other than the decennial population census, disaster relief duties, relating to elections to the local authority or the State Legislature or Parliament as the case may be"
42. S. Viswanathan's article in the feature ONLINE AND OFF LINE in *The Hindu*, dated April, 12, 2010.
43. *Ibid.* (Kernal of a para).
44. "India's Children have a precarious right". (Krishna Kumar – *The Hindu* dated April 3, 2010).
45. Section 12 (1) C (Chapter IV) reads: " Specified in the sub-clause (iii) and (iv) of clause (n) of section 2 shall admit in class I to the extent of at least twenty five percent of the strength of that class, children belonging to weaker sections and disadvantaged

groups in the neighbourhood and provide free and compulsory education till the completion".

46. Krishna Kumar in the Hindu, April, 3, 2010 (*op. cit*).
47. *RTE Act: Some Rights and Wrongs* (Pushpa M. Bhargava – *The Hindu* July 26, 2010).
48. *Ibid.*
49. *Ibid.*
50. Krishna Kumar in his article, *The Hindu*, April 3, 2010 (*op. cit*).
51. Refer *Eenadu* dated Sept, 7, 2010, p. 5.
52. *The Hindu*, in a special news item "*Muslim Community Split on RTE Act*," has published the views of some Muslims on the RTE Act (Refer the Hindu – 13th July, 2010), p.10 of Hyderabad. ed.)
53. Refer "*Primary Education – Constitutional Chameleon: A Fundamental Right: Burning Issue*" by Arvind Kumar Agrwal in "*Dimensions of Education under the Indian Constitution*". (Ed. G. Manohar Rao) Gogia Law Agency, Hyderabad. 2003.
54. Peggy Mohan has expressed views of the experiments of Trinidad and Tobago in her article "*Right to Education: Lessons from Trinidad and Tobago*" published in the Economic and political Weekly, May 29, 2010.
55. Points taken from "*The Constitution (86th Amendment) Act, 2002: Right to Universal Compulsory Primary Education in the reference to child labour*" of Dr. Madabhusi Sridhar (Refer Dimensions of Education under the Indian Constitution, *op. cit*) p. 109.
56. *op.cit.* 110.
57. *op.cit.* 113.
58. *Ibid.*
59. *op.cit.* 114.
60. *op.cit.* 115.
61. *op.cit.* 116.
62. *op.cit.* 117.
63. *op.cit.* 118.
64. *op.cit.* 121.
65. Refer the foot notes No. 22.
66. Refer the foot notes from 6 to 10.

ENLIGHTENED DEMOCRACY, EDUCATION AND EMPOWERMENT

A. V. Satish Chandra

In my personal opinion one of the greatest treatises to be written on education is Emile by the French Philosopher Jean Jacques Rousseau. The work was condemned because it stood for revolutionary principles that were inconvenient to the Catholic Church and to European society in general. However over a period of time there has been recognition of this work and any teacher worth his/her salt should have a look at it. In this context of course, the book and its contents have an immediacy which is even more poignant, because in this work of Rousseau that one sees the true meaning of equality and empowerment. I therefore think that it would be in the fitness of things to start with the preface that Rousseau himself wrote to Emile.

"I began this disorderly and almost endless collection of scattered thoughts and observations in order to gratify a good mother who knows how to think. At first I had planned a memoir of only a few pages, but my subject carried me along in spite of myself, and imperceptibly the memoir became a kind of treatise, too large indeed for what it contained but too small for the matter with which it deals. For a long time I hesitated whether to publish it or not, and I have often felt while working upon it that writing a few brochures does not teach one how to compose a book. After vain attempts to improve it, I believe I must give it over as it is, since it is important to direct public attention to this subject. And whenever my ideas are bad, if I make others come up with good ones I will not have completely wasted my time. A man who from a solitary retreat casts his writings before the public without any one to advertise them, without any party to defend them, without even knowing what is thought and said about them, need not fear that if he is wrong people will accept his errors without examining them.

I shall say very little about the value of a good education, nor will I stop to prove that the customary method of education is bad. Thousands of others have done this before and I do not wish to fill my book with things that everyone knows. I will merely state that since the beginning of time there has been a continual outcry against the established practice without anyone suggesting how to propose a better one. The literature and science of our century tend to destroy rather than to build up. When we censor others we take on the tone of a pedagogue. But to propose something new we must adopt a different tone, one less gratifying to the philosopher's pride. In spite of all those books whose only aim, so they say, is public utility, the most useful of all arts — the art of training men — is still neglected. Even after Locke's book my subject was completely new, and I strongly fear that it will still be so after mine.

We know nothing of childhood, and with our mistaken notions the further we advance the further we go astray. The wisest writers devote themselves to what a man ought to know without asking what a child is capable of learning. They are always looking for the man in the child without considering what he is before he becomes a man. It is the latter study to which I have applied myself the most; so that if my method is unrealistic and unsound at least one can profit from my observations. I may be greatly mistaken as to what ought to be done, but I think I have clearly perceived the material that is to be worked upon. Begin thus by making a more careful study of your pupils, for it is clear that you know nothing about them. If you read this book with that end in view I think you will find that it is not entirely useless"[1].

Rousseau argued that we are inherently good, but we become corrupted by the evils of society. We are born good - and that is our natural state. In later life he wished to live a simple life, to be close to nature and to enjoy what it gives us - a concern said to have been fostered by his father. Through attending to nature we are more likely to live a life of virtue. Jean-Jacques Rousseau was interested in people being natural. "We are born capable of sensation and from birth are affected in diverse ways by the objects around us. As soon as we become conscious of our sensations we are inclined to seek or to avoid the objects which produce them: at first, because they are agreeable or disagreeable to us, later because we discover that they suit or do not suit us, and ultimately because of the judgements we pass on them by reference to the idea of happiness of perfection we get from reason. These inclinations extend and strengthen with the growth of sensibility and intelligence, but under the pressure of habit they are changed to some extent with our opinions. The inclinations before this change are what I call our nature. In my view everything ought to be in conformity with these original inclinations"[2].

One can say that "From the outset Rousseau had drawn inspiration from his own heart and found philosophical truth in the depth of his own being"[3] . His later writings, especially *Reveries of the Solitary Walker*, show both his isolation and alienation, and some paths into happiness. "Everything is in constant flux on this earth"[4], he writes.

"But if there is a state where the soul can find a resting-place secure enough to establish itself and concentrate its entire being there, with no need to remember the past or reach into the future, where time is nothing to it, where the present runs on indefinitely but this duration goes unnoticed, with no sign of the passing of time, and no other feeling of deprivation or enjoyment, pleasure or pain, desire or fear than the simple feeling of existence, a feeling that fills our soul entirely, as long as this state lasts, we can call ourselves happy, not with a poor, incomplete and relative happiness such as we find in the pleasures of life, but with a sufficient, complete and perfect happiness which leaves no emptiness to be filled in the soul. Such is the state which I often experienced on the Island Of Saint-Pierre in my solitary reveries, whether I lay in a boat and drifted where the water carried me, or sat by the shores of the stormy lake, or elsewhere, on the banks of a lovely river or a stream murmuring over the stones"[5].

In India there were a few fundamental mistakes committed in providing education to the people of the country post-Independence. On the one hand the first Prime Minister of the country, Pandit Jawaharlal Nehru talked about the necessity for a temperament that was based in an understanding of science[6], but permitted the setting up of schools which were to impart education in the vernacular. What was overlooked (those who are more sympathetic to Nehru's problems are more charitable in describing the scenario as 'inevitable' due to the lack of an English educated workforce of teachers) was that there was no translation of the requirements of modern society in knowledge terms in the vernacular languages. Regional media therefore failed in imparting the kind of education that was necessary for the continuance of the spirit of modernity and scientific inquiry. This has led to different gaps in Indian society, vis-a-vis the educated in English and the educated in regional languages.

Regional media for education were introduced in India in tearing hurry and that has led to the destruction of the education system. There can be no argument over the fact that socially, politically and medically relevant knowledge has to treat the world as its constituency. When the world is the constituency for knowledge, the language used for understanding this should have the flexibility and openness to describe and analyze situations and diseases etc. Now local languages are precisely that. Since every language evolves from within a culture its structures and vocabulary pertain to that culture. English too was a local language once. But with colonialism and with the spread of English to most parts of the world and because it was the language of the powerful, English became the language which was better equipped than most to deal with new and emerging forms of knowledge. These developments meant that for a local Indian language to be enriched it needed translations from English. However, the problem with that is that it requires persons who have a good grasp and control over both the languages, English and the other language into which things are being translated. It also means that the translator will have to be knowledgeable of technical terms and the technicalities of the languages concerned. A tall order. For a nation in a hurry to establish itself as the equal of all others such an exercise proved to be time consuming. Instead, of then saying that English would be the language of instruction till such time that bodies of knowledge were adequately translated into Indian languages, to satisfy the jingoistic concerns of some, regional media of instruction were introduced taking education to where it is today. The consequence was inequality among educated people and all those who have been educated in the regional media and are hopeless about their future are a big constituency of lumpen elements whose services can be hired by politicians for whatever purposes they have in their minds. Otherwise how does one explain educational institutions becoming breeding grounds for all activities political, revolutionary or otherwise.

One of the biggest casualties of the regional medium and vernacular education, in India, have been the social sciences. In the Western world one saw the social sciences incepting in an atmosphere that was conducive to free thinking[7]. Free thinking was the desire of the individual to define and organize oneself on rational grounds in a way which would facilitate that individual's realization of the true potential of the self. Into this scenario were born the social sciences which took advantage of the liberality of a society that allowed the individual to do what I have talked about in the preceding sentences. The social sciences then were an extension of the liberal arts and at best a slightly more pompous version of the arts. All things considered pretensions apart the subject matter of the social sciences and the liberal arts is the same. Therefore that which is considered to be "social scientific" knowledge is one that still deals with the question of the individual and his/her place in society. Karl Marx, in his attempt to ground the study of human society in what he called "objective material conditions"[8] created an epistemological break by seeking to eliminate the one variable for whose sake the study was being carried out - the human being. But by and large the agenda that even the Marxists and Marx had was very much consistent with that of the liberal arts.

The state of social science education in India is poor. There are many reasons for this but the most significant of them is the fact that the social sciences have got lost in an ocean of stupidity. After the attaining of independence the spirit was such that people took pride in their own culture and justifiably so. But when this pride in one's own culture is stretched to illogical levels, it only becomes jingoism that is completely devoid of any meaningful content. And that is what happened with the education system in India and especially so the social science education. One may ask why the social sciences especially? If that is your question you will find the answer to that in the following sentences. Most of the time when certain words find circulation in the sphere of public speech they begin to lose their true import and meaning. After a while they remain merely words with no specific content or meaning and therefore they become vacuous. Nevertheless they continue to circulate in the public sphere with people talking at each other than to each other. Education, the term or the word, has sadly met the same fate. People today talk about education without having the faintest idea about what is involved in it. For most education is a degree that one receives, to some it is a sacred cow and if you are in Andhra Pradesh it is a business opportunity. None of these correspond to what education is or should be. Armed with this inability to properly define education we have successfully created stereotypes about what it is and therefore we think that one who has 95% marks is educated or one who has a good job is educated and so forth. The furtherance of these stereotypes has created a mess that is now very difficult to clean up. In all this the very elementary purpose of education - that of enlightenment - has been forgotten. Compounding the situation is the pursuit of money and material happiness.

In this process the social sciences have suffered more and disciplines such as history have been reduced to the documenting of fictitious and puerile things. They have also become weapons in the hands of bigots. So why did this happen. The answer is simple. The social sciences when they were born in the West had a form that was consistent with the content. It has remained more or less like that till date. However, in India it is a different story. We have taken the form and have tried to stuff it with whatever we thought was the appropriate content. This parody of sorts happened because of the desire to study in one's own tongue and when there is no body of knowledge to support that ambition or aspiration, things are bound to go wrong. The true pursuit of social science entails either a translation of all Western content into whichever language that one wished to study in or the creation of an alternative body of knowledge. In India's case neither has happened and as a result people study the same book in their mother tongue, from class eleven to Ph. D. This means that higher qualifications are awarded for studying the same book. What is even better is that in spite of the ten odd years that go into the study of the same book, the students are still at a loss to explain what it contains. Social scientific education is a necessity in any society, for it is the tool that one can use to have an audit of the functions of society, politics and governance. Not only can it audit, it can also provide with good alternatives to bad policies and programmes. It is also a necessity for a good and enlightened democracy[9]. In the case of India, the necessity for proper social sciences is even more heightened for obvious reasons. A society that has become fissiparous and threatens to fall apart needs good social sciences. And that is missing. Are the other sciences any better? The answer will be yes, but only a little. The other sciences are armed with mathematics and numbers which are considered to be lingua pura and therefore they are not bogged down so much by the problems of language. It is therefore completely a categorical imperative[10] in order create a proper social scientific knowledge and once again create the globally competitive Indian.

All problems affecting this country today are those that go back to the lack of a good system of education. Let me draw a parallel here. The old USSR imploded mainly because it tried to something which was not sustainable. To understand what I am saying better, let us look at the structure of what was the USSR. There were sixteen republics and they lynch pin among them was Russia. A feudal colonial power that brought the fifteen other republics under its control through the usual violent means. In the post Second World War days, especially under the rule of Stalin, Russia pursued its imperial intents under the garb of World Communism. The fifteen other republics were already co-opted into the process by being part of the USSR. At this point I would like to state though there was supposed to be the use of the principle of self determination used in the formation of the USSR, it is well known that most became a part of it since they were not allowed any other option. Russia tried to take on the best imperial powers such as the West European nations and the USA in their own back yard. It believed that through military might the rest of the world could be brought down on its knees. So it accelerated the arms race and in the process spent its precious resources on military might while at the same time starving the people of the USSR literally. The collapse of the Soviet economy was that which led to the implosion and every republic went it's way peacefully, except Georgia and Chechnya.

For those among you who are wondering as to what this bit of Russian history has to do with the present post, I am drawing a parallel between the Indian education system's present plights with that of the economy of the erstwhile USSR. What makes the parallel possible is the underlying cause which is unrealistic ambition and a foolish determination to prove to the world that you are among the best when actually the basic frame work to getting there does not exist. Russia and the USSR tried to become the most powerful without having the economic strength that is necessary to satisfy such an ambition. India too is trying to climb up the ladder to becoming a brain power while in effect; every step that it takes on this ladder is pulling the ladder down. And that is happening because the basics of what should be good education are not in place. Even though this may entail a repetition of some issues that I have written in other posts, I will go ahead and say that the first big mistake was in expanding the education system without considering the hurdles that it would create. The second big mistake was the government's pursuit of socialism and therefore its inability to invest properly in the educational sector. The setting up of all the huge public sector where there were six supervisors for one worker saw a drain on the resources. This meant that the government had no money to nurture an education system which will feed the developmental process for a long time to come. The result was the almost complete abandoning of the primary education sector and concentrating on the higher education sector. The government was building the IIT's and the IIM's and at the same time creating schools that no one went to at the primary level, simply because there was no infrastructure such as buildings, black boards, teachers etc. The primary and secondary education sector went into the hands of the private sector which in order to sustain itself and to grow required to charge a fee, which millions of poor Indians could not afford to pay. Education was accessible only to the affluent and most that belonged to this category came from the upper castes who had built a base for themselves right from the days of British Imperialism.

This led to the creation of educated elite, one that generally abhorred the other Indians who represented for them everything that they did not want to be. A couple of generations which emerged out of this primary education system went on to fulfill the aspirations of the IITs and the IIMs as institutions. They were able to churn out students who could compete globally and on equal terms with the rest of the world. At this juncture two things need to be looked at. This globally competitive Indian did not see his/her future in India. America for them was the new land of milk and honey and therefore they went that way. Products of the elitist education system who paid for their primary and secondary education and also for a very subsidized higher education did not invest their abilities back in India. So there is in effect no growth in the number of properly educated people contributing back to the system that they came from. As generations of good teachers retired from schools and with not many to replace them the primary and secondary sectors of paid and private schools has also started suffering from the lack of good teachers. Therefore contributions from the private primary sector has also started slow down to a trickle and today it only succeeds in putting out disinterested, illiterate nuveau riche elites, who wannabe but cannot be.

The Universities do not seem to attract any talent available and I read with dismay and horror the news that the Central Government in India is not setting up some of the new Central Universities that it proposed to, due to the lack of employable talent. It did not say there were no people holding the required certificates. It only said that the certificate holders (including Ph. Ds) were unemployable[11]. There are two ways of looking at this, horror (for obvious reasons) and relief, because it means that there is a realization that there is no necessity to employ and feed people who will only be a burden on the system. In a democracy where vote banks are of the utmost importance, it is quite necessary to satisfy the will of the people. The huge pool of the lumpen students is readily available for demonstrating the strength of the issue. So we have a situation where education institutions instead of enlightening people are serving the cause of the dark side of politics.

Most students of social sciences don't seem to have an idea as to what the State is and what its responsibilities are. We also seem to treat it as the 'other' that is distinct from the people and that which is responsible for the miseries and misfortunes that we as people suffer. Institutions such as the police which are seen as enemies are not seen as those which are empowered and legitimized by the State which is itself legitimated by the people. Most people are happy to identify democracy with just procedures such as voting and no more. People do not seem to understand the idea that democracy is self governance of the people in substance, with the procedure of voting put in, to simply identify representatives of the people, who will work for the welfare of their constituents. In my previous posts I have been saying that what is missing in Indian democracy is the deliberative component, which is obviously the key requirement. We do not seem to be able to connect institutions such the Parliament and State Legislative Assembly to the notion of deliberation. We don't seem to realize that these institutions are provided with the idea that they will serve as platforms for people's representatives to discuss the problems and prospects of their constituents, and also to find mechanisms of problem resolution. Contributing to this lack of understanding is the behaviour of our politicians who use the Parliament or the Assembly (if and when they go there) to behave boorishly. My question then is where is the substance of democracy in India? Only in procedures? Add another variable to this and it becomes even more confusing. Could we possibly have societies without power relations in them?

Power is one of the crucial variables that we need to understand when looking at the functioning of society. Otherwise why would we require authority? Authority should be seen as the official and legitimate empowerment of offices and officials so that these can deter naked power. The existence of authority is the acquiescence to the existence of power relations. Democracy seeks to overcome naked power and jungle law through a deliberative process and hence deliberation is at the centre of all democratic thinking. But it seems when judging the functioning of institutions and offices it seems as if we see authority abstracted from the context of naked power in which it exists and hence our disbelief in police and the State. Contributing to this are politicians who use the authority vested in them by their constituents as naked power rather than legitimate authority. How else does one explain the distancing of elected representatives from their people?

Politicians have by and large misused the trust of the people to get into manipulations that have very little to do with the interests of their constituents. The interest of the constituents is used as a facade for the pursuance of the politicians own ends, which rely heavily on the politicians ability to extend their naked power. When what should have been legitimate authority begins to act in the manner of naked power, there is a cascading effect that extends to all other institutions as well. We therefore forget that the police and bureaucracy are at one level people common people but those who can go against the disempowered people by serving the interests of various contending paradigms of naked power. Separatists movements and secessionist movements like the onetime Khalistan movement and the present Kashmir movement or extremist movements like Maoism are all conjured by politicians by pitting people against people for the furtherance and fulfillment of their (politicians) own goals of power mongering.

When the UPA was voted into power in the year 2004 and when the Sensex crashed by then unprecedented four hundred points in one day. This crash happened because of the combine of Communist parties had sixty two seats in the Lok Sabha and the fate of the Congress led UPA was felt to be very much in the hands of the Communists. The then Finance Minister, Mr. Chidambaram had to speak to the captains of the industry and allay their fears. Then this piece appeared on one of the websites[12] where the writer claimed that the will of two billion Indians was less significant than the economic activity in a two kilometre radius in Mumbai. The writer of that piece was clear about where his loyalties are. They are with the people, their will and democracy. How I wish the argument was so simple. What constitutes the Will of the People has the potential to fall into the gamut of rhetoric and an empty one at that. To demonstrate proof of what I am saying let me tell you a story here. I once got into an argument with Prof. Gurpreet Mahajan of the Centre for Political Studies, JNU. I had gone to do a refresher course and Prof. Mahajan was speaking about John Rawls, Multiculturalism and Democracy. She concluded that the definition of democracy should be "fairness". She told me then that to always stick with the definition of democracy as will of the people was untenable.

Over the years (there have been almost thirteen of them now) I have time and again pondered over this question without getting anywhere close to an answer. Really democracy in operation does not lend itself to any easy definitions. Prof. Mahajan had pointed out to me that it was not easy or possible to establish what the will of the people was[13]. Is it unchanging and always well deliberated? Is it the majority will and in that case what about those who do not subscribe to that majority will? Difficult questions indeed and that is why I have asked myself if democracy is a problematique (as in a source from which a number of problems emanate). And to me it seems that it is. In India majority opinion is "demonstrated" as being in favour of something or someone when the powerful support or espouse a cause. It can be seen as the demonstration of might. It is for reasons such as this that philosophers such as John Stuart Mill warned of a "tyranny of the majority" [14]when majority opinion becomes the order of the day.

It is very true that might can become right and I think it is for this reason that Rousseau had talked about the untenability of a democracy based in the show of strength of any kind by a majority. I am at this ripe old age beginning to understand the true brilliance of people like him and what he meant when he talked about the General Will and in what seemed an idiosyncratic move proposed the alternative of a single Universal Legislator who could embody and act for the good of 'ALL' when instances where direct democracy is not possible or fails[15]. He shrewdly suggested two alternatives so one could take over when the other failed. But coming to the context of India coalition politics and a general tendency to favour aggressive groups who threaten, blackmail and disrupt society has now firmly come to the forefront and the only solution to that is an enlightened people. But the failure of the education system in the last 63 years has ensured that enlightenment of the people is a distant dream. The only way that one can break out of this particular problem that the country faces is by building a solid system of education that will enlighten its citizens sufficiently enough for them to participate in various deliberations that concern them and their welfare. That would ensure that power mongers, power brokers do not hijack the agenda of democracy or the democratic process away from the general interest of all people to that of only the few. Education therefore is the most critical variable that makes possible the most primary of all forms of empowerment.

Notes

1. Rousseau, Jean-Jacques, Emile, New York, USA, Basic Books, 1979, p. 4.
2. From Boyd, William. *The Educational Theory of Jean Jacques Rousseau*. London, England Longmans, Green and Co., 1911. p. 14.
3. *ibid.*
4. Rousseau, Jean-Jacques, Emile, New York, USA, Basic Books, 1979, p. 7.
5. *ibid.*
6. See Nehru, Jawaharlal, "Discovery of the World", New Delhi, India, Surjit Publications, 1979.
7. See Wood, Gordon S., "Democracy and the American Revolution", Oxford, England, OUP.
8. See, Marx, Karl, "The Capital", Moscow, USSR, Progress Publishers, 1972.
9. Lloyd, G.E.R., Democracy, Philosophy and Science in Ancient Greece, in Dunn, John edited "Democracy – The Unfinished Journey, Oxford, England, Oxford University Press, p. 47.
10. See, Kant, Immanuel, Metaphysical Foundation of Morals, New York, USA, Modern Library Press, p. 46.
11. There is a constant chatter in various newspapers and magazines about how the 'educated' are in a situation where they need constant training and how this costs the companies a colossal sum of money apart from wasting their (the companies') time.
12. The website was rediff.com and the author did not put his signature on the piece.

13. Also refer: Mahajan, Gurpreet, "Identities and Rights", New Delhi, India, Oxford University Press.
14. Read: Mill, John Stuart, "On Liberty and Other Essays", Oxford, England, Oxford University Press.
15. Refer to: Shklar, Judith, "Men and Citizens" Cambridge, England, Cambridge University Press.

EMPOWERMENT OF FEMALE HEADED HOUSEHOLDS CASE STUDY:
"Sedighin" Charity Institution in Iran

SEYED HOSSEIN ZARHANI

INTRODUCTION

The household is regarded as the fundamental social and/or economic unit of society. Transformation at the household form, therefore, has impact at the aggregate level of a country. For instance, changes in household composition and structure have an impact on the distribution of goods and services, and on the planning of the public institutions, requirements for schools, housing and health infrastructure.

In recent decades the new form of households emerged. House headed by women have become more significant phenomenon worldwide in the last half of 20th and 21th century (Baros & Fox, 1997, p. 231).In 1960 only 9 per cent of families with children in united state were headed by none married women; by 1999 the number was over 20 per cent. (Min & Michael, 2003, p. 191).

A more recent occurrence in this direction is the increasing number of women headed households in developing countries that are emerging as a result of economic changes, economic downturns and social pressures, rather than as a product of cultural patterns. In many countries in the third world, like Asian or Latin

American countries, in recent years, there has been a significant increase in the percentage of female-headed households (FHH).

This is critically important when considering that female-headed households (most of which are headed by lone mothers, are rising in number and proportion in most developing regions, currently constituting an estimated 13% of all households in the Middle East and North Africa, 16% in Asia, 22% in sub-Saharan Africa, and 24% in Latin America. (Bongaarts, 2001) As the study of the status of female household heads and their households is becoming important and is given a fairly new emphasis among women's issues, it is the belief of both policy makers and functionaries working in the area of gender and development that researches on areas related to female heads and their households should be given special priority and concern.

FHH DEFINITION

Primary, the difference between family and household is discussed. A family, by definition, is a social institution that has a personal function of the reproduction and replacement of members (Schultz, 1976, p. 81). It is a social group characterized by common residence, economic cooperation and reproduction. It includes adults of both sexes, at least two of whom maintain a socially approved sexual relationship, and one or more children, owned or adopted, of the sexually cohabitant adults. (Murdock, 1949). In contrast the household has another meaning and it is "the basic residential unit in which economic production, consumption, inheritance, child rearing, and shelter are organized and carried out"; [the household] "may or may not be synonymous with family (Haviland, 2003).

The headship of the household is usually identified with the person who has the greater authority in the family or household. Power and authority in turn may be vested in the member who has control over the general affairs of the family unit, including decision-making concerning its economic, social and political interactions. (Sanni, 2006).

Illo (1989) however cautions that while females are recognized as potential household heads, in reality, [official] data collection, men are most often ascribed the headship position "a practice that still subscribes to the patriarchal view that men provide for the family while the women nurture it. Thus, headship may be assigned without due regard to the actual economic contributions of the female members.

The gender of the head of the household is one of the most important characteristics of the household. When households are headed by women, it is generally hypothesized that these households are more likely to be economically deprived and to lack the proper emotional environment for psychosocial development in children.

Fuwa (1999) gives three broad categories of FHH definitions: self-reported, demographic, and economic. The self-reported household category is often created based on respondents statements in surveys and censuses, although there is no precise definition. Demographic definitions take account of FHHs where there is male partner that is temporarily not present, and of FHHs where the female head is separated, divorced, widowed or single (1999). Further disaggregation of households can be done in terms of de facto and de jure FHHs. De facto FHHs are those households where the self-reported male head is absent the majority of the time (Fuwa, 1999). De jure female-headed households are those usually headed by widows or unmarried, divorced or separated women. Finally, FHHs may be defined depending on the level of economic contribution of females to the household. Fuwa (1999) suggests defining headship in terms of the largest cash earner in the household. Rogers (1995) advocates a distinction in terms of the 'major earner,' i.e. an earner who contributes 50 per cent or more to the household earnings. Gammage (1989) uses the term 'female- maintained' to describe this particular type of household. Moreover, Rosenhouse (1989) uses the working head definition for the household member most heavily engaged in income-generating activities, which includes activities in the Labour market as well as family Labour (but excludes household chores or child care) in order to emphasize the dual burden attached to female workers.

The definition of female-headed household adopted for this study, is the one given by International Labour Organization (ILO): Household where either no adult males are present, owing to divorce, separation, migration, non-marriage or widowhood, or where men, although present, do not contribute to the household income. (The ILO Thesaurus, 2005).

REASONS OF CREATION AND PROLIFERATION OF FHH

According this definition there are many reason for creation of FHH. Among the main reason, we can imply to male migration, the deaths of males in civil conflicts and wars, divorce, and family disruption.

In respect of routes into female household headship, it is fair to say That these are more usually 'involuntary' than 'by choice' i.e. in cases Where women get pregnant and do not marry, or fall victim to Separation or divorce, men are more often the ones in the position of Determining and/or instigating the process. This is partly because in most societies the pressures on women to contain their sexuality within a stable partnership and/or to keep marriages afloat are greater than for men. (Chant, 2007).

What are the reasons behind the proliferation of FHHs? They vary, but in Europe and the United States an important reason has been the greater longevity of women compared with men, and the large percentage of women aged 60 and above (United Nations, 1995) Another reason, pertinent to these regions, is the greater social acceptability of single mothers, female participation in the modern economy, and access to housing. Who constitute female-headed households? It is helpful first to distinguish between de jure and de facto FHHs. De jure FHHs maintain their households alone, while de facto FHHs may include men who are unable or unwilling to work. Female-headed households may consist of elderly women (widowed or divorced) with no dependents, or younger women (divorced or never-married) with dependent children. FHHs may be permanent or transitory or embedded in a wider kin network of support. They may represent family breakdown or a conscious lifestyle choice. (Moghadam, 2005, p. 10).

The majority of women in FHHs in developing countries are widowed, and to a lesser extent divorced or separated. In the developed countries most female-headed households consist of women who are never married or who are divorced. Perhaps because of flexible definitions of female headship, as well as inadequate data, estimates on the extent of FHHs tend to vary.

ECONOMIC AND SOCIAL RESULTS OF HOUSEHOLDS WITH FEMALE SUPERVISOR

Thus, female headship is a concept that attracts policy attention as a social and economic issue in many cases. Since a substantial segment of female- headed households are "man less" households or households with no permanent male resident contributing to household income, female headship may imply a heavy economic burden on women who have the responsibility of maintaining the households. The situation is assumed to be particularly critical in developing countries like Iran where social welfare systems which could support this group are nonexistent or inadequate.

In developing countries, the majority of households that are headed by women have many economic and social problems. FHH often faced with issues such as cultural discrimination, lack of access to job opportunities, low literacy and lack of regular income. Socio-Economic factor of poverty directly and indirectly affects on the cultural, social and ecological condition of FHH.

Poverty in female headed households is not an isolated case as literature maintains that women make up a disproportionate number of the poor. The United States also found that, of the world's poor, 60-70 per cent is women. (Dungumaro, 2008).

Two African scholars asserted that there exists a strong relationship between female headed households and the incidence of poverty. There are several persuasive factors that attribute to the prevailing perception of feminization of poverty (Kimenyi & Mbaku, 1995, p. 44). They include disparities in rights, entitlements and feminization of Labor.

Rosenhouse (1989) termed such economic disadvantages as "triple burden." They are; (i) disadvantage that women experience in Labour market and other means of income (ii) dual task which places time constrain (iii) higher dependency burden as in most cases women in these households are single earners as opposed MHHs who are mostly joint earners.

The feminization of poverty is key concept for describing FHH social and economic level. The feminization of poverty is the process whereby poverty becomes more concentrated among Individuals living in female-headed households. (Asgary & Pagán, 2004, p. 97).

The term "feminization of poverty" originated in the United States in the late 1970s, when it was discovered that the fastest growing type of family structure was that of female-headed households (Pearce, 1978). Moreover, because of the high rate of poverty among these households, their increase was mirrored in the growing numbers of women and children who were poor. By the mid-1980s, it was believed that half of all the poor in the U.S. lived in families headed by women in various stages of the life-cycle (Moghadam, 2005, p. 6).

U.S. census data showed that between 1966 and 1986, women consistently represented the majority of the poor population (56-57 per cent female and 42-43 per cent male). This was in part due to the lower wages earned by women compared with men. By the mid-1990s, about 20 per cent of all U.S. households were headed by women, and of these, some 39 per cent were below the poverty line. In 2000, the U.S. poverty rate was about 13 per cent; that is, there were over 34 million impoverished individuals, and the majority of the poor are women and children. Even some workers with full-time, year-round labor force attachment earned poverty-level wages. (Moghadam, 2005, p. 7). At the same time as the U.S. studies, Women in development research was focusing on female household headship and its importance to development planning, particularly in light of rural poverty and labor migration (Buvinic & Youssef, 1978) Studies proliferated on female-headed households (FHHs) in sub-Saharan Africa, Latin America, and the Caribbean and to a lesser degree, in South Asia (Dwyer & Bruce, 1988)These and other empirical studies found that women who head households have greater constraints in obtaining resources and services in housing and agriculture. Because women have less access to land, credits, capital, and

Box 1: Common Characterisations of the 'Feminisation of Poverty (Chant, 2007)'

- Women experience a higher incidence of poverty than men
- Women experience greater depth/severity of poverty than men (i.e. more women are likely to suffer 'extreme' poverty than men)
- Women are prone to suffer more persistent/longer-term poverty than men
- Women's disproportionate burden of poverty is rising relative to men
- Women face more barriers to lifting themselves out of poverty
- The 'feminization of poverty' is linked with the 'feminization of household headship'
- Women-headed households are the 'poorest of the poor'
- Female household headship transmits poverty to children ('inter-generational transmission of disadvantage').

jobs with good incomes, and because they are likely to have dependent children, they are disadvantaged and more vulnerable to poverty. The women in development studies thus recommended that poverty-alleviation policies explicitly target FHHs. (Moghadam, 2005)According chant (2007, p. 7) feminization of poverty has some familiar feature.

FHH IN IRAN

Iran also is facing this problem. In recent years, Statistics show that divorce, unexpected accidents, immigration, crime and imprisonment have caused to increase of the number of female headed households. Female-headed families have been viewed as a sign of social pathology and the disruption of family and social values, resulting in poverty and economic inequality. According to official Iranian statistics, 9.45% of the country's households have female providers in 2006.

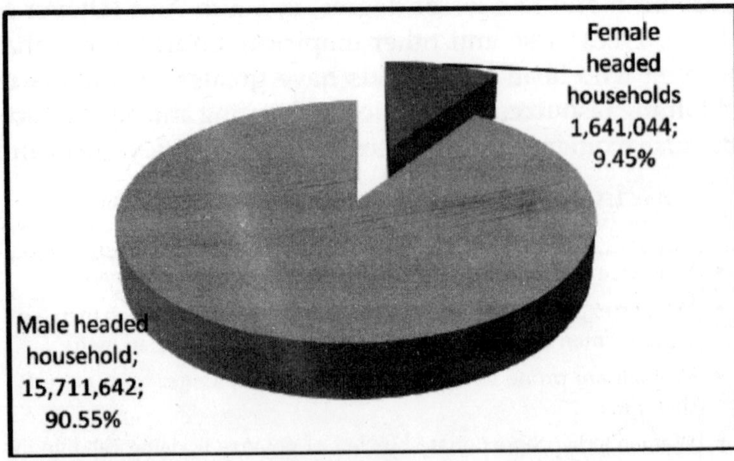

***Chart 1: Number of households in Iran based on Gender of households* (Normal households, according gender and age of head of households and the number of people in household: Persian date Aban 1385, 2006)**

Existing data on tells a considerable realities, including a growing number and proportion of Female heads of households during the last four decades is such that in the years 1976, 1986 and 1996, female head of households have formed 7.1, 7.3 and 8.4 per cent of the total Iranian households. (Women headed households become poorer and more every day, 2005).

According to Statistical center of Iran, nowadays near 10% of the country's households have female providers, but some sociologist claims that the real number is closer to 15%. The authorities only count widows and divorced women in their statistics. (Kristiansen, 2003) Nevertheless, there are many women who are heads of their households of other reasons, because the husband is in jail, is a drug addict, old, ill or disabled. Or because the husband has left the family to find works in the city or abroad, or has fled Iran of political reasons.

Another significant issue is typology of Female Headed Households in Iran. According chart 2 65 per cent of single person households have been formed by women. On the other hand, with the increasing of the number of household members, the percentage of households with female head is reduced. Hence this fact can be observed that the lowest number of female headed households were in households with seven or more members.

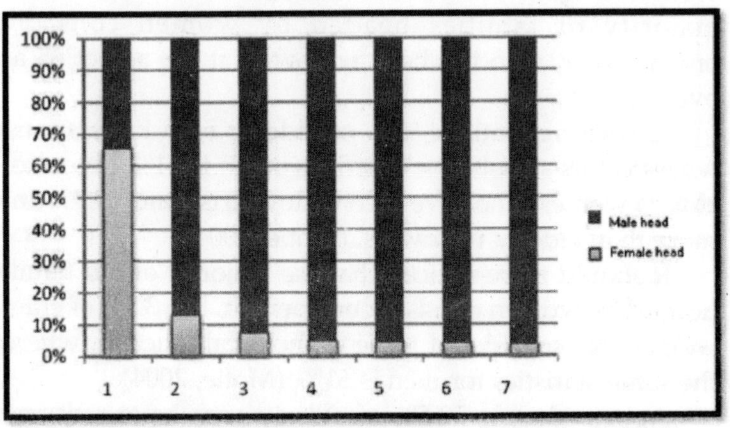

Chart 2: Numbers of member households regarding to gender of head of household in Iran-2006 **(Popu'ation Statistics, 2008)**

According chart 3, the majority of families headed by women consist of one member, who has been widowed at the age of 60 and over.

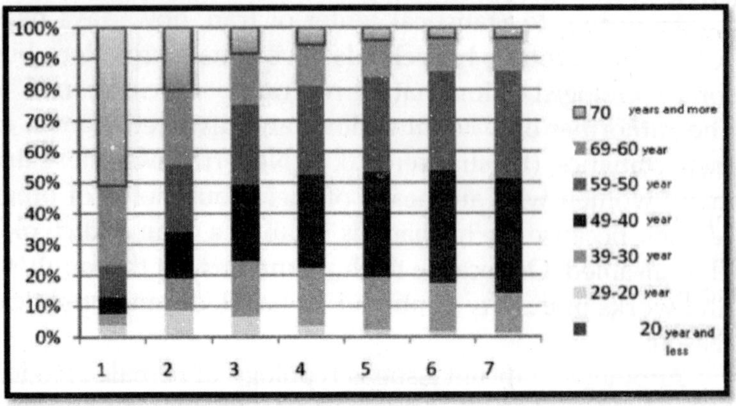

Chart 3: Number of persons in households with female head based on age group of head of household-2006 **(Population Statistics, 2008)**

Finally it is concluded that the number of dependants in families headed by women is fewer than families headed men and majority of single person household in Iran is consisted from old widow women. In other word, the majority of families headed by women consist of one member, who has been widowed at the age of 65 and over.

According statistic 90% of elderly men have spouses whereas this statistic for elderly women is 51%.The ratio of elderly women who have been widowed is almost 4.9% times more than elderly widowers. (Motie, 2004).

It should to be noticed that the majority of old families headed by women consist of one person. But 3.3% of elderly women are considered to be economically active, whereas the same statistics for men is 61%. (Motie, 2004).

Approximately 72.5% of elderly men have retirement benefits or income not related to employment, these statistics regarding women is approximately 27.5%.

Another important aspect of FHH in Iran is employment. 14.06 Women heads of households out of the entire number, (9.4%) are employed and 86% are not directly active in job market and have another way for earning money.

Table 1

FHH's Activity Status -2006 (Population Statistics, 2008)

Activity status	*Total*	*per cent*
Employed	230748	14.06
Unemployed	9611	0.59
Student	18501	1.13
No working income	791917	48.26
Homemaker	508981	31.02
Other	75111	4.58
Undeclared	6175	0.38
Total	1641044	100

The majority of urban women heads of households are employed in service industries, whereas in rural areas these women mainly consist of simple agricultural workers. Over half of internal immigrants in this country are women, the majority of whom travel to large cities for education and employment purposes. Only 22.5% of women heads of household are active in the formal sector. In Iran's urban society 31.4% women heads of household are employed or have income unrelated to employment, 62.4% are housewives. This statistic in the rural societies is respectively 44.2% and 49.4%. In other words the majority of urban and rural women heads of household relies on financial supports from other members of their families and do not have a stable income. Moreover inadequate pension of women heads of household has often resulted in their employment in the private and unofficial sectors. (Motie, 2004).

One third of the poor women worked, but because there are no good and cheap day care systems, working at home was the most typical, like laundry and sewing. Some of them also brought their young children to work. 70% of the women were not working and lived on support from the government or family. (Kristiansen, 2003)

Literacy status of women headed households is as follows: In terms of literacy, 71% of illiterate women headed households compared with the average amount of illiteracy in Iran shows a huge gap. (Women headed households, 2007) In addition the poor women in had low reading and writing skills, but this was not true of their children. Almost all of the children that participated in the study went to school, and none of them were school dropouts. The literacy rate or levels of education of women's heads of household is far lower than that of men. Therefore, women heads of household have far less access to higher income jobs.

For more than half of the poor women the cause of headship was their husbands' deaths, while divorce was the reason for 18%. The others stated the reason for headship that their husband was drug addict, refugee, in jail or disabled. In families where the husbands were not totally absent, many of women reported great problems with bad treatment from their ex-husbands, like violence or threats of violence. Furthermore women looked upon kinship and the family network as important, especially mother and sisters. More than half of the poor women lived together with their own parents or other family members in their own family, while one quarter lived with husband's family. This means that women without husbands mainly are supported by their own family. So in spite of laws and traditions that prescribe that married women belong to the husband's family; it is the women's families that support them when poverty prevails. (Kristiansen, 2003).

But in the old people different situation is observed. The demographic decline in families and changing attitudes in inter-generation relations deteriorates care taking of the elderly, whereas their need for care is higher than ever. This issue affects old women more. With the increase in the age of head of household, the economical well-being of the family decreases. Considering the average age of women heads of household, these families are placed in the lowest income brackets. (Motie, 2004).

According Shadi Talab study (2004, pp. 63-54) While more than 50 per cent female head of households has formed the poorest groups, male head of households are 16 per cent. In other words, women headed households represent "poorest poor" social groups. The main findings of this study indicate that women are at increased risk of poverty and that the poverty rate of female headed households is higher than the poverty rate of male headed households, but the gap between the two groups has diminished. While the poverty rate of female headed households in urban areas has decreased, uneducated and low literate female headed households remain at high risk of poverty. Also, the study indicates that as the number of income earners in these families increase, the likelihood of poverty in the poorest segments of this population decreases. Female headed households of Iran, because of low education levels, small families and fewer numbers of income earners within the family can be classified as the poorest groups living in poverty.

According to Imam Khomeini Relief Committee 29 per cent of households below the poverty line are households with female head.

GOVERNMENT POLICIES FOR REDUCING POVERTY AMONG FHH

For fighting against FHH's poverty some work has been done by government of Iran. Today some organization like Imam Khomeini Relief Committee, Ministry of Welfare and Social Security and Behzisti (welfare organization) are trying to reduce poverty among FHH.

Principles of constitutional law and civil laws in Iran have referred to special support of the women and procurement of their salary. By virtue of the fourth plan of development, the government is obliged to take action regarding preparation of master plan for empowering the women supervising their family. This plan can be implemented on the basis of cooperation of the organizations, foundations, and nongovernmental associations. In recent years, number of the families which are managed by women and live under poverty line is increasing due to traditional and legal limitations and social and economic problems.

After Islamic Revolution, "Imam Khomeini Relief Committee", a charity organization affiliated with the government, dealt with female headed household welfare issues. Imam Khomeini's Relief Committee was founded in March 1979 as a charity organization to provide support for poor families. The aim was to help such families regain financial stability. This foundation is supported by Iranian government and also receives the Islamic taxes of *Khums* and *Zakat*, as well as voluntaries aids.

For the poor women, charity organizations are important for economic support, while there was little help to get from the government. The support that according to the law of 1992 is supposed to be given to needy women and children only covers 5-10% of the total expenses of a family of five persons. (Kristiansen, 2003).

The Imam Khomeini Relief Committee covered 1023773 female headed households with 1997995 members in 2008. (Statistical Yearbook 1387, 2008).This charity pays 30$ each FHH per month as the Pension. Moreover 174000 women headed households are covered by Behzisti (welfare organization) in 2010. These people are paid monthly pension (Barimani, 2010).This data shows that more that 70% of FHHs in Iran need assistantship of Charities. If this statistic is compared with percentage of employment of FHH employment this fact is found that FHH have not Ways and means.

According section L article 97 The "law of Fourth social and economic and cultural development plan in Iran "(2005-2010) with purpose of reducing and preventing social calamities, government is bound to take measure and prepare comprehensive plan to increasing monthly pension of needy and unprotected families and women heads of households under patronage of protective organization on the base of at least 40% of the salary and wage in the first year of plan. (Law of the Fourth social,economic and cultural development plan of the Islamic Republic of Iran, 2004).

But actually monthly pension of women heads of households has been remained on level of 10 to 20 per cent annual minimum wage since the first year of plan. (Mohammadi, 2009).

In fact the highest amount that protective organizations are paying to under patronage FHH as the pension is 60 dollars. This 60 $ is paid to the woman who has five members in her household. Otherwise, to single person or small household as pension 32 dollars are paid. The Ministry of Labor and Social affair announced 305 dollars as 2010 minimum salary. According law 40 per cent of minimum wage are equivalent of 120 to 130 dollars. On the contrary what the women headed households reaches is finally 60 dollars. (Report on the status of women headed households in Iran, 2010).

Despite government's effort for better financing for FHH, growing rate of creation of this type of households requires more resources. Mr. Musa Reza Servati, Member of Parliament's social commission, said: The budget of women headed household's protective organization has been increased 20%. He remarked that Behzisti's (Welfare Organization) Budget in 2007 years has been approximately 457 million dollars and it was increased to 473 million dollars in 2008.He also remarked 20% of budget of the Welfare Organization in current year is allocated women headed households. More over Iran's parliament has allocated 1,186,000,000$ for Imam Khomeini Relief committee in 2007 and billed 1,400,000,000 in 2008. The parliament also determined 20% of credit this year for women headed households. (Abadi, 2009).

This means that despite the enormous budget allocated to women headed households practically between 20 and 30 dollars has been paid as pension to every household. In addition the government presently owes considerable sums to the social security fund which it will not be able to pay in the near future.

It should be mentioned that the latest research and statistics of Imam Khomeini Relief Committee shows 7,050,000 people are protected by the Relief Committee. Furthermore This Committee is paying pension to approximately 4,000,000 people. According this data these people are living under the absolute poverty line. (Samadi, 2009).

This problem mostly affects the disabled, the elderly and women heads of household, who will be likely to suffer the most as result of inadequate resources in the system.

In addition to the Social Security Organization Behzisti Organization, which is also responsible for supporting women heads of household, families without heads and their children has not been able to achieve the Third Development Plan objectives financially. Moreover with same situation it cannot realize Fourth Development plan goals.

Finally, despite the noticeable increase in funds of Imam Khomeini Relief Committee and Behzisti (welfare organization) they have not effectively been able to meet with basic needs of the urban and rural elderly and women heads of household.

EMPOWERMENT AS A SOLUTION

However restrictions on financial resources and increase the number of FHH caused to policymakers pursuit empowerment policies rather than direct contribution. Moreover direct payment makes dependent these households to government and they cannot be independent and active unite in the society. In this framework, the empowerment approach focuses on mobilizing the self-help efforts of the poor, rather than providing them with social welfare. Economic empowerment is also the empowering of disadvantaged sections of the population like FHH.

The empowerment prepares a framework for the FHH in which they can be independent, productive and active in the society. Then the main question is what women's empowerment?

The word "empowerment" is used in many different contexts and by many different organizations. For example, literature about "empowerment" is found in the fields of education, social work, psychology, in US radical politics in the 1960s and community development groups in the North and South, as well as in the work of feminist and development organizations. (Oxaal & Baden, 1997, p. 1).

The concept of women empowerment was introduced at the international women conference at NAROIBI in 1985. Women's empowerment has five components: women's sense of self-worth; their right to have and to determine choices; their right to have access to opportunities and resources; their right to have the power to control their own lives, both within and outside the home; and their ability to influence the direction of social change to create a more just social and economic order, nationally and internationally. (Sushama, 1998, p. 11)

The idea of power is at the root of the term empowerment. Power can be understood as operating in a number of different ways:

Table 2
Definitions of Power and Empowerment in Practice
(Williams, Seed, & Mwau, 1994)

power over	This power involves an either/or relationship of domination/subordination. Ultimately, it is based on socially sanctioned threats of violence and intimidation, it requires constant vigilance to maintain, and it invites active and passive resistance;
power to:	This power relates to having decision-making authority, power to solve problems and can be creative and enabling;
power with	This power involves people organizing with a common purpose or common understanding to achieve collective goals;
Power within	This power refers to self confidence, self awareness and assertiveness. It relates to how can individuals can recognize through analyzing their experience how power operates in their lives, and gain the confidence to act to influence and change this.

UNICEF has adopted the Women's Empowerment Framework, developed by Sara Longwe, as an appropriate approach to be used in mainstreaming gender. The framework states that women's development can be viewed in terms of five level of equality in which empowerment is an essential element at each level. The levels are:

1. **Welfare**: this addresses only the basic needs of women, without recognizing or attempting to solve the underlying structural causes which necessitate provision of welfare services. Women are merely passive beneficiaries of welfare benefits.
2. **Access**: equality of access to resources such as educational opportunities, land and credit is essential for women to make meaningful progress. The path of empowerment is initiated when women recognize lack of access to resources as a barrier to their growth and overall well-being and take action to redress this.
3. **Awareness-raising**: for women to take appropriate action to close gender gaps or gender inequalities

there must be recognition that their problems stem from inherent structural and institutional discrimination. They must also recognize the role that women themselves often play in reinforcing the system that restricts their growth.

4. **Participation**: this is the point where women take decisions equally alongside men. Mobilization is necessary in order to reach this level. Women will be empowered to gain increased representation, by organizing themselves and working collectively, which will lead to increased empowerment and ultimately greater control.
5. **Control**: The ultimate level of equality and empowerment, where there is a balance of power between women and men and neither has dominance. Women are able to make decisions regarding their lives and the lives of their children and play an active role in the development process. The contributions of women are fully recognized and rewarded. (UNICEF, 1994).

THE ROLE AND POSITION OF NGOS IN EMPOWERMENT

Furthermore The Human Development Report (UNDP, 1995) stresses that empowerment is about Participation. Development must be *by* people, not only *for* them. People must participate fully in the decisions and processes that shape their lives. but at the same time promotes a rather instrumentalist view of empowerment; Investing in women's capabilities and empowering them to exercise their choices is not only valuable in itself but is also the surest way to contribute to economic growth and overall development.

This concept of empowerment without public participation is unimaginable. Empowerment is essentially a bottom-up process rather than something that can be formulated as a top-down strategy. Understanding empowerment in this way means that development agencies cannot claim to "empower women". Women must empower themselves. Devising coherent policies and programs for women's empowerment requires careful attention, because external agencies/bodies tend to be positioned with "power-over" target populations. The training of development professionals, in government, NGOs or donor agencies does not always equip them to consult and involve others, which supporting empowerment requires. (Oxaal & Baden, 1997, p. 6).

The current popularity of the term empowerment in development coincides with recent questioning of the efficacy of central planning and the role of the state, and moves by donor governments and multilateral funding agencies to embrace NGOs as partners in development. Political and institutional problems have gained prominence on the development agenda with a focus on human rights, good governance and participation. (Razavi & Miller, 1995).

Hence central planning for FHH empowerment in Iran, need to increasing financial and human recourses, and the government could not afford it. Consequently the way for the presence of civil society organizations was paved by government. A large number of educated women heads of households voluntarily created NGOs to empower poor FHH. These NGOs observe empowerment in various aspect such as Education (Life skills, job oriented, health, and law), Entrepreneurship (job loan, technical aids), counseling and employment.

NGOS AND FHH EMPOWERMENT IN IRAN

Women Non-governmental organizations (NGOs), in the form of charities that provide services such as food, medication, and education, became formally recognized entities in the aftermath of the 1906 constitutional revolution (Kazemi, 1996). But they had a low profile in Iranian society.

At the time of the 1979 revolution, there were 45 NGOs working on women's issues, predominantly on economic issues. They generally dealt with poor women and single-parent families, offering grants or self-employment loans. (Namazi, 2002).

Most were linked to the state, and many were abolished after the revolution. Following the 1979 revolution, a number of new NGOs emerged with the goal of furthering Islamic values. They were politically motivated organizations, committed to presenting an "authentic" image of the "Muslim Woman."

With Khatami's election in 1997 and the increased attention given to women and civil society during his administration, there was a sudden proliferation of women's NGOs. According to Khatami's advisor on women's affairs, Zahra Shojaie, the number of NGOs rose by 318 per cent during his presidency. (Women's Rights and Democracy:Peaceful Transformation in Iran, 2006).

Some of these organizations went beyond charity, education, and reproductive health and became engaged in political, cultural, and legal aspects of women's rights.The shift have happened because women believe that fundamental changes are possible within the society. Women NGOs had a very active role in changing the focus of attention from reform through the state toward reform through civil society.

With the understanding that increased awareness among women was a vital factor in promoting democracy and women's rights, activists set out to launch campaigns focused on information and capacity building, education and communication, and domestic violence. Attention was also given to building the capacity of fledgling NGOs; however, most NGOs avoided taking on the issues in an overtly political manner, and opted instead to lay the in civil society (Women's Rights and Democracy:Peaceful Transformation in Iran, 2006).

SEDIGHIN CHARITY INSTITUTE (SDI)ON EMPOWERING THE FAMILY SUPERVISING WOMEN

Finally as a case study "Sedighin charity institution" is chosen to analyze and we explain its function and influence on FHH empowerment.

One of the most important NGOs emerged in Khatami Era is Sedighin charity institution. This paper regards some concerns which Sedighin Charity Institute mentions about problems of the supervising women in different societies and Iran as well as presentation of some solutions for solving the problems of this group of women and their families.

Sedighin Charity Institute started its activity in Dec. 2001 by aiming at empowering the supervising women under registration No. 43/76993 by Ministry of the Interior. The mission of this institute is to empower supervising women and their families and all activities of this institute is nonpolitical and non profit in accordance with Article 2 of Articles of Association. (Shababi, 2010, p. 2).

This NGO created by educated women heads of households and managed by them. All of this people are supervisor of their family and have job and high social position in Academic or economic aspects.

Table 3
Mangers and Board of Sedighin Charity (Seddighin Charity Website)

Name	*Responsibility*	*Degree*
Zahra Bonyaniyan	Managing Director	MA-International Law
Mehrshad Shababi	Chairman	PhD - Political Science
Maliha muazzin Qamsari	Board Member	MA–Public Administration
Fatemeh Hajian Moghadam	Board Member	PhD students - Cultural Management
Shahnaz Pezshek	Board Member	MA - Anthropology

Main objective of this institute is support and empower the target groups by giving financial and non- financial aids and legal, family, economic and employment consultations as well as to create job opportunities for this group of women and their children and to fulfill mental, psychological and cultural needs of their children through cultural-recreational activities and to promote cultural and educational levels of the women in order to prevent from social damages of these groups and those supervised by them.

Sedighin Charity Institute suggests some plans and methods for removing deprivation from this class all of which are summarized in empowering process. Empowerment is a complex process of changes of mental, psychobiological, spiritual, social and cultural factors and indices. Failure to promote each one of these sections can damage empowerment process; as a result, it is necessary to take action regarding realization of the following goals in accordance with empowerment master plan. (Shababi, 2010).

As referred above, empowerment is a complex process of positive and continual changes in mental, psychobiological, spiritual, social and cultural factors and indices. Goals of the empowerment master plan are as follows:

1-Mental Empowerment of the Assistance Seekers

- Study on mental health condition of assistance seekers and intervention for problem solving (removal of the tensions and problems which are serious obstacles to empowerment).
- Preparation of the assurance seekers for conscious entrance and active participation in empowerment process
- Increase of compatibility skills in assistance seekers
- Promoting management power in themselves and families (All of these cases are performed through

individual and group consultations and formation of teamwork with use of experienced professors in the field of consultation and psychology)

2-Social and Cultural Empowerment of the Assistance Seekers

- promoting level of knowledge, technical and vocational skills and life skills in assistance seeker (by creation of necessary facilities for the assistance seekers in order to continue studies and necessary coordination so that her education and training don't damage her work and care of the children).
- Promoting social identity and active participation of the assistance seeker in social activities (by providing the opportunities for the assistance seeker to have social participation in addition to work).
- Promoting suitable relation level in the family (by providing the opportunity for the these persons to use pilgrimage and tourism trips with their families as well as holding classes for increasing skill of relationship with family member).
- Promoting social interactions in accordance with social customs

3-Biological Empowerment

- helping teat the diseases and train how to prevent from diseases (by covering them under Therapeutic services insurance as well as identifying charitable physicians and introducing them to the assistance seekers in need and giving necessary information regarding prevention from diseases).
- Empowering the assistance seeker regarding health with emphasis on suitable and varied nutrition.
- Training and building culture of sport.

4-Spiritual Empowerment

- reinforcing spiritual morale and feeling of confidence in the assistance seeker.
- reinforcing religious morale through thinking and religion.

5-Economic Empowerment

- helping the assistance seekers promote on the educational or technical and vocational basis in accordable with needs of the labor market.
- making effort to employ the assistance seekers and promote their job skill, satisfaction and security.
- providing necessary services for economic empowerment with emphasis on assistance seeker.
- making effort to make the assistance seeker independent (self employment) It is necessary to note that this plan can be generalized in the country and be implemented in many other countries with partial differences commensurate with customs of the countries.

EMPOWERMENT ACTIVITIES

Of activities of this institute are to establish Pazhoohesh Gostar Service Company under registration No. 188817 and to establish Soorchin semi industrial kitchen as well as to create and equip dressmaking workshop under trade name of Piratan and to train the assistance seekers with use of professors of Alzahra University which was confirmed by Islamic Development Bank (IDB) granting $19000 to the institute. These actions led to employment of many assistance seekers covered by the institute. Design of ATEK (Education, experience, work) empowering model which is herewith attached and implementation of the related model and creation of educational workshops: dressmaking, computer, repair of mobile, photography, cinematography and assembly are of other activities of this institute. It is necessary to note that more than 400 assistance seekers have been trained in ATEK design and more than half of them were empowered. (Shababi, 2010) In table 3 elaborated empowerment programs is summarized:

Table 3
Empowerment Activities in SCI

Job oriented Traning	Counseling	Entrepreneurship
• Sewing • Soldering iron work • Computer Training and Internet Marketing • Compiling and assembling • Cell phone repairing • Accounting	• Legal counseling • Religious counseling • Psychological counseling • Health counseling • Job couseling	• Career Advice and employment center • Job loan • Technical aids • Obtaining insurance deductible employer contribution (20% employer premium contribution)

SDI offers both of formal and informal educational courses for Female heads of households. Sedighin charity institution succeeds to obtain license of Vocational Training Educational Complex. All of these courses are job oriented. These courses include: information technology (hardware and software), sewing and Finance, Commerce and Accounting.

CONCLUSION

In many developing countries as elsewhere, there has been a significant increase in the percentage of female-headed households (FHH) in recent years. Among the main causes are male migration, the deaths of males in civil conflicts and wars, unpatented adolescent fertility and family disruption. Development initiatives have often tried to direct resources and services to FHHs on the assumption that they were poorer than households headed by men (MHHs) and less able to improve their situation without special help.

In Iran, On the basis of census of 2006, more than 1,641,000 (9.45%) households headed by the women have been identified. Increase of these households is considerable in recent years due to increase of other social phenomena such as divorce and addiction and unemployment of husband. On the basis of statistics in 1976, 1986, 1996, families managed by women have comprised of 7.1, 7.3 and 8.4% of the total Iranian families respectively.

On the basis of results of this census, out of 1,641,000 women supervising the family in the country, more than 1,410,000 ones i.e. about 86% have been unemployed and only 14% has been employed.

More than 50% of the families managed by women are in the first and second deciles i.e. the poorest groups. 71% of the women supervising their families have low education or are illiterate and poverty and illiteracy have direct and indirect effect on physical and mental health and cultural and social status of these women and their families.

Unfortunately, many women supervising the family are in poor, low income group and those lacking necessary skills for employment and there are other barriers to their growth and development.

Despite the noticeable raise in funds of Imam Khomeini Relief Committee and Behzisti (welfare organization) to more than 1.5 billion $ in year (2008) they have not effectively able to meet with basic needs of the urban and rural women heads of household. These organizations pay between 30$ to 60$ to more than 1,200,000 FHH as pension. But most of FHH are living under poverty line.

Hence, limitations on fiscal resources and raise the number of FHH led to policymakers pursuit empowerment policies rather than direct contribution. Furthermore direct payment makes needy these households to government and they cannot be self-sufficient and active unite in the society. In this framework, the empowerment approach emphasized on mobilizing the self-help efforts of the poor, rather than providing them with social welfare. Economic empowerment is also the empowering of disadvantaged sections of the population like FHH.

In this paper according Nairobi conference, Women's empowerment has five components: women's sense of self-worth; their right to have and to determine choices; their right to have access to opportunities and resources; their right to have the power to control their own lives, both within and outside the home; and their ability to influence the direction of social change to create a more just social and economic order, nationally and internationally. But it should be mentioned that empowerment is about Participation. Development must be by people, not only for them. People must participate fully in the decisions and processes that shape their lives. but at the same time promotes a rather instrumentalist view of empowerment; Investing in women's capabilities and empowering them to exercise their choices is not only valuable in itself but is also the surest way to contribute to economic growth and overall development. Hence central planning for FHH empowerment in Iran, need to increasing financial and human recourses, and the government could not afford it. Consequently the way for the presence of civil society organizations was paved by government. A large number of educated women heads of households voluntarily created NGOs to empower poor FHH. These NGOs observe empowerment in various aspect such as Education (Life skills, job oriented, health, and law), Entrepreneurship (job loan, technical aids), counseling and employment.

One of the most important women NGOs emerged in Iran is Sedighin charity institution. Sedighin Charity Institute is seeking the solution for problems of the supervising women in Iran through empowerment. Sedighin Charity Institute suggests some plans and methods for removing deprivation from this class all of which are summarized in empowering process.

It is necessary to note that this sample can be generalized in Iran and be implemented in many developing countries with partial differences commensurate with customs of the countries.

Bibliography

The ILO Thesaurus. (2005), Retrieved September 16, 2009, from International Labour organization (ILO) Web Site: *http://www.ilo.org/public/libdoc/ILO-Thesaurus/english/tr3578.htm*

Abadi, M. H. (2009), Women in the maze of life. *Resalat Newspaper*, p. 6.

Asgary, N., & Pagán, J. (2004), Relative Employment and Earnings of Female Household Heads in Mexico, 1987-1995',J. *Journal of Developing Areas* , 1 (38), 93-106.

Barimani, S. (2010), *50000 Women Heads of Household Welfare are Waiting for Welfare Organization.* Retrieved October 3, 2010, from Mehrnews: *http://www.mehrnews.com/fa/newsdetail.aspx?NewsID=1149220.*

Baros, R., & Fox, L. (1997), Female Headed Households, Poverty and Welfare of Childeren in Urban Brazil. *Economic Development and Cultural Change* , 45 (2), 231-257.

Bongaarts, J. (2001), *Household Size and Composition in the Developing world.* newyork: Population Council.

Buvinic, M., & Youssef, N. (1978), *Woman-headed Households: The Ignored Factor in Development Planning. Report submitted to the Office of Women in Development,.* USAID. Washington, DC: ICRW.

Chant, S. (2007), *Children In Female-Headed Households:Interrogating The Concept of An 'Inter-Generational Transmission of Disadvantage' With Particular ReferenceTo The Gambia, Philippines And CostaRica.* London School of Economics. London: Gender Institute.

Dungumaro, E. W. (2008), Gender differentials in Household Structure and Socioeconomic Characteristics in South Africa. (Report). *Journal of Comparative Family Studies.*

Dwyer, D., & Bruce, J. (1988), *A Home Divided: Women and Income in the third world.* . Palo Alto: Stanford University Press.

Fuwa, N. (1999), *The Poverty and Heterogeneity among Female Headed Households Revisited:The Case of Panama.* Matsudo-City: Chiba University.

Gammage, S. (1989), *The Gender Dimension of Household Poverty: Is Headship Still a Useful Concept?'.* International Center.

Haviland, W. (2003), *Anthropology.* Belmont, CA: Wadsworth.

Illo, J. F. (1989), "Who Heads the Household? Women in Households in the Philippines". *The Filipino Women in Focus* .

Kazemi, F. (1996), Civil Society and Iranian Politics. In A. R. Norton (Ed.), *Civil Society in the Middle East.* New York: Brill.

Kimenyi, M. S., & Mbaku, J. M. (1995), "Female Headship, Feminization of Poverty and Welfare. *Southern Economic Journal,* 62 (1), 44-52.

Kristiansen, N. (2003, 08 18), *Iranian Female Headed Households.* Retrieved 4 2010, 18, from KILDEN-Norwegian Information and Documentation Centre for Women's Studies and Gender Research: *http://eng.kilden.forskningsradet.no/c52778/nyhet/vis.html?tid=53514*

Law of the Fourth Social, Economic and Cultural Development Plan of the Islamic Republic of Iran. (2004), Retrieved April 17, 2006, from United Nation Public Administration Network: *http://unpan1.un.org/intradoc/groups/public/documents/APCITY/UNPAN021522.pdf*

Min, Z., & Michael, S. (2003), Assets, Expectations, and Children's Educational Achievement in Female-Headed Households. *The Social Service Review* , 77 (2), 191-211.

Moghadam, V. (2005), *The 'Feminization of Poverty'and Women's Human Rights.* Division of Human Rights, Gender Equality and Development Section. Paris: UNESCO.

Mohammadi, E. (2009), *Women Headed Households Requires Immediate Consideration of Government.* Retrieved April 26, 2010, from khabronline: *http://www.khabaronline.ir/news-3170.aspx*

Motie, N. (2004), *Women and Poverty.* NGO Reports on B+10, Situation Analysis of Women in Iran 10 Years After Beijing, Asian Pasific Women's Watch.

Murdock, G. P. (1949), *Social Structure.* Newyork: The Macmillan co.

Namazi, B. (2002), *Study on Community Organizations and Non-Governmental Organizations in Iran.* (S. Akhtary, Trans.) Tehran: Municipality Publication.

Normal Households, According Gender and Age of Head of Households and the Number of People in Household: Persian Date Aban 1385. (2006), (s. c. Iran, Producer, & Statistical Center of Iran) Retrieved 4 30, 2010, from statistical center of Iran Web site: *http://amar.sci.org.ir/Detail.aspx?Ln=F&no=262987&S=TP*

Oxaal, Z., & Baden, S. (1997), *Gender and Empowerment: Definitions, Approaches and Implications for Policy.* Institute of Development Studies, BRIDGE (Development - gender). Brighton: University of Sussex.

Pearce, D. M. (1978), The Feminization of Poverty: Women, Work and Welfare. *Urban Social Change Review,* 28-36.

——(2008), *Population Statistics.* Tehran: Center for Women and Family Affairs-president of Islamic Republic Office.

Razavi, S., & Miller, C. (1995), *'From WID to GAD: Conceptual Shifts in the Women and Development Discourse'.* Geneva: UNRISD.

Report on the Status of Women Headed Households in Iran. (2010), Retrieved April 22, 2010, from Radio France International Web site: *http://www.persian.rfi.fr/node/16434.*

Rogers, B. L. (1995), Alternative Definitions of Female Headship in the Dominican Republic. *World Development,* 23 (12), 2033-2039.

Rosenhouse, S. (1989), *Identifying the Poor: Is 'Headshipa Useful Concept?'.* World Bank Living Standard Measurement Study.

Samadi, N. (2009), *The Variables of Poverty line in Iran.* Retrieved April 2010, 22, from Mowj News Agency: *http://www.mojnews.com/fa/Miscellaneous/ViewContents.aspx?Contract=cms_Contents_I_News&r=378791*

Sanni, L. (2006), Comparative Study of Female-headed Households in the City of Ibadan. *Jenda: A Journal of Culture and African Women Studies,* 2 (8).

Schultz, R. W. (1976), Marriage, Family, Capital and Fertility. *Journal of Political Economy,* 81.

Seddighin Charity Website. (n.d.), Retrieved April 2010, 22, from *http://www.seddighin.com/fapage.aspx?5*

Shababi, M. (2010), *Empowering the Family Supervising Women.* Retrieved April 2010, 11, from Office of high commisioner of human right-UN.

Shadi Talab, J. (2004), The Poverty of Female Headed Household. *Womén Research (in persian)*, 2 (1), 49-70.

Statistical Yearbook 1387. (2008), Retrieved April 2010, 23, from Imam Khomeini Relife Committee: *http://www.emdad.ir/gozareshat/files/s/1387/fasle3.pdf*

Sushama, S. (1998), "*Women and Empowerment*. New Delhi: Discovering House.

UNDP. (1995), *Human Development Report 1995*. Oxford: Oxford University Press.

UNICEF. (1994), *'Gender Equality and Empowerment of Women and Girls: A Policy Review'*. UNICEF Programme Committee.

United Nations (1995), *The World's Women 1995: Trends and Statistics.* New York:: UN.

Williams, S., Seed, J., & Mwau, A. (1994), *Oxfam Gender Training Manual*. Oxford: Oxfam.

Women headed households (2007), Retrieved April 2010, 16, from Expediency Discernment Council of the System: *http://www.maslehat.ir/Contents.aspx?p=18cfba1c-1010-4b1e-b7ac-eda00fdf3302*.

Women Headed Households become Poorer and More Every Day. (2005), *Kar va Kargar Newspaper (in persian)*.

——(2006), *Women's Rights and Democracy: Peaceful Transformation in Iran.* Hunt Alternatives Fund, The Initiative for Inclusive Security Policy Commission. The Initiative for Inclusive Security Policy Commission.

DALIT WOMEN EMPOWREMENT THROUGH SHG'S-A CASE STUDY OF NALGONDA DISTRICT

P. MANJULA

> In order to awaken the people it is the woman who has to be awakened. Once she is on the move- the family moves, the village moves, and the Nation moves.
>
> —*Pandit Jawaharlal Nehru*

EMPOWERMENT

The Oxford dictionary defines empowerment as the action of empowering the state of being empowered. It also defines the word 'Empowerment' is to give power to make them able (person/group). The term "Empowerment" is a multidimensional process of creating power within which enables individuals or groups to such an extent to realize their identity and power completely in various aspects and all spheres of life. In the context of women it is a process to participate effectively in decision making that affects women ability to help their family, community and higher levels of the political process (Pandey, 1991).

WHO ARE THE DALITS?

"The term "Dalit" is Inclusive of all the oppressed and exploited sections of society. Etymologically the term is inclusive of meanings such as: downtrodden, disadvantaged, underprivileged, dispossessed, deprived, handicapped, abused, humble, prostrate, etc., it does not confine merely to economic exploitation in terms of appropriation of surplus, but also relates to suppression of life and value system- and more importantly the denial of dignity. The term Dalit includes Scheduled Castes (SCs) Scheduled Tribes (STs) and other backward classes (OBCs). The women of the Dalit are socially humiliated and economically backward".

STATUS OF WOMEN IN ANDHRA PRADESH

India predominantly consists of rural areas and nearly two-third of the population lives in villages. According to the 2001 census, in India the total population is around 102.52 cores. Out of which Andhra Pradesh population is 7.26 cores and rural population of Andhra Pradesh figures around 5.53 lakh. Among districts of Andhra Pradesh, Nalgonda district occupies the top-most position in population. Out of this, the population of SC women is 575.788 lakhs (17.73%) and that of ST women is 342.676 lakhs (10.55%).

This shows that the population of SC women is more compared with other communities in the districts.

The world experience reveals that empowering women is critical to achieve the transition of development. The major aspects to achieve empowerment of women are by bringing socio-economic and political awareness; providing them with education, health and employment opportunities they need, to realize their full potential. To achieve this transition of development, women should have the socio-economic and political awareness. Further, to realize this they should be provided with health, education and employment opportunities.

The success of any strategy of women empowerment depends upon the following factors:

(1) Level of education, Hard work

(2) Socio-custom

(3) Family planning, Small family
(4) Health, Medical Services, Cleanliness
(5) Environment, Tree growing, Kitchen Gardening.

The empowerment of women has to become the primary focus to all those concerned with the emancipation of women. It implies a process in which building of capacity, self-image, confidence, self-assertion are expected to take place. Increasing involvement, individual and collective action, self generated momentums are also other desirable factors to be promoted in the process. In brief, empowerment implies a fundamental redistribution of power between different groups which include families, communities and classes.

Various case studies show that there is a positive correlation in credit availability and empowerment of women. So the emphasis is to lay on the empowerment of rural women focusing on the following aspects.

(a) Direct involvement of women in programming and management.
(b) Effective collaboration with community organizations.
(c) Organizing and strengthening of women's self help groups.
(d) Sensitization and advocacy for Gender Just Society.
(e) Identifying women's needs and priorities while generating employment.
(f) Organizing women in groups to undertake certain productive activities to earn their livelihood and to develop the rural community.

THE PARAMETERS OF WOMEN EMPOWERMENT

(1) Enhancing self esteem and self –confidence of women.
(2) Building a positive image of women by recognizing their contribution to the society, polity and the economy.
(3) Fostering decision making and action through collection processes.

(4) Providing information, knowledge and skill for economic independence.

(5) Enhancing access to literacy and information relating to their rights and entitlements in society (Khan and Sharma 1993).

DWCRA IN ANDHRA PRADESH

Andhra Pradesh is a pioneer state to introduce DWCRA schemes in all the districts to achieve self-sufficiency and to bring social transformation among the rural women living below the poverty line. The DWCRA program is a successful program among all the programs initiated by the Government of India. Recently the DWCRA program has changed its nomenclature as 'SELF HELP GROUPS' (SHG) in the year 2002. The Government of India has given top priority and allocated special funds in 9th and 10th five year plans. The development agenda of the state aims at keeping rural women in the forefront to facilitate formation of a large number of self-help groups throughout the state. Over 30 lakh women belonging to the weaker sections of the society have become members of these self help groups. A majority of them according to the government reports developed the habit of saving a rupee a day, paving the way of socio-economic development. The state government has drawn a long-term action plan for women's employment through SHGs. The World Bank task force committee officials praised SHG programmes as "Creating a silent revolution in the lives and status of the women". About 45 lakh rural poor families in the state covering a population of 2.50 crores have become the members of SHGs. The state government is making all efforts to assist these self help groups by providing revolving fund nearly 40 per cent of the SHGs in the country are formed in Andhra Pradesh itself.

The Government of Andhra Pradesh (1998) lists the following criteria for empowerment through SHGs approach.

- To enjoy equal status with men in the family;
- To live in dignity (freedom from humiliation)
- To get basic needs like drinking water, fuel for cooking nutritious food for the family, safe livelihood and adequate shelter;
- Self sufficiency
- Health and education
- Government within reach
- Decision making capacity within and outside the household
- Leisure
- Freedom form violence, conflict, war
- Mobility
- Ability to make choices.

The SHGs are helping the women for their empowerment and to grow, develop as well as come together on a common platform of equality and development. In relation to these objectives of the effect of SHG program on women empowerment the present study entitled as "Dalit Women Empowerment through Self Help Groups": is proposed in four Mandals of Nalgonda district, i.e., Bhongir, Aler, Garidepalli and Neredcherla are chosen for data collection within five parameters of development, which are Self Help Group's "education, health, political participation, economic empowerment and social status", selected for the study.

THE OBJECTIVES OF THE STUDY

(1) To study the individual and social features that introduced women to participate in a self help group.

(2) To study the extent of participation of SHG members in decision making in various activities undertaken by the group.

(3) To study women's place in enjoying equal status within the family and society to live in dignity (freedom from humiliation)

(4) To study the role of micro credit in the socio- economic empowerment of women.

(5) To study the role of group participation and initiation on education of women and their children.

(6) To study the extent of participation of self help group members in political participation at various levels.

(7) To study women's improvement in area of politics by participating in group activities and awareness generation.

HYPOTHESIS OF THE STUDY

(1) The higher participation of self help groups the greater the chances of taking part in decision making

(2) To study whether the economic status influences the Social status

(3) To study whether economic status affects the lifestyle.

METHODOLOGY

The study carried out original research based on the primary survey and secondary data. The methodology and implementation plan for the study is as follows.

Selection of Mandals and Villages

Being a resident of Nalgonda district the researcher is well acquainted with this district. As a result this district is selected for the study. Further it was identified among the highest SC populated mandals. Along with ST population it was selected the same way as we have selected the four villages from each mandal. According to the 2001 census SC and ST Women population in Nalgonda district is 17.78 per cent and 10.29 per cent respectively. The study selected Alair, Bhongir,

Garedpally and Neredcharla mandals and are representative of Scheduled Caste and Scheduled Tribes population of the state respectively. According to the 2001 census the percentage of SC population is 21 per cent and ST population is 3 per cent in Alair mandal. In Bhongir Mandal the percentage of SC population is 16 per cent and ST population is 4 per cent. In Garedepally the SC population is 21 per cent and ST population is 9 per cent. In Neredcherla Mandal the SC population is 20 per cent and ST population 14 per cent respectively. The mandals from this district were selected based on discussion with senior district level officials and considering the nature of village population type, extent of women's participation, role of women self help groups etc.,

Collection of Primary Data

Primary data was collected from SC SHG members administering of the questionnaires and conducting group interviews.

Collection of Secondary Data

The existing of Research works on the Research topic has studied to the maximum extent. Further secondary data related to SHG's and mandals was collected form the district head quarters, mandals and libraries the data consisted of published and unpublished sources and converted to the following, demographic, socio economic profile, and groups' formation, role of the group and institution, progress of schemes, financial gains with special focus on dalit women aspects

ANALYSIS OF DATA

The collected primary and secondary data was analyzed keeping in view the objectives and chapterisation of the study. The secondary data was analyzed primarily to provide inputs into the status of district, mandals and villages in implementation of development programmers and schemes.

The primary data was analyzed mainly to understand and assess the role or SHG and participation and formation of SHG's over all impact on the development and improvement. The data had been analysed with the help of a computer. It had been transformed into computer code and analysed. Statistical tools such as average, percentage, has been used to analyze the data.

EMPOWERMENT

Empowerment literally means 'giving power to creating power with in and enabling. It is a multidimensional process, which enables individuals and groups to realize their full identity and power in all spheres of life.

The Oxford Dictionary defines empowerment as the action of empowering, the state of being empowered.

According to Shyam Sundhar Singh Chowhan, empowerment is nothing but a religious cultural and legal struggle against oppression, injustice and discrimination. Empowerment expresses the bold idea that all people have claims to social arrangements that protects them from the worst abuses and deprivations and secures the freedom for a life of dignity.

"The Economic Empowerment" implies a better quality of material life through sustainable livelihood owned and managed by women. By "social empowerment" we mean a more equitable social status for women in society. "Legal Empowerment" is the provision of an effective legal structure, which is supportive of women's empowerment and "Political Empowerment " means a political system in favour of the participation in and control by women of the political decision making process and in governance.

STATEGIES FOR WOMEN'S EMPOWERNMENT

The strategies for women's empowerment are three-fold. The first is related to education that promotes building a positive self – image and self-confidence among women and develop the ability to think critically. The second strategy implies skill development and empowerment for economic independence. The third is concerned with increasing awareness among women about health, nutrition, environment, economic and political conditions to ensure equal participation in the process of social change and development.

The above three aspects are interdependent and consequently depend on and lead to total development process. It implies that women's empowerment is a prerequisite for the development of a nation. But constraints are there which stop women from going forward. These include social, economic, traditional and educational constraints.(Chowdhry and Anand-1996).

INNOVATIVE SCHEMES

Ever since independence, a number of innovative Schemes have been launched for the upliftment of women in the country with empowerment as the goal. Regarding the empowerment of rural women, focus is laid on the following aspects.

(1) Direct involvement of women in programming and management.

(2) Effective collaboration with community organizations.

(3) Organizing and strengthening of women's self-help groups.

(4) sensitization and advocacy for gender just society.

(5) Identification of women's needs and priorities while generating employment and

(6) Organizing women in different groups to undertake certain productive activities to earn their livelihood and to develop the rural community.

PLANNING: WOMEN EMPOWERNMENT

From the very beginning of independent India's developmental planning process, one of the main issues has been that of providing equal status of women. While the thrust of the first four plans was on organizing various welfare activities and giving priority to women's education. However the fifth and sixth plans witnessed the shift from "welfare to development" or women with thrust on health, education and employment of women. The stress of the seventh plan was on identifying and promoting beneficiary oriented programmes with a view to extending direct benefits to women. The eighth plan (1992-1997) promised to ensure that benefits of development from different sectors do not bypass women.

The Ninth plan (1997-2002) made two significant changes in the strategy of planning for women, firstly empowerment of women became a primary objective and secondly the plan attempted "convergence of existing services available in both women – specific and women related sectors.

The Tenth Plan (2002-2007) had made a major commitment towards "empowering women as the agent of socio-economic change and development" based on the recommendation of national policy for empowerment of women. For their purpose a sector specific three – fold strategy has been adopted.

DALIT WOMEN

The role of women in development is initially related to the goal of comprehensive socio-economic development. Any development strategy which perceives women as a specific interest issue and designs programmes to generate income or meet their basic needs will not serve the purpose. There have been infinite variations of the status of women, differing according to the cultural milieu, family structure, caste class occupation; property rights etc. all these factors are significant determinants of variations in their position in different groups. The scheduled caste woman who constitutes a sizable population of India is subjected not nearly to gender bias, but also to indignities arising out of the age old tradition of unsociability from which incidentally the entire social group of scheduled castes suffer. The deep rooted social discriminations have compelled this section of India's population to lead a life of bare subsistence level, both in economic terms and human values (NCW, 1998).

The reports of the national commission on scheduled caste and Scheduled Tribes are a grim reminder that the vast majority of the dalits remain poor ,illiterate, lack requisite skills for competing in the modern world, enjoy unequal access to productive resources, and remain deeply tied to land and traditional occupations which offer limited possibilities of upward mobility. Untouchability, though banned under the law, continues to be widely practiced.

Of the 407 Million total women of India (1991 census), 66-29 million i.e. 16 per cent belong to the scheduled caste communities constitute a sizeable percentage of rural peasantry and laborers. Having occupied the lowest rank in the social hierarchy, these communities, generation after generation, have been the victims of age old practice of untouchability. Because of the consequential social and economic disabilities, the development problems of the scheduled caste women get compounded. The various prejudices and discrimination against them come in the way of their personal development. The scheduled caste women thus form a category of their own which is more deprived of access to development resources, social, economic and political than their counterparts in the general population needing special attention in the empowerment programmes for women (NCW, 1996).

It is a well known fact that SC women are exploited a lot. Economic dependence on others is the prime reason for such a state of affairs. A number of welfare schemes have been launched in the country for the upliftment and development of scheduled caste in previous two decades.

The Andhra Pradesh government headed by Telugu Desham party under the dynamic leadership of Nara

Chandra Babu Naidu came up with new, innovative programmes in empowering and bringing all backward class women on the main stream of the economy and society.

The women led self help groups in Andhra Pradesh have successfully demonstrated how to mobilize and manage thrift, appraise credit needs and enforce financial self discipline. The SHG Groups in Andhra Pradesh reveal the effectiveness of these groups with linkage programme and awareness among the rural folk about the significance of women empowerment and rural credit. Self help groups thus become forums for the collective voice of the poor against common oppression and exploitation to understand individual and common problems and improving the skills and capacities to manage resources. Another rational behind the group approach is to facilitate mobility of rural women, which is otherwise restructured due to socio cultural factors. Being in a group provides them with collective strength and helps them in taking initiatives.

The development strategies and programs formulated by the Andhra Pradesh government is a stepping stone for the economic empowerment of women at the grassroots. Effective implementation of these programmes enables women to operate small savings and micro credit facilities and convey out small investment in income generating activities at the village level. Several developmental agencies have promoted and inspired formation of diverse kinds of thrift and credit groups in Andhra Pradesh to channelise the various poverty alleviation and social development programs. These groups vary widely in terms of their membership size, decision making process and methods of group activities.

Women empowerment especially economic empowerment is closely linked with the levels of education. Women illiteracy, low level of education and skills many a time create hindrance for their advancement. Ways and means to provide reasonable level of education, skills and literacy for SC women will have to be vigorously pursued.

In this sector, the role of NGOs should be further strengthened through supporting financially and other incentives. The long term objectives of development programmes for SC women, as also for women in general population should be raised for their economic and social status to bring them in to the main stream of natural development in the process and due recognition should be accorded to the role and contribution of women in various social-economic political and cultural activities.

Empowerment is viewed as a process in which all voices will be encouraged and heard for the ultimate goal of securing mutually beneficial solution. Government agencies have supported policies and programmes, which will reduce women's inferior status that hinders their development, thus as a major initiation from government, self help groups have evolved for empowering and stabilizing women.

SELF HELP GROUPS FORMATION OF SIGNIFICANCE

Women form a vital part of the Indian Economy constituting one third of national labor force and a major contributor to the survival of a family. More than 90% of Indian rural women are unskilled and these are confined to low paid occupations. They constitute 60 per cent of the rural unemployed and 56 per cent of the total unemployed in India. Many analyses reveal that Indian women are relatively disadvantaged in matters of health, finance, nutrition, literacy, freedom and productivity.

Women are generally under-employed due to their limited command over resources and regulatory institutions, particularly, rural women face greater problem than their urban counterparts with no source of livelihood other than agriculture. Hence the Government has been adopting various programmes for empowering rural women in the country. The introduction of development of women and children in rural areas (DWCRA) was one such scheme. The DWCRA scheme was introduced in the year 1982 as a pilot project in fifty selected districts. By the end of VII plan (1985-90), it was extended to 162 districts. During their period 28,000 groups were formed with a membership of 4.60 lakh women as against the target of 35,000 groups. During 1990-91 against a target of 7,500 groups, 7,139 groups were formed. This figure jumped up to 15,483 in 1993-94 and 19,000 groups in 1994-95 which covered about 3.19 lakh beneficiaries. However, its several short comings leading to its failure paved the way for the introduction of self-help groups (SHGs) scheme, a sub programme under Swarnajayanthi Gram Swarozgar Yojana(SGSY). The SHGs scheme is specially aimed at increasing women's the earning and making them self-confident. It has been regular component of the Indian financial system since 1996.

DEFINITION AND FORMATION OF SHGS

NABARD being the principal agent in rural development in India has defined the concept of SHGs as "small economically homogeneous affinity groups of rural poor, voluntarily formed to save and mutually contribute to a common fund to be lent to its members as per the group member, decision".

(In India, through SHGs are formed for various purposes, the principal objective ordinarily lies in the promotion of livelihoods of their members through collective saving and investment activities).

A Self Help Group can be defined as a voluntary association of the poor with a common goal of social and economic empowerment. The purpose behind the formation of self help group may be to pool in the resources of members to meet their needs.

SHGs have an in-built mechanism where emphasis has been given over the capacity building of woman through developing their confidence, communication skills, decision making ability, co-ordinating etc., social mobilization through 'Self Help Groups' is inevitable for economic empowerment and poverty alleviation. The concept of SHGs exists prior to any intimation. A common bond like caste, blood / community and place of origin or activities of interest links the members in these natural groups of 'affinity'.

The 'Self Help Groups' provide economic benefits in certain areas of production process by undertaking common action programs like cost-effective credit delivery system, generating a forum for collective, learning with rural people, promoting democratic culture, fostering an entrepreneurial culture, providing a firm base for dialogue and co-operation in programmes with other institutions, possession of creditability and power to ensure participation and helping to assess an individual members management capacity.

Self Help Groups enhance the equality of status of women as participants, decision makers and beneficiaries in the democratic economic, social and cultural spheres of life. The SHGs have inculcated a great confidence in the minds of women to succeed in their day-to-day life.

Self Help Groups broadly go through three stages of evaluation:

1. Group formation
2. Capital formation through the revolving fund and skill development.
3. Taking up economic activity for income generation.

FORMATION OF SELF HELP GROUPS

A SHG is a group of rural poor who have volunteered to organize themselves into a group for eradication of poverty of the members. They agree to save regularly and convert their savings into a common fund. The members of the group agree to use their common fund and such other funds that they receive as a group through a common management. The group formation will keep in view the following broad guidelines. A self help group may consist of 10 to 20 persons. In the case of minor irrigation and in the case of disabled persons, the members may be a minimum of five.

1. The group corpus fund should be used to advance loans to the members. The group should develop financial management norms covering the loans sanction procedure, repayment schedule and interest rates.
2. The members in the group meetings should take all the loaning decisions through a participatory decision making process.
3. The group should be able to priorities the loan applications, fix repayment schedules, fix appropriate rate of interest for the loans advanced and closely monitor the repayment of the loan installments form the loans.
4. The group should operate a group account so as to deposit the balance amounts left with the groups after disbursing loans to its members.
5. The group should maintain simple basis records such as minutes books, attendance register, load ledger, general ledger, cash book, bank pass book and individual passbooks.

SHG is a group of rural poor who have volunteered to organize themselves into a group for eradication of poverty of the members. They agree to save regularly and convert their savings into a common fund. The member of the group agree to use their common fund and such other funds that they may receive as a group through a common management.

The poor may organize themselves, into small groups up to 20 persons, known as self-help groups (SHGs) to inculcate the habit of thrift and credit operations among themselves. Other than immediate investment the groups saving of self help groups serve a wide range of objectives.

- Improves discipline on group members in developing the saving habit.
- Savings enhances self-confidence of the individual as it is a sign of group involvement.

- Group savings of the poor can demonstrate the strength of unity of members.
- Savings can cover the individual rise against normal business risk.

SHGs may be organized in clusters of blocks/districts either by reputed voluntary agencies / NGOS or at the initiative of branch managers of commercial, cooperative and regional rural bank.

Under SGSY, a self help group may consist of 10 to 20 persons. In the case of minor irrigation, and in the case of disabled persons, their number may be a minimum of five.

All members of the group should belong to families below poverty line. The group shall not consist of more than one member from the same family. A person should not be a member of more that one group.

The SHG will be an informal group. However, the groups can also register themselves under the societies registration act the state cooperative act or as a partnership firm. The SHGs can be further strengthened and stabilized by federating them at say, village level. This would facilitate regular interaction and exchange of experiences including flow of information from DRDAs and other departments.

AIMS OF THE SELF HELP GROUP

The aim of the SHG is to bring out all-round sustainable development of the members, families and villages.

Main Aims

1. To create appropriate awareness among the members for their all round development in the society.
2. To promote co-operation and self help attitude, good habit of savings among the members and voluntary collective works.
3. To promote savings attitude and habit among the members for their future and to encourage the members to commit themselves to regular savings.

4. To meet the credit needs of the members in time for consumption, income generation, asset formation and other appropriate purposes.
5. To help members in acquiring and use of appropriate technical knowledge and managerial skills in relation to their occupation in order to increase productivity.
6. To create awareness and work for human health development.
7. To improve the basic facilities of the village viz., drinking water, sanitation, etc.
8. To arrange for the availability of improved agricultural equipments, implements, etc., for the villages and to run a service country for the benefit of the members.
9. To give special attention to population control measures.

DISTRICT PROFILE

Nalgonda district is one among the backward districts of Telangana region. This district was originally known as Nilagiris. This district underwent territorial changes several times. In 1985 the administration units in the district were changed i.e., the then existing 15 Taluks were reorganized into 59 mandals. Nalgonda district has been divided into four divisions. Nalgonda Revenue Division, Suryapet division, Miryalguda division, Bhongir division. Bhongir mandal and Alair mandal fall in Bhongir division and Naredcherla and Garidepally mandal fall in Mirylalagulda division.

Nalgonda district is at a great, advantageous position with regard to many national resources which could be profitably exploited for its rapid progress and industrial development. Demographic figures indicate that the population of the district has been increasing decade after decade. According to 2001 census figures the total population of the district was 32,38,449 of which 28,08,99 are rural population and 4,29,258 are urbanites. According to 2001 causes in Nalgonda district the total SC population was

575,788 which accounts to 17.73 per cent to the total population. Similarly the ST population in the district was 342,676 which accounts for 10.55 per cent of the total population.

The total SC women population was 283,828 which accounts to 17.78 per cent to the total population and similarly ST women population in the district was 164,303 which accounts for 10.29 per cent to the total population. Basically, Nalgonda district depends upon agriculture. Truly speaking, this district is not developed industrially. However, cooperative segment has played a significant role in this district. Handloom weaving rescued the rural peoples upliftment in this district. There is no dearth of tourist spots in the district. Prominent among those are Yadigirigutta, Pillalamarri, Bhongir etc.

The soil of the district is very poor and mostly consists of red soil. The fertile black soil forms only 9 per cent and occupies the bank of Krishna and isolated patches here and there. Among the red soil, 47 per cent is Dubba (ilamy sands) which has very low moisture retaining capacity and the rest is chalka soil forming 44 per cent.

The flora of the district is very poor when compared to other districts of the state. Of the important rivers flowing in the district are Krishnna, Musi and Dindi etc. Nagarjunasagar is the only major irrigation project benefiting 15 mandals; among them two are Neredcherlla and Garidepalli.

Mandal Significance

1. Bhongir
2. Aler
3. Naredcherla
4. Garadepally

CONCLUSION

It is impossible to think about the welfare of the world unless the condition of women is improved.

The empowerment or women has to become the primary focus to all those concerned with the emancipation of women. It implies a process in which building of capacity, self-image, confidence, self-assertion are expected to take place. Increasing involvement, individual and collective action, self generated momentums are also other desirable factors to be promoted in the process. In brief, empowerment implies a fundamental redistribution of power between different groups which include families, communities and classes.

DWCRA

Most of the developmental programmes for rural women focus on subsidiary occupations, which generate regular income through gainful employment. One such program is DWCRA i.e., Development of Women and Children in Rural Areas. Andhra Pradesh is the pioneer state in introducing

DWCRA schemes in all the districts to achieve self sufficiency and to bring social transformation among the rural women living below the poverty line. It has been widely recognized that unless the potentialities of women are properly developed, no social transformation and economic development is possible. The three objectives of the DWCRA scheme are to improve economic, health, education and social status of rural women by providing them assistance and generating employment opportunities to earn their lively hood.

ANALYSIS OF DATA

The research in general and educational Status of the members of the Self Help Group conducted in all the mandals revealed that the groups are the association of poor people, preferably from the same socio economic back ground and caste.

The scheme of SHGs has transformed the real economic power into the hands of women and has considerably reduced their dependence of them. This has helped in empowerment of women and building self confidence but lack of education often comes in the way and many SHGs are considered as some of the most significant tools to adopt a participatory approach for the economic empowerment of women, it is an important situation for improving the life of women on various social components.

From the table it is observed that 26 per cent of the members in the self help groups in all the four mandals of Nalgonda district possess own agriculture land where as 74 per cent of the SHG members in the 4 mandals do not have agricultural land. This shows that most of the women do not have income from agriculture. This shows the poor financial status of the members. The average family income of the members in the four mandal i.e. Bhongir, Aler, Naredcharla and Garadepally is Rs. 15,980/- per annum. As the groups in the mandal have applied for loans, this shows that the financial assistance provided itself is the inspiration for the members to join and start a group. The economic support provided for the establishment of the group by the government, banks and NGO's is the reason for women's participation.

The distribution of the activities of the members in four mandals is different depending on their resources, skills and strength of the members. 27 per cent of the SHGs are engaged in vegetable selling, 7 per cent are involved in kirana shops, 1 per cent are involved in chappal making, 4 per cent are preparation of food items, 3 per cent are involved in dress making, 5 per cent of the SHGs are running tea stalls, 25 per cent of them are into buffalo rearing 10 per cent are running phone booths, 2 per cent pickles, 1 per cent is T-shirts making, 2 per cent are preparing papad, 3 per cent are into tailoring, 2 per cent are in goat business, 1 per cent are in candle making and 6 per cent of the SHG members are running shops. The financial output of the SHG members in all the mandals together is Rs. 79420. It is observed that the group on an average is to save Rs.755 but is able to save Rs.861. This shows that there is an improvement and development in the financial outcomes of the group which, if further increased, can strengthen women's socio-economic status

Self Help Groups enhance the quality of status of women as participants, decision makers and beneficiaries in the democratic, economic, social, political and cultural spheres of life. SHGs have inculcated a great confidence in the minds of women to succeed in their day to day life.

Among the SHG interviewed in the four mandals 75 per cent of the groups participate in the political activities whereas 25 per cent of them are not involved in any political activities.

The long standing SHGs brought attitudinal change among their members. By making their activities commercial, the SHGs created a sense of productive partnership among members. They are trained in discharging group responsibilities. Though majority of them are illiterate they have learnt keeping accounts. The SHGs imbibed in them a sense of democratic spirit and secular approach. The attitudinal changes of women have brought perceptible changes in social, cultural and political life of the rural folk.

The SHGs in India have proved beyond doubt that if the women, however poor, illiterate and ignored are organized and guided, they realize their problems, and can create wonders in their own lives and improve the lot of their families.

The social status of Self-Help Groups of the four members shows that the permanent resident members, participation is more in self help groups than the temporary and recently settled. From the study it is observed that all the members are happy working in the group .The interaction among the members in the group is highly significant. It is found that the SHGs members, social and economic status has improved after joining the scheme.

The SHG has fully proved to be helping women in attainment of employment. The prevalence of casteism in rural areas acts as a strong determinant to take the poor marginalized women in the group. But the SHG program has helped women come forward for equal participation and further improvement in their social status.

The impact of modernization on changes in the status of women could be seen through social, economic, occupational, structural and cultural changes. These will also lead to changes in the education, health, nutrition and sanitation. The economic activity is the primary motivating factor to change from tradition to modernity. According to the respondent's statements and from the findings of the study it is clear that this program has helped in improving their living conditions and social status. The strength of the group helped them to build confidence and competence to take part in decision making concerning their own development.

Though certain operational inconsistency is present in the program functionally, the SHG program has proved in attaining women empowerment through SHGs.

REVIEW OF LITERATURE

Anjugam and Alagumani (2000)[18] studied the impact of micro finance through self-help groups. The study revealed that SHGs helped them to use loans properly and repayment was 100 per cent. It increased the awareness of members for girls' education, improved outside contact and decision- making skills. This case study has clearly indicated that if the group formation is correct, then definitely there will be a positive impact on all aspects.

"Working and impact of Self-Help Groups in Goa" by Gaonkar (2000)[21] highlight that SHGs have made a lasting impact on the lives of the poor, particularly women, whose quality of life has been improved to a great extent. The members gave the following responses relating to social and economic aspects leading to empowerment in the quality of life in terms of increase in the family income, increase in savings, increase in consumption expenditure, gaining self-confidence, productive use of free time, getting an opportunity to improve the hidden talent and gain greater importance in the family etc.

Ayalakshmi. K. (2001)[23] in her study examined the pre and post status of SHGs groups and the members and the operational issues pertaining to the scheme. The study found that in each of the Mandals (SHG& DWCRA) together there were more than 400 groups. Each of them was saving Rs.20-30 per month. With 10-15 in a group it was not very homogeneous in nature with women from different social and economic status coming and forming a group.

B. Suguna (2006)[30] in her study examined the impact of SHGs in bringing empowerment among women in rural areas. The study focused on several aspects, such as the role of SHGs in the social, economic and political empowerment of women, the functioning of SHGs and the awareness and participation of women in SHGs etc. As such it also examined the different kinds of problems of beneficiaries with regard to savings, revolving fund, productivity and marketing etc. It is observed that the impact of SHGs on rural women brought change in their status with economic improvement and with the increase of social mobility through exposure to outside world. The study further observed that there is an improvement in the health status of women through greater awareness and better utilization of health services. Thus it is understandable that progression in various aspects has been taken place in the lives of rural women with the impact of SHGs.

References

Naidu Ashok (2006), 'Empowering Women', Jayaprakash Narayan Institute of Social and Economic Studies, Vision, vol. no .xxvi, Jan June, p. 1-2.

Rasimi Rekha Das. (2002), "Socio- Economic Allotment of Rural Women in India- the Role of Education" vision (vol.xxI) pg. no. 99.

Ghanshyam Shah (2002), "Dalith and the State an Overview" pg. no. 16.

M. K. Ghadaliya (2004), "Empowering Women through Self-Help Group : Role of Distance Education, Google Search .com pg. no 12.

Ibid reference 2.

Dr. H. D. Dwarakanth (1999), "DWCRA in Andhra Pradesh" Kurukshetra, Vol. 47, No. 12, sep-pg. no. 15-16.

Ibid –reference pg. no. 4.

Shyam Sundhar Sing Chowhan and Bansal Gaurar, "Various Dimensions of Women Empowerment" Social Welfare. Vol.49, No. 5., Aug. 2002.

Chodhry, Anand, Meenaxi, (1996), "Empowering Strategies for Rural Women In India". Kurushetra, Vol. 47, No. 6, March pp. 18-23.

Dr. H. D. Dwarakanath (1999), "DWCRA in Andhra Pradesh" Kurukshetra, Vol. 47, No. 12, pp. 15-16.

Banerjee N. K. (1975), 1990; Grassroot Empowering Adiscussion Paper No 22Center for Women Development Studies, New Delhi 1995. p. 8.

D. Chennap (2006), Women 'Emopowerment through SHGs Acase Study of SHGs at UPPAL Kalan Municipality. 'Selp Employment and Government Policy. Anmol Publication, New Delhi. pp. 338.

Bimal, K. Mohanty (2005), Women In SHGs. Issues and Evidence. Vision' vol XXV, No 1-2, july-sep.pg. 27-28.

G. Sreeramulu (2006), Empowerment of Women through Selp help Groups, Kalpaz Publication, New Delhi, pp. 123-124.

District Collector Offoce, Nalgonda 2001 Census.

Anjugam, M. and .Alagumani. T. (2000), Impact of Micro Finance though Self help Groups- A Case Study. Sreeramulu. G. (2000), Empowerment of Women through Self Help Groups. Page no. 46. Kalpaz Pulblication, New Delhi.

Gaonkar. R. R. (2000), Working and Impact of Self Help Groups, *Indian Journal of Agricultural Economics'*, July – September. 2001. pp. 469.

Jayalakshmi. K. (2001), Deepam Scheme in Andhra Pradesh, *Indian Journal of Agricultural Economics*, July-September, PP.

Suguna B. (2006), "Empowerment of Rural Women through Self Help Groups", Discovery Publishing House, New Delhi.

BENEFICIARY PERCEPTIONS OF ACCION FRATERNA'S WATERSHED DEVELOPMENT PROGRAMMES - WITH REFERENCE TO WOMEN EMPOWERMENT

P. Arjun Rao, M. Srinivasa Reddy and
P. Raja Narender Reddy

Watershed programmes, inter-alia, changed the very face of rural India. This has resulted, to some extent, in stopping the migration of rural population to towns and cities in India. Smaller and marginal farmers could earn their living without succumbing to various undersired pressures. The watershed programme has come to stay in rural India. This research paper highlights the perceptions of beneficiaries of watershed programmes taken up by AF[4], an NGO, which earned the positive reputation for having been engaged in the rural development arena. AF, an active NGO in Anantapur district in Andhra Pradesh had entered into several areas of rural development. The office bearers of AF are associated with several programmes taken up by Panchayatraj institutions. The office bearers of the NGO are on most of the development committees of Panchayatraj Institutions (PRIs). In a way the NGO under discussion had officially become a party in the rural development activities undertaken by PRIs. Watershed is one of the rural development programmes actively sponsored by AF. The study desired to understand the perception of beneficiaries of watershed programmes managed by it and know the merits and demerits of the said programme. The research describes in detail about the perceptions of beneficiaries on several aspects associated with the watershed programmes and suggests certain corrective measures in the light of the findings of the research study.

Some estimate that by 2020, the national demand[5] for groundwater in India will exceed its availability for irrigation by nearly 30%. The next two to three decades may also see a doubling in demand for domestic water use, which will lead to increasing competition and conflict if adequate measures are not taken[6]. Meanwhile, drinking water supplies from traditional open wells and bore wells have often been negatively affected as the agricultural areas under irrigation increased[7]. Issues surrounding water use and management are thus now at the forefront of many development efforts.

Andhra Pradesh (AP) is a drought-prone and resource-poor area of southern India, where issues pertaining to the livelihoods of the poor - particularly, water resource management - are of vital importance. Approximately three-fourths of the state's population i.e. around 75 million people live in rural areas. While the share of the state's overall income from agriculture has been declining in comparison with other sectors, the overwhelming majority of the people continue to be employed in agricultural work. As so many people depend on rainfed agriculture, the loss of productivity due to drought can have serious consequences in many areas of the state. The Government of India is spending over $500 million annually on watershed development projects[5]. Thus the successes and shortcomings of these initiatives have potentially enormous financial outcomes.

AF, a non-governmental organisation founded in 1982 as a subsidiary of the Rural Development Trust (RDT), has taken a leading role in watershed development in the

Anantapur District of AP - an area of the state that has lowest rainfall. Its activities range from watershed development works to promotion of self-help groups for targeted communities.

The present study was undertaken at the request of the Andhra Pradesh Rural Livelihoods Programme's PSU Coordinator, in order to better understand and document the perceptions of the intended beneficiaries of the various projects of AF. There has been increasing recognition over the past several years, especially with the adoption of the new guidelines for watershed development in 1995 that the success of many watershed programmes is highly dependent upon the level of participation of the community members it aims to benefit[8]. It is hoped that an investigation into stakeholders' perceptions of programme impacts may provide insight into aspects of projects they believe have been most beneficial, challenges to be met, and potential areas for future focus.

Watershed Programmes, in a way, gave the opportunity for women to participate in several of the programmes and prove their capabilities not only to cope with the problems but face challenges posed by the nature. This article gives an insight of women participation in various Watershed Programmes and also their perceptions about the activities taken up by Accion Fraterna.

METHODOLOGY

Background information on the main villages included in the study, as well as on facets of AF's various programmes, was provided by AF staff from their fieldwork and previous studies. The perceptions of villagers regarding the impacts of AF's projects were gathered through focus group discussions and individual interviews. The researchers, accompanied by a team of six AF staff familiar with the villages, made six field visits, to conduct discussions and interviews. Focus group discussions involved participants selected according to the primary projects they benefited from one of the six sectors: horticulture, rainwater harvesting, employment generation, bio-gas promotion, soil moisture conservation, and women's leadership development. These categories were not meant to be mutually exclusive, as many of the participants often benefited from more than one type of AF project. Practical considerations also limited the number of participants that could be included from any given list of potential beneficiaries. It should be noted that this was not a random sampling procedure, and the participants were largely male landowners from the non-poor castes, and in many cases were part of decision-making bodies (for example, as members of the watershed committees). The group sessions were conducted in a semi-structured format, lasting between 1½ to 2½ hours. Semi-structured interviews were conducted with some individuals selected from among the participants in the group discussions, which lasted from one to two hours. Semi structured formats were chosen for discussions and interviews in order to balance the desire on the part of the researchers to investigate specific topics, while still allowing some flexibility for the participants to discuss issues that they saw as relevant.

It should be noted that participants' comments in this study may have been influenced by, among other factors, their familiarity with one of the researchers (in some instances, leading to a clear desire to make a case for more funding), and their unfamiliarity with the other (whose presence, as a foreign national, caused more than a little disturbance in the villages). Truly "individual" interviews were also almost impossible to conduct, as other family members, former employers, husbands and other men (in the case of interviewing women), random onlookers, and occasionally AF staff were present for most of the duration. In addition, when referring to project donors, funding sources, and implementing agencies, there was frequently confusion in people's minds as to which entity or organisation was responsible for which project - particularly regarding the distinction between those projects under the support of the RDT, and those undertaken by AF. Any such ambiguities were left uncorrected - as part of people's perceptions throughout the report.

The villages selected for the present study are here under:

1. Mallapuram;
2. Kadiridevarapalli and Thimmapuram;
3. Settur;
4. H.R. Palli and Seeboi;
5. Kundurpi.

WOMEN'S LEADERSHIP AND EMPOWERMENT

This group had nine women, though the watershed committee president did all the talking.

Livelihood activities reported by this group included small business, rainfed farming, agricultural labour, labour exchange (landed women working in each other's fields), paddy and sunflower cultivation, horticulture, and watershed works (such as contour bunding). Some do tailoring (for both household and business purposes) – which they learned in Kalyandurg from tailor shops – and basket making during non-work hours. Some also purchase fruits and vegetables from Kalyandurg and within the village, and sell these in the village or surrounding areas. One member owns a store, and one is a teaching assistant in the ICDS (*anganwadi*) centre.

All present in the group are active in the watershed committee and various watershed works. Some of the important activities and achievements of the committee were then discussed. These included the promotion of horticulture and associated works (pit-digging, planting, etc.). The motivation of residents to participate in *sramadan* (cooperative, voluntary labour) has also been one of their objectives. Other areas included family planning, encouragement of school dropouts to re-enroll, lobbying for school expansion (to include students above 7th class), and discouraging agricultural labour for children under 14.

They noted that women's participation in village meetings has increased, as has their participation in other events – such as International Women's Day – since the inception of the RDT programme, and the self-help groups in particular. They now feel freer to approach officials about issues of their concern. They have also participated in "exposure trips" to learn more about agricultural management practices for implementation in their own fields.

The main benefit of the RDT programme that they repeatedly stressed was their increased ability to express themselves at various levels. One tangible benefit of this was felt recently, as they were able to resolve an ongoing dispute with a wealthy person who had barred their access to some of the temple lands, which are an important common property resource. The women used funds from their self-help group to pay for transportation to visit various officials – including the collector – and seek action concerning this unjust situation. As a result, the wall that the person had constructed was eventually recognised as illegal and dismantled.

For the future, they plan to use the watershed development funds that are collected from people's contributions to pay for needed projects and maintenance of watershed-related structures. They did not mention any other significant challenges.

VILLAGE PROFILES AND CASE STUDIES

The watershed development programme was initiated in Kundurpi in 1999. It is notable that both the Kundurpi and Karriganipalli watershed committees are comprised solely of women members. All four villages have watershed projects funded by AF. There are 33 self-help groups in Kundurpi, six of which are supported by RDT.

Kundurpi, which is the *Mandal* headquarters, is located 33 kilometers from the town of Kalyandurg, and 80 kilometers from the district headquarters Anantapur. It has a population of 7061, and out of a total of 703 households, less than 1 per cent is ST, 26 per cent are SC, 58 per cent are BC, and 15 per cent are OC. Eighty of the families are landless. The landed farmers irrigate an area of about 758 acres.

FINDINGS FROM FOCUS GROUP DISCUSSIONS

Women's Empowerment and Leadership

This group consisted of 13 women from Kundurpi and the nearby villages of Karriganipalli, Bandameedapalli, and Nijavalli.

Participants in this discussion included farmers with irrigation facilities, as well as landless labourers. Some managed small businesses and others did agricultural wage labour and watershed work. Many reported participating with their husbands (as "helpers") in such activities as sheep and goat rearing, sericulture, black smithy, carpentry, and cutting hair in barbershops. Many of their activities were promoted through RDT self-help groups. In addition to income-generating work, they did household work such as fetching water and collecting fuel wood.

Members from the three villages near Kundurpi all reported involvement in avenue plantation work. The watershed committees of their respective villages monitor their work and pay them Rs. 15 per plant for watering and maintenance. The high survival rate of the plants (around 95%) has led to their reputation as being good caretakers.

When asked about the effects of drought, their first concern was the reduced agricultural employment. One woman in the group indicated that she was eating less. Many are now involved in separating seeds from the groundnut harvest (for which they are paid by the kilogram). For those with land, some exchanged labour by working in each other's fields.

One participant indicated that the women's groups are using their power to strike for better government assistance through increased drought-relief works. They have also given presentations to various officials regarding this need. Incidentally, during our discussion, a few members of the group left to participate in a demonstration demanding more government assistance during the drought.

Over a year ago, some of the members fought for a drought-relief fund to help cover the losses they incurred from the rainfed groundnut crops. As a result of their action Rs. 500 per acre were paid this year. They believe that if the present drought continues, they will have to resume demonstrating for government assistance as soon as possible, especially for help with obtaining inputs for future crops. There have been problems regarding inequitable distribution of the relief assistance given to date, so they have to continue fighting for those who have been overlooked. Their advocacy on other issues has led to benefits provided for the elderly and widows, as well as ration cards for the landless from the government.

One of the challenges they expressed was the lack of time to do both agricultural and household work. In order to help alleviate this problem, they requested gas cylinders for cooking use – as an alternative to wood-fired stoves. Two group members have acquired gas cylinders, as well as bio-gas generation systems. The cylinders were made available through a government scheme, with RDT facilitation. It costs Rs. 300 to buy one cylinder, and it is difficult for them to afford it during the drought, but using gas saves time and energy that would otherwise be spent on collecting fuel wood. Burning gas instead of wood also produces less pollution in their homes. Others in the group reported cost was a factor preventing them from acquiring these systems. They did not acquire the bio-gas systems either, because they need to have at least four cattle for dung. It is not possible to freely collect dung from other people's animals, as it is highly valued as a source of fertilizer for fields.

They gather minor forest produce, fuel wood, and graze livestock in the nearby revenue hills. For village development as a whole (including road and lighting improvements), they valued the annual money-raising auctions of village lands near the tanks. In Nijavalli, the village woodlot area was previously not maintained well, and generated only Rs. 12,000 through the auctions. The all-women watershed committee then took over management of the area, and it now generates Rs. 30,000 through auctioning. A large portion of this money has been used for school improvement.

In Karriganipalli, the unopposed selection of an SC woman as *Sarpanch* of the *Gram Panchayat* was rewarded by RDT with Rs. 25,000, in addition to Rs. 45,000 for an entry-point activity designed to promote collective village development work. Out of this Rs. 20,000 went towards the construction of a watershed office, and the remainder was used for a drinking water pipeline.

In Bandameedapalli, the watershed committee raised money to improve access to the local school. In villages where schooling is available only up to primary level leads to a number of students –especially girls – discontinuing school. School up gradation, expanding to include upper primary classes, is thus a very important issue to many families. The scarcity of teachers can be overcome in some cases with the temporary employment of volunteers to fill in gaps, with contributions from parents towards their salary.

One woman in the group is the current village development committee/watershed association president. Proud of her 40 years of service as a communist party member, she says she was impressed with the watershed development programme activities from the start, and so decided to become involved. In her position, she conducts and participates in *Grama Sabhas* and watershed committee activities "without a profit motive." She participates in *sramadan*, and various watershed works, such as maintenance of the water-harvesting structures. She stated that a 100 per cent rate of collection of contributions has been achieved under her leadership, by convincing farmers to partake in the watershed activities. As a result of the watershed development programme, she has also had the opportunity to approach government officials concerning the implementation of various social programmes for her community.

As a result of the RDT programme, and subsequently the AF programme, women's leadership emerged. In particular, the self-help groups have given many women the opportunity to participate in a meaningful way in a variety of activities. Formerly, most women would not attend government meetings. Since the inception of the watershed programme activities, women's attendance has increased at *Gram Panchayat* meetings, as well as *Mandal*- and district-level meetings. Most of the group members attended the recent International Women's Day celebrations in Anantapur. Due to the equal wages paid to men and women for watershed activities, the gender disparity in agricultural wages was reduced substantially, as increasing numbers of women pressed farmers for more equitable pay.

They cited various watershed works to be most beneficial to them. The wage labour available for watershed works has been important to many during the lean season, when agricultural employment is difficult to find. Additionally, the watershed self-help groups offered members a source of loans, as an alternative to the wealthy farmers. The backyard horticulture and kitchen garden projects have been highly useful, as the AF subsidies have made inputs for growing coconuts, sweet limes, and mangoes. AF provided such plants for Rs. 15 per plant, whereas the same plants would have cost Rs. 50 through most private vendors.

As the returns from groundnut crops are never guaranteed, they expressed a need for financial incentives to promote mango cultivation – a more reliable source of income. They also would like to see greater promotion of non-farm activities, through either the government or RDT, in areas such as training for other skills and crafts (for example, making bullock carts) and marketing. Another area for future development is the promotion of dairy activities. While the men in their families were doing agricultural work, they would prefer to raise milch animals if they could get assistance in acquiring them, and if a milk-collection centre were available in their local area.

Individual Interview 1

M. Gangamma, 45, belongs to the SC community. Her family has nine members, including two men and two women who are working. One of her sons received his bachelor's degree, and is presently unemployed. Her elderly husband is dependent on her. She is currently a watershed committee member, self-help group executive committee president, and ward member of the Gram Panchayat.She has seven acres of land, two of which are irrigated while the rest is devoted to rainfed groundnut. She also does some sericulture. The main limitation to her livelihood activities at present is the lack of water in her borewell. She also does agricultural wage labour in others' fields. Her daughter-in-law works with her, but her sons do not work in others' fields. She does not do watershed work. The watershed development programme has benefited her with increased water available in her borewell, and allowed her to double the area under irrigation (from one acre, to two). However, due to the drought conditions, two of her crops failed recently, and there has been a lack of adequate water in the borewell.Six months ago, RDT constructed 10 houses for SC colony, where she lives, and also installed a hand pump for household use. She reported no problems with the drinking water availability or quality. She previously lived in a hut, and considers the RDT housing an improvement.Prior to the drought, her groundnut harvest amounted to over 40 bags, but has been reduced to only eight bags recently. The loss of income, in addition to major expenses – including her son's bachelor's degree, daughter's marriage, and digging a borewell – has led her to become highly indebted - totaling to Rs. 90,000. Now there is pressure on her to repay the loans and the creditors have threatened to seize her home and other assets. Her positions as a watershed committee member and Gram Panchayat member have served as a temporary coping strategy for dealing with her creditors.Important sources of assistance for her have included interest-free loans from the permanent drought fund, which enabled her to purchase groundnut seeds this year. As part of her self-help group, she promotes dairy activities to raise income for its members. She would like to become involved in tamarind cultivation, which she sees as less risky than growing mangoes.

Individual Interview 2

V.S. Premalatha is a young woman (she has passed 10th class) from the OC community and is president of the watershed association. Her family owns 80 acres of land, 20 of which are hers since the recent division of land among her siblings. One month ago, she separated from her joint family household, and now lives with her husband and their two daughters.She has been president of the watershed association for the past six months, after taking over from her mother-in-law, who quit due to poor health. The watershed committee unanimously accepted her at that time. Her husband is the president of the sericulture farmers' committee, of which she is a member. All of her 20 acres of land is under irrigation, with 15 acres devoted to mango, along with some sapota and tamarind. Intercropped with these trees are Ragi, groundnut and sunflower crops. She also has five acres of papaya trees. Last year, the income from these crops was Rs. 45,000; this year, it has been reduced to Rs. 35,000 due to drought. Watershed development activities in her lands have included the construction of two check dams, contour bunding, backyard horticulture, and kitchen gardening projects. RDT gave them various financial incentives for mango cultivation (pit-digging, watering, and related activities). They now lease out their mango plantation for the duration of the crop year (from January to May or June annually).From RDT, she also received three units (1 unit = 1000 worms) of vermi-compost. As part of this programme, RDT supplied 10 units of vermi-compost and training to interested farmers in the village, with the expectation that the farmers would provide the necessary labour. As a result, for the past four years she has been practicing vermiculture composting. In addition to increasing the yields on their own plots, she and her husband have also been able to make a substantial sum (Rs. 110,000) selling the surplus vermicompost they have produced.For the future, she would like the promotion of dairy development in small groups, through assistance in purchasing mixed-breed buffaloes.

WOMEN'S LEADERSHIP DEVELOPMENT

As a result of the RDT programmes and, subsequently, the AF watershed development programme, the active participation and leadership of women in decision-making has become an important characteristic of many villages. In particular, many women have taken the opportunity through self-help groups to increase their participation in a variety of activities.

Since the inception of the watershed programme, women's attendance has increased at *Gram Panchayat* meetings, as well as *Mandal* and district-level meetings. Formerly, most women would not attend government meetings. Now, many feel they can approach officials about issues of concern to them, such as drought-relief works, equitable distributions of benefits, compensation for agricultural losses, and other issues. Many members of the women's groups also attended the recent International Women's Day celebrations in Anantapur.

Equal pay for men and women through watershed works has been an improvement over the gender disparity in traditional agricultural labour. Due to this the gender disparity in agricultural wages was reduced substantially, as increasing numbers of women asked farmers why wages were not equitable.

Women reported increased productive activities available for themselves through RDT self-help groups. In addition, instead of borrowing from rich farmers, they use the groups as an alternative source for loans. In one village, women's management of common property land near a tank has increased its value. Fund-raising for village development through auctioning of the land, has led to greater funds for roads, lighting, and school improvements.

The lack of local schooling above primary level causes some students (especially girls) to dropout. To rectify this situation, women have been advocating for school up gradation. Another issue of concern to them was the demands on women to do both income-generating activities and household work.

MAINSTREAMING GENDER AND ORGANIZATIONAL DEVELOPMENT

It is in this process of continuous organizational change, that AF realized that to enhance the effectiveness of its work, apart from strengthening village level institutions, further understanding and addressing organizational issues (e.g. mainstreaming gender, PME, OD Processes) is extremely important. Thus, AF entered into a new phase of institutional learning and development.

AF began in early 1990s with efforts to increase the participation of women in CBOs and their involvement in decision making of watershed development. Gradually since 2002, AF has been making efforts to integrate gender in AF and in programmes through recruiting more women staff at senior level and developing greater contact with women at village level. The learning's from these attempts created a demand for building perspectives on gender across the organization and work towards mainstreaming of gender.

The process of organization level reflection and learning on this issue resulted in;

- Moving towards a holistic perspective on gender and its mainstreaming in the organization and in programme.
- Increased women's participation in watershed activities and institutions.
- Promoted women leaders with an objective that they take up village issues.
- Efforts made to understand the role and participation of women and innovative attempts to integrate women in NRM.

Apart from the above, a holistic 'ecological perspective' started emerging as an integrative framework to address issues related to agriculture, NRM, livelihoods and community empowerment. AF feels the need to further explore this perspective that enables further understanding on interfaces and linkages between NRM and gender, social institutions and technology.

GENDER TRAININGS

Gender is a cross-cutting theme in all AF's program activities. In order to bring the gender balance in program activities gender trainings / (separate and combined) are organized in all 240 villages twice in a year.

The main aspects focused in the trainings are: Disparities between men and women in education, health, employment, income opportunities control over assets, personal security, work load, early marriages, and participation in AF's program activities, and decision making, power etc: Under each training 30 men and 30 women are covered.

WOMEN'S DAY

Women's Day is planned at cluster level, covering 200 women and men from all villages, every year in the month of March. Aspects related to empowerment of women, participation in AF's program activities, government policies and program like NREGP, livelihood program, social welfare schemes are discussed in this gathering. The purpose of the gathering is to share their experiences and feelings to others who come from different villages. The Women's Day is happy occasion for them to express their feelings, views and enjoy the day besides taking some decisions related to their future role in family on community / society. From each village, 30 women and 10 men will attend to these Women's Days.

G. Indiramma - House Wife, Battuvanipalli Village said, "...Biogas is very useful to our family. I don't have to go for fire wood collection now. My kitchen is clean because it does not produce smoke. I am free from smoke hazards like burning eyes, cough etc. It is easy to clean cooking utensils also...."

Saraswathi Mahila Women Group Members, Bandameedapalli village said,"....Tamarind trees on lease have earned me around Rs. 25,000/. We have mobilized a loan of Rs. 98,000/- from Gramykya Sangham (VO). With this amount we took Tamarind trees on lease and earned Rs. 25,000/-. We could provide employment for 60 labourers in the process. Further we mobilized loan from RDT to an extent of Rs. 38,500/- and with that amount all the group members purchased two ram lambs each. We reared them for one year and got profits up to Rs.1,000/- on each lamb....."'

Anjinamma - SHG member, Palavenkatapuram village said, "Now, I don't have to depend on my husband for small needs..." and she also said,"...*After joining SHG, I have taken a loan and set up a small petty shop at my house. Now I don't have to depend on my husband for small needs. Now my husband is also taking my opinions in agricultural works, crops etc. I am taking some of the family decisions and my husband is also supporting me. I am feeling very happy now and I thank AF for that...*"".

Laxmi Devi - User Group Member, Yerraborepalli village said, "...Village meetings and trainings helping me ..." and she also said, "*.... I am attending out-of-village meetings and trainings at Kalyandurg and even staying there for one or two days, sometimes. My husband is also supporting me and he and his mother are even taking care of my small children at home.....*""

Govindamma - SHG member - Kambalapalli village said,"...Even men are also encouraging us to participate actively and our opinions are also valued..." and also explained, "*in combined meetings with men, we are sitting in the front rows and freely expressing our opinions. Even men are also encouraging us to participate. So we are very happy that we are participating actively and our opinions are also valued.*"

Watershed Development Committee Members, Rudrampalli village said, "...Living with dignity..." and extend their views,".... there are four destitutes in our village. We collected contributions from people to help them. We paid them Rs. 1,250/- each during Grama Sabha. We are also collecting food grains. We are trying to make them live with dignity....""

Santhamma, House Wife, Diguva Thanda village opined,".... I am saved from health hazards like burning eyes...."

"".....AF has supplied smokeless chulha to our family. It is mobile and I can take it anywhere indoor or outdoor. The consumption of fuel wood is less. I am saved from health hazards like burning eyes....""

Akkamma, Women farmer, M. Venkatampalli village said, "... My husband supported my decision...."

Rangamma, SHG member, Kariganipalli village said, "....Last year we planted fruit plants in our land. I decided on the number of plants to be raised i.e. in 1 acre. My husband supported my decision. Informally, the plantation is also in my name. I am very happy about this....". "....I got a profit of Rs. 4000 ..."

Jyothi – Women Labour, Veligonda village said,".....My husband and I are working as labourers in Kariganipalli watershed. During these 3 years we have saved Rs.2,800/- from our earnings in bunding work. Recently we purchased 4 ram lambs from this amount and we are expecting a profit of Rs.4,000/- after 6 months. We are thankful to AF for providing us work...."

"... We also have a chance to express our opinions... We are attending meetings on watershed and village developmental works. We also have a chance to express our opinions. The committee members are listening to my opinions and discussing them. I am feeling very happy about this..."

CASE STUDIES

A few following Case studies are given to show the women Empowerment.

A Tailoring Centre is Established with Young Girls' Initiative: A Case Study of Mahantapuram Village

There is high demand for garments in the surrounding areas of Settur. Two girls Roja and Shilpa of Mahanthapuram village in Settur area used to go to the Mandal head quarters for learning tailoring. Daily they used to leave at 8.00 a.m. and return by 6.00 p.m. to their village. They felt it difficult to do so every day. They gathered 23 girls, who were also interested in tailoring, contacted AF staff, expressed their problem and asked for a solution.

AF staff, in turn contacted JSS (Jana Shikshana Samsthan) a Government Agency in Anantapur which provides skills training for rural youth. Then AF staff conducted a meeting for the girls and their parents and explained the terms and conditions involved for establishing tailoring center in their village.

Within a week's time the contribution amount was collected from the members and handed over to JSS official, who got the proposal sanctioned.

> *"We are thankful to AF for helping us in the establishment of a tailoring center in our village. It saved our time and money. Our parents are also feeling relaxed as there is no need for us to go to far-off places to learn tailoring. We are thankful to JSS for the help they have extended to our village-* ***Girls of Mahanthapuram***

The center was started on September 13th and AF staff took the responsibility of follow-up, checking the attendance of the members and the tutor regularly, conducting tests every month etc.

Here they learn not only normal cloth stitching but also the fancy hand works, Zigzag, embroidery etc. After completing this training the interested girls will be sent to nearby towns and cities for learning advanced courses in fashion designing. The other girls can do the garments in the village itself and sell in their village as well as in surrounding villages.

An Initiative by Women Groups to Solve the Seed Scarcity for the Poor Farmers in Manirevu Village

The farmers of Manirevu village were having acute scarcity of Groundnut and Red gram seed. They had to purchase seed from the town market or from the middlemen for which they had to pay a high price and there was no guarantee of quality. AF staff noticed this problem and motivated the representatives of the existing 20 women groups (SHGs) from the two Village Organizations called Sai and Sailatha, to establish a seed bank in the village itself which could also be a seasonal livelihood opportunity for them.

Later AF staff and group leaders organized a meeting for the farmers and discussed with them, and identified the farmers in need of seed, particularly the poorest farmers. They were formed in to a seed user group. The V.Os. provided Rs. 3,00,750/- credit to the group for starting a seed Bank. (The group purchased 23,200 kgs of groundnut and 400 kgs. of red gram from the co-operative society). AF's agriculture officers helped them to buy good quality of seed. Then they supplied the entire seed to 48 needy farmers of Manirevu for a fair price. The planning and implementation of this activity was monitored by the Village Organizations. As a result:

- The needy farmers got quality seed, for a fair price and in time, on credit.
- They could repay the credit after the crop was harvested and sold.
- The group also made a reasonable profit from this activity.

The women group's representatives in the *Sanghas* expressed their happiness for gaining reasonable profit in this process, while fulfilling the seed needs of poor farmers in the village. The farmers were immensely happy as they got good quality seed at a fair price in time on credit. They were happy to repay the credit.

Gainful Employment Is the Key for Better Living of the Poor: The Story of Mrs. Laxmi Devi, alone Labourer in the Family:

Family information

Mrs. Lakshmi Devi has been working as labour in Seeboi watershed, being implemented by Accion Fraterna (RDT) since 6 years. She is the leader for her 15 member labour group. She has been selected as leader since she has studied 5th class and is 'able to convince others'.

Family Conditions before Watershed Programme

1. Mrs. Lakshmi Devi - Family head
2. Mr. Thippe Swamy - Husband
3. Mrs. Thimmakka - Grand mother
4. Shanthi - Daughter – Studying 8th class
5. Chandra - Son – Studying in Pre Primary

Mrs. Lakshmi Devi was only earning member in her family. Her husband was not able to work because of his overweight, due to some disease. The family migrated many times from the village as there was no labour work throughout the year and faced many a hardship. They were not having enough food, clothes, house and other basic amenities. They had to depend always on others for their health and other small needs. And they were not able to cultivate their 5 acres of land due to lack of investment. They were under employed, underpaid, and lived in severe poverty.

Effective Use of Earnings from Labour

Only Mrs. Lakshmi Devi worked in the watershed programme for 100–120 days in every season and earned about Rs. 4,000/- per Annum at the rate of Rs. 35 – 50 per day. She had earned about Rs. 25,000/- over the past 6 years. When the watershed works were not there, she went for agriculture labour work within the village and earned Rs.20 to 25/- per day. Since the agriculture work was seasonal and not continuous, her earnings in the rest of 240 to 260 days were almost equal to her watershed earnings in 100 to 120 days. She was very wise in spending the amount for her family development.

- One buffalo was purchased for Rs. 5000/-
- Rs. 5000/- was money lended for interest.
- Spent a lot of money for the medical treatment for her grandmother and husband who often fell sick.
- Pebble bunding was done in 2 acres of her land with the assistance from Watershed Programme. She paid 10% of the cost as farmer's contribution to the watershed committee.
- Spending money for her 2 Children's Education who are studying at Kalyandurg.

It was really interesting to note that her son who was about 4 years is sent to a lower kindergarten primary school, and her daughter is also studying in a private school at Kalyandurg town which is 15 Kms. away from her village. They are paid schools!

That showed how much she liked to educate her children! It is very unusual for a lone woman labourer in the family to send both her children to a paid private school. The family is leading 'a normal life' even though severe drought conditions are prevailing in the area for the last 3 years.

CHANGE IN QUALITY OF LIFE

Mrs. Lakshmi Devi expressed that lot of change had taken place in their daily life of the family. They have now enough food, proper clothing and a place to live. They are cultivating their 5 acres of land by purchasing seed, fertilizer and pesticides. Food and clothing pattern is changed. They consume milk and curd that come from the buffalo. Their health condition has improved. Both the children are studying in good schools. The family established good relationship with farmers and other people in the village and get due respect and recognition from them. Lakshmi Devi is an active member in labour groups and participates 4 times in a year in Shramadan activities. She said that she would like to participate as much as possible in making her village as a model village!

CONCLUSION

Mrs. Lakshmi Devi is a living model for other labour in the village in improving social and economic status of a family. Watershed programme is bringing in a positive change in the lives of the poor (like Laxmi Devi) through employment opportunities besides natural resources development. Mrs. Lakshmi Devi is positively motivating and inspiring the labour in the watershed programme.

She was not alone in this category. There are about 5000 such poor families who avail employment opportunities every year in the AFs Eco-employment and watershed development programme. They are able to improve their living condition and overcome their poverty. They are able to gain respect and recognition and are able to live in dignity. They are able to create some productive assets, provide education for their children, care for their health, redeem from the bondage, repay the old debts etc.

Livelihood Diversification Led to Improved Quality of Life

Rangamma and her husband Obanna are living in Ragula padu village of Uravakonda Mandal with their 7 family members. Both of them are members in AF's Livelihood group. The returns from their 5 acres of land are very minimal due to frequent droughts. They took loans from the money lenders to meet their family needs like food, health and education of their children. They were struggling a lot to repay the debts and cope-up with drought. Previous year AF's staff explained them the opportunities of getting more income by developing backyard poultry. Being a member in Velugu group Rangamma took Rs.3,000/- loan from the group and started back yard poultry with 20 country birds. Today they have 120 birds in their farm. They invested the profits from the poultry on their land and increased their crop yield. With AF staff's encouragement they bidded the tamarind trees produce in auction for Rs.30,000/-. They borrowed Rs.20,000/- from bank and Rs.10,000/- from Velugu group as loan on 12% interest per annum. They harvested tamarind, graded and sold it for Rs.47,200/- and earned a net profit of Rs.17,200/- from tamarind business.

> *"We are very much thankful to AF staff for providing support by suggesting backyard poultry and tamarind business... By joining AF's Livelihood group we are able to utilize many of the Government schemes and developed profitable livelihoods and solved our economic problems. Now we are in a position to provide higher education to our younger children."-**Rangamma, Ragulapadu.***

Now they are repaying their loans regularly. Rangamma has also started saris (ladies garment) selling business with Rs. 5,000/-. She purchased 25 saris at Rs.150/- to 300/- each from a wholesale shop and sold 20 saris with a profit of Rs. 25/- on each sari. She earned a total profit of Rs. 500/- and this time she want to increase the investment. She got a house sanctioned under State Government's Housing programme. Now the family is leading an improved quality of life due to diversification of income opportunities.

SHG Leaders and Farmers Benefit from Better Marketing Strategy - A Case Study of Gangavaram Village

Lalithamma, Dhonamma, Mumtaz, Kamalamma, Shivamma, Lakshminarasamma and Erriswamy are the leaders of SHG groups of Gangaveram village in Kalyandurg Area. They discussed the problems in marketing the farm produce and the exploitation by the middlemen in their network meetings. They decided to explore all possibilities to get a fair price for the farm produce from their village. They went to agriculture market yard in Anantapur and learnt about marketing techniques and market prices. Then they created awareness amongst the farmers of their village on the market prices and the tricks played by the middle men in duping the farmers. They also discussed about the benefits and problems in self marketing. All the farmers gave their support to this group. Being members of *Velugu* group they took loan from the group and purchased 52 quintals of Bengal gram from the farmers for Rs. 93,600/- at prevailing rates. Then they sold the stock for Rs. 1,09,200/- at market yard after two months. They also appointed a three member committee for better transparency. As a result of this initiative:

- Farmers could get price for the exact quantity of their produce (they used to lose 8 – 10 kgs of their produce through defective weighing by the middle men).
- They did not lose 2-3 kgs. of their produce, which they had to give as commission (Riwaj) to middlemen.
- They could get their money, immediately after selling the produce (The middlemen used to pay them in installments).
- The SHG leaders earned a net profit of about Rs. 14,000/-, which they shared amongst themselves @ Rs. 2,000/- per person.

The farmers and SHG leaders are very happy about this. They said they will continue the practice in future and try to avoid middlemen altogether.

CONCLUSION

The detailed study indicates that the women are active in various developmental programmes and are proved to be partners in the bread earning to the family. Watershed Programmes gave scope for women to exhibit their leadership qualities. With this programme, to some extent, the rural face is certainly changing by stopping migration, mitigating the rural drinking water problems etc. The women participants are happy and vocal in conveying the researchers as to how best they could utilize the opportunities provided to their advantage and bring a meaningful change in their lives .... to say that the programmes gave opportunities for Women empowerment.

Women reported benefiting from the programme in various ways, from greater empowerment in decision-making (especially for those now serving on the watershed committees), to time-saving on household work by using bio-gas systems. Many also benefited indirectly from the programme, as the gender-equitable wages paid for watershed work led in some cases to less disparity in wages for other agricultural work as well. However, the sample size in the present study was too limited to address the question of how widely the benefits to women were distributed.

This is a micro-study and findings may not be treated as comprehensive and universal. This study leads to suggest macro level study across the country and the resultant findings would enlighten to take steps for a major policy decision.

Notes

1. Accion Fraterna, a non-governmental organisation, established in 1982, as a subsidiary of the Rural Development Trust (RDT), has played a leading role in watershed development in Anantapur District of Andhra Pradesh, by taking up several programmes to strengthen watershed development.
2. Rao, C.H.H. (2000), Watershed Development in India: recent experience and emerging issues. Economic and Political Weekly 35(45). November 4, 2000.
3. Butterworth J, YV Malla Reddy and Charles Batchelor(2001), Addressing water needs of the poor in watershed management, Paper Prepared for the 27th WEDC Conference, People and systems for water, sanitation and health, Lusaka, Zambia,20-24, August.
4. Saxena, N. C. (1999), Forward in: Farrmgton, J., C. Turton and A. J. James (Eds.). Participatory Watershed Development: Challenges for the Twenty-First Century. Oxford University Press, New Delhi.

EMPOWERMENT OF OBCs:
A Case Study of Munnuru Kapus in Telangana

P. VENKATESWAR

INTRODUCTION

According to sociologists, caste is defined as a hereditary, endogamous, usually localised group, having a traditional association with an occupation and a particular position in the local hierarchy of caste. The Other Backward Classes (or OBCs) in India are a group of citizens other than the Scheduled Castes and the Scheduled Tribes as may be specified by the Central Government in their lists. The list presented by the commission is dynamic (castes and communities can be added or removed) and will change from time to time depending on Social, Educational and Economic factors. The Constitution recognizes the need to extend reservations to this section. For example, the OBCs are entitled to 27% reservations in public sector employment and higher education. In the constitution, OBCs are described as "socially and educationally backward classes", and government is enjoined to ensure their social and educational development. Until 1985, the affairs of Backward Classes were looked after by the Backward Classes Cell (BCC) in the Ministry of Home Affairs. With the creation of a separate Ministry of Welfare in 1985 (renamed as Ministry of Social Justice and Empowerment on 25th May 1998) the matters relating to SC, ST, Other Backward Classes (OBCs) and Minorities were transferred to the new Ministry. The Backward Classes Division in the Ministry looks after the policy, planning and implementation of programmes relating to social and economic empowerment of OBCs. It also looks after matters relating to two institutions set up for the welfare of OBCs: National Backward Classes Finance and Development Corporation (NBCFDC) and the National Commission for Backward Classes (NCBC).

Under Article 340 of the Constitution, it is obligatory for the government to promote the welfare of the Other Backward Classes (OBC). Article 340(1) states, "The President may by order appoint a commission, consisting of such persons as he thinks, fit to investigate the conditions of socially and educationally backward classes within the territory of India and the difficulties under which they labour and to make recommendations as to the steps that should be taken by the union or any state to remove such difficulties and as to improve 'their condition and as to the grants that should be made, and the order appointing such commission shall define the procedure to be followed by the commission." Article 340(2) states, "A commission so appointed shall investigate the matters referred to them and present to the president a report setting out the facts as found by them and making such recommendations as they think proper." Despite the fact that the term 'backward class' has appeared more than once in the Constitution of India, it has not been defined clearly in the Constitution. Thus there was a need to determine backwardness by means of adopting suitable criteria and identify all those who come under the backward classes category.

COMMISSIONS

First Backward Classes Commission

The First Backward Classes Commission was set up by a presidential order on January 29, 1953 under the chairmanship of Kaka Kalelkar. The commission submitted its report in March 1955. It had prepared a list of 2,399 backward castes or communities for the entire country and of which 837 had been classified as the "most backward". Some of the most notable recommendations of the commission were:

1. Undertaking caste-wise enumeration of population in the census of 1961;
2. Relating social backwardness of a class to its low position in the traditional caste hierarchy of Indian society;
3. Treating all women as a class as "backward";
4. Reservation of 70 per cent seats in all technical and professional institutions for qualified students of backward classes.
5. Reservation of vacancies in all government services and local bodies for other backward classes.

The commission in its final report recommended "caste as the criteria" to determine backwardness. But this report was not accepted by the government as it feared that the backward classes excluded from the caste and communities selected by the commission may not be considered and the real needy would be swamped by the multitude and would hardly receive special attention.

Mandal Commission

The decision to set up a second backward classes commission was made official by the president on the 1st of January 1979. The commission was popularly known as the Mandal Commission as it was headed by B P Mandal. It submitted the report in December 1980. The recommendations of the commission were: The population of OBCs which includes both Hindus and non-Hindus is around 52 per cent of the total population according to the Mandal Commission. However, this finding was criticized as based on "fictitious data." The National Sample Survey puts the figure at 32%. There is substantial debate over the exact number of OBC's in India, with census data compromised by partisan politics. It is generally estimated to be sizable, but lower than the figures quoted by either the Mandal Commission or and National Sample Survey. Twenty seven per cent of reservation was recommended owing to the legal constraint that the total quantum of reservation should not exceed 50 percent. States which have already introduced reservation for OBC's exceeding 27 per cent will not be affected by this recommendation.

With this general recommendation the commission proposed the following overall scheme of reservation for OBC's:

1. Candidates belonging to OBC's recruited on the basis of merit in an open competition should not be adjusted against their reservation quota of 27 per cent.
2. The above reservation should also be made applicable to promotion quota at all levels.
3. Reserved quota remaining unfilled should be carried forward for a period of three years and de-reserved thereafter.
4. Relaxation in the upper age limit for direct recruitment should be extended to the candidates of OBC in the same manner as done in the case of SCs and STs.
5. A roster system for each category of posts should be adopted by the concerned authorities in the same manner as presently done in respect of SC and ST candidates.

These recommendations in total are applicable to all recruitment to public sector undertakings both under the central and state governments, as also to nationalised banks. All private sector undertakings which have received financial assistance from the government in one form or other should also be obliged to recruit personnel on the aforesaid basis. All universities and affiliated colleges should also be covered by the above scheme of reservation. Although education is considered an important factor to bring a desired social change, "educational reform" was not within the terms of reference of this commission. To promote literacy the following measures were suggested:

1. An intensive time-bound programme for adult education would be launched in selected pockets with high concentration of OBC population;
2. Residential schools should be set up in these areas for backward class students to provide a climate specially conducive to serious studies. All facilities in these schools including board and lodging should be provided free of cost to attract students from poor and backward homes;
3. Separate hostels for OBC students with above facilities would have to be provided;
4. Vocational training was considered imperative.
5. It was recommended that seats should be reserved for OBC students in all scientific, technical and professional institutions run by the central as well as state governments. The quantum of reservation should be the same as in the government services, i.e., 27 per cent.[1]

RISE OF MANDAL POLITICS

Mandal politics owes its name and origin to a 1990 decision taken by the VP Singh government at the Centre to implement the Mandal Commission's recommendation of reserving 27 per cent of all central government jobs by way of affirmative action for Other Backward Classes (OBCs), just as 22.5 per cent had been kept for Scheduled Castes and Tribes (SC/STs). While millions of OBCs found a voice of assertion in the plan, it provoked a severe backlash from urban India's upper-caste youth who saw job quotas as cramping their career prospects, thus creating a new fault line in Indian politics.

Issues of caste identity attained sudden salience, with Mulayam in UP and Lalu in Bihar the chief OBC beneficiaries in VP Singh's Janata Dal party—which later split, with the two running their own shows. The Mandalisation of Indian politics saw OBCs exercising socio-political power for the first time ever, with the mass backing of Muslims (and even Dalits in Bihar), in opposition to upper-caste domination.

However, this phase also saw a hardening of identities, which rarely happens without conflict. Mandal politics in the north was accompanied by the rise of Hindutva, a reactionary upper-caste mobilisation roused by saffron slogans of a Ram Temple to replace a 16th century mosque in Ayodhya, UP. This agitation peaked on 6 December 1992 with the Babri Masjid demolition. The event not only led to a surge in saffron support, but also communal violence in many parts of India and a mass switchover of Muslim loyalties from the Congress—seen as twiddling thumbs while the BJP staged its Hindutva act—to Mulayam and Lalu in UP and Bihar. As it turned out, the Yadav duo's success acted as a bulwark against the north's saffronisation. Soon enough, the Muslim-Yadav (M-Y) vote became a winning combination in these states. In effect, Mandalisation found consolidation. The BJP did make some gains. But the Congress collapsed.[2]

Once the original Janata Dal fragmented, successor parties were often hostile to each other. Also, the turn towards identity politics spawned several other formations as well. If the BJP had upper-caste support, the BSP took over Dalit loyalties in UP. In multi-cornered contests, the threshold voteshare to win elections was so low that small shifts, one way or another, spelt big changes.

THE POLITICAL ADVANCEMENT OF MUNNURU KAPUS IN TELANGANA

Munnuru Kapu's are primarily concentrated in Telangana region of Andhra Pradesh. By occupation they are farmers. The name Munnuru seems to be of a recent origin, which means three hundred. They were a part of the Telaga community and were the Imperial guard of the Tanjore Nayaks. The nawabs of Hyderabad requested the Tanjore Nayaks to send a battalion of his best infantry and cavalry for his personal security. The Tanjore Nayak dispatched three hundred Telaga men and their families. The descendants of these three hundred families are now called Munnuru Kapu. The Munnuru Kapu's have always been associated with one Kingdom or the other in the form of Interior Palace Guards like Tanjore Nayaks, Patels, Devarakonda, and Nizam etc.

Over the years, Munnuru Kapus in the Telangana region of Andhra Pradesh acquired political dominance. As yet, they are a powerful electoral block in the region that makes or mars the prospects of parties eyeing for political power in the state. Munnuru Kapus are spread in 10 districts of the region. Agriculture is their main occupation. Though they gained significantly in terms of power politics – right from 1989 – they have often failed to capitalize on the development front. They were the most visible and articulate caste formulation in the 2004 and 2009 elections which were fought in the backdrop of prolonged agitation for a separate Telangana state by the Telangana Rashtra Samiti led by Velama leader K. Chandrasekhar Rao.

It is really strange then that most of the Munnuru Kapus residing in the rural areas are very backward economically and educationally. For lack of awareness, they could not make best use of the government schemes/projects for their overall development. Like the Yadavs of UP and Bihar, they remain at the bottom of human development index.

The agriculture crisis has forced many of the Munnuru Kapus to take to occupations like labour, goldsmith, carpentry etc. A majority of the population is poor though their leaders call the shots at the state capital. However, there is a growing feeling among the rural people to form caste associations to advance their socio-economic interests collectively and away from political glare. The idea of creamy layer is also taking ground among some of the sections of Munnuru Kapus who feel that the elite among their caste is making best use of government schemes/projects aimed at their development. Unless, this political assertion and awareness takes roots in the ordinary masses belonging to Munnuru Kapus, there can be no real social justice for them.

CONCLUSION

Caste formulations play a key role in the electoral politics of India, particularly so in the case of Andhra Pradesh. The Telangana region has a dynamic political nature with other backward classes competing between themselves for political hegemony. In contrast to the Yadavs of North India, Munnuru Kapus could not gain political power either on their own or on the strength of coalition of various social groupings. The MY (Muslim-Yadav) combination in Bihar and Uttar Pradesh was potent enough to bring political power to Lalu Prasad and Mulayam Singh. Such a combination could not be repeated in the Telangana region on the plank of self-respect and social justice. Also, the region is inherently feudal in nature with a dash of communal overtones. This political behavior is on account of the long Nizam rule. Unless, political assertion and awareness take roots at the base in Munnuru Kapus, there can be no real social justice and political empowerment for them.

Notes

1. Ramaiah, A (1992) "Identifying Other Backward Classes", *Economic & Political Weekly*, pp. 1203-1207.
2. *www.openthemagazine.com* (accessed 15th April 2010)

References

Acharya K.R. *Samakaleena Rajakeeyalu* (Telugu) Hyderabad: Priyadarshini Publications, 1991.

Ahmed, I & Saxena, N.C. Caste and Land and Political Power, Rawat Publications, Jaipur, 1999.

Almond Gabriel and Powell, G.B., Jr., Comparative Politics: *A Development Approach*, Bostan: Little Brown, 1966.

Bernstorff, Dagmar, Political Leadership in Andhra Pradesh: 1956-1973, in Pandey, B.N. (Ed.) -, Leadership in South Asia, Vikas Publishing House, New Delhi,1977.

Elliott, Carolyn M., "Caste and Faction Among the Dominant Caste: The Reddys and Kammas of Andhra", in R. Kothari (Ed.), Caste in Indian Politics, Orient Longman, New Delhi, 1970.

Ghanshyam Shah. Caste, Caste-conflict and Reservations, R. K. Publications, Bombay, 1980.

Ghurye G. S. *Caste and Race in India*, Bombay: Popular Prakashan Pvt. Ltd., 1979.

Kaka Kalelkar Commission Report, Government of India, New Delhi 1955.

Mandal Commission Report, Government of India Publications, New Delhi, 2000.

Hanumantha Rao. Party and Politics in Andhra Pradesh, (1956-2003), A. B. A. Publications, Hyderabad, 2005.

Kothari, Rajni. (Ed.), Caste in Indian Politics, Orient Longman, New Delhi. 1970.

Mathew George (Ed.), Shift in Indian Politics: 1983 Elections in Andhra Pradesh and Karnataka, Concept Publishing Company, New Delhi, 1984.

Ram Reddy, G. "Politics of Accommodation: Caste, Class and Dominance in Andhra Pradesh", in Francine R Frankel and M.S.A. Rao (ed.), Dominance and State Power in Modern India: Decline of Social Order, Vol. I, Oxford University Press, New Delhi.

Tirumali, Inkonda. Dora against Nizam, Peoples Movement in Telangana, Kanishka Publications, New Delhi, 2009.

AMBEDKAR AND EMANCIPATION OF DALITS: A CRITICAL ASSESSMENT

V. VIJAYA BHASKAR AND V. BHUMAIAH

The country today is beset with innumerable social, political problems and communal threatening the very existence and integrity of the millions. Particularly the Dalits, backward classes, minorities and powerless. It gives us an opportunity to examine and assess the great man like Ambedkar's contribution not only to his caste or group but also to the entire Indian Society. He was the champion of the cause of the oppressed and he fought for the social justice.

Ambedkar was an erudite and versatile person and one of the greatest builders of Modern India. He has been regarded as more than an institution - a social reformer, a redeemer, the lawmaker and so on. His socio - economic and political philosophy and his views on religious, economics and politics and his sermons are very much relevant even to the present time.

Ambedkar stood for the progressive transformation of the society, removing glaring social and economic inequalities. He opined that in Indian context political or religious exploitation is no less oppressive than economic exploitation.

The concept of economic development according to Ambedkar, means eradication of poverty, elimination of inequalities of income and means of production and to save the masses from exploitation. He preferred industrialisation with in the framework of the mixed economy, where state management and state ownership of industry were necessary. He opined that economic emancipation is the very foundation for the social progress.

Ambedkar always stood for the casteless and classless society but not stateless society. To him, a good state was that which guaranteed protection against internal disturbances, violence and disorder. He regards rights as natural and inherent in the individual.

For him the state existed only to prevent injustice, tyranny and oppression. Rights are protected not by law but by the social and moral conscience of society. He tried to seek harmony between the people and the legal powers of the state.

Religious awakening and social reform become the touchstones of his life mission. He opined that a developing society could not flourish with out a balance between the material and spiritual awakening. His program of Humanism is basically concerned with the emancipation of the oppressed classes of the society. The social humanism, which was the gospel of Ambedkar, aims at securing an integrated human personality as well as emotional integrated society. It implies to regard every human being as an end in himself with a right to his own development in his own way.

Ambedkar saw the Indian caste system as a serious obstacle in the path of democracy, equality and justice. Indian society was divided and graded on the basis of caste and therefore it is not democratic society. The caste system is a specifically Indian expression of institutionalised inequality and indignity. Untouchability is part and parcel of the caste structure. The abolition of this untouchability for securing human dignity is the significant step towards equality and social justice.

Ambedkar wanted the contradictions in Indian society to be removed at the earliest possible moment i.e., the contradictions between formal political equality on one side and the actual denial of social and economic equality on the other. Equality and justice were the key elements of his life and mission. Hence, the avoiding concern of Ambedkar for the principles of equality, justice, liberty and fraternity was enshrined in the preamble to the constitution of India.

The most important contribution of Ambedkar is the consistent and relentless struggle against the institution of caste. Several people have written on caste in India and Abroad. But none of them except Ambedkar has used it as a political weapon to fight against it.

Sharply reacting to the inhuman caste practices, Ambedkar affirmed that annihilation of caste is one way of achieving human emancipation for the Dalits. In India, even after 50 years of independence there are Scheduled caste people who live on the out skirts of the villages and towns. Though the untouchability has disappeared to some extent, yet prejudice against them is there for all to see. Ambedkar wants such a society where all people treated equally. No one is high or low simply because of the accident of birth in a particular caste. He said there could be the division of labour in society, but not the division of labourers in watertight compartment.

Ambedkar aimed at the reconstruction of society devoid of class and caste divisions, and free from dehumanisation. He stressed that the path shown by Buddha was the right path to achieve the cherished goal of social justice for all irrespective of birth, class or caste. The main object of his life was to bring social revolution. He wanted to break the system of Varna and caste so that every one gets the opportunity of self-development. For this he adopted a democratic and constitutional means. Therefore, his thinking was dominated by constitutional and democratic ideologies. He wanted to transform the political democracy into social democracy.

The social revolution was not for removing the disabilities to the particular class only, but to remove all the man-made barriers of caste by providing equal opportunities to all to rise to the highest position and making no distinction between man and man so for as civil rights are concerned. Ambedkar said that the movement stands for strength and solidarity, for equality, liberty and fraternity. He refused to be controlled and bound by the Shastras and Smrities composed in the dark ages and based his claims on Justice and humanity.

He launched a heroic, countrywide battle against the oppressive, in human features of Hindu society. He elevated the people, who were living a life worse than beasts, to human dignity. Ambedkar alone, though he a social leper, economically poor and political depressed, accomplished by his relentless struggle and supreme sacrifice. Ambedkar through all the available means worked for eradication of untouchability, casteism and repression of the lower caste. Ambedkar was truly a man of simplicity and greatness; by virtue of sheer hard and sustained work he rose to prominence in public life. He was greatly concerned with the living condition of the poorer sections of the society and hence championed for their rights self respect and dedicated his life for their upliftment and betterment.

Ambedkar's approach towards religion is not traditional one but rational, social and utilitarian. He believed that religion is necessary to govern the mind and behaviour of a man. To him, religion must mainly be a matter of principle only. It can not be a matter of rules. The Hindu religion he believes is a religion of rules, which practices caste system and untouchability. Hence he rejected Hinduism. He treated Hinduism as a mass of sacrificial, social, political and sanitary rules and regulations: all mixed up. To him religion must be judged by social standards based on social ethics.

He strongly believed that the religion which teaches man to behave with man in an inhuman manner, and a religion which does not recognise a human being as a human being and the religion in which the touch of human being pollutes is not a religion but the mockery of religion.

Ambedkar took the stand that religion must provide guidance in the major values and principles that should govern human relations. The religion should not only recognise the spiritual brotherhood of mankind, but also should recognise the dignity of the individual human being and his right to opportunity to growth. The religion should recognise the role of love and compassion but not one that preached paternalistic charity, which hurt human dignity. He formed these values and promise of rational action in Buddhism and he expected that reason and a universalistic set of moral values would guide this religion.

Ambedkar recognised that all human beings were not equal in all abilities, but there had a right to equal opportunity, social dignity and equality in civic and political life. Equality was the touchstone, which he applied to religion and the social order.

Ambedkar was not against the very existence of Hinduism, but was against its wrong ideals and the tenacity with which the Hindu leaders adhered to them. According to him Hinduism gave no support to social unity. Hinduism and social union is incompatible. Its traditional structure is the greatest obstacle to Hindu unity. Religious awakening and social reform became the touchstones of his whole thinking process.

According to him caste was incompatible with conversion, which dragged Hinduism into a religion of inequality. He wanted the Hindu society to be organised on two main principles; equality and the absence of casteism. He regarded that the caste system must be annihilated, because it was inhuman and detriment to the upward march of the Dalits. Ambedkar advised his people to struggle because "lost rights are never regained by begging and by appeals to the conscience of the usurpers, but by relentless struggle. He laid emphasis on the collective aspects of human life. He thought that the balance between material and spiritual awakening must be struck; as with out it a developing society could not flourish.

Ambedkar's social reform scheme i.e., abolition of caste and untouchability was an integral part of his radical religious out look. His emphasis was on reason and rationalism as against blind faith and superstitious practices and a sociological approach to religious problems. He carried out a relentless struggle for the social elevation, political liberation and the economic emancipation of the down trodden people.

His chief concern in life was to meet the challenge of wrongly idealised social relations, which threatened the whole of human existence and shook the foundations of a moral and just social order. His aim was not communal and limited to personal benefit, but it was essentially social and human, which was related to all who suffered from slavery, injustice, tyranny and exploitation. His purpose was practical rather than speculative and his philosophy of life was essentially a development and evolution under conditions and circumstances that prevailed in Indian society.

He broke the shackles of traditionalism, religious orthodox and blind superstitions of the Hindu society and looked every problem in a broader view of life and considered them collectively. He sacrificed his life for the dignity and upliftment of the oppressed. As a spokesman of ignored humanity, he created human rights for all and brings all men on socially equal plane. He stood for all scientific and artistic activities, which enhanced the cause of human progress and happiness.

Ambedkar could not tolerate the unjust social, economic religious and political environment, which had been holding humanity in clutches (fetters) for many centuries. He stood for human dignity and freedom, for simplicity, integrity, liberty, equality, social and economic justice, material prosperity and spiritual discipline and he was opposed to any social order or institutions or any practices which involved injustice, suppression, violence which stood as an obstacle for the development of the human personality.

He should be remembered not only as a great social reformer, a patriot, a vigorous champion of Justice and freedom but much more as a great constitution - maker that the nation could ever produce. His contribution to the making of constitution is undoubtedly of the highest order. Indeed he deserves to be called the father or the chief architect of the Constitution of India.

Ambedkar's contribution to the evolution of free India lies in his striking for secularizing Indian politics, State and society and his struggle for making out political, social and economic justice to one and all as a humanist. He breathed the sprit of liberalism and Nationalism into the lives of not only the Dalits but of all the Indians. His courage and conviction was something astounding, which would not bend him down to a compromise his principles. In his capacity as the chairman of the Drafting committee, he hammered out a comprehensive workable constitution into which he incorporated some of his strong views. He gave free India its legal frame work and the people the basis of their freedom. To this task his contribution was significant, substantial and spectacular.

Ambedkar's socio-economic and constitutional philosophy is reflected in the constitution of India. He played a significant role in making the constitution of India as a Sovereign, Democratic, Secular and Socialist Republic. The commendable service rendered by him in piloting the Draft constitution passing through the very rough and tough weather of the Constituent Assembly sessions, was universally acclaimed and acknowledged by all sections of India and in which he exhibited great erudition and skill in constitutional law and other related disciplines.

The constitution of India is committed to establish an Egalitarian Social order based on the principles of Equality and Liberty. It provides for a legal mandate in the form of Fundamental Rights (part-III) and Directive Principles of State Policy with a view to promote respect for Fundamental human rights such as Freedom of speech, Right of Equality, Right to Life and Liberty and to preserve and protect the Interests of Scheduled Castes and Scheduled tribes in order to ameliorate the conditions of the neglected sections in the Indian Society.

The very Preamble of the Constitution (stresses) echoes the Egalitarian principles of Social Justice, Equality, Liberty and Fraternity on the foundations of which the so-called Parliamentary democracy and Welfare State are built up. The V and VI schedule and Part XVI of the Constitution contain the provisions for the promotion of Welfare and well being of the Scheduled Tribes.

Ambedkar was a strong advocate of Federal structure of the union and states and staunch supporter of parliamentary democracy based on the principles 'Strong Centre' and 'Independent States' and the principles of social democracy. Ambedkar also did great service to the nation by proposing the institution of unified judicial system, uniformity in laws and common All India Services with a view to strengthen the National unity and Integrity.

It was his strong belief that Federalism would rest on a balance between the centre and the Federal units. What is needed according to Ambedkar is the interdependence, which creates harmony, orderly progress and prosperity.

He was also a strong advocate of parliamentary form of Government right from the inception of Government of India Act of 1935. He believed in the peaceful democratic methods of legislation, persuasion, discussion, consensus etc., as the most appropriate means for achieving socio-economic change. He firmly believed that the parliamentary system of Government alone could usher in an egalitarian society through the application of principles of social democracy such as socio-economic justice and equality amongst the people. Ambedkar was of the view that no democracy can function successfully without an active responsible opposition party. He also viewed that for the success of the parliamentary democracy, free and fair elections is needed. In the absence of any one of these, democracy degenerates into mobocracy and dictatorship in the name of democratic form of Government.

Ambedkar preferred parliamentary democracy as the best model suitable to conditions in India though he was conscious of the inherent defects in it. The major weakness of this system is that essential change like the realization of social and economic justice and equality cannot be expedited and promises made could be fulfilled only as a slow pace (or in a long run). This obviously leads to the discontentment and unrest among the people who may in turn revolt against the system. Therefore, watchful, vigilant public opinion and effective implementation of laws and responsible executive, committed legislature and impartial judiciary are very much essential to the success of parliamentary democracy. Then only it could bring socio-economic justice to the people.

He suggested that this Government should always struggle for the common good of all its citizens of the country irrespective of caste, creed or religion. He strongly believed that democracy of whichever type it may be would only survive when healthy conventions based on moral principles are evolved. To him, no democratic form of Government shall survive without observing the principles of constitutional morality.

This constitutional morality would also mean an effective coordination between conflicting interests of different people and the administrative co-operation to resolve them amicably without any confrontation amongst the various sections (groups) working for the realization of their ends at any cost. For Ambedkar, morality of the State, governance and the governed must be strong.

Ambedkar being influenced by western ideals like equality and egalitarianism rejected the basis of Hindu

Orthodoxy and preached the gospel of equality. Ambedkar espousing the cause of backward classes declared that caste inequality is man made rather than ordained by God. It was mainly because of his dramatization that of the cause of depressed classes, the Constitution included the policy of compensatory discrimination under the Fundamental Rights.

The most significant feature of the Fundamental Rights chapter is that these rights are made 'justifiable'. The right to move the Supreme Court for enforcement of Fundamental Rights under Article 32 is itself a Fundamental Right. Ambedkar suggested that without Article 32 the insertion of Fundamental Rights in the Constitution would have become meaningless, as rights are real only if remedies accompany them.

The another important contribution of Ambedkar is reflected in the protective discrimination scheme or the "Reservation Policy" of the Government envisaged under some provisions of Part III Fundamental Rights and many of Part IV provisions dealing with the constitutional mandate to ameliorate the conditions of the so called Scheduled Castes and Scheduled Tribes and the other Backward classes. With these provisions, Ambedkar contemplated that the oppressed classes could try selflessly to uplift their brethren and integrate themselves with the mainstream. He however thought that such reservations/ provisions must be able to protect the interests of the Scheduled Castes, Scheduled Tribes and other backward classes as a part of the society as a whole. Therefore, he made it his life mission to uplift these down trodden people from the unequal position of inferiority to that of an equal position of parity in socio-economic status with other so called high caste Hindus. It was for achieving this goal, the 'Reservation Policy' or the scheme of protective discrimination was advocated and achieved by him to ameliorate the conditions of the various depressed downtrodden sections of the Hindu Society.

Caste created a social order that was divisive in character resulting in fragmentation of the society. He emphasised that freedom in such a society would be impossible. Ambedkar was pointing to the very character of the Indian Society in which politics was nothing but "theology in action". Unless that was cast off and the society was secularised, representative government could not function at all. So long as this theological character of the society was preserved, the depressed classes needed to be protected by special safeguards.

Ambedkar was against the policy of a perpetual reservation system for the simple reason that it would perpetuate inferiority amongst the reserved categories who should develop themselves on the basis of self-reliance and self-help by developing self-confidence but not on the charity of somebody else. Reservation policy is (not a matter of charity but) a legal obligation on the part of the government to improve the conditions of the many innocent neglected sections of Indian people. Being a great humanist Ambedkar always stood for high standard of human values and dignity of human persons.

He had indomitable faith in democratic values, firm determination to emancipate the depressed classes, fraternal compassion with the suffering humanity, objective-oriented strategic policy. He however visualized a new social order based on liberty, equality and fraternity, in which every one would secure Justice. In his new society (social order) there would be neither castes nor classes.

He thought that the caste and class were bound by cause and effect relationship and believed that economic equality is not divine, but a direct natural consequence of exploitation of the weaker section by the priestly class or its protagonists. Therefore, he wanted to break the cast-property relations under his state socialism, which he was incorporated in the Constitution so that it could be beyond the reach of the privileged classes to abrogate it.

His towering personality could illuminate, influence and mould the politics in the contemporary India by his thoughts and deeds. Politics for him was a mission and not a trade. Politics is not poly-tricks for acquiring power, post, prestige and selfishness. He believed that politics must be value-oriented.

His political thought is not a speculation regarding Utopian ideal, but is an attempt to provide empirical solutions to the complex (vexed) problems of the society. He believed in rationally solving the problems. He utilized all his scholarship, intelligence and energy in endeavoring to solve the problems of the society confronted during his days. He inquires into the problems from objective point of view, analyses and interprets them rationally. He applies his inquisite mind to them and provides a right solution. He takes nothing for granted, absolute and final. Hence, his inquiry is exceptionally scientific.

To him all the institutions like state, government, constitution etc., are the means to achieve the end. As the end is good, means also must be good. He had utmost faith in constitutional means for achieving the ends. However he would not hesitate to resort to unconstitutional means when the constitutional means prove to be ineffective. He thought that means should be judged by utility in real perspective.

His thoughts were undoubtedly pragmatic and he has provided with a key of scientific inquiry to unlock and vexed problem and find a solution. His thoughts are based on the given situation. Hence, they are bound to change with the change in situation. Therefore, his thoughts cannot be treated as dogma, but a dynamic thought.

His thoughts on Abolition of untouchability eradication of poverty making a united and strong nation, solving the communal problem and so on were still very much relevant to the present situation. All most all the present communal, regional and economic problems owe their origin to inequality in the society. Therefore he stressed for the principles of liberty, equality and fraternity.

Ambedkar's thoughts would lose their original sense and spirit behind them if the interpretation of his thoughts were partial or improper. Hence, it is necessary to interpret his thoughts in their real perspective. While constructing his philosophy, one must take into account his whole life, the mission, thoughts and underlying spirit as well as the socio-political environment, in which he lived and reacted.

He gave to India a new vision, a new philosophy and a new way to march on to progress. His sincere efforts to bring himself up as the emancipator of untouchable and the series of his constructive and ameliorative programmes and demonstration to redeem from the grip of slavery and socio-economic and disabilities and his genuine interest in finding solutions to the vexed social wrongs of Indians society are the real bases to evaluate his political ideology.

He committed himself to instill and inculcate a spirit of self-respect and revolt in the minds of the Dalits to fight against the untold humiliation and injustice thrust on them. He focussed all his time, energy and resources to educate and organizes depressed classes to agitate against 'untouchability' and fight for Social Justice.

He gave a message to the people in general and the Scheduled Castes in particular that they should "Educate, Agitate and Organise". To him, there is no disaster parallel to ignorance. The mind properly educated would certainly agitate against all injustices and exploitation that prevails in the society.

According to him the untouchables were mostly landless labourers, semiserfs or engaged in the worst position of occupations. They suffered from two-fold evils namely, economic and social. Ambedkar wanted to fight against the old tyranny and oppression of caste Hindus and secure social equality for millions of untouchables.

Untouchables are the depressed classes, though a part of the Hindu religion has suffered persecution of all kinds for centuries. They were victims of suppressed class to a peculiar socio-political and religious persecution. If at all there was any class that needed immediate emancipation, it was these depressed classes. Ambedkar was the principal personality who deeply concerned with this task of emancipation. As a born untouchable he had experienced all humiliations to which his brethren were condemned by the Hindu society. The four fold classification of the Hindu society stood in the way of an integrated life and free development of a human personality. He realized that it was a deeply entrenched problem with a religious sanction behind it.

The Ambedkarian ideology is rapidly emerging as the counter to the upper caste dominant ideology and as a result of which Dalits and oppressed classes all over the country are awakened about their plight and rights. Ambedkar was ardently worked for justice to the Dalits and oppressed classes in a just society through secular politics.

In reality, Ambedkar was advocated an open society which would truly accord with the principles of democracy. He had made it amply clear that political and economic reform should be preceded by social reform in the social order. A just social order cannot be built on a defective base like the unreformed, traditional Hindu society. His approach to the problems was more scientific and comprehensive. He spoke pure politics by using terms like democracy, equality and justice. He left an indelible imprint on the minds of the Indian people both old and new generations and have carved out a place of their own in the history of India.

EMPOWERMENT OF TRIBALS IN ORISSA: ISSUES AND DIMENSIONS

BISHNU CHARAN CHOUDHURY

INTRODUCTION

Empowerment, a recently coined term, is a derivative word from 'power'. To empower means "to authorise" or "to give power". Empowerment is generally being interpreted as giving people power, but it is more appropriate to call it as "making people powerful". But empowerment as seen in its use in recent times does not reflect this meaning. Andre Beteille analysed empowerment from the sociological point of view. For him empowerment is about radical social transformation and can virtually be invoked in any context – in speaking about human rights, about basic needs, about economic security, about capacity building and skill formation or about the conditions of a dignified social existence. Thus, the idea of empowerment implies a certain theory of social change, in particular a change from a hierarchical to an egalitarian type of society and for an aristocratic to a democratic type of society. Empowerment is a process whereby constraints that impede equal participation are reduced. It also means gaining of knowledge and interest in politics of status and visibility of consciousness and confidence, and of awareness.

TRIBALS IN INDIA

The tribals are the indigenous[1] inhabitants of India. They constitute a disadvantaged sector of the Indian society.[2] Their political awareness is very low because of their poverty, illiteracy and social backwardness.[3] They have long been living in different parts of the country before the Aryans penetrated into India. The tribals have lived far away from the mainstream for centuries, in the relatively isolated, inaccessible, less fertile and less agriculturally productive region of forests, hills and mountains.[4] In the Indian context, 'tribe' has never been defined precisely and satisfactorily. It was used, at one time, to denote a bewildering variety of social categories that were neither analogous nor comparable. In the later usage, it referred only to the primitive groups and aboriginals. The term "Adivasi" ('Adi' – aboriginal and 'Vasi' – inhabitant) has become popular among certain people. The International Labour Organisation has classified such people as 'indigenous'. These tribal groups, for historical reasons, have remained socially and economically backward. The term *'Adivasi'*, *'Girijan'* and *'Vanyajati'* and so on are of recent origin. The administrators, lawyers and social scientists have taken different criteria, such as, the colour of the skin, social organisation, religion, customs, language, and habits etc. as the basis of their definitions. The Indian Constitution defines it under Clause 25 of Article 366 when it says "Scheduled Tribes mean such tribes or tribal communities or parts of or groups within such tribes or tribal communities as one deemed under Article 342 to be Scheduled Tribes for the purposes of this Constitution". India's tribes, therefore, have a social, cultural and legal identity. The tribal segment of the Indian population has been distinguished from other ethnic groups in terms of ecology, demography, economy, politics and other social behaviour. The anthropologists have traced certain common traits among the tribals such as the absence of the urge to acquire property, reluctance to do any more work than which is absolutely necessary, and their love for hunting, drinking and singing.[5]

Although "tribe" is customarily viewed as a dimension of African politics, one of the largest tribal populations in the world lives in India. The tribes of south and south-east Asia live on cultural margins of societies with great traditions. In language, religion, social structure, cultural outlook and their self-consciousness and identity they are apart from the larger societies in which they live.[6] There are 425 tribal pockets in the country. As per 1971 census the percentage of tribal population in India was 6.94 of the total population. The tribal population rose up to 8.19 per cent of the total population as per 2001 census. The percentage of male tribal population is 4.14 as against 4.05 of female. It is important to note that while tribals are a national minority in India, they constitute a majority of the population in several parts of the country.[7]

TRIBALS IN ORISSA: A PROFILE

Orissa occupies a unique position among the Indian States for her tribal concentration, next only to that of Madhya Pradesh, as per 1991 census.[8] However, as per the 2001 census its tribal population comes to 81,45,081 as against 1,22,33,474 of Madhya Pradesh and 85,77,276 of Maharashtra. The population of the Scheduled Tribes in the State is 22.13 per cent of the total population as per 2001 Census. There are 62 categories of tribes in Orissa. There are a few tribals, who have not been classified. The tribals reside in a contiguous belt. The districts of Mayurbhanj, Koraput, Malkangiri, Nowrangpur, Rayagada, Gajapati, Sundargarh, Keonjhar, Phulbani and Sambalpur have a high concentration of tribal population. The districts cut by Eastern Ghats and the Vindhya ranges have a large percentage of tribal population.[9] The diversity among the tribes is as kaleidoscopic as the non-tribal population. They are in various stages of development in economic, educational and cultural fields. Out of 62 tribes,

13 have been identified as primitive tribes in consideration of their pre-agricultural level of technology, low level of literacy and a stagnant or diminishing population.[10]

The sixty-two tribal communities that inhabit the state are widely different from one another in terms of demography, house pattern, dress and ornaments, economic life, social organisations and religious practices, plastic and performing arts and traditional crafts, language and degree of acculturation.[11] There are 15 major categories of tribes having a population of more than one lakh. They are: (1) Bhathudi, (2) Bhottuda or Dhotada, (3) Bhuiya or Bhuiyan, (4) Bhumiji, (5) Gondo, Gand, (6) Kharia or Kharian, (7) Khand or Kond and Nuguli Kondh, (8) Kisan, (9) Kolha, (10) Munda, Mahalis, Munda-Lohara Junda, (11) Oran, (12) Paraja, (13) Santal, (14) Saora, Sahara, Savar or Saura and (15) Shabar or Lodha.

District-wise S.T. Population in Orissa as per 2001 Census

Bargarh	1,29,546
Jharsuguda	1,59,757
Sambalpur	3,22,770
Deogarh	92,103
Sundargarh	9,18,903
Keonjhar	6,95,141
Mayurbhanj	12,58,459
Balasore	2,28,454
Bhadrak	25,141
Kendrapara	6,822
Jagatsinghpur	8,640
Cuttack	83,591
Jajpur	1,25,989
Dhenkanal	1,36,501
Anugul	1,32,994
Nayagarh	50,836
Khurda	97,186
Puri	4,482
Ganjam	90,919

Gajapati	2,63,476
Kandhamal	3,36,809
Boudh	46,557
Sonepur	52,978
Bolangir	2,75,822
Nuapada	1,84,221
Kalahandi	3,83,573
Rayagada	4,63,418
Nowrangpur	5,64,480
Koraput	5,85,830
Malkangiri	2,89,538

The Adivasis or the Scheduled Tribes of Orissa have been roughly classified ethnically into three groups: (i) Munda (Austric), (ii) Dravidian and (iii) Indo-Aryan. Some tribal communities are typical to Orissa as they are not found anywhere else. They are Juang, Bonda, Kutia, Dongria, Lanjia, Paudi Bhuyan, Didayi, Pengo, Jatapu, etc.

Distinct Identity

The tribes of Orissa have their distinct identity, which is overtly marked in their social organisation, language, culture, rituals and festivals, dress, ornaments, art and craft, beliefs and value judgements and the lifestyle. These things descended from antiquity have been preserved till date. On the other hand living with nature has taught them to love, respect, fear and worship the force of nature. The tribal societies share some common characteristics, which make them distinctly different from advanced complex societies.

PROBLEMS OF THE TRIBALS: ISSUES AND DIMENSIONS

During the pre-independence period, the British Government was inclined to leave the tribesmen alone. It was partly because of their perception that the task of carrying on administration in inaccessible areas would not only be difficult but unrewarding. This policy of partial exclusion of the tribal areas helped the tribals in preserving their distinctive lifestyle and cultural traits unaffected by the currents of change. But such a policy was not conducive for the growth and development of the tribal areas. The tribal areas of Orissa remained isolated from the rest of the areas. Later the policy of indirect rule of the British acted as an impediment to the participation of the tribals in the broader regional and national life. The tribal areas were excluded from the purview of normal administration and were kept under Special Agents. Thus the word 'Agency' came to be applied for tribal areas. The opening of tribal areas through the development of communication facilities by the British, have brought significant changes in these areas. The most important being the entry of non-tribals, who started as traders and settled down as exploiters. Another act of the British that affected the tribals was their Forest Policy, which largely restricted the utilisation of forests for various purposes. The oppressive role played by the local Zamindars and Muttadars, the exploitation of traders and moneylenders led to the indebtedness and land alienation in tribal areas.[12] The curbing of their rights on forest and the evil effects of contact had adversely affected their life pattern.

The Government of India Acts, 1919 and 1935 incorporated special provisions for administration of 'excluded areas' and 'partially excluded areas'. These special laws laid the emphasis on preserving peace and did not do much for protecting the economic interests of the tribals or uplift their condition. The tribals were subjected to a three-pronged exploitation by the chiefs or headmen of the villages, the non-aboriginal moneylenders and the petty officials. It may be noted here that Naba Krushna Choudhury, the former Chief Minister of Orissa, then as a member of the Partially Excluded Area Enquiry Committee, 1940 in the Minutes had recorded his note of dissent in the following words:

> The dismal story of *Bethi, Mamul, Gudam, Gothi,* etc. related in the report of the Committee sufficiently

demonstrate the unreality of the kind of the special protection of the aboriginal and backward tribes, in the name of which these tracts have so far been kept out of the purview of the popular legislatures and under the unlimited control of the Executive Officers responsible only to the British Government. The usual plea put forth in support of this policy of Special Protection has been that the interests of the aboriginal tribes are likely to be overlooked by the advanced people of the plains who constitute the majority in the Provincial Legislature. But how this policy has been worked out in practice? In the course of tours and investigations as members of the Committee we found as a matter of fact and history that backward tribes of the tracts under our enquiry had been left completely at the mercy of the non-aboriginal Mahārajas, Rajas, Hill Chiefs, Bisoyis, Patros, etc. and what appeared to me to be the worst aspect of thing is that whereas these non-aboriginal local overlords in the pre-British days had been often been kept in check in their dealings with the hill-tribes which were then quite militant, by the fear of a violent rising against them, the British Government removed that natural check on their capacity and medieval tyranny by making it abundantly clear to the tribes that the mighty British Government stood behind the chieftains and that they would be crushed in the name of law and order if they dared to rise against the latter. Naturally most of these tribes have been thoroughly emasculated in the process; but for a few Christian Missionaries and much few humanitarian officers, and tribesmen's contact with the people of the plains had not in the least improved their material and moral condition.[13]

Low Level of Literacy

It is a fact that the Scheduled Tribes of Orissa are in the lowest rung of literacy ladder. The female literacy rate is still very low as compared to male literacy. The difficulties that stand in the way of promoting education among the Scheduled Tribes are varied. For a tribal family, to send a boy or a girl to school is a matter associated with their economic conditions and involves dislocation in the traditional pattern of division of labour within the family. Many parents are, therefore, not inclined to send their children to schools.

Right to education in India enjoys the constitutional status. There is no denying the fact that education is a great liberating force without which one cannot earn a rightful place in society. Lack of education has hindered the occupational capability of the tribals. It has also kept them away from the modern system of communication, which can usher in modernisation. Most of the tribal children have not got the benefit of even primary education. It is because of poverty that tribals are not in a position to send their children to schools. On the other hand, the children are engaged to supplement the income of the family. Another handicap has been the medium of teaching. The tribal children find it difficult to be taught in Oriya language. So alternatively, the Government should take suitable steps to teach them in local languages like Santali, Kui and the like. The parents must also be made conscious of the benefit of education before they send their children to schools.

It is widely recognised that rapid spread of education among the tribals is one of the foremost requirements for their progress and development and in the ultimate analysis their assimilation into the mainstream of national life. Education would also help them to save them from exploitation and make them conscious of their constitutional rights and privileges. It would be difficult to break through the barriers of their age-old social customs, habits and superstitions unless they are educated.

Tribals and Linguistic Identity

The language of each community is an expression of its cultural tradition. The Indian tribal communities are classified into four broad categories according to the language they speak. They are (a) Indo-Aryan speakers, (ii) Dravidian speakers, (iii) Tibeto-Burmese speakers and (iv) Austric speakers. However, there are no Tibeto-Burmese speaking tribe in Orissa. Despite such linguistic diversity, there are striking socio-cultural similarities among the Odissi tribes. In Orissa about 30 tribes have their own dialects. The rest speak one of the regional Indo-Aryan dialects. Most of tribals are bilingual. They use their own language at intra-community level and the Indo-Aryan language at the inter-community level. Four of the tribal languages, namely, Santali, Soura, Ho and Kui have devised scripts for writing. Each language has its rich oral literacy tradition. Some written literatures have been created and published in the Ol-Chiki script of Santali and Soran Sompen script of Saora. Oriya has been made the medium of instruction all over the state. This to a large extent has prevented the learning process of the tribal child and become a hindrance to individual development at a faster pace.

WELFARE AND PROTECTIVE MEASURES FOR THE TRIBALS IN ORISSA

The first Congress Ministry (1937-39) of Orissa led by Biswanath Das appointed a Committee under the Chairmanship of A.V. Thakkar of the Harijan Sevak Sangh, an eminent freedom fighter and social worker to examine the laws, regulations governing the administration of the Partially Excluded Areas and "to recommend any special measures which may be deemed necessary in the interests of the aboriginal tribes in these areas and the agency by which such measures may be extended with particular reference to public health, medical aid and education and the cost thereof. The Committee was also to enquire into the abuse of *'bethi'* and *'beggari'* and to make recommendations as to the means by which they may be abolished". The Thakkar Committee in its report submitted in 1940 recommended the creation of a separate department of Government with a special staff. In 1947 a full-fledged department was created to deal with the backward classes kept under the charge of a Minister. The department was later renamed as Tribal and Rural Welfare Department to plan and carry out various measures of welfare on the lines recommended by the Thakkar Committee and Dr. Elwin.[14]

Since independence, there has been much emphasis on tribal development programmes. To improve the quality of life of tribal populations and to integrate them with the mainstream of Indian population, various development programmes were launched through different government agencies and departments. The schemes of the Government of Orissa for uplift of the aboriginals were broadly divided into three categories, namely, (1) economic uplift, (2) education and (3) public health. Under the economic uplift the main sub-heads were: (i) provision of land including settlement in colonies, (ii) restoration of land taken from aboriginals by the non-aboriginals, (iii) relieving indebtedness, (iv) stoppage of all forms of exploitation including *Gothi, Bethi* and *Mamuls,* (v) establishment of organisations to sell cheap, ordinary articles required by the communities and purchase from them their produce at fair rates, (vi) encouragement of cottage industries and (vii) providing industrial employment in mines and large-scale industries in tribal areas.

Tribal Developments in the Post-Independence Period

In the post-independence period the Government of Orissa had taken action in solving some of the problems faced by the tribals. *Bethi* or forced unpaid labour was discontinued. Steps were taken by legislation to eradicate the *Gothi* system of labour; and *Mamuls* i.e. the customary payment made to Patros and Bisoyis in the Ganjam Agency were also discontinued. Action was taken to stop transfer of land from hillman to non-hillman. The Agency Tracts Interest and Land Transfer Act, 1948 was enforced with suitable modifications to serve this purpose. In cases where such transfers have been legally made in the past, steps were taken to restore such lands to the original tribal owners. The officers of the Revenue Department were instructed by the State Government to give top priority to hillmen in the matter of leasing out wastelands.

Scheduled Areas in Orissa

The Scheduled Area[15] of the State accounts for 44.7% of the State's geographical area. It comprises the entire district of Mayurbhanj, Koraput (undivided), Sundargarh, Kandhamal, Balliguda and G. Udayagiri Tahasil of Phulbani district. R. Udayagiri Tahasil, Gunna and Rayagada blocks, Sorada tahasil, excluding Gazabadi and Gochha Panchayats of Ganjam district, Kuchinda tahasil of Sambalpur district, Telkoi, Keonjhar, Champua and Barbil Tahasils of Keonjhar district, the Rampur and Lanjigarh blocks of Kalahandi and Nilgiri block of Balasore district.

Tribal Development Blocks

In the early 1950s the normal Community Development Programme made some impact on the economic development of the tribal communities. It was, however, found that the tribal areas required intensive treatment due to prolonged neglect in the past. This led to the formation of Tribal Development Blocks. Out of 314 Blocks in the State, 75 Blocks were identified as Tribal Development Blocks.

Tribals and Legal Protection

There are several welfare regulations made by the State Government to protect the tribals. These are:

- The Orissa Scheduled Areas Transfer of Immovable Property (by Scheduled Tribes) Regulation, 1956, briefly called Orissa Regulation 2 of 1956. It was promulgated on 1st October 1956. An amendment declaring a transfer of immovable property in favour of a female member of a Scheduled Tribe who is married to a person not belonging to Scheduled Tribe was made with effect from the 22nd January 1977 to check fraudulent transfers.

- The Orissa (Scheduled Areas) Debt Relief Regulation, 1967, briefly called Regulation 1 of 1968 (to provide relief from indebtedness).
- The Orissa (Scheduled Areas) Moneylender's Regulation, 1967 briefly called Regulation 2 of 1968 (To control and regulate money-lending).

Besides, there are other general laws which are in force for protecting the interests of the tribals in respect of land and labour and against exploitation.

- Orissa Moneylenders Act, 1939.
- Orissa Agency Rules (Orissa Amendment) Regulation, 1946.
- The Agency Tracts Interest and Land Transfer (Orissa Amendment) Act, 1948.
- The Minimum Wages Act, 1948.
- The Orissa Debt Bondage Abolition Regulation, 1948 (Applicable to the Ganjam Agency Tracts and Koraput District excluding Kashipur Tahasil).
- The Protection of Civil Rights Act, 1955.
- Orissa Land Reforms Act, 1960.
- The Orissa Cooperative Societies Act, 1962.
- The Orissa Land Reforms Act, 1964.
- The Orissa Reservation of Vacancies in Posts and Services (for the Scheduled Castes and Scheduled Tribes) Act, 1975.
- The Orissa Legal Aid to the Poor Rules, 1975.
- The Bonded Labour System (Abolition) Act, 1976.
- The Protection of Civil Rights Rules, 1977.
- The Scheduled Castes and Scheduled Tribes (Prevention of Atrocities) Act, 1989.
- The Protection of Human Rights Act, 1993.

- The Panchayats (Extension to the Scheduled Areas Act), 1996 (PESA), which *inter alia* provides the following:
  - (a) Substantial power to the Scheduled Tribes with regard to resource management and self-governance.
  - (b) Gram Sabhas are empowered to preserve their cultural identity, community resources, modes of dispute resolution and the right to approve government plans, programmes and projects within their jurisdiction.
  - (c) Gram Sabhas have to be consulted before acquiring land for development in the Scheduled Areas.

Tribal Sub Plan Approach

The Tribal Sub Plan (TSP) aims at the integrated approach and development of tribal areas, in which all the programmes of the government irrespective of their sources of funding operate in unison with a view to bring the area at par with the rest of the State and for welfare and development of Scheduled Tribes. In Orissa, there are 21 Integrated Tribal Development Agencies (ITDAs) which cover 55.46 lakh tribals. Beyond the Scheduled Area, there are 46 Modified Area Development Approach (MADA) pockets and 14 Clusters. Besides, there are 17 micro projects, which have been functioning for the all-round development of 13 primitive tribal groups. The effective implementation of these projects/programmes will go a long way in ensuring the socio-economic development of the tribals.

73rd Amendment Act: A Step in the Direction of Empowerment of Tribals

In December 1992 the Indian Parliament passed a new amendment to the Indian Constitution to revive and revitalise the Panchayati Raj. This amendment gave a constitutional mandate for democratically elected Panchayats at the village, district and intermediary levels in the whole country. The

73rd Constitutional Amendment Act of 1993[16] ushered in a new era in the political and social transformation of India. The amendment made provisions for delegation of substantial powers to villages, which hitherto were under the stringent control of both the union and state governments. This legislation introduced reforms to the moribund Panchayati Raj institutions. Even though Panchayati Raj institutions have existed since independence, they were for all practical purposes non-functional because of lack of functional autonomy. Under 73rd amendment, elections were made mandatory every five years. There were provisions of 33 per cent reservation of seats for the women, the Scheduled Castes and the Scheduled Tribes and other backward castes in proportion of their population. The 73rd Amendment was a step in the right direction by the government for empowerment of the people. The government felt that a democratic framework at the local level was indispensable for responsive administration. People at the grassroots level should be elected to manage their affairs through democratic decentralisation of power.

PROBLEMS ASSOCIATED WITH DISPLACEMENT

The forced displacement for the purposes of various development projects, such as big dams, large industrial or mining projects, highways and flyovers, and so on, has been going on in India for a very long time. The instrument of displacement was the Land Acquisition Act, 1894, under which private land could be acquired by the State for a 'public purpose'. A study at the national level reveals that there are about 19 lakh cases of alienation of land which have been officially reported by 2001. However, restoration has been effected only in four lakh cases.[17]

The development projects particularly the major irrigation projects and setting up of major industries have invariably resulted in the displacement of tribal people from their land in which they have lived for generations. This problem had surfaced in the recent years in Kashipur in Rayagada district where the proposal for setting up of some industries is in progress.[18] In Kalinga Nagar in Jajpur district, 12 tribals were killed in police firing on January 2, 2006 while demanding for stoppage of construction of boundary wall for a proposed 6 Million Tonne Steel Plant by the Tata Steel. The tribals of Kalinga Nagar have been demanding proper rehabilitation for those who lost land and homes to industries. In Kalinga Nagar under the banner of *Visthapan Virodhi Janamanch*, the tribals started their agitation. They are being supported by some civil society organisations. Those supporting the agitation have been demanding, suspension of industrial activities in the area; immediate cessation of land acquisition; proper rehabilitation to those displaced by earlier development projects and immediate withdrawal of mining concessions given to private parties.

The problem of project displacement was never paid any attention in the past. In recent years, however, the problem has come to the forefront as most of the sanctioned industries are proposed to be located in the tribal dominated areas. The large-scale mining activities in the State have adversely affected the tribals. Most of the iron-ore mines and deposits are located in the tribal dominated districts of Keonjhar and Sundargarh. Due to continuous mining activities, the tribal people of these districts have lost their homes and with the destruction of forests and water sources, their livelihood. The tribal people never made any organised protest in the past, as most of the projects were done in the name of greater public good. The threat of displacement and its consequences forced them to oppose new industries. The resentment became acute as more and more companies and monopoly houses evinced interest in setting up their industries/ projects.

A survey reveals that about 2 million people have been displaced by development projects in the State between 1951 and 1995, of whom 40 per cent were tribal people. About 25 per cent of the displaced people were never resettled. The project managers and the authorities have been totally insensitive to the issues of displacement, rehabilitation and resettlement.

In the present context, the industrialisation and major projects in certain tribal belts of Orissa has affected the tribals. These measures of development have resulted in uprooting the tribal villages, loss of traditional occupation and land. While it is not desirable to halt the process of development, the government must contemplate built-in safeguards for the interests of the tribals in these areas. Measures should be taken to stop further encroachment on tribal land and exploitation of tribal resources. Steps have to be devised to accelerate the process of smooth transformation. A proper policy of relief, rehabilitation and resettlement for the displaced tribals must be formulated and implemented. It may be noted here that in the event of their displacement, they must be given reasonable and adequate compensation. They must be shifted and resettled in an alternative site. Land with assured irrigation facilities and with Record of Right (*Patta*) should be provided to them. The landless tribals must also be provided means of subsistence through employment in project activities. The rehabilitation of tribal people should have a forest bias. The concerns of those tribals who are adversely affected must be addressed in a fair, humane and equitable manner.

Resettlement and Rehabilitation Policy, 2006

Orissa is regarded as the pioneering state in respect of formulation of Resettlement and Rehabilitation Policy, 2006. It contained a number of provisions which addresses most of the critical areas of concern that have been raised by different stakeholders and also the displaced people. The main aim of this policy is to ensure sustained development through a participatory and transparent process. The basic objectives of the policy are:

- to avoid displacement wherever possible and minimise it exercising available options otherwise.

- to organise voices of displaced communities emphasizing the needs of the indigenous communities and vulnerable sections.
- to ensure environmental sustainability through participatory and transparent process and
- to help guiding the process of developing institutional mechanism for implementation, monitoring, conflict resolution and grievance redressal.

FORESTS AND TRIBAL LIFE AND ECONOMY

Forests are intimately connected with tribal life and economy. To a vast majority of the tribal people, the forest is their well-loved home, their livelihood, and their very existence depends on forests. Apart from the forest usufruct and fuel obtained by the tribal, the minor forest produce is second only to the agriculture produce for the sustenance of the tribals. In the category of minor forest produce fall various items like Kendu leaf, Siali leaf, broomsticks, medicinal herbs, honey, resin, myrobalam, tamarind, arrow-root, Sal, Karanj and Kusum seeds. In some parts of the State, the tribals have also taken to sericulture of *Asan* trees. The Kendu leaves provide them considerable employment from January to June every year. Mohua flower is collected abundantly during February to April and is used for food and liquor. Tribals enjoyed the freedom to use forest products or hunt animals from time immemorial and this has given them a conviction that remains even today deep in their hearts that the forests belong to them. This state of affairs continued till the middle of 19th century. The gradual extension of authority of the government and interference of people from outside had an impact on the tribals and disturbed the tribal economy. It affected all those tribals not primarily dependent on agriculture. They were forced to engage themselves in cultivation. It is also pertinent to note that the tribals, who had inherited rich forest and had adjusted their life patterns on this resource-base, are now finding it more and more difficult to sustain it in view of increase in their population.

The forest wealth is being over-exploited. This has caused serious shortfall in the supply of forest-based items, which used to meet various needs of the tribals. This has resulted in socio-economic dislocation. By 2000, India's recorded forest cover was 76.52 million hectares, which included 14.8 million hectares of protected areas and national parks. The remaining 61 million hectares of forest land includes approximately 14 million hectares of degraded forest lands. Predominant causes for India's dwindling forest wealth have been identified as explosion of human and livestock population, over-exploitation, over-grazing, illegal encroachments, unsustainable practices, forest fires and indiscriminating use of forest areas for development projects. In 1981 the total forest cover area of Orissa was 59,963 square kilometres, which was 38 per cent of the entire area of the State and 8 per cent of the total forest cover of the country. By 1997 it was reduced to 58,135.47 square kilometres. The loss of forest cover has many environmental consequences, such as, depletion of soil fertility, deepening of aquifers, dysfunctionality of the tradition system of irrigation, loss of birds etc. The tribals have shown great adaptability to the environment around them.[19]

Policy of Sustainable Development

The latter part of 1980s saw the shift of focus towards sustainable development, in which the link between social and environmental concerns was much more forcibly articulated. The 1988 Forest Policy explicitly recognised the linkages between the tribals and forests and the need to involve tribal communities in the management of forests. It also emphasised that domestic requirements of firewood, fodder and minor forest produce should be the first priority of forest management, not commercial or industrial needs. Subsequently, the 1990 Government Order on Joint Forest Management (JFM), while giving communities adjacent to reserved forests usufruct rights, was also aimed at improving the protection of forests.

Scheduled Tribes and Traditional Forest Dwellers (Recognition of Forest Rights) Act, 2006

The Scheduled Tribes and Traditional Forest Dwellers (Recognition of Forest Rights) Act, 2006 is a piece of landmark legislation in independent India which recognises and vests forest rights and occupation in forest land to forest dwelling Scheduled Tribes and other traditional forest-dwellers who have been residing there for generations, but whose rights could not be recorded. This would undo the historical injustice done to the forest dwelling Scheduled Tribes. The other highlights of the Act are: [20]

- It provides for recognition of forest rights of other traditional forest-dwellers provided they have for at least three generations prior to 13.12.2005 primarily resided in and have depended on the forest or forest land for *bona fide* livelihood needs. A "generation" for this purpose would mean a period of 25 years.
- The cut-off date for the recognition and vesting of forest rights under the Act will be 13.12.2005.
- It provides for the ceiling of occupation of forest land for purposes of recognition of forest rights to the area under actual occupation and in no case exceeding an area of four hectares.
- It provides for conferring rights in the national parks and sanctuaries also, renamed as "critical wildlife habitat" on a regular basis.
- It provides for the right to hold and live in the forest land under individual or common occupation for habitation or for self-cultivation for livelihood by a member or members of a forest-dwelling Scheduled Tribe or other traditional forest-dwellers.
- It recognises the right of ownership access to collect, use, and dispose of minor forest produce which has been traditionally collected within or outside village

boundaries. The Act has defined the term minor forest produce to include all non-timber forest produce of plant origin, including bamboo, brush wood, stumps, cane, tussar, cocoons, honey, wax, lac, tendu or kendu Leaves, medicinal plants and herbs, roots and tubers.

- It recognises the right to *in situ* rehabilitation including alternative land in cases where Scheduled Tribes and other traditional forest-dwellers have been illegally evicted or displaced from forest land of any description without granting their legal entitlement to rehabilitation prior to 13.12.2005.
- It provides for the forest right relating to the government providing for diversion of forest land for the purpose of schools, hospitals, *anganwadis*, drinking water supply and water pipelines, roads, electric and telecommunication lines, etc.
- The rights conferred under the Act shall be heritable but not alienable or transferable and shall be registered jointly in the name of both the spouses in the case of married persons and in the name of the single head in the case of a household headed by a single person, and in the absence of a direct heir the heritable right shall pass on to the next of kin.
- It provides that no member of a forest-dwelling Scheduled Tribe or other traditional forest-dwellers shall be evicted or removed from forest land under his occupation until the recognition and verification procedure is completed.
- Under this Act the Gram Sabha has been designated as the competent authority for initiating the process of determining the nature and extent of individual or community forest rights or both that may be given to the forest-dwelling Scheduled Tribes.

POLITICAL PARTICIPATION AND REPRESENTATION OF TRIBALS

A study of the political participation of the tribals of Orissa suggests that many tribals have not only been elected to the Parliament but also to the State Legislative Assembly since 1951-52. They have occupied different positions in the power structure. Two tribal leaders could become the Chief Ministers of the State. It may be noted here that Juel Oram from Orissa has to his credit is the first among the tribal to become a Union Minister of the Cabinet rank since Independence. The details are given below:

As Chief Ministers

Hemananda Biswal	7.12.89 to 4.3.90:	2 months 27 days
	6.12.99 to 5.3.2000:	2 months 29 days
Giridhar Gamang	17.2.99 to 6.12.99:	9 months 19 days

As Union Ministers

Name	*Status*	*Period*	*Portfolio(s)*
C.P. Majhi	Deputy Minister	17.10.74 to 3.1.76	Petroleum & Chemicals
		3.1.76 to 24.3.77	Chemicals & Fertilisers
Giridhar Gamang	Deputy Minister	1982	Supply & Rehabilitation
	Deputy Minister	1982-83	Labour
	Deputy Minister	1985-88	Welfare
	Minister of State	1988	Tourism
	Minister of State (Ind.)	1988-89	Communication
	Minister of State (Ind.)	1991-93	Food Processing Industry.
	Minister of State (Ind.)	1993-94	Planning and Programme Implementation
	Minister of State (Ind.)	1995-96	Mines
Bhagey	Minister of State	1989-90	H.R.D.
Gobardhan	Minister of State	1990	H.R.D.
Juel Oram	Cabinet Minister	1998-99	Tribal Welfare
	Cabinet Minister	1999-2000	Tribal Welfare

As Cabinet Ministers in Orissa

Name	*Year*	*Portfolios*
Sonaram Soren	1946	T & R.W., Labour and Commerce
Sonaram Soren	1954	T & R.W., Labour and Commerce
Toyaka Sanganna	1963	T & R.W.
Toyaka Sanganna	1965	T & R.W., Excise, Revenue (Regn.)
Toyaka Sanganna	1967	T & R.W.
Man Mohan Tudu	1967	T & R.W.
Kartik Chandra Majhi	1967	U.D., Works, Transport, P.H. (E)
Gangadhar Pradhan	1967	Home (Jail), Agriculture (Animal Husbandry and Fisheries)
Sidhalal Murmu	1971	Labour, Employment and Housing
Gangadhar Pradhan	1971	Forests & Animal Husbandry
Rama Chandra Ulaka	1975	Tribal and Rural Welfare
Rama Chandra Ulaka	1976	Food & Civil Supplies
Bhagiratha Gomango	1976	H & F.P.
Ghasiram Majhi	1979	T & R.W., Health & Family Welfare
Rama Chandra Ulaka	1980, 1981, 1984	Harijan and Tribal Welfare
	1989	Irrigation and Power (Hemananda Biswal Ministry)
Dambaru Majhi	1989	H & T Welfare
C.P. Majhi	1990	Education and Y.S.
Ghasiram Majhi	1990	Health & F.W.
Hemananda Biswal, Deputy Chief Minister	1995	P.R., Housing, Public Grievances & Pension Administration.
Rama Chandra Ulaka	1995	Forest, School and Mass Education
Rama Chandra Ulaka	1998	Welfare
Gajadhar Majhi	1999	ST & SC Development
Saraswati Hembram	1999	Women & Child Development
Gajadhar Majhi	1999	S.T. & S.C. Development and Minorities and Backward Classes Welfare.
Saraswati Hembram	1999	Women and Child Development
Mangala Kishan	2000	S.T. & S.C. Development and Minorities and Backward Classes Welfare.

Mangala Kishan	2002	Water Resources
Mangala Kishan	2004	Water Resources
Golak Naik	2004	Fisheries & Animal Resource Development, Textiles and Handlooms
Bijay Ranjan Singh Bariha	2009	ST & SC Development, Minorities & Backward Classes Welfare

N.B.: Besides, many other tribal MLAs have been taken as Minister of State (Independent Charge), Minister of State and Deputy Ministers in various Ministries.

Women Ministers in different Ministries of Orissa

Name	*Year*	*Status*	*Portfolios*
Saraswati Hembrum	1981 to 1985	Deputy Minister	C.D. & P.R.
Frida Topno	1985	Minister of State	Fisheries & A.H.
Frida Topno	1986	Minister of State	Education, Sports & Youth Services
Parama Pujari	1986	Deputy Minister	Harijan & T.W.
Saraswati Hembrum	1986	Deputy Minister	C.D. & P.R.
Frida Topno	1989	Minister of State	Education & Y.S.
Saraswati Hembrum	1989	Minister of State	C.D. & P.R.
Parama Pujari	1989	Deputy Minister	Health & F.W.
Saraswati Hembrum	1999	Cabinet Minister	Women & Child Dev.
Parama Pujari	1999	Minister of State	R.D. & P.R.
Saraswati Hembrum	1999	Cabinet Minister	Women & Child Dev.
Parama Pujari	1999	Minister of State	S.T. & S.C. Development & Minorities and Backward Classes Welfare
Draupadi Murmu	2000	Minister of State (Independent charge)	Commerce and Transport

Deputy Speaker of State Legislative Assembly

Prahallad Dora 1990-95 and 2004

Lal Bihari Himirika 2009 (continuing)

Organisational Responsibility

Giridhar Gamang	President, PCC
Hemananda Biswal	President, PCC
Sushila Tiriya	General Secretary, PCC and Joint Secretary, AICC.
Gasiram Majhi	Secretary, Swatantra Party State Unit
Raghunath Hembrum	President, Orissa Unit of All India Jharkhand Party
Juel Oram	President, BJP State Unit.

The tribal MLAs have expressed their desire to fulfil the following objectives:[21]

- Tribal development and upliftment.
- Social reforms among the tribals.
- Modernise the tribals and to acquaint them with modern culture and civilisation.
- Removal of social evils from tribal communities.
- Safeguard social customs of the *Adivasis*.
- Promote *Adivasi* welfare activities.
- Development and promotion of tribal languages
- Promote and protect tribal culture.
- Establish educational institutions to educate the tribals.
- Expand facilities of education of tribal women.
- Enforce Family Planning and Prohibition.
- Eradication of Illiteracy.
- Campaign against dowry.
- Write Articles on life and culture of the *Adivasis*.
- Facilitate socio-economic transformation of the tribal communities.
- Fight against corruption
- Create awareness against liquor
- Fight against sexual exploitation of tribal women.
- Elimination of poverty among the *Adivasis*.

Tribals who won from the General Constituencies:

Bijay Ranjan Singh Bariha	-	Padmapur.
Dhaneswar Majhi	-	Kesinga
Duryodhan Majhi	-	Khariar
Surendra Singh Bhoi	-	Saintala
Ghasiram Majhi	-	Nawapara

Major Tribal Communities who won in different Elections to the State Legislative Assembly and both the Houses of Parliament:

The leaders of the following tribal categories who won in different elections are: Santal, Kandha, Gond, Sabar, Kolha, Kisan, Bhatudi, Paraja, Bhatoda, Bhuyan and Oram.

A study on the political recruitment of the tribal leaders reveals that they have joined the active politics through the following movements/organisations:

- Freedom Movement.
- Jharkhand Movement
- Panchayati Raj Institutions.
- Adivasi Students Association.
- Adivasi Sangha
- Congress Seva Dal.

Besides, some of them left the Government and non-Government jobs to join active public life.

The following tribal women have been elected as MPs and MLAs:

MP (Lok Sabha)

Name	Constituency
Frida Topno	Sundergarh
Sushila Tiriya	Mayurbhanj
Hema Gamang	Koraput

MP (Rajya Sabha)

Sushila Tiriya

MLAs

Name	Constituency
Saraswati Hembrum	Kuliana
Parama Pujari	Umerkote
Phulamani Santa	Dabugam
Chandrama Santa	Pottangi
Frida Topno	Raghunathpalli
Mamata Madhi	Chitrakonda
Draupadi Murmu	Rairangpur
Bhagabati Pujari	Kodinga
Hema Gamang	Gunupur
Ajayanti Pradhan	G. Udayagiri
Sarojini Hembram	Bangiriposi

Tribal Representation (Rajya Sabha)

C.P. Majhi

Debananda Amat

Chandra Mohan Singh

Birabhadra Singh

Bhagirathi Majhi

Mangala Kisan

Academic Profile

A study of the academic profile of the tribal leaders reveals that some of them are highly qualified. The details are as follows:

Damburu Majhi	B.A., LL.B.
Kartik Chandra Majhi	B.A., LL.B.
Arjun Singh	B.A., B.Ed.
Sonaram Soren	B.A., B.L.

Bhage Gobardhan	B.Sc. (Hons.), M.Sc. (Technology), IAS (June 1963).
Rama Chandra Ulaka	B.Sc.
Frida Topno	B.A., B.Ed.
Raghunath Hembrum	M.A.
Mangala Kissan	B.A.
Durjyodhan Majhi	B.A.
Gajadhar Majhi	B.Sc., B.Ed.
Jadav Majhi	M.A.
Laxman Majhi	M.A., LL.B.
Sudam Marandi	B.A.
Ajey Murmu	B.Com.
Sadan Nayak	M.A., LL.B.
Juel Oram	Diploma (Elec. Engineering)
Bijay Ranjan Singh Bariha	M.A. CPS (JNU, New Delhi)
Padma Charan Haiburu	M.A.
Haldhar Karjee	M.A., LL.B.
Mamata Madhi	B.Sc., Diploma in Computer Sc.
Saharai Oram	B.A.
Ignace Majhi	M.A., LL.B., Bar-at-Law (London)
Dr. Giridhar Gamang	B.A., Doctor of Science (Hony.)

Tribal Leadership: An Elitist Orientation

A study on the political participation and representation of the tribals in Orissa suggests that there is an elitist orientation. Many of the tribal politicians have been elected several times to the Parliament and the State Legislature.

Elected more than once as MP (Lok Sabha)

Giridhar Gomang	1972, 1977, 1980, 1984, 1989, 1991, 1996, 1998, 2004
T. Sangama	1951-52, 1957
Rama Chandra Ulka	1962, 1967
Khagapati Pradhani	1967, 1971, 1977, 1980, 1984, 1989, 1991, 1996, 1998
Debananda Amat	1967, 1977, 1989
Salkhan Murmu	1998, 1999
Bhage Gobardhan	1989, 1991
Man Mohan Tudu	1971, 1980
Frida Topno	1991, 1996
Juel Oram	1998, 1999, 2004
Govinda Munda	1977, 1989, 1991
Parsuram Majhi	1999, 2004

Elected more than once as MLA

Hemananda Biswal	Man Mohan Tudu
Ghasiram Majhi	Gangadhar Madhi
Rama Chandra Ulaka	Gangadhar Pradhan
Bhagirathi Gomanga	Chotray Majhi
Saraswati Hembram	Jagateswar Mirdha
Parama Pujari	Frida Topno
Jayaram Pangi	Dambarudhar Ulaka
Basudev Majhi	Raghunath Hembram
Gajadhar Majhi	Mangala Kissan
Duryodhan Majhi	Juel Oram
Jadav Majhi	Nagarjun Pradhan
Prahallad Dora	Haladhar Karjee
Ananta Ram Majhi	Golak Naik
Govinda Munda	Saharai Oram
Gopal Pradhan	

Tribal Representation in Different Ministries in Orissa

Year	*Ministry*	*Chief Minister*	*CabinetMinisters including CM*	*State (Ind.)*	*State*	*Deputy*	*Total Strength*
1946	Congress	H.K. Mahtab	4(1)	-	-	5	09
1954	Congress	N.K. Choudhury	6(1)	-	-	7	13
1956	Congress	H.K. Mahtab	4	-	-	5	09
1957	Congress	H.K. Mahtab	10	-	-	4(2)	14
1959	Congress	H.K. Mahtab	11	-	-	-	11
1961	Congress	Biju Patnaik	7	-	-	-	07
1963	Congress	Biren Mitra	9(1)	-	-	5(2)	14
1965	Congress	Sadasib Tripathy	7(1)	-	-	7(1)	14
Mar. 1967	Swa-J.C.	R.N. Singh Deo	14(3)	-	-	5(2)	19
Sept. 1967	-do-	R.N. Singh Deo	12	-	-	7(4)	19
Aug. 1969	-do-	R.N. Singh Deo	14(3)	-	-	5(2)	19
1971	Swa-U.C. & Jharkhand	Biswanath Das	14(2)	-	-	12(5)	26
1972	Congress	Nandini Satapathy	9(1)	-	5(2)	1	15
1974	Congress	Nandini Satapathy	6	-	8(2)	3(1)	17
1975	Congress	Nandini Satapathy	7(1)	-	8(1)	3(1)	18
1976	Congress	Binayak Acharya	9(2)	-	4	1	14
1977	Janata	Nilamani Routray	9	-	6(4)	-	15

contd. next page

Year	Ministry	Chief Minister	CabinetMinisters including CM	State (Ind.)	State	Deputy	Total Strength
1979	-do-	Nilamani Routray	12(1)	-	13(5)	-	25
1980	Congress	J.B. Patnaik	8(1)	-	10(1)	1(1)	19
1981	Congress	J.B. Patnaik	7(1)	-	10(1)	1(1)	18
1984	Congress	J.B. Patnaik	7(1)	-	8(1)	1(1)	16
1985	Congress	J.B. Patnaik	6	-	10(4)	-	16
1986	Congress	J.B. Patnaik	9	-	12(4)	2(2)	23
1989	Congress	Hemananda Biswal	8(3)	-	15(3)	2(1)	25
1990	Janata	Biju Patnaik	14(2)	-	11(5)	1	26
Jan. 1991	Janata	Biju Patnaik	22(2)	-	15(6)	-	37
1995	Congress	J.B. Patnaik	12(1)DCM	4	5(1)	-	21
1998	Congress	J.B. Patnaik	15(1)	9(2)	5(1)	-	29
1999	Congress	Giridhar Gamang	13(2)	5(1)	9(3)	-	27
1999	Congress	Hemananda Biswal	14(2)	8(1)	9(2)	-	31
2000	BJD-BJP	Naveen Patnaik	15(1)	6(2)	4(1)	-	25
2002	-do-	Naveen Patnaik	14(1)	6(1)	4(2)	-	24
2004	-do-	Naveen Patnaik	15(1)	7(1)	-	-	22
2009	BJD	Naveen Patnaik	12(1)	9(1)	-	-	21

Note: Number of Tribal Ministers of different categories has been mentioned in the brackets.

A study on the tribal political participation and leadership pattern has the following inferences:

- The old *Garhjats* covering the undivided districts of Bolangir, Kalahandi, Sundargarh and also the district of Koraput with concentration of the tribals were the citadel of the Ganatantra Parishad, a regional political party. Subsequently the tribals have shifted their loyalty to the Congress and now majority of them have been identified with parties like the BJP and the Jharkhand.
- The tribal legislators have not been given proportionate representation in the various ministries in Orissa except in 1971, 1979 and 1991. They were entrusted with mostly the Tribal and Rural Welfare portfolios. The so-called prized portfolios like Home, Revenue, Finance or Rural Development were not allotted to them. These portfolios have been monopolised by leaders belonging to the upper castes.
- Not a single tribal legislator has been elected as the Speaker of the State Legislative Assembly.
- Young leaders, because of their educational attainments, have an edge over the leaders of the older generation. It is believed by the tribals that young leaders can bring more funds from the Government. They are given tickets by the political parties basing on their hold on the community and their influence in the area. Thus, the ability to win is the main criterion.
- A very few among the tribal legislators are very articulate inside the State Legislative Assembly while participating in its debates, but most of them are not up to the mark.
- There is an emergence of tribal elites in the politics of the State after independence. F.G. Bailey calls these

tribal elites as the linkman. They are responsible for the economic and political development of the tribal areas and act as torchbearers, educators and communicators. They try to establish link between the government and the mass. They act as the catalysts of change in traditional societies. The tribal elites are born in rural areas, but get their education from the urban areas of the inland districts. The bulk of the elites are from agricultural background.

- In recent years a few tribal women could carve out *niche* for themselves in the politics of the state.

CONCLUSION

India, like other developing countries, is facing rapid socio-economic and political changes. In this vast country with a variety of peoples including ethnic minorities, called "Scheduled Tribes", development has not been uniform. This is a legacy of the history, geography and ethnic background.[22] The tribals have led a life of silent suffering in the dark jungles. The tribals have been victims of the various types of exploitation since time immemorial. Therefore, their development is of prime concern today, without which our independence would be reduced to a mere slogan.[23] A majority of them have not taken the advantage of legislative and administrative measures by the Government because of their illiteracy, ignorance and poverty. There has been a great deal of transfer of agricultural land and other immovable property from the tribals to non-tribals. The tribals are not only exploited by the non-tribals but also tribal village chiefs and tribal elites. Some of the tribals who are educated and nearer to political leaders take advantage of all developmental benefits that are meant for poor tribals. They flourish, at the cost of the vast majority of tribals who suffer from poverty and starvation. Thus the tribals are subjected to exploitation from within and without. The external exploiters include the traders, moneylenders and officials.

The tribals have actively participated in various struggles, struggles against outside infiltration, against land alienation, against harassment, falling wages, loss of economic benefits against forest and excise contractors and against the arbitrary actions of the Government. Some struggles have been spontaneous in nature and some are organised. These struggles from time to time however could force the state to adopt certain development programmes and ensure certain concessions in the use of forest and land resources.

Tribes are inseparable parts of Orissan life. One cannot think of Orissa without her tribal communities. There is need to know about these tribes and preserve their socio-cultural identities. Tribal areas of the State are known for their rich natural resources and yet one of the poorest and most exploited region. There is also a need to harmonise national and tribal interest. In other words, the tribals have to find themselves a place in Indian society consistent with their conception of honour. It has been rightly observed that "once the fear of the minorities, that their culture and language will become subordinate to that of the dominant group, is removed, political integration will become much easier, a reality".[24] The Scheduled Areas and Scheduled Tribes Commission was of the view that "the problem of problems is not to disturb the harmony of tribal life and simultaneously work for its advance; not to impose anything upon the tribals and simultaneously work for its advance; not to impose anything upon the tribals and simultaneously work for their integration as members and part of the Indian family. These objects were in the minds of the framers of the Constitution when they provided special measures in the Constitution.[25] Keeping in view the gross social injustice and disabilities suffered by the tribals for centuries, the founding fathers of the Indian Constitution incorporated special provisions with a view to promote and safeguard their social, educational and economic interests.

It has been suggested that the Government should reinforce the cultural traits of tribals, raising forest as common property resources, emphasis on tribal literacy and afforestation. Special attention has to be given to the social, economic and cultural development of the tribals, so as to bring them to the national mainstream. Otherwise, it may give rise to social conflicts and violent agitations having an adverse impact on the democratic process.

Notes

1. Verrier Elwin, *New Deal for Tribal India* (New Delhi: Ministry of Home Affairs, Government of India, 1963), p. 1.
2. Myron Weiner and John Osgood Field (eds.), *Electoral Politics in the Indian States, Three Disadvantaged Sectors,* Vol. II, Delhi: Manohar Book Service, 1975.
3. F.G. Bailey, *Tribe, Caste and Nation: A Study of Political Change in Highland Orissa* (Bombay, 1963) and L.P. Vidyarthi and N. Mishra, *Harijan Today* (New Delhi, 1977).
4. Bhupinder Singh, "Tribal Development in the Fifth Plan – Some Political and Administrative Aspects", *ADIBASI,* Vol. XIV, 1972-73, No. 4, Tribal & Harijan Research-cum-Training Institute, Bhubaneswar, Orissa, pp. 1-10.
5. Part I of Part IV of the Memorandum for Grants-in-Aid from Government of India, Orissa Legislative Assembly, Proceedings, Vol. I, Part II, No. 55, 9th July 1952 – Appendix G PL XXVIII.
6. Myron Weiner and John Osgood Field (eds.), *Electoral Politics in the Indian States, Three Disadvantaged Sectors,* Vol. II, *op. cit.,* p. 106.
7. *Ibid.,* p. 80.
8. "Tribal Sub-Plan", 1993-94, Government of Orissa, Harijan and Tribal Welfare Department, 1992, p. 1.
9. Shreeram Chandra Dash, *States of Our Union: Orissa,* Ministry of Information and Broadcasting, Government of India, Publications Division, New Delhi, September, 1970, p. 9.
10. Population of as many as 27 tribal communities in Orissa has shown negative growth rate. Population of 13 tribes has gone down below 3,100.

11. Nityananda Patnaik, *Anthropological Studies on Indian Societies*, Modern Book Depot, Bhubaneswar, 2001, p. 102.
12. P.V. Rao, *Institutional Framework for Tribal Development*, Inter-India Publications, New Delhi, 1988, p. 22.
13. *Orissa Legislative Assembly Proceedings*, July 1952, *op. cit.*, p. LXXIX.
14. Dr. Verrier Elwin, Honorary Anthropologist to the Government of Orissa.
15. In pursuance of the orders of the President of India issued under Paragraph 6 of the Fifth Schedule of the Indian Constitution.
16. The 73rd Amendment Act came into force on 24 April 1993.
17. Roy Mathew, "A Triumph for the Tribals", *The Hindu*, Visakhapatnam, October 28, 2001, p. 25.
18. Three tribal people were killed in police firing in December 2000 for resisting setting-up of an Alumina Refinery at Kashipur in Rayagada district.
19. Rohit Shukla *et al* (eds.), *Forest and Tribal Life (Study of a Micro-Region)*, (New Delhi: Concept, 1990), p. 105.
20. *Frontline*, Vol. 25, No. 4, February 16-29, 2008, p. 8.
21. Refer *Who is Who of the Orissa Legislative Assembly*, 1967, 1971, 1974,1980, 1985, 1995 and 2000.
22. L.K. Mohapatra, "Social Movements among Tribes in Eastern India with Special Reference to Orissa: A Preliminary Analysis", *Adibasi*, Tribal and Harijan Research-cum-Training Institute, Bhubaneswar, Vol. 9, No. 1, 1967-68, p. 37.
23. K.K. Misra, *Social Structure and Change Among the Ho of Orissa* (Delhi: Gian Publishing House, 1987), Preface.
24. K.M. Panikkar, "Its Plurality of Culture that Binds US", *Yojana*, January 26, 1987, Vol. 3, Nos. 1 & 2, p. 53.
25. *Report of the Scheduled Areas and Scheduled Tribes Commission*, Vol. I, 1960-61, p. 6.

POLITICAL EMPOWERMENT OF INDIAN MUSLIMS: SOME ASPECTS

M. A. Hussein's

A nation is empowered by its people. People are empowered by their capabilities. People's capabilities are created by investments in their education, well being and skills and providing them with opportunities for gainful productive employment. People are also empowered by the freedom they enjoy. In the World, in which we live today, no country can feel empowered unless all its citizens feel empowered.[1] When a child, a woman, a person belonging to a weaker section or a minority community or group of any kind feels disempowered we all lose something in us. This well being of each of our citizens empowers every one of us.[2]

For a healthy nation it is necessary that all sections comprising it should develop together. If any section of the society lags behind or is not able to benefit from development policies, the nation ought to be concerned.[3]

It has been a continuing complaint of Muslims that the process of development witnessed by the country has bypassed them and they were being left high and dry.[4]

The Muslims inhabiting the Indian sub-continent comprise the largest concentration of the community in the World. The 120 million Muslims constitute the largest minority in India. Partition of India gave them hard blows. The political power they could have wielded in the

Independent India was totally undermined by their division and being orphaned in the process.

Helplessly outnumbered, they are today victims of fascist propaganda. Educationally backward, ill at ease with the native languages, the Muslims today are unable to explain their case before their countrymen. Their image has suffered due to this. Myths are concocted about them with ease and distorted history poisons the minds of the innocent citizens. Their lapses are exaggerated and achievements belittled or obscured.[5]

Constitutional democracy allows Muslims to be as much participants in the national polity as any member of the majority community. But vested interests often seen as a participant in the malignity campaign against minorities and thus denies them the right to be fairly represented. The myths abound because of deliberate mischief by the communal elements in league with media and also because of the innocent misgivings about Muslim culture, history and society.[6]

Some of the myths are:

1. Muslims came as invaders. And they are responsible for the division of the country.
2. They demolished temples and constructed mosques.
3. They converted large number of people to Islam.
4. Muslims oppose Family Planning.
5. Muslims are generally polygamous.
6. Islamic family laws are biased.
7. Purdah/hijab keep the women backward
8. Muslim Personal Law is a privilege for Muslims.
9. The Indian Constitution guarantees special rights to minorities under Article 30 to run their educational institutions.
10. Muslims do not need reservation because Islam does not recognize the Caste System.

11. Islam inspires Terrorism. India is a victim of Islamic Terrorism.
12. Muslims want India to remain secular but whenever they are in majority they want the country to be Islamic.

If viewed objectively, most of the myths have no basis. Public image of Muslims has therefore taken a serious beating and Hindu-Muslim relations have much to do with this kind of an image.[7]

ISSUES INVOLVED IN MUSLIM RESERVATIONS

In the context of the demand for reservation for Muslims there are two approaches employed by Muslims in their argument for addressing the acute condition of their being in the least privileged even below SCs, STs and non-Muslim OBCs. Both approaches affirm reservation in jobs and education as important ingredients in trying to uplift them from the disturbing condition of backwardness. Backwardness of Muslims is also a hindrance in the path of national development, within days of the Sachar Committee Report being tabled. The media announced that Prime Minister Manmohan Singh had told the National Development Council that Muslims (now statistically proved to be at the bottom of the development pole) should have "FIRST CLAIM ON RESOURCES." The BJP the then President Rajnath Singh said that "INDIAS' RESOURCES ARE NOT TO BE DIVIDED ON COMMUNAL LINES."

The Rajender Sachar Committee Report appointed in 2005 by the Central Government has analysed the data pertaining to Muslims educational, economic and social status.[8] Also a National Commission on Backward Religions and Linguistic Minorities was appointed in 2004 under Justice Ranganath Mishra.[9] The Commission submitted its Report in 2007, making a recommendation, among, others, for 15% reservation for the religions, minorities, of which 10% was to be exclusively for Muslim Community.[10]

SACHAR COMMITTEE RECOMMENDATIONS

1. 94.9% of Muslims in Below Poverty Line (BPC) families in rural areas.
2. While only 3.2% Muslims get subsided loans, just 1.9% of the Community benefit from Anbyodaya Assna Yojala Scheme, a programme meant to prevent starvation among the poorest of the poor by providing food grains at a subsidised rate.

60.2% of Muslims do not have any land in rural areas. The national average is 43%. Only 0.8% Muslims in rural areas are graduates although in urban areas nearly 40% of the Muslims now receive modern education, only 30.1% of the Community in urban areas are graduates. Just 1.2% are Post-Graduates.

Further it is essential to point out that if 94.4% Muslims below the poverty line do not get free food grains, the fault does not lie in the allocation of the budget but in the delivery system.

The Sachar Committee Report pointed out that Muslims have become, more backward than Dalits, especially with regard to employment.[11] The Sachar Committee report belies the allegation of the BJP and other Hindutva forces that Muslims are being appeased. Significantly, the Sachar Committee report does not propose reservation for the Muslim Community as a whole. It recommends "multifarious measures including Reservation only for Muslims with traditional occupations comparable to those of SCs and STs.[12]

The Sachar Committee has derived the population data for Muslim OBCs (Dalit Muslims included) from the 55th (1999-2000) and 61st (2004-05) rounds of NSSO returns wherein for the first time since Independence the data pertaining to the OBC category was obtained. From the 55th round returns, the population of Muslim OBCs was estimated at 31.7 per cent of the Muslim population (for general

Muslims it was 68.3%) and from the 61st round returns the estimate of Muslim OBCs was 40.7 of the Muslim population (for general Muslims it was 59.3%). This shows the growth of about 9% in just five years.

The Sachar Committee Report when outlining the social stratification of Muslims in India States:

Thus one can discern three groups among Muslims.

1. Those without any social disabilities, the ASHRAFS.
2. Those equivalent to Hindu OBC's, the AJLAFS and
3. Those equivalent to those who are referred to as Muslim OBCs combine (2) and (3).[13]

One approach seeks to identify that the Muslim Community as a whole is a backward community economically and therefore socially and educationally backward. This approach implies that "Muslim Community" by religion is also a 'Class' on economic class of people sharing the same relations to the forces of production. This leads to the necessity of seeing the second approach of argument in demanding reservation for Muslims.

The second approach is being derived from the heterogeneous Muslims being divided into many castes – like BIRADARI groups. Muslim Society in India is divided into segments in caste-like groups. Given this reality many Muslim organizations representing groups mostly from 'AJLAF' category argue for the demand for reservation of their respective Muslim caste like groups expressing the fear that the event of giving reservation to the Muslim Community as a whole, the better-off groups under the category of so called "ASHRAF" might appropriate the better part of the benefits, thus undermining the very purpose of empowering the weak and the underprivileged. Thus, this approach expresses the desire for inclusion of backward Muslim Castes like groups in the OBC Category. These two broad approaches are a part or the effort by the under privileged sections to improve their lot working with the system. As a matter of fact, "inclusive growth" may be possible only in an "inclusive democracy."[14] Concluding that Muslims are a deprived lot, the Sachar Committee has favoured reservation for the most backward in the Muslim Community, creation of an Equal Opportunity Commission and a nomination procedure for their politics at the grass root level.

MUSLIMS DEMAND IMPLEMENTATION OF RANGANATH MISRA REPORT OF THE NATIONAL COMMISSION FOR RELIGIOUS AND LINGUISTIC MINORITIES (NCRCM)

Many Muslim organizations are raising the demand for reservation in education and Jobs. They were not making a communal demand but were simply making the case that Muslims as a whole were backward and entitled to reservations under the "socially and educationally " backward category. Many Muslim organizations were opposed being accommodated within 27% OBC quota. The backwardness of the community had been established twice over – first by the Sachar Committee which concluded that Muslim deprivation levels almost equaled those of the Scheduled Castes, and now by the Ranganath Mishra Commission, which recognized Muslim backwardness recommended a 10% Quota exclusively for the Muslim Community.

Further the Ranganath Mishra Commission Report also says "we recommend that all these classes, sections and groups among the minorities should be treated as backward whose counter parts in the majority community are regarded as backward under the present scheme of things.[15]

EMPOWERMENT OF MUSLIMS IN ANDHRA PRADESH

The Late Dr. Y. S. Rajashekara Reddy's government n Andhra Pradesh has introduced and issued an order and provided 4% reservations for Muslims in Jobs and in educational institutions in 2007. It calls for the inclusion of socially and educationally backward classes of Muslims and category "E" in the list of Backward Classes (G.O.M.S.No. 23) Backward Classes Welfare (C2), 7th July, 2007. A VHP leader Muralidhar Reddy challenged in the A.P. High Court the Muslim Reservation Act. The Andhra Pradesh High Court in its recent Judgment on 8th February, 2010 has termed a separate quota for Muslims as unsustainable and unconstitutional as 5 Judges of the High Court led by the then Chief Justice had pronounced. The B.J.P. hailed the High Court Judgment and said that it was unconstitutional to have religion based reservations but the MIM Party workers and supporters stormed into Andhra Pradesh Secretariat shouting slogans against the Government and against the High Court Judgment.

ANDHRA PRADESH

The Andhra Pradesh Government in 2006 led by late Dr. Y.S. Rajashekara Reddy granted 5% reservations to Muslims, but the legislation was struck down by the Andhra Pradesh High Court as the Indian Constitution does not allow Religion based reservations. The Constitution says "CLASS". "If Caste could be interpreted as class, then why not religions?" said Ilyas of the All India Muslim Personal Law Board.

Ilyas says there is no 'confusion' among Muslims and wants the entire community declared backward with reservations given to all, minus the creamy layer. His reluctance to accept SC/ST/OBC categorization for Muslims is opposed by Muffi Mukharam Ahmed of Delhi, Fattepuri Mosque who does not want a section of Muslims calling themselves "Dalits."

The Andhra Pradesh Government approached the Supreme Court against the High Court Judgement recently on Muslim reservations and on 25th March, 2010 in what could be a momentous step for the Andhra Pradesh Government, the Supreme Court has ordered a stay on the Quota. The Quota will be applicable to 14 of the Muslim Communities that were identified by the State Government. The matter has not yet been closed, though a Constitutional Panel will hear the case on 12th August, 2010 when it yet to come for hearing.[16]

Before we discuss the case for the OBC/Dalit reservations for the Indian Muslims let us point out the strategic concerns.

1. There is no constitutional impediment to declaring a religious group as a "backward class" in a normative sense. We must also admit that there is a historical baggage attached with the "MUSLIM IDENTITY" in the public perception. Even as the revisionist historical scholarship has now convincingly demolished the over stated onus for the partition tragedy on the Muslim elite and has consequently underscored the role of "Hindu Elite" and the Colonial Government as being also in large measures responsible for it, the truth remains that Muslims has become the despicable 'Other' in the Indian Society.
2. Some excellent and institutional's propaganda by the SAFFRON Brigade has wrought out a magnified, villainous image of the Muslims in the consciousness of Indian masses.

An expert panel set up in 2007 to look into the structure and functions of an Equal Opportunities Commission[17] has recommended that the benefits of the Commission shall be made available to all social groups that feel discriminated and not only to SCs/STs, Minorities or any other pre-defined groups. The Five Member Equal Opportunities Commission consisted of Javed Alam, Satish Desh Pande, Yogendra Yadav and Gopal Guru. The Panel suggested the following recommendations:

1. It is important to go beyond "purely formal approach" to Equality.
2. "Deprivation Index" should be the key for establishing the Equal Opportunity Commission

3. Education and Employment Sectors should be the priority for the Panel and
4. A publicity debated criteria of evidence is needed for establishing Equality of Opportunity.

The above Panel has also argued for extending the jurisdiction of the commission to the Private Sector as well since the Public Sector occupies a small and shrinking part of the economic opportunities in India.

The price of ignoring Dr. Gopal Singh Committee, the Rajender Sachar Committee and Justice Ranganatha Mishra Committee reports may be lethal in the near future. The frustration, resentment and anger of many young Muslims at their utter marginalization from the mainstream National life may well prompt them to embrace the sense of a minion and the belief in apocalyptic redemption that holds out to its adherents.

Reaching out to people who are untouched by the growth in the Country's economy can be achieved by broadening the reservation system giving to people and helping out Muslim Community who are deprived of Reservations is not wrong. So please support the poor sections of the Muslim Community and empower them to come out of poverty.

The argument being made against Quotas for Muslims is that they will create resentment and generate a backlash. This is a weighty argument and it is almost certainly true, although it is unlikely that the victims of the backlash will be the same as the beneficiaries of Quotas.[18]

Quotas by their very nature directly benefit only a few individuals and their extended families. Does that not create resentment among hapless many against the resourceful few who have learnt to manipulate the regime of Quotas to manipulate advantage?

There are as yet no Quotas for religious minorities, but we can form some Judgement of their possible consequences from our long experience of Quotas for the SCs and STs and the other backward classes.

In India, the Constitution and the laws have been committed since Independence to the Principle of Equality of Opportunity. But translating that principle into practice is no easy matter.

As R.H. Tawney, who was inspiration for the Welfare State in Britain, pointed out that the existence of equality of opportunity depends not merely on the absence of disabilities but also on the presence of abilities.[19] Affirmative action is important because it serves to create those very abilities without whose presence Equality of Opportunity remains only a formal principle.[20]

Numerical Quotas undermine that difficult and delicate process by putting individual effort at a discount and reinforcing the sense of in capacity from which disadvantaged castes and communities feel they are doomed to suffer.[21] As Pratap Bhanu Mehta who is President, Centre for Policy Research, Delhi commented, "A democracy prizes individuality. Quotacracy prizes group think. Democracy values self-identification. You should be whatever you wish to or choose to be or name yourself. Quotacracy is premised upon ascription you can be this and no other."[22]

Notes & References

1. Atul Kohli (ed.), India's Democracy – An Analysis of Changing State – Society Relations (New Delhi: Orient Longman, 1991), p. 10.
2. Raktahari Chatters (ed.), Politics in India – The State – Society Interface, (New Delhi, South Asian Publishers, 2009), p. 335.
3. B.S. Baviskar & George Mathew (ed.), Inclusion and Exclusion in Local Governance (New Delhi: Sage Publications, 2009), p. 5.
4. Loya Hasan, "Muslims in India: Why are they excluded and Discriminated?" A Concept note prepared for DFID.
5. Abusalen Shariff, "One the Margins: Muslims in a State of Socio-Economic Decline," The Times of India, Bangalore, Dated 22.10.2004.

6. Asghar Ali Engineer, Identity and Social Exclusion – Inclusion: A Muslim Perspective File: Identity and Social Exclusion – Inclusion – A Muslim Perspective – htm, Centre for Study of Society and Secularism, Mumbai, Dated 13.4.2010.
7. South Asia Politics, New Delhi, February, 2008. Vol. 6, No. 10, p. 41.
8. Rajendra Sachar Committee Report, New Delhi, Government of India, 2005.
9. Report of the National Commission for Religious and Linguistic Minorities (NCRLM) popularly called Justice Ranganath Mishra Commission Report, New Delhi, Government of India, 2007.
10. Syed Shahabuddin, "On Equitable Implementation of the Mishra Commission Recommendation," Mainstream, New Delhi, Vol. XLVIII, No. 16, April 10, 2010, p. 17.
11. Khalid Anis, Ansari "Debating Muslim Reservations." Mainstream, New Delhi, Vol. XLVIII, No. 16, 2010, p. 19.
12. The Hindu English Daily Newspaper, A.P. Edition, Dated 2.12.2006.
13. The Indian Express, English Daily Newspaper, Coimbatore Edition, Dated 1.12.2006.
14. Arjun Sengupta, "Inclusive Development Vs. Equitable Growth" article contributed in Deccan Chronicle Newspaper, Hyderabad, Dated 29.6.2009.
15. "Muslims Reservations in Andhra Pradesh," Andhra Pradesh Government G.O. on Muslim Reservation Government of Andhra Pradesh, Hyderabad, Dated 7.7.2007.
16. *Ibid.*
17. Imtiaz Ahmed, 'Sachar Committee Report," Yojana, February 2007, p. 51.
18. Andre Betelle "Brake the Quota Routine," The Times of India, English Newspaper, New Delhi, Dated 15.6.2009.
19. *Ibid.*
20. *Ibid.*
21. Pratap Bhanu Mehta, "Our Wonderful Quotocracy, The Indian Express, English Newspaper, New Delhi, Dated 15.3.2010.
22. *Ibid.*

DEMOCRATIC DECENTRALISATION, EMPOWERMENT AND INCLUSIVE GOVERNANCE: STATE AND CIVIL SOCIETY PERSPECTIVE

SATYANARAYANA SANGITA

I

INTRODUCTION

India globalised its economy with the liberalisation of trade and investment in the 1990s. Foreign capital and trade increased many times over. Disinvestment took place in a big way in the public sector. Unlike in other developing countries, many initiatives were taken in India to counter the negative implications of globalisation and protect the rights and livelihood of the disadvantaged, particularly in the rural and backward regions. The plan allocation for social security, health and education among others, has increased since the era of liberalisation in the early 1990s. Programmes like the National Rural Employment Guarantee Schemes (NREGS), National Rural Health Mission (NRHM), universalisation of education (Sarvashiksha Abhyan), national drinking water and sanitation and slum improvement schemes under the Jawaharlal Nehru Urban Renewal Mission (JNURM) were initiated. The Eleventh Plan aims to promote inclusive growth, revive dynamism in agriculture, build necessary infrastructure in rural areas and expand access to health and education. Along with this, the three-tier structure of local self government at the district, taluk, and village level has come into existence through the 73rd Constitutional Amendment in the late 1990s to empower the rural people, particularly the disadvantaged, to protect and promote their rights, interests and needs. Even the Right to Information Act came into existence in 1996 to empower the people and bring transparency in governance.

This paper examines the role of decentralised governance in empowering the disadvantaged and promoting inclusive governance. The second section deals with the empowerment and capacity of the people, through decentralisation, to raise their voices and preferences for their welfare. The third section deals with the provision of services through decentralised governance in an efficient and equitable manner to the satisfaction of the needy. The fourth section focuses on the enabling conditions for the success of democratic decentralisation for promoting inclusive governance. The last section concludes with the policy implications.

II

DECENTRALISATION AND INCLUSIVE GOVERNANCE

Devolution of powers strengthens democracy and enhances the legitimacy of the political system. It facilitates people's participation in decision-making and reflects their needs and preferences. It promotes representative and responsible grassroots level leadership. It generates incentives for people to own the local government with newly assigned responsibilities and resources relevant to them. Decentralised governance makes it easier for the citizen to hold the government accountable through voter information, participation and monitoring. It promotes legitimacy, transparency and accountability, devolution of powers, responsibilities and resources to local government facilitate better service delivery.

Democratic decentralisation tends, strongly, to enhance speed, quantity and quality of responses from government institutions. Local governments have both authority and resources to respond quickly to problems and pressures from citizens without waiting for approval from higher levels. It helps to mobilise both human and financial resources as well as to contain corruption and ensure accountability. Decentralised governments have more and better information regarding their constituents and are able to enforce and coordinate policies and programmes more efficiently (Bardhan 1996). Thus, decentralisation promotes expected improvement in allocative efficiency, welfare and equity through increased participation, transparency, empowerment, responsiveness and accountability.

Economists tend to frame their analysis in terms of costs and benefits of decentralisation while other social scientists and practitioners are generally concerned with the processes and democratic aspects of the processes (Blair 2000 cited in Mark Robinson, 2007). This paper deals with the expected results of democratic decentralisation in the context of globalisation - the processes and outcomes. The processes ensure empowerment and autonomy of the local people and governments in influencing the policies benefiting the people and bring political stability and social harmony. The second dimension is provision of various public services to the people efficiently and equitably. The provision of affordable, accessible and appropriate services to all categories of a population in equal measures is not only a universal standard (efficiency) but a social justice perspective on provision of privileges directly to economically and socially marginalised groups. Democratic decentralisation does not affect the outcome–provision of service in terms of quantity, quality or equity-directly but through its process variables like participation, empowerment, responsiveness and accountability.

DEMOCRATIC DECENTRALISATION IN INDIA

India is one of the few developing countries that have been experimenting with the democratic decentralisation to promote development since independence. A major initiative was launched with the introduction of the three-tier structure of local self-government known as the Panchayat Raj Institutions (PRI) at the district, taluk and village level in the late 1950s. The third tier of government (along with the central and state governments) for rural and urban areas with independent powers and resources was constituted in the 2000s with the 73rd and 74th amendment of the Constitution of India.

After the constitutional amendment, the PRIs emerged as units of local self-governments for promoting development programmes. The PRIs enjoy political, administrative and financial autonomy in many respects. All major responsibilities along with resources (central and State plan schemes and other resources) rest with the PRIs. Many centrally sponsored programmes have been transferred to PRIs in many states. All 29 functions as mentioned in schedule and resources have been transferred to the PRIs (assigns 30 specific subjects to VPs, 28 to TPs and 28 ZPs in Karnataka). The PRIs can prepare plans for agriculture, animal husbandry, primary and secondary education, public health, rural roads and housing, women and children, social welfare, public distribution, public libraries and so on. The GPs can undertake regulatory functions such as issue of licenses, approval of building plans, and maintenance of common properties, assets and buildings. They can provide basic services such as drinking water and sanitation and maintain village roads, buildings and streetlights. The elected heads of the PRIs are entrusted with executive powers and control over officials. The State Election Commission is entrusted with the responsibility of holding free and fair elections to PRIs. The State Finance Commissions were constituted to devolve financial resources to the PRIs.

III

DEMOCRATIC DECENTRALISATION AND EMPOWERMENT

Democratic decentralisation empowers the people to articulate interests and improve livelihood. People are also mobilised through other democratic movements (civil society/political parties) to counter the negative implications of globalisation. Democratic decentralisation makes participation easier and makes empowerment more feasible at the local level than at the national level, especially for minorities and vulnerable groups. Firstly, democratic decentralisation enables the people to participate in the country's governance. The establishment of small and decentralised governance structures/units like the VPs ensures proximity to the people (6,000 and 400 population for GP and ward, respectively) and regular elections motivates people to participate in the election of responsible leaders and selection of relevant development policies (responsiveness). The high turnout in PR election reflects this trend[2].

Secondly, the mobilisation of people through elections (contesting, campaigning, and voting and so on) brings awareness among the rural people about their rights and entitlements. Elections also bring information about the leaders and political parties and their programmes and policies. Even the Grama Sabha (Village Assembly) and Ward Committee meetings make the people aware of the relevant schemes and resources available with the PRIs to take correct decisions. As a result, the poor people's dependence on the rural rich has come down. This is evident from the people's assertion and articulation in defeating the sitting members and incumbent regimes in PR elections. Even the poor can now raise their voice if their needs are not fulfilled through wrongdoings of the PRIs.

Thirdly, decentralisation has also opened a wider political arena for the disadvantaged to take up leadership positions in the PRIs. Reservation enables disadvantaged groups to occupy seats of power. For instance around 36-38 per cent of women, 17-20 per cent SC, and 7-11 per cent ST got elected to the VP, TP and ZP accounting 27,31,199[3].

This representation has helped the disadvantaged to improve their administrative skills and articulate in local governance. For instance, women's association with PRIs has brought transformation in terms of empowerment, confidence and political awareness. Some studies have revealed that the women who reluctantly entered into politics showed great maturity in outlook, enthusiasm in strengthening their political consciousness and fine-tuning their perception of their role and responsibility. Most of the women who were elected for the first time without political experience, started asserting control over resources and officials and challenging male authority and supremacy. Initially many of the women who were first-timers and illiterate depended upon their men folk (husbands and other male representatives) to conduct the panchayat activities and to shield them from the PR officials. Gradually, they become independent and exercised control over the officials. This has also resulted in a positive change in the power equation between husband and wife.

Besides, the women from the lower caste take much interest in the PRIs than their counterparts from the higher castes. Studies have found that the participation of the weaker sections (SC/ST, women) in meetings and in decision-making is quite satisfactory (Litvack et al. 1998; Klitgaard 1988). It was reported that about 80-90 per cent of women, particularly from the lower income group, attend the PRIs meeting regularly. Women are responsible for changing the work culture in PRIs and in articulating issues related to women. Chattopadhyay and Duflo (2001) found that the women leaders of village councils concentrate more on developing infrastructure that is relevant to the needs of the rural women (drinking water, fuel and roads). The power of the weaker sections over resources has increased through the PRIs.

Studies have also pointed out that reservation has improved the perception levels of women and has created an urge in them to participate in the governance. Twenty-five per cent of the women members found visible change in their status within the family after they had been elected. About 60 per cent of women said that they would encourage women to contest election. About 60 per cent is contemplating to contest the forthcoming elections (PRIA, 2000). In the all-women GP of Mydolalu in Karnataka it was found that the women fared better than men in implementing development programmes. Interestingly, all the women in this GP had been elected for the first time and had no previous experience. Similar observations were recorded regarding other disadvantaged groups such as the SC/ST/OBCs.

VILLAGE PANCHAYATS VOICES AGAINST MEGA PROJECTS

Many VPs have protested against multinational companies (MNCs) and mega projects that have come up as a result of globalisation. For instance, the Plachimad VP in Kerala voiced concern over Coca Cola for exploiting ground water. Even some VPs opposed the acquisition of land for the Special Economic Zones (SEZ). Similarly many VPs in Goa have raised their voice against mega projects. The GSs have passed resolutions for cancellations of licences for housing projects obtained by fraudulent means. Expert committees were appointed to scrutinise the licences given to the builders. Even demands were made for investigation by the Vigilance Commission in the dealings with the builders. The VPs have also gone to court for cancellations of mining permits and have also succeeded in securing compensation for the loss of agricultural crops from the mining companies[4]

DEMOCRATIC (PEOPLE/CIVIL SOCIETY) MOVEMENTS

Many civil society movements have come into existence to take up issues relating to plight of the poor and the environment in the context of globalisation. The people have rallied against the SEZs over acquisition of land and compensation to the farmers. For instance, Singer, Nandigram, Narmada and many other movements can be mentioned in this regard. Farmers in Maharashtra voted against the acquiring of land for SEZ by Reliance. Similarly the farmers in Singur and Nandhigram in West Bengal stalled the Tata's small car project and SEZ, respectively. In Andhra Pradesh the notification of acquiring land for the Coastal Corridor in between Kakinada and Vishakapatnam was cancelled after a movement was launched by the opposition parties. As a result, a new rehabilitation package to protect the interests of the farmers was implemented.

Apart from this, political parties are also mobilising people against the negative implication of globalisation. Competitive politics compelled the political parties to promote welfare schemes in the government's plans, budgets, programmes and election manifestos as well. In recent times, both DMK and AIDMK in Tamil Nadu and Congress and Telugu Desam parties in Andhra Pradesh announced popular schemes like waiver of loans and free electricity for farmers, Rs 2 per kg of rice, houses, pension, health care and insurance to win the elections. For instance, the Congress party under Ms Sonia Gandhi introduced popular schemes like the NREGS, NRHM, and so on, to promote inclusive growth. Political parties are going slowly in the introduction of economic reforms (labour laws, FD in banking and insurance sector, disinvestment in PSUs and so on) due to fear of losing the people's support. Reform regimes under Vajpayee at the centre and Chandra Babu Naidu, S M Krishna and Digvijay Singh at the state levels faced defeat in the 2004 elections.

DECENTRALISATION AND SERVICE DELIVERY (ALLOCATIVE EFFICIENCY)

Democratic decentralisation not only generates allocative and productive efficiency but also accelerates service delivery. Allocative efficiency is high in decentralised governance rather than the government at a higher level. It facilitates a perfect match between resources and needs. Local information and needs can be ascertained by local governments more accurately and thereby identify projects/ schemes that have maximum utility or welfare gain. Selection/location of projects/members is very effective, whenever the local people participate in the process. The involvement of the GS has brought down the selection of wrong places and persons. This is more so where needs are more diversified. For instance some village needs water facilities rather than roads. In such situation the utilisation of the former is more than the latter, which is provided by the government at a higher level through uniform policies and guidelines. Many centrally-sponsored rural development programmes in the past have failed due to wrong priorities, design and location. Infrastructure facilities like roads, school buildings, hospitals, water and field channels have not been used because they have not been strategically located to suit the needs of people. Similarly, many hand pumps are out of order because the people did not feel the pride of ownership. Ultimately maintenance and sustenance of such projects and schemes under decentralised governance was very high (Sangita, 2002). It was found that many assets created under various central schemes were under-utilised.

DECENTRALISATION AND SERVICE DELIVERY (PRODUCTIVE EFFICIENCY)

Productive efficiency is also high in decentralised governance due to people's participation in the implementation and monitoring of the development programmes. Firstly, people's involvement in the formulation and implementation of development programmes results in reduction in transactional cost (such as administrative costs, salaries, complex procedures, waste, leakages and corruption). The former Prime Minister, the late Rajiv Gandhi, used to say that only 15 paisa out of one rupee spent reaches the poor through various anti-poverty programmes.

Decentralisation contributes towards better compliance and enforcement with low cost because decisions regarding selection of schemes and design of projects are taken in consultation with the various stakeholders. This is particularly so in the management of community property resources like forests and water tanks where law enforcement and punitive regulations are minimal.

When the people monitor the implementation of programmes and projects, wastages and leakages are minimised. Their close observation prevents the procurement of substandard inputs like goods and materials. Close monitoring by PRIs helps to improve the attendance of teachers and doctors in schools and hospitals, respectively. Regular monitoring by elected representatives (monthly review and surveys) ensures that the policies and programmes serve the intended purposes. Further, the increased transparency and accountability that results from such vigilance by civil society enhances efficiency by decreasing the potential for diversion of resources due to patronage or corruption (Brinkerhoff, 2000: 604).

Productive efficiency also increases due to transparency and accountability in delivery of services. PR election has become a powerful mechanism for ensuring accountability. If the elected leaders do not work for the uplift of rural society, they will not be able to win the next election. The defeat of a large percentage of sitting members in PR elections reflects this trend. Studies have even mentioned that the accountability of officials to the elected representatives has improved. Responsible officials (like PHC medical officer, agricultural and veterinary officer etc.) can be asked to attend

PRIs meetings. In the meeting an officer may be asked/ questioned for his/her performance. Productive efficiency can also be improved through social auditing and monitoring. Social audit (Jamabandhi) through Gram Sabha (GS) and Ward Sabha (400 population) in Karnataka has enabled citizens to monitor the progress of works and ensure administrators accountable for the entrusted tasks and responsibilities (Sivanna N, 2004).

Productive efficiency can be achieved by reduction of corruption under PRIs. A study found that decentralised governance enhanced greater transparency and reduced the incidence of corruption. Another study found that corruption among PRI functionaries was minimal where media and civil society were effective. Rent rates are higher in areas where institutions like the Grama Sabha, the media and civil society organisations are not functional[5]

Productive efficiency can also be improved in decentralised governance by mobilising additional resources (voluntary contribution like land, capital and labour) for promoting rural development. Such contributions accounted for 20 to 40 per cent of the expenditure of the community development blocks in the 1950s. Many villagers donated land for construction of schools and hospitals and even provided resources for the repair of field canals and tanks and construction of buildings and roads. The people's involvement has also helped in managing village common property resources and improvement in collection of levies and betterment and user charges. For instance, PRI functionaries and representatives in Belandur and Kinnigoli GPs have taken many innovative measures to mobilise local resources and promote development[6]

DECENTRALISATION AND SERVICE DELIVERY

Decentralisation has improved the provision of the services to the public in sectors like education and health. It was observed that there was a significant improvement in the area of medical and public health facilities and the supply of drugs in Karnataka. The attendance of doctors and paramedical staff improved considerably under the constant monitoring of local leaders in many PHCs and hospitals. VP leaders played a positive role by exerting moral pressure on the staff not to avoid their regular duties. Availability of doctors and para-medicals in medical centers are 74 per cent and 93 per cent, respectively. With regard to behaviour of doctors and teachers, 31 and 26 per cent of households, respectively, expressed satisfaction. The utilisation of resources, which has been transferred to the PRIs, was much better than it used to be under the respective departments. Developmental works are being executed more speedily under PRIs (Meenakshi Sundaram 1994).

DECENTRALISATION AND SERVICE DELIVERY (EQUITY)

Decentralised governance ensures effective delivery of services like poverty elimination programmes. Decentralised governance is more sensitive to poverty and unemployment according to the World Bank (2002) and John (2000). According to these studies, PRIs in India have done remarkably well in respect of devolution of power and implementation of the centrally sponsored employment generating and anti-poverty programmes (NREP, PDS, and IRDP) especially in Karnataka, West Bengal, Andhra Pradesh, Madhya Pradesh, Rajasthan and Kerala and other states.

Westergard's (1986) study suggested that NREP had considerable success in providing employment to the rural poor. Some studies found the food-for-work programme successful. Dreeze (1990) also found that the IRDP overwhelmingly benefited landless labourers. Swaminathan (1990) noticed similar success while comparing the state performance in implementing IRDP in West Bengal and Tamil Nadu. Webster (1992) found that the benefits under the employment generation programme and IRDP had gone to the poor and improved their living conditions.

Leakages and wastages have come down under PRIs in implementation of poverty alleviation programmes. Bardhan and Mookherje (2000) in their study of the IRDP and agricultural mini-kits during 1978-98 in West Bengal found that the proportion of Gram Panchayat (GP) seats secured by landless doubled (10 per cent to 20 per cent). Distribution of the IRDP leakage rate to the medium and large landowners was quite low (less than 4 per cent) as against 87 per cent of benefits for small and marginal farmers.

IV

STATE (GOVERNMENT) AND CIVIL SOCIETY FOR SUCCESS OF DECENTRALISATION

The success of decentralisation depends upon the commitment of the central and state governments and the support of civil society organisations and movements as well. Political regimes (parties and leaders) with strong commitment to decentralisation and development are responsible for delegating adequate power and resources to local governments. For instance, the PRIs came into existence at the initiative of the Congress party under the leadership of Jawaharlal Nehru and S K Day in the late 50s. Similar attention was given by Rajiv Gandhi in the 90s that ultimately resulted in PRIs acquiring constitutional status. Janata Party Chief Minister Ramkrishna Hegde along with a dedicated band of bureaucrats was responsible for delegating major powers along with resources to PRIs in the 80s in Karnataka.

The Left governments in Kerala and West Bengal passed supporting legislation along with the resources to strengthen the PRIs to reduce poverty and promote social development. At the same time, civil society organisations and movements were instrumental in mobilising the people for devolution of powers and resources to PRIs. Political parties in Kerala and West Bengal with reforms on their agenda created opportunities for collective action from the grass root level by mobilising small and marginal farmers and the landless to take advantage of the benefits of PRIs and the anti-poverty programmes (Mark Robinson, 2007). Even civil society organisations and movements mobilised the people to delegate powers and resources to PRIs. Some of them have empowered PRIs through protests, advocacy, capacity building and so on. In recent years, NGOs in Karnataka have fought for the rights of the PRIs, when the state government tried to dilute the powers given to PRIs. Similarly, the Kerala Sastra Sahitya Parishad played a significant role in shaping and implementing the people's campaign for decentralised planning in the late 1990s (Mark Robinson, 2007; David A. Crocker, 2008).

V

CONCLUSION

It is evident from the above review, that democratic decentralisation along with civil society organisations can play a significant role in empowering the disadvantaged to raise their voices against the negative implications of globalisation. Democratic decentralised institutions like the PRIs create awareness among the rural people to articulate their interests and protect them from the negative implications of globalisation. The intensive electoral battles among the candidates and parties for positions in PRIs have liberated the rural poor from the influence of traditional leaders and the rural rich. It has also enabled them to elect the leaders of their choice and raise their voices without any fear.

Leaders elected to PRIs from the disadvantaged groups through affirmative action are effective in taking decisions independent of their mentors. Many women (who initially depended on the male members in their household and administrators) are asserting their control over local governance and influencing the policies benefiting them. Many of these leaders, particularly those representing VPs are opposing mega projects (including MNCs) that affect the livelihoods of the local people. PRI leaders along with civil society organisations are preventing over-exploitation of natural resources and protecting the rights of the disadvantaged.

Democratic decentralisation is also promoting inclusive growth through effective provision of public services meant for the rural poor. Wastages and leakages have come down in major social security programmes initiated in the context of globalisation. Major efficiency gains have been noticed in the delivery of health, educational and other services. Thus democratically governed institutions, along with civil society organisations and movements have acted as the filters in protecting the interests of the disadvantaged groups. The benefits of globalisation can be harnessed and spread positively and evenly. The negative shocks associated with globalisation can be prevented with effective implementation of social welfare policies and antipoverty programmes. The positive effects of globalisation on growth and equity can be found when institutional conditions are tempered by participatory, democratic, transparent and accountable mechanisms to manage social, economic and political conflicts arising out of globalisation.

Notes

1. **Decentralisation and Voting:** In its study of 53 villages in Rajasthan and MP, for instance, the World Bank found that voter turnout in PR elections was well over 90 per cent for all categories (in terms of gender, class and caste). This is significantly higher than the turnout in 1998 *Lok Sabha* elections, which was 61 per cent for women and 65.9 per cent for men17.

2. **Elected Panchayat Members**: Rural people and disadvantaged were empowered after the 73rd and 74th of the Constitutional amendments. The total elected representatives in 539 district Panchayats was 15,759 (as on 1st December, 2006) out of them, SC constitutes: 2769 (17.57 per cent), ST 1680 (10.66 per cent) and women 5821 (36.94 per cent), 58328 members were selected

in the 6105 intermediate Panchayats. Out of this, SC were 33128 (21.08 per cent), ST 11538 (7.34 per cent) and women 58328 (37.11 per cent). 2657112 members were elected for 2, 33,251 GP's in which SC accounted 491305 (18.49 per cent), ST 314942 (11.85 per cent) and women 975723 (36.72 per cent). Prior to the 73rd constitutional amendment, women representatives in PRIs were from the dominant caste/class (Maratha families above twenty acres of land in Maharashtra and lingayats and vokkaligas in Karnataka).however, after the amendment, majority of members were illiterate and lower income strata. They were comparatively younger and predominantly first-generation entrants in politics (Nirmala Buch, 2000).

3. **Cheyyar Panchayats Oppose Special Economic Zone**: Eight of the ten VPs of Cheyyar taluk in Tiruvannamalai district, Tamil Nadu, passed resolutions at their GS meetings on October 2, 2008 against the government's move to acquire 2,200 acres of land for the expansion of the Cheyyar Special Economic Zone. The villagers of these VPs have been agitating against acquisition of agricultural land under the banner of the Tamil Nadu Movement Against Special Economic Zone (*Sirrappu Porulaathara Mandala Ethirpu Eyakam*) for the last six months. They have already expressed their objections orally and in writing to the District Collector (Panchayat Raj Update, Institute of Social Sciences, Vol. XV (10), October 2008).

   Panchayats Raise Their Voice Against Mega Projects: Many VPs in Goa raised their voice against mega projects that were given permission through illegal means. For instance, Benaulim VP in Goa (following the growing movement against mega projects led by Ambelim, Nuvem and Curtorm panchayats) in its meeting on June 2, 2008, after three marathon sessions, demanded the revocation of construction licenses of all the four mega projects which were executed. The GS demanded that the replies received from the builders are to be scrutinised by the committee consisting of villagers, legal experts and architects so as to prepare a watertight case against mega projects and not let the builders take advantage of any loophole. It also adopted a resolution demanding an enquiry by the vigilance commission into all the construction licenses issued by the VP for the last 10 years. Even the villagers marched to

Panaja city to protest against the director of panchayats for favouring builders. Similarly, Kolva panchayat on June 3, 2008 revoked the license of mega housing projects for not adhering to the regulations based on the GS resolution. The VP decided not to issue occupancy certificate unless the matters related to garbage, road, power and water were resolved. Villagers of Sirsaim on June 16, 2008 unanimously resolved not to permit any mega projects. The VP had issued licenses for the project comprising 22 bungalows, 10 apartments, one tennis court and two swimming pools without consulting the GS. They gave permission overlooking several technical discrepancies and illegalities relating to approach road, sewage treatment plant, garbage disposal, water availability[4] (Panchayat Raj Update, Institute of Social Sciences, Vol. XV (6), June 2008).

High Court Stays Government Order the Gujarat High Court has stayed industries and mines department's decision to lease 140-acre gauchar land of Bhimdeval village in Junagadh district to Gujarat Heavy Chemicals Ltd. The GP of Bhimdeval has been contesting grant of lease of this disputed land to Gujarat Heavy Chemicals for the last three decades. In 1976, a sarpanch and her husband got false documents drawn up to help state government departments to give the plot to Gujarat Heavy Chemicals[5] (Panchayat Raj Update, Institute of Social Sciences, Vol. XV (10), October 2008).

Panchayat Succeeds in Securing Compensation for Crop Loss: Mining companies will pay Rs.3.40 crore to 761 farmers of Suriya village in Goa as compensation for crop losses. This is the largest ever compensation for crop loss in the state. The petition had been filed by the Suria panchayat seeking compensation for crop loss due to mining activity of seven companies. The petitioners said that because of dumping of mining rejects, crops in the adjacent fields had been damaged and soil adversely affected Panchayat Raj Update, Institute of Social Sciences, Vol. XV (6), June 2008.

4. **Decentralisation and Corruption:** In Karnataka during the late 1980s, the overall amount of money stolen from local development funds plummeted. People who had earlier stolen between 25 per cent and 40 per cent of these funds behind closed doors - without the knowledge of ordinary people - now

found that they could pilfer no more than 5 per cent or so because the new system was so transparent. But that very transparency persuaded citizens that more money was now being stolen {James Manor, 1997}.

5. **Experience of Belandur VP in Bangalore District:** Belandur has the most successful VP with an income of more than Rs 1.7 crore and 100 percent tariff collection. It has underground drainage system and garbage collection facilities. It has provided mini water schemes with 5 overhead tanks to every ward. The GP has made by-laws for fair delivery of water to all households. A penalty of Rs. 2000 can be levied for illegal water connection or the regular connection may be disconnected for a period of six months. About Rs 25 lakh has been spent on the construction of a drainage system. Toilets are being constructed for all the households, including those living below the poverty line. There is no evidence of open defecation in the panchayat area. In 2001-02, about 365 toilets were constructed in this panchayat under different schemes. The GP took a mandatory decision that it will construct more than 40 latrines in a year. Factors that play a crucial role for the success of the VP are many. However the important factor is the quality of leadership as provided by the president of the panchayat and his team (**Source**: Nayak, Bhargava and Shubha 2004).

Experience of Kinnigoli VP in Dakshina Kannada: This VP demonstrated that water supply schemes can be maintained successfully by collecting tariffs from the households. The scheme comprises bore-wells that feed 5,000-litre capacity overhead tanks. There are nearly 100 pipe connections to individual houses. The total cost of the scheme was estimated at Rs 7 lakh of which 10 per cent was contributed by the villagers. The VP ensured regular water supply to all the households. The VP expected to levy and collect a one time advances charge of Rs 1000 for each connection but failed to collect the water charges. It was decided to levy a higher rate on higher incremental consumption. A new tariff formula was devised for the *Guttakaadu* scheme based on monthly consumption(Rs 50 for 3-10 Kls, Rs. 100 for 15 -30 Kls, and Rs 350 for above 30 Kls. Water meters are fixed for all 133 house pipe connections. A separate electric meter is fixed for a submersible pump to keep a proper account of electric power consumed. The system is working very well and the cost collection is 100 per cent (**Source:** Deccan Herald, April 19, 2003).

References

Atradi, V and Sala-i-Martin X (2003), The Economic Tragedy of the XX Century: Growth in Africa. *Working Paper, No. 9865.* Cambridge: National Bureau of Economic Research.

Bardhan, Pranab (1996), The Nature of Institutional Impediments to Economic Development. *Working Paper, No. 1041.* U C Berkely: Institute for Business and Economic Research.

Bardhan, Pranab and Dilip Mookherjee (2000), Capture and Governance at Local and National Levels. *American Economic Review,* 90(2): 135-39.

Barro, J. Robert (1991), The Economic Growth in a Cross Section of Countries. *The Quarterly Journal of Economics,* 106(2): 403-43.

Brinkerhoff (2000), Democratic Governance and Sectoral Policy Reform: Tracing Linkages and Exploring Synergies. *World Development,* 28(4): 601-615.

Chattopadhyaya, R. and E. Duflo (2001), Women as Policy Makers: Evidence from an India Wide Randomized Policy Experiment. Unpublished, Cambridge Mass.

David A. Crocker (2008), *Ethics of Global Development: Agency, Capability and Deliberative Democracy,* Cambridge, New York.

Dreeze, Jean (1990), Poverty in India and the IRDP Delusion. *Economic and Political Weekly,* 25(39): 95-104.

Gidden, Anthony (1990), The Consequences of Modernity. Cambridge: Polity.

Hamelink, C. J. (1994), The Politics of World Communication: A Human Rights Perspective. U.K.: Sage Publication Ltd.

Harvey, David (1990), The Condition of Post Modernity: *An Enquiry into the Origins of Cultural Change.* U.S.A.: Blackwell Publishing Ltd.

Hirst, Paul and T Thompson Grahame (1996), Globalization in Question: The International Economy and the Possibilities of Governance. Cambridge: Polity Press.

James Manor (1997), 'The Political Economy of Decentralisation', *The World Bank*, August.

Klitgaard, E. Robert (1988), Controlling Corruption. Berkley: California University Press.

Litvack, Jennie, Junaid Ahmad and Richard Bird (1998), Rethinking Decentralization in Developing Countries. Washington D C: World Bank.

Mankiw, G. Romer, D. and D. Weil (1992), A Contribution to the Empirics of Economic Growth, *Quarterly Journal of Economic*, 107(2): 407-427.

Mittleman, J. H. (1996), The Dynamics of Globalization. In James H Mittelman (Ed.), (1996). Globalization Critical Reflections Boulder, U.S.A.: Lynne Rienner.

PRIA (2000), Programme for Strengthening Panchayati Raj Institutions: Narrative Report. New Delhi: PRIA.

Sachs, Jeffrey and Andrew Warner (1995), Economic Reform and the Progress of Global Integration. Harvard I.E.R. *Working Paper, No.1733*. Harvard: Harvard Institute of Economic Research.

Sangita S. N. (2002), Administrative Reforms for Good Governance, *The Indian Journal of Political Science*, 63 (4), December 2002.

Sangita S NS (2007), Decentralisation for Good Governance and Service Delivery in India: Theory and Practice, *The Indian Journal of Political Science*, Vol. LXVIII (3), July Sept., 447-484.

Schiller, Otto (1969), Cooperation and Integration in Agricultural Production Concepts and Practical Application: An International Synopsis. London: Asia Publishing House.

Sivanna N. (2004), Panchayat Jamabandhi in Karnataka: A Case of Transparency and Accountability in Good Governance, No. 142, ISEC, Bangalore.

Srinivasan, N. (2003), Federalism, Decentralization, Globalization and Economic Reforms: Some Issues by Center for Research on Economic Development and Policy reform. *Working Paper*,

No.158. Stanford University: Center for Research on Economic Development and Policy Reform.

Sundaram, Meenakshi (1994), *Decentralisation in Developing Countries*. New Delhi: Concept.

Webster, Neil (1992), Panchayati Raj and the Decentralisation of Development Planning in West Bengal. Calcutta: K P Bagachi and Company.

Westergaard, Kirsten (1986), *"People's participation, Local government and Rural Development: The case of West Bengal"*. CDR Research Report.

World Bank (2000), 'Decentralisation: Rethinking Government' in *Entering the 21st Century World Development Report 1999/2000*, Washington, 107-124.

World Bank (2002), Decentralizing Indonesia: A Regional Public Expenditure Review, Overview Report "East Asia". Washington D C: World Bank.

EMPOWERMENT OF THE SOCIALLY DEPRIVED CHILDREN – A CASE STUDY OF CHILD LABOUR SCHOOLS IN KHAMMAM DISTRICT

S. K. Maheboob Bakse

Millions of children in today's world undergo the worst forms of child labor, which includes child slavery, child prostitution, child trafficking, child soldiers. In modern era of material and technological advancement, children I almost every country are being callously explo9ited. The official figure of child laborers worldwide is 13 millions, but the actual numbers are much more higher.

Of the estimated 250 million children between the ages of 5 and 14 who are economically active, some 50-60 million between the ages of 5 and 14 are engaged in tolerable forms of labor.

Among the 10-14 year old children the working rate of 41.3 per cent in Kenya, 31.4 per cent in Senegal, 30.1 per cent in Bangladesh, 25.8 per cent in Nigeria, 24 per cent in Turkey, 17.7 per cent in Pakistan, 16.1 per cent in Brazil, 14.4 per cent in India, 11.6 per cent in China.

India has the dubious distinction of being the nation with the largest number of child labourers in the World. The child labour endure miserable and difficult lives. They earn little and struggle to make enough to feed themselves and their families. They do not go to school, more than half of them are unable to learn barest "skills " of literacy. Poverty is one of the main reasons behind the phenomenon.

With official estimates 12.6 million children in hazardous occupations. India has the highest number of labours in the World under the 14 years of the age.

SECTORS INVOLVED IN CHILD LABOUR

1. **Beedi** – Manufacture: According to 1994 to 1995 survey revealed that, child labour workers comprise of more than 30 per cent of total hired workers in the beedi manufacture.
2. **Diamond Industry**: According to estimation of I.L.O. 25 per cent of the child labours are working in Diamond factores of Surat. Where the majority of the World Diamonds are cut and polished while workers are often paid only fraction of 1 per cent of the value of the stones they cut.
3. **Fireworks – Manufacture**: Fireworks manufacture in "Sivakasi' had along been criticized for their use of child labour. 3000 children still work at every stage of the manufacturing process with wages as low as Rs. 20/- per day.
4. **Silk-Manufacture**: According to human rights estimation at least 3,50,000 children are employed by the Silk Industry in India.
5. **Domestic-Labour:** According to official estimation child labour in domestic and in restaurants is more than 25,00,000, whole NGO estimates the figure to be around 20 million.

"Child Labour" is a socio-economical problem. In order to find out solutions to this problem, there has to be necessary enlightenment on certain factors, those are as follows:

1. Poverty
2. Unemployment
3. Over population

4. Illiteracy
5. Child-marriages
6. Breaking of joint family systems
7. The tradition of family
8. The Role of Industrialist, Capitalist and Big Farmers, Middlemen etc.
9. Defective-education and bad habits
10. Caste System and racial-discrimination
11. Children of died/martyr army man
12. Transition from centrally planned to a market economy

In order to eradicate child labour, there were exists number of child labour protection acts, those are as follows:

1. 1881: factories Act: It is one of the initial act, which was came into existence. The main aim of the act is, prohibition of employment of children of minimum age of seven years. In 1891, the age was increased upto 9 years, further, raised to 15 years in 1948. The act provided maximum working hours of (9) hours a day with atleast for holidays in a month.

In 1891, working hours were reduced to (7) hours with prohibition of work at night was modified 7 P.M. and 5.30 P.M.

I. The Mines Act – 1901: The act of 1901 prohibited, employment of children under the age of (12) years. In 1923, age was raised 13 years, in 1935, it was further raised to (15) years. It further provided permission of employment of persons, between 15 and 17 years only on production of certificate of physical fitness granted by a qualified medical practitioner.

II. 1931: The Indian Ports Act: It is laid down 12 years as the minimum age that could be prescribed for handing goods in ports.

III. 1932: The Tea Districts Act: This act was passed to check migration of labourto Assam provided, that no under-age child is employed or allowed to migrate unless the child was accompanied by either her parents or adults on whom the child was dependent.

IV. 1933: The Children Pleading Act: Prohibited pleading of children – i.e. taking of advances by parents and guardians in return for bonds, pledging the labour others children.

V. 1938: The Employment of Children Act: Children under the age of 13 years shall not be employed or work in the transport of passengers or goods or mails, by rails, etc.

The act prohibited the employment of child. Under 15 years in occupations , connected with transport of goods, passengers, mails on railways.

1951: The Plantation Labour Act: Prohibited the employment of children under the 12 years in plantation.

1958: The Merchant Shipping Act: Prohibits children under 15, to be engaged to work in any capacity in any ship.

1961: The Apprentices Act: Prohibits the apprenticeship/ training of the person under the 14 years of age.

1966: The Beedi and Cigar, Workers Prohibit Act: The Employment of Children, under the (14) years in any industrial premises manufacturing, beedies or cigars.

1986: The Child Labur (Prohibition and Regulation) Act: The Act 'ban' on the children under the (14) years of children in specified occupations and processes. (Neary 100 above).

The Role of the Constitution to eradicate child labourers:

1. **Article – 23:** Prohibition of traffic in human beings and forced labour.
2. **Article – 24:** Prohibition of employment in factories etc.

3. **Article - 39(e) and (f):** The State shall in particular, direct it spolicy securing that the health and strength of workers, men and women. (f) That children are given opportunities and facilities to develop in a healthy manner and in condition of freedom and dignity.
4. **Article – 41:** The Right to work, to education and to public assistance in particular circumstances.
5. **Article – 45:** 'Provision' for free and compulsory education for children.
6. **Article – 47:** Responsibilities of the children to raise the nutritional levels and standards of living of its citizen and to improve the public health.

Implementation of Various Acts: The high introduce of child labour in India, the poor implementation of the Acts stands predominant. As matters relating to children receive low priority, when it comes to implementation.

1. In addition the existing enforcement, machinery very often does not have proper orientation or inclination to deal with the problem.
2. Most of the inspections conducted on child labour law do not end up in prosecution, because during the inspection. Some of the provisions of the Act or the Rules are lost sight of.
3. For the Inspections under the Act to be purposeful and effective should always be surprise, because of the employers, who employ children send to children away or hide the children and destroy the evidence about employment of the childe,
4. As employers, generally do not keep record of child labour 'frequent' inspections are necessary.
5. Prosecutions do not result in convictions very often because of the failure on the part Inspections to gather sufficient and reliable evidences during the course of Inspections.

6. The most common among the reasons for acquittal cases are delay in filling the case.

'Moreover, analyzing, the various legal measures, concerning child labour reveals that the problem, w ere often approached, within narrow perspective, which ignore the causes which are deep rooted. Such an approach the children are the generation of the future and their normal, development is an important determinant of the future of the country.

"N.C.L.P. – Started in 1987": National Child Labour Project (N.C.L.P.)

N.C.L.P. oriented towards the objective of freeing children from the exploitative conditions and to provide space and opportunities for their full fledged development. The main activity of N.C.L.P. is to identify, release and rehabilitate child workers.

Coverage of N.C.L.P. Schools

There are (1130) special schools sanctioned to A.P. State and out of this (1032) schools are actually operational. Nearly 50,000 children are enrolled in these schools with (57) per cent of them girl children. The average enrolment per school works out to 53. All the (23) districts covered under N.C.L.P. n Andhra Pradesh.

Management of N.C.L.P. Schools

The 95 per cent of the N.C.L.P. schools are run by N.G.O. in Andhra Pradesh State. It is found in some districts that the schools are entrusted to SHG and Youth clubs.

Khammam N.C.L.P. Project

In Khammam District National Child Labour Project initiated in 1995. Approximately (40) schools were sanctioned to operate child labour schools. Under the supervision of Project Director, Misses, Leelavathi Madam (P.D.).

There has been no clear cut guidelines provided, by the State authorities in the past on running of N.C.L.P. societies at the district level. During April, 2007 clear guidelines were issued to all the district collects from the State Project Director, SSA, Andhra Pradesh. Those are as follows:

1. The 'Child Labour Schools' children certificates issued by labour officers to the effect that they were relieved from from hazardous or non-hazardous occupations shall only be admitted in N.C.L.P. schools.
2. The children between 9-14 age group shall only be admitted in N.C.L.P. schools.
3. The N.G.O.'s with good track record only be permitted to run the N.C.L.P. schools
4. N.G.O.'s who came with their own list children seeking approval of N.C.L.P. and shall not be considered, without proper verified of all 100 per cent cases.
5. N.C.L.P. schools shall be run only as per the N.C.L.P. Norms and Conditions.

The researcher has been selected 15 school to collect sample data, from different Urban and Rural areas. From each school 15 (respondents) have been chosen for interview. The Interview – Questionnaire, mainly emphasized on different perception, broadly such as, Health, Education, Infrastructure, facilities of the school and Soio0Economcal backgrounds of the respondents.

Based upon the Survey Report, these facts which has been find out. Those are as follows:

1. Among the respondents, especially in the parents, majority people were illiterate.
2. When we were taken family structure, most of the families were "Nuclear" families. Traditional Joint Families were broken out, because of the Industrial Revolution.

3. Among the respondents, family members also so high not below than the 4 members.
4. Majority people, Income (monthly) was just (Rs. 1000/- to Rs. 3000/-) below only.
5. Their expenditure is (monthly more than their earnings)
6. Most of the people, spending their income to drink 'Alchohol' and other bad habits.
7. Other finding was they were having, 'family tensions' each and every house.
8. According to views of the parents school are running in good manner has to be continued it.
9. There were no, 'optimistic' – Vocational training Centres, except the 'Screwing Machines.'
10. B.K. Schools, teachers are being attended schools regularly.
11. According to their 'opinion' (Teachers) the government should not, put, the restriction upon the age of child admitting in the school.
12. Most of the students come from the SC/ST/BC/ Minority Communities only.
13. Regarding to 'food' of B.K. Schools, more or less good.
14. Only few schools are having, playing material in the schools.
15. No B.K. School is having sufficient 'facilities'. Every one schools is only running 'tentative' – huts, tiles and rooms only.
16. Majority opinion of the respondents were after joining in the B.K. Schools, learners behaviour has been changed.
17. The B.K. Schools, children facing the facilities problem also. (bathroom, toilets, drinking water, etc.).

18. Recently – 'Rice' also curtailed by the Central Government to students because of State Government is arranging food.

19. Per candidate, they are going only 200 paise per day to students for nutritious food. It is also severely criticized by the people.

CONSTITUTIONAL PROVISIONS AND WOMEN EMPOWERMENT IN INDIA

S.A. Palekar

In India, there are many constitutional provisions to safeguard women interests in social, economic and political life. In order to improve the well being of women in society, the Government has made a significant shift in the approach from "Welfare during fifties" to "Development during seventies" and to "Empowerment during the nineties". During nineties major thrust in respect of women was to make them economically independent and self-reliant.

Today, women are engaged in all activities of the economy. Their economic and social status has improved and they are more educated and their awareness has increased. Though they are marching forward day-by-day, they have still many problems due to gender bias and sex discrimination. There are inter-state and intra-state disparities regarding social and economic status of women. Much has been done but more efforts are still required to make women as important agents in the process of social and economic development.

In this paper an attempt has been made to highlight the need and importance of the issue of women empowerment and also constitutional provisions and other legal provisions in India, made to safeguard the interest of women and to ensure their rights. The paper also presents an overall scenario of women empowerment in India. The paper also discusses efforts, programmes and policies of women empowerment in India under Five year plans and other government schemes. Lastly, paper deals with concludes the important findings of this study and provides fruitful suggestions to improve the social and economic status of women in India.

WOMEN EMPOWERMENT: NEED AND ISSUE

During the post-independence era, India took a path of directed social change based primarily on constitutional and legal reforms, planned economic development and state support for social welfare activities to create a democratic, equitable and prosperous society in which there would be no discrimination on the basis of sex, caste and creed. To this end, a major policy thrust was laid on the education of women. The advent of the green revolution during mid-sixties which helped in linking the rural and urban areas, brought rural women gradually within the purview of education. However, it was only with the formulation of the Sixth Plan draft (1980-85) that a separate section on women's employment was incorporated while the New Policy of Education (NPE) 1986, made special provisions for the education of the women. These developments gave a fillip to the education of women and helped them to enhance their status by seeking diversified employment opportunities at the various levels of education. However, the educational opportunities have not been uniformly spread over all the states of the Indian Union.

The need to bring women into the mainstream of development has been a prime concern in India. It is so because they are the principal provider of care and support to infants and children. Thus, the investment towards woman capacity building and empowering them to exercise their choice is not only valuable in itself but also the surest way to contribute to economic growth and overall development of the society.

Empowerment may be defined as a "Process which increases the assets and capability of the poor people – women and men and other excluded groups to participate, negotiate, change and hold accountable institution that affect this well being" (Deepa Narayana, 2000).

In this way, empowerment is closely related to human resource development and human capital building, which is the process of increasing capacities of people in society (Reddy, 2002). Capacity defines the potential for development, like the capacity to generate local resource and the capacity to use resource effectively, while performance represents the degree to which that potential is realized in actual achievement. Capacities of people also mean health condition, education level, use and control over resources/ public services and social and political strengths.

At the level of individual development, Amartya Sen's work on human capabilities stresses empowerment as both a means and an end. It is a process of development of individual capacities through gaining education and skills in order to empower individuals to fight for a better quality of life (1990, 1995). Looking at the lack of attention to the political processes required for equitable resource distribution in Sen's view, Batliwala (1994) insists that women's empowerment must include transforming political action as well. Rowlands (1997, 1998), drawing on feminist writings, argues that 'empowerment is more than participation in decision making; it must also include the processes that lead people to perceive themselves as able and entitled to make decisions. To her, it is personal, relational and collective.

CONSTITUTIONAL AND OTHER PROVISIONS

The Principle of gender equality and justice and protection of women's rights have been the prime concerns in India thinking from the days of the independence. Accordingly, the country's concern in safe guarding the rights and privileges of women found its best expression in the constitution of India. While Article 14 confers equal rights and opportunities both to men and women in the political, economic and social spheres, Article 15 prohibits discrimination against any citizen on the grounds of sex, religion, race, caste etc and Article 15 (3) empowers the state to make any special provision in favour of women and children. Similarly, Article 16 provides for equal opportunities in the matter of public appointment for all citizens. Yet, another Article 39 mentions that the state shall direct its policy towards providing to men and women equally the rights to means of livelihood and equal by pay for equal work. Article 42 directs the state to make provisions for ensuring just and humane conditions of work and maternity relief. Article 51 (A) (e) impose a fundamental duty on every citizen to renounce the practices derogatory to the dignity of women. Certain legislations relating to safeguard the interest of women and girls are like the Dowry Prohibition Act, 1961, The Child Marriage Restraint Act, 1929 (as amended in 1986), the Immoral Traffic (Prevention) Act, (as Amended and retitled in 1986), Indecent Representation of Women (prevention) Act. 1986 etc have also come about in the recent times. The landmark achievements of both the 73rd and 74th constitutional Amendments in 1993 have also empowered women by participation in the grass-root democracy through the Panchayati Raj Institutions (PRIs) and Local Bodies.

The other main acts/provisions for providing social securities and equal rights etc. to women are- The factories (Amendment) Act, 1976, The women Factories Act, 1976, Industrial Dispute Act, 1947, The employee's State Insurance Act. The Medical and Sickness Benefit, The contract Labour Act, The Equal Remuneration Act. 1976 & 1978, The Immoral Traffic (Prevention), Act. 1956, the marriage Law Amendment Act 1976, The Special Marriage Act. 1954, Hindu Wives' Adoption and Maintenance Act, 1956, Family Courts,

Indecent Representation of Women (Prohibition), Act 1986, The Commission of Sati (Prevention) Act. 1987 and National Commission for Women Act. 1991 etc.

WOMEN EMPOWERMENT EFFORTS

Women constitute the most important target groups in the present day context of development planning. It is urgently felt that women be empowered economically and socially to become a strong and vigorous force in the development of the country. To empower women, efforts are being made; (i) to finalise the draft National Policy for Empowerment of Women. (ii) to legislate reservation of not less than 1/3 seats for women in the Lok Sabha and in the State Legislative Assemblies so as to ensure adequate representation of women in decision making; (iii) to adopt an integrated approach towards empowering women through effective convergence of existing services, financial and human resources, and infrastructure in both women-specific and women related sectors; (iv) to organize women into self-help groups. A task force on Women and Children has been constituted to review the existing legislation and Government schemes for improving the asset base of women to improve their social status. The Women's Component Plan (WCP) introduced as a major strategy for the first time during the Ninth Five-Year Plan (1997-2002) was reviewed in August, 2000. It took note of funds having been made available by a number of Ministries/Departments such as Health and Family Welfare, H.R.D., Labour, Agriculture, Rural Development, Social Justice and Empowerment, Tribal Affairs, etc. to benefit women. Some states such as Gujarat, Himachal Pradesh, Karnataka and Kerala have also earmarked funds under WCP.

Under the Five Year plans, several efforts have been made to enhance the status of women in India. The First Five Year Plan (1951-56) envisaged certain welfare measures for women. The Central Welfare Board (CSWB) was established in 1953 which symbolized the welfare approach to women's problems.

Under Second Five Year Plan (1956-61) the need for the organization of women as workers was recognised. Further, to enable women to compete for higher jobs, it suggested provision for their training also.

Female education, as a major welfare strategy was emphasized in the Third and Fourth Five Year Plans. The Fifth Five Year Plan coincided with the International Women's Decade (1975-85) and the submission of the Report of the Committee on the Status of Women in India (CSWI). United Nations declared 1975 as International Year of Women and now thereafter every year 8th of March is celebrated as International Women's Day all over the world. All these initiatives helped at least to focus attention on the problems specific to women.

In the Sixth Plan, for the first time, a shift was perceived from welfare to development approaches for women. This plan devoted a whole chapter to women and development.

The Seventh Five Year Plan envisaged operational concern for equality and empowerment articulated by the International Decade for Women. Then came the 1990s, an era of structural reforms, where much emphasis had been on privatization and deregulation of domestic economies. Under this new regime, it appears that the issue of employment which had been accorded high priority during the four decades preceding 1990, has now in late nineties suddenly, became a less important issue. Many experts feel that the new economic policies are increasingly marginalizing women from their traditional occupations, and very little has been done to prepare them for alternative, newer or better avenues of employment.

Focusing on gender issues in the context of the social sector development means empowering women as agents of socio-economic change. The Ninth Plan (1997-2002) specially stipulated identifying "Women Component Plans" for which at least 30 per cent of funds should flow to women development schemes. There are women specific welfare schemes/programmes that receive funds under the annual Budgetary allocations such Mahila Samridhi Yojana, Balika Samridhi yojana, Working Womens Hostels, Swashakti Project and other schemes – 29 identifiable women specific schemes that received Rs. 856.64 crores allocation in 2000-01 Central Government Budget as against Rs. 605.46 crore in 1999-2000 (RE). The Department of Women and Child Development sponsored study undertaken by National Institute of Public Finance and Policy in its interim report: 'India-Gender Budgeting' in December 2000, has assembled very useful information that can help in focusing greater attention on women specific issues and can facilitate greater inflow of development funds for women/child welfare schemes.

Some interesting features of this study are highlighted below:

1. Apart from promoting equality among citizens, gender equality can benefit the economy through efficiency gains. For example, the likelihood of children being enrolled in school goes up with their mother's educational level. Women's extra income also has a greater positive impact on household investments in nutrition, health and education of children, relative to extra income accruing to the father. From the efficiency point of view, what is important is the social rate of return of investment in women, and in many cases, this can be greater than the corresponding rate for men.
2. While many public goods and services like defence are not amenable to gender partitioning, many others have a differential impact on the two sexes. For example, outlays for augmenting the supply of safe drinking water can benefit women more than men by cutting down on the time spent in fetching water

from the river or ponds. The existing practice of budgeting does not pay any special attention to the impact of budgets on women.

Some programmes have also been undertaken which can be called women-specific employment cum training programmes. These comprise Development of Women and Children in Rural Areas (DWCRA), Indira Mahila Yojana (IMY), Support to Training and Employment Programme (STEP), 1991. In addition, the Rashtriya Mahila Kosh (RMK), which works through the medium of NGOs, is an innovation venture to facilitate credit support to poor and asset less women struggling in the informal sector. Further, the Rural Women's Development and Empowerment project (RWDEP) was sanctioned in October, 1998 as a centrally sponsored project aimed at crating an environment for empowerment of women in six states of Bihar, Haryana, Karnataka, Gujarat, Madhya Pradesh and Uttar Pradesh. The government has also set up a National Commission for Women (NCW) to safeguard the rights and interests of women through review of laws and intervention in social harassment of women at the work place and in specific individual complaints of atrocities.

In addition to the government, the voluntary non-government organisations have also come into existence in the country in a comprehensive way. They are mobilizing women by making them conscious of their rights and preparing them for collective action. To mention a few examples, 'Jago Bahana' on Bihar (In the leadership of Dr. Shanti Ojha, President Awardee), the Rajasthan Women's Development Programme, the Mahila Samakhya, Chipko, SEWA, Annapurna, the All India Women's Conference, the Gandhi Smarak Nidhi, the Kasturba Trust and the Khadi and Village Industries Commission are doing great deal of work for women, both in the rural and the urban areas of the country. The role and contribution of women in economic activities should be given its due place by enabling them to unleash their creative potentials and entrepreneurial talents apart from being proud mothers of future citizens. There exists a great need to promote a number of N.G.O. type of organisations to harness this hidden resource. Moreover, Education of the 'Girl Child has received more importance in recent times.

CONCLUSIONS AND SUGGESTIONS

The important conclusions of this study are:

1. Issues of gender bias were taken seriously during mid nineties and especially from Ninth Five Year Plan in India. We have so many constitutional provisions/ amendments and other legal provisions to safeguard the socio-economic status of women in India.
2. Reduction of gender inequality and increasing economic empowerment of women has a positive relation to the social and economic development of the country because increase in female literacy, income and opportunities provides the basis to develop them as a human resource in the process of development.
3. A number of programmes and policies were launched for this purpose and they have had a successful effect in empowering women socially and economically.
4. In the liberalisation phase, more benefits have been availed by the urban female as compared to rural women; therefore, the participation rate of women has increased in the secondary and tertiary sectors. Similarly, women participation in decision making services and entrepreneurship have also increased but once again these fruits are obtained more by urban women who have better education, skill opportunities, exposure and good standard of living.
5. In the rural sector, there is still a lack of awareness, education, opportunities and basic facilities for women for economic empowerment.

6. Women education is still low as compared to men, and dropout rate from schools for the female child is high, thus, creating hurdle in the process of their empowerment.
7. Most of the working females are in rural areas and in the unorganised sector but they receive less income, whereas, in urban areas, females have skilled jobs, more income and in the private sector, their participation has increased. The maximum employment growth of females has been observed in the service sector.
8. Unfortunately, the crime rate against women has increased which shows that women have not obtained their desired social status yet and social thinking has still not changed much.

SUGGESTIONS

Some important suggestions for women empowerment in the present day context are:

1. Since 1990, economic reforms, new economic policy, awareness and efforts for women empowerment came side by side. As a result, no doubt the literacy gap between male and female has narrowed down but still female education should be at top priority and there is a need to increase primary education for females and to check out their dropout rate.
2. It is true that educated and trained women are finding and will find increasing avenues for employment in all sectors in the growing economy. So, women have to improve their skill and qualify themselves for semi-skilled and skilled jobs. For this, educational programs will have to be restructured and emphasis should be laid on girls' education.
3. There is a need to promote the health of mothers and children with an emphasis on individual

reproductive choice, access to information and health services.

4. A quantum jump is necessary to promote quality skill and productivity of women with the support of government, NGOs and social thinkers.
5. Proper institutional support for credit, information, and guidance is necessary to support self employed women in rural and semi urban areas, because females in these areas are behind in terms of all these things as compared to urban employed women and women entrepreneurs. The procedure of getting finance should be simple also.
6. To encourage women entrepreneurship, encouragement to technical and professional education is necessary. Easy education loans are essential for this purpose.
7. There is a need to strengthen legal and regulatory measures for equal opportunities.
8. It is important to organise and train poor, dalit and tribal women to take part in Panchayat elections.
9. In the decade of economic reforms, in case of economic empowerment of women we have some success but on the social front the status of women is still poor. So, more constitutional amendments and legal provisions along with their effective implementation are highly desirable to enhance the social status of women.

Empowerment of women would depend upon change in the value systems, attitudes and social structure prevailing in the country. Women have to change their attitude towards women. This would necessitate coordinated and concerted efforts on the part of our political leaders, social reformers and other members of social strata, including the women themselves. Mere reservation for women in local, state and national bodies will not solve their problems unless everybody realized that man and woman are equal. We also need a fundamental change in our mindsets.

References

Leslie J. Calman (1992), *Toward Empowerment: Woman and Movement Politics in India*, Boulder, Westview Press.

Karl, Marilee (1995), *Women and Empowerment–Participation and Decision-Making*, London & New Jersey, Zed Books.

Sen, G. Germain, A. and Chen, L. C. (eds.) (1994), *Population Policies Reconsidered – Health, Empowerment and Rights*, Boston, Massachusetts, Harvard School of Public Health.

Anker Richard (1998), Gender and Jobs: Sex Segregation of Occupation in the World, ILO, Geneva.

Jain, A. K. and P. K. Bhargava (1989), "Role of Women in Economic Development: The Case of Women workers in India," The *Indian Journal of Economics*.

Banerjee, N. and S. Mitter (1998), "Women Making a Meaning Full Choice", *EPW*.

Census of India, 1991 and 2001, Govt. of India.

Employment Review, Various Issues, Ministry of Labour, Govt. of India.

Economic and Political Weekly, Various Issues.

Government of India (1988), "Report of the core Group, National *Perspective Plan for Women*. 1998-2000 AD".

Mohd. Muzammil, "Improving the Economic and Social Status of Women, VARTA, Vol. XVII & VIII, Oct. 96, 97.

UNDP, Human Development Report-1995, Oxford University Press, Delhi.

World Development Report, Issues 1997, Onwards.

THE BSP AND DALIT EMPOWERMENT IN UTTAR PRADESH: DILEMMAS AND CONTRADICTIONS

SHYAM SINGH

INTRODUCTION

Dalit Empowerment has been on the top of the priorities of contemporary Dalit Movement in the country in general and Uttar Pradesh in particular. The perception of the Dalit leaders about the empowerment has broadly been surrounded by two strategies. First is to capture the office of the government at the both levels – central and state, and second is to benefit Dalits by introducing exclusive public policies in the domain of social welfare and social security. The logic behind these two strategies is that if political power rests in the hands of Dalits they would feel their social status enhanced, and their economic status would boost up when they get benefits from public policies exclusively designed for them. BSP's project of Dalit Empowerment in Uttar Pradesh has been underwritten in these lines since it got power in the state for the first time. But, the contradiction took place when these two strategies became two priorities, dominating first on the second, for the BSP. For the BSP, the Herculean task is to retain state power while not losing its paternal electoral base i.e. Dalits. The BSP is compelled to share the benefits of public policies with upper castes, which is one of its constituencies along with Dalits, and Dalits are being compensated through the introduction of symbolic and cultural politics. Therefore, for the BSP, the project of cultural and symbolic politics becomes more important than the social development of the Dalits.

But, historical reality of depravedness and cornering them in public domain put a strong need to give special attention to them. This attention becomes necessary when the government is elected and headed by them. Arrangements of positive discrimination in the constitution have not been effective for the Dalits and they need a much more focused approach for their upliftment. Hence, agenda of Dalit Empowerment becomes crucial for both, the BSP and the Dalits. This paper is an attempt to analyze both perspectives. The questions which are to be asked in this paper are as to how the present BSP Government in Uttar Pradesh is responding to the Dalit empowerment, on what junctures need Dalit empowerment and BSP's politics for the Dalits reconcile, and how a common man from Dalit community understands the BSP's agenda of Dalit empowerment and the Dalit politics. Methodologically, paper is based on primary fieldwork. In-dept interviews with the BSP leaders at the district level and BSP cadres at the village level are the main instruments to get answers to the above asked questions.

The paper is divided into three sections. The first section gives details about the BSP's priorities of the social welfare and social security policies in three social sectors – Health, Education and Health. This section looks at the BSP's efforts for the welfare of the Dalits and others. The second section contains a discussion on the cultural and symbolic policy of the BSP. This section analyzes how the BSP is giving dominant priority to its cultural policy. Third and last section provides analysis of understanding of common people from the Dalit community about the BSP's efforts for the empowerment of the Dalits and its *Sarva Samaj* Policy. The analysis of this section is based on the interviews with the 100 beneficiaries of different social security schemes of Health, Education and Housing sectors and 100 local BSP cadres from 6 villages in UP. The last section is followed by the conclusion.

BSP'S PRIORITIES OF THE SOCIAL WELFARE AND SOCIAL SECURITY

BSP's priorities of social welfare and social security have been surrounding around the Dalits in Uttar Pradesh. During the first three tenures of the BSP in the office of State Government (1995, 1997, 2002-03) in Uttar Pradesh exclusive public policies and programmes were introduced to benefits Dalits from many ways. During its initial tenures in Government, BSP advocated a one point programme: proportional representation to all groups in government, bureaucracy and educational institutions. It solved all aspirations of Dalits which the Congress had neglected (Hasan, 2002). This concept provided rationale to the BSP to originate some exclusive public policies for the Dalits. Therefore, BSP took both sort term and long term efforts to benefit Dalits. Under sort-term provisions, some arrangements like scholarships, compensation for deaths, injuries and atrocities to SCs, and marriage and illness contingencies were provisioned by the then BSP led governments during first three turns. And, as a long-term agenda, the BSP has introduced Ambedkar Village Programme (AVP) which was to be introduced only in the villages having domination of SCs in population. So much so that, in 1995, the then Chief Minister Ms. Mayawati had given an order to stop all the welfare programmes going on in the state so that funds could be diverted to the villages selected under the AVP (Dainik Jagran, 1995).

Therefore, the guiding principle of the BSP politics i.e. proportional representation to all the groups was restricted only to the Dalits, though the principal talks about giving priority to all the sections of society according to their proportion in the population, and other sections were left out without giving any attention to them. The BSP was so serious about the implementation of Dalit-oriented programmes, that it had deputed special officers from the Dalit community in important departments of each district so that schemes and programmes for the Dalits could be implemented properly. To make this happen, the BSP governments in 1995, 1997 and 2002-03 had done large scale transfers of administrative and police officers. Tenures of the BSP governments during these periods were vey small and the party had to rely on the others to be in the office of the government. It compelled the BSP to change its political strategy. Change in the political strategy for any political party in a democratic system is not an easy task, especially when it is in a competitive democratic system. Changes have to be reflected in the major ideological perspective; then only that party can present its rationale before the masses. The BSP has gone in the same lens. For expanding its electoral base, BSP brought a policy called for *Sarva Samaj* which provides a framework to accommodate every section of society along with the Dalits. Though, strategically, this policy targeted upper castes, mainly Brahmins, the BSP chief, Mayawati, referred to her party icon B R Ambedkar to prove this ideological change valid: "Ambedkar not only accepted a *Brahmin* surname given to him by a *Brahmin* teacher but also married a *Brahmin*." She also termed *Brahmins* as '*manav*' (humans) and not '*manuwadis*', and as leaders of social change (Verma, 2005).

The change in the political strategy of the BSP has also brought about changes in the party's policy preferences. For example, earlier AVP was to be implemented in only villages where share of SC population is more than 50 per cent but now the present BSP government (2007) is intended to implement this programme in each and every village of the state. The implementation of plan will be completed within five years in five stages. And also, earlier benefits of plan were given exclusively to the Dalits but now benefits of this plan are available for high caste people too, under the AVP. After adopting the *Sarva Samaj* policy, policy initiatives are highly inclined towards the new social bases of BSP. Mayawati is also repeatedly advocating for reservation for the poor among higher castes and for that she demands amendment in the constitution of India (Singh & Kumar, 2009). To keep the broader look at the BSP's priorities for the social welfare and social security under the *Sarva Samaj* agenda, here we discuss schemes and programmes in three social sectors – health, education and housing in Uttar Pradesh. The points of our analysis in these three sectors are: to look at the status of social security schemes and programmes initiated by both Central and State Governments and to look at the quantity and quality of the social security schemes initiated by the present BSP Government in UP.

Health is an important constituent of human development. The state of health in UP is a human development challenge (HDRUP, 2003). Health Services in UP are not impressive and have been declining over time. Though, UP has a large public sector health infrastructure, only 9 per cent of it makes use of this facility for treatment of ordinary illnesses and has to depend on private healthcare. UP stands at 11th rank among Indian states and reserved 63.8 percent life expectancy rate in 2001, while the life expectancy rate of India for same year was 65.4 percent. Infant mortality rate in UP in 2002 was 80 (16th among all Indian states) much higher than average IMR of India (63). In 2007, infant mortality rate for UP came down to the level of 69, but was still much higher than India (55). Only Orissa (71) and MP (72) are lagging behind from UP. The percentage of safe deliveries is very less in SC/STs. The rate of undernourished children in UP is 51.7 per cent and stood at 22nd position among 25 Indian states. Per capita health expenditure of UP for 2003-04 was Rs 91.43 only above the Bihar (Rs. 76.73). All

India per capita health expenditure for same period was Rs. 214. 62.

Among the existing measures of health in UP arė mostly financed and initiated by the central government under the umbrella of National Rural health Mission (NRHM). The major components under the NRHM are- Reproductive and Child Health (RCH) services which include maternal and child care benefits and facilities, Village Health Plan, District health Plan and District Health Fund, upgrading Community Health Centres to the Indian Public health Standard and State health Mission. Broadly, NRHM takes care of major health requiremenst including the development of infrastructure and social security services. The major intervention by the central government gives a free hand to the state government. Therefore, the present BSP government has not initiated any of social security schemes in health Sector except SSMY which is being financed by the central government under NRHM. It should be noted here that there are no exclusive health services available exclusively to benefit Dalits, though they are being benefited among all other sections of society.

Education is another important area of human development. Aggregate Literacy Rate of UP is 56.3 per cent which is lower that the Indian average i.e. 64.8 per cent. The female literacy rate in UP (42.2 per cent) is also lower than all India average Female Literacy Rate (53.7). About 36 per cent of rural males and 70 per cent of rural females are illiterate. Only 15 per cent of rural persons and 37 per cent of urban persons are reported to have received education up to secondary level or above and only about 14 per cent of the urban people and 2.8 per cent of the rural people had received education up to graduate level or above. The aggregate dropout rate in class I-X in UP for 2005-06 is 42.26 per cent. The dropout rate of boys and girls are 39.5 per cent and 47.36 per cent respectively. In this respect UP is in a better position than the all-India average which claims 60.41 per cent for boys and 63.44 per cent for girls. Drop-out rate in lower social

Table 1
Existing Health Security Schemes in UP

Schemes	*Nature of the Benefits*	*Target group/s*	*Sponsorship*	*Initiator*
Janani Suraksha Yojana (JSY)	Maternal benefits: financial and medical help in public health centers	Pregnant women from BPL families (no caste restriction)	Central Government	Central Government
Saubhagyawati Surakshit Matretev Yojana (SSMY)	Maternal benefits: financial and medical help in private health centers	Pregnant women from BPL families (no caste restriction)	Central Government	*BSP Government*
School Health Programme (SHP)	Medical checkup and medicine	Students in primary and junior schools (no caste restriction)	State Government	Earlier state government but not BSP Government

groups in UP is very high. For SC, it is 72.56 per cent which is more that the all India average of 70.57 per cent.

In the Education sector, the central government is making huge contribution through Sarva Siksha Abhiyan (SSA) in terms of funds being provided under it. As far as the BSP government is concerned, it has initiated one scheme for the girl students of secondary classes (11th and 12th). They are provided one bicycle and a sum of Rs 25000/ in two installments during a period of two years. This scheme is fully financed by the state government. Although, the state government is also contributing in the scholarship for the pre- and post-metric students for all categories- general, OBCs and SC/STs (table 2). Therefore, in comparison to the health sector, the BSP government is more concerned with education. But, again the point to be noted is that benefits under the social security schemes in the education sector are entitled to the poor from all sections of society rather than restricted to the Dalits only.

Uttar Pradesh is the most populous state in the country. Huge numbers of people live in mud houses. NSSO data shows that in rural UP, 23 per cent of households have katcha houses. In urban slums and squatter 12 per cent houses are katcha houses (NSSO, 2002). These people have a strong need to get pakka houses. The government of Uttar Pradesh along with the central government is implementing some housing security schemes aiming those poor people who either don't have houses or have mud houses. The BSP government seems to be impressive in the housing sector as against its less interest in health and education sectors. The government has initiated two housing security schemes in addition to the central government scheme i.e. IAY (table 3). For the urban houseless poor, KSGAY has been introduced by the BSP which, interestingly, provisions major parts of the benefit to poor people from general castes. OBCS get 23 per cent and SCs get 27 per cent of total benefits under KSGAY. Central government sponsored IAY (state share is only 25 per cent)

Table 2
Existing Education Security Schemes in UP

Schemes	*Nature of the Benefits*	*Target group/s*	*Sponsorship*	*Initiator*
Scholarships	Financial help	Pre- and post-metric students	Central & State Government	Central & State Government
Savitribai Phule Balika Shiksha Madad Yojana (SBSMY)	Rs 25000/ and one bicycle	Girls students form BPL families (no caste restriction)	BSP Government	BSP Government
Mid Day Meal	Day-food	Students of primary and junior schools	Central Government	Central Government

Table 3
Existing Housing Security Schemes in UP

Schemes	*Nature of the Benefits*	*Target group/s*	*Sponsorship*	*Initiator*
Indira Awaas Yojana (IAY)	Financial benefits to construct or upgrade the house	BPL Families (no caste restriction)	75:25 share of central and State Governments	Central Government
Mahamaya Awaas Yojana (MAY)	Construction or up gradation the house	BPL SC/ST families	BSP Government	BSP Government
Kanshi Ram Shahari Gareeb Awaas Yojana (KSGAY)	To provide fully furnished houses	BPL families 50%- General, 27%- SC/ST, 23%- OBCs	BSP Government	BSP Government

is already being implemented in rural areas. In this case BSP is trying to keep balance while introducing MAY which provides housing security exclusively for SC/STs in rural areas.

While summing up this section it can be concluded that the BSP's attention on the Dalits has been reduced. During earlier tenures of the BSP Governments in UP, most of the social sector benefits were reserved for the Dalits. But, in the present tenures, attention on Dalits has been diverted. The BSP is sharing the benefits with other social sections, especially general castes which were totally neglected during earlier tenures of the BSP in power in UP. At the same time, it can also be concluded that the BSP's attention on the social security of the poor has been reduced. The details about the ongoing social security schemes in three sectors under the BSP government given in the tables- 1, 2 & 3 reflect that there is no attention from the BSP government on the health services. However, a little attention has been given for secondary education by arranging one scheme for girls to attract them to higher education. The BSP has given considerable attention to housing security for the poor.

CULTURAL AND SYMBOLIC POLICY OF THE BSP

The BSP, in its fourth tenure in office in Uttar Pradesh, has divided its political preferences into two different priorities. One is to include all sections of society, keeping focus on the upper castes, into the party's social welfare agenda. Secondly, the party has concentrated on the work to glorify Dalit History. During earlier tenures of the party in government, the BSP's agenda of social welfare was cornered around only Dalits and a cultural policy was implemented in a modest way. The names of many districts were changed and the new districts were named after Dalit icons. The BSP has established many Ambedkar statues in villages and town squares during its previous three tenures, but it did not work because the people simply discarded the BSP's agenda because the common man perceived Ambedkar more as the founder of the Constitution than as a Dalit icon. Therefore, the BSP is now focusing also on parks and monuments in the name Kanshi Ram and Mayawati, even though there is widespread protest from other political groups (Singh, 2010). In the present tenure, this policy has received significant attention, probably more than any other policy from the BSP. For balancing the act between the Dalits and non-Dalits, the BSP is addressing the Dalits' sentiments and emotions by building monuments and memorials in the honor of Dalit icons.

The cultural policy of the BSP incurs huge public expenditure and that has limited the government's ability to use funds for some other important concerns like social welfare or rural development or environment. A according to one estimate, the cost of the 60 stone elephants set up in Ambedkar Memorial, one of the BSP's dream projects in Lucknow, the government has spent Rs.60 lakh per piece per stone elephant. But for creation and maintenance of a special elephant reserve, the state government is sparing only Rs.50 lakh. The state's forest department decided to allocate an annual budget (for the year 2009-10) of Rs.50 lakh for the elephant reserve to come up in Bijnore district under Project Elephant.[1] Similarly, the Uttar Pradesh Chief Minister Mayawati has shown an inability to implement the Right to Education (RTE) Act 2010 because of UP has no funds. RTE insures free education to children of 6-14 years age group. Nearly two crore children in UP fall under the RTE and this would cost total Rs 18000/crore. According to the provision of RTE 45 % or Rs 8000 of total funds should be arranged by the UP government (Times of India, 2010a). In another development, for example, the UP government has indicated that it does not have funds to provide electricity to 10,000 Ambedkar villages in the state. It should be noted that 1, 28,518 hamlets in the state are yet to receive any electrification -solar or thermal. The UP government sent a proposal comprising Rs 10,407/ crore for electrification of its villages under phase II of the Rajiv Gandhi Grameen Vidyutikaran Yojana (RGGVY), where the centre provides 90% subsidy, while the remaining 10% is loaned to the state government (Times of India, 2010b).

During May 2007-August 2009, the BSP government in UP has spent around Rs 4,500 crore on memorials and parks in Lucknow. Rs 8.54 crore has been spent on two stone plaques at Kanshiram Smarak Sthal. Over Rs 300 crore has been spent on construction of statues and murals in Lucknow in first two years of BSP rule. Over Rs 150 crore has been spent on boundary walls to protect different memorials and statues in Lucknow. Rs 5.64 crore was spent on construction of a 530-meter boundary wall at Kanshiram Smarak i.e. one meter of boundary wall costs over Rs 1 lakh (Indian Express, 2010). Among some other constructions, Gautam Buddha Samta Moolak Sthal- 90 crore, Buddha Vihar Shanti Upwan- 15.15 crore, Manyawar Kanshi Ram Yaadgar Vishram Sthal- 12 crore, Kanshi Ram memorial- 370 core, Ramabai Ambedkar Maidan- 54 crore, Kanshi Ram eco Park- 4 crore and Samajik Parivartan Sthal – 150 crore are the costliest constructions done by the BSP Government[2].

The BSP government has also set up a special protection force consisting of ex-army men to protect these memorials and parks arguing that if any harm is done to these memorials, a massive social unrest may take place. The government has started recruitment of 1200 personal for this purpose which would cost approximately 9 crore per annum. Though, the government is looking for 2 lakh such security personals with the cost of approximately 67 crore per annum[3]. In that way, BSP has built up an entire strategy to keep its core constituency, the Dalits, within the basket of the party. According to Badri Narayan, the BSP's "politics of memorials" works at four levels[4]. "The first is the local heroes of yore at the village level. Their contribution to the Dalit cause is highlighted by putting up their statues and distributing printed material on a massive scale". At another level, the legacy of well-known poets and warriors from the community is publicized. "The next level is Ambedkar. The last is Kanshi Ram and Mayawati".

Despite of maintaining the Dalits' association with the party for long, the BSP's cultural and symbolic politics is trying to hit another ambitious objective. This objective has a two-fold strategy. The first is to break the dominion of the upper castes in colonial history, which was the result of a long independence movement under the leadership of the Congress. This hegemonic domination was further accentuated by the developmental projects run by the Congress governments in terms of establishing monuments, parks, museums and libraries that glorified the contributions made by its leaders. This helped the upper castes and the Congress to establish and maintain their dominance in politics for long periods. The second strategy of the BSP is to establish the same order of dominance as the Congress had enjoyed in Uttar Pradesh for first 40 years after the independence. It can help the BSP to hold the political power for long (Singh, 2010).

BSP's move towards the symbolic politics and its conscious unwillingness to underestimate other more important public concerns is a restless effort to woo the Dalits, no matter that other social groups have strong discontentment. Being a product of the century-long Dalit movement, the BSP gets reasonable rationality to argue in the favor of its memorials and symbols. Because social movements always find their roots in the interpretation of historical junctures, possibly in terms of historical struggle or indigenous liberty or natural rights or something else. The party is presenting its symbolic politics as a result of prolonged efforts of the Dalit Movement which took place under the guidance of a line of leaders started from Phule to Ambedkar to Kanshi Ram and now Mayawati.

DALITS' RESPONSE TO THE BSP'S SOCIAL WELFARE AND *SARVA SAMAJ* POLICY

It is very important to see that how those people feel about the government who are taking benefits of government's schemes and programmes related to the health, educational and housing security. Table 4 presents a set of quite dispersed opinions of beneficiaries of different social security schemes. In table 4, the figures are drawing attention to three points. One is reducing attention of BSP Government on SCs, as only 29 per cent respondents consider that BSP' focus of social welfare is only on SCs. Second is the widening horizon of social security schemes to the upper castes along with the SCs, as 33 per cent respondents support this view. Third and most important is the reluctance of a significant section of respondents (21 per cent) saying that BSP's focus is on nobody.

Table 4
BSP Government's focus of Social Welfare

Opinion of Beneficiaries	*Caste Affiliation of Beneficiaries*				*Total*
	General	*OBCs*	*SCs*	*Muslims*	
Focus is on only SCs	1	14 (41)	11 (20)	3	29
Focus is on SCs and only Brahmins		2 (6)	1 (2)		3
Focus is on SCs and all upper castes including Brahmins		12 (35)	21 (37.5)		33
Focus is on all sections of society		3 (9)	6 (11)	5	14
Focus in on nobody	1	3 (9)	17 (30)		21
Total	2	34 (100)	56 (100)	8	100

* Figures in parentheses are percentage of respondents to the respective caste total

These three points have also been verified by the SC respondents who are supposed to be BSP's paternal social base (Table 4). Only 20 per cent SCs say that BSP's focus is on SCs exclusively. While 37.5 per cent SCs say that BSP government's focus of social welfare is on SCs and upper castes both. Similarly, 30 per cent SCs say that the BSP government's focus of social welfare is on nobody.

Table 5
Changes in the Priorities of BSP after it has Adopted *Sarva Samaj* Policy-I

Question	*Response*	*Caste Affiliation of Respondents*				
		General	*OBCs*	*SCs*	*Muslims*	*Total*
Do you feel any change in the priorities of	Yes	1	19 (56)	47 (84)	1	68
BSP government of the	No		10 (29)	6 (11)	1	17
social welfare after it has adopted Sarva	Don't Know	1	5 (15)	3 (5)	6	15
Samaj policy?	Total	2	34 (100)	56 (100)	8	100

* Figures in parentheses are percentage of respondents to the respective caste total

The diversion of the BSP's attention from SCs to other sections of society is being perceived as a potential consequence of BSP's *Sarva Samaj* Policy. Remarkably, 68 per cent beneficiaries support this view in against a tiny number (17 per cent) who say that there is no change in BSP's policies. Importantly, out of total 68 per cent respondents 84 per cent are from SC community have supported this view. Only 11 per cent SC beneficiaries say that there is no diversion in BSP's attention on SCs because of *Sarva Samaj* policy (table 5). Similarly, 56 per cent of OBC beneficiaries support this.

If we look at that what kinds of changes have occurred in BSP's priorities to social welfare after it has adopted *Sarva Samaj* policy, majority of respondents feel that BSP has reduced its attention on social welfare in comparison to its earlier tenures in the office of UP government (table 6). Out of 68 respondents who say that changes have been occurred in the priorities of the BSP Government on social welfare, 81 per cent (55 respondents) say that these changes are negative i.e. priorities of the BSP government on social welfare has reduced. This fact has also been supported by SC respondents. Total 42 respondents (89 per cent) out of 47 who accept the changes in BSP's priorities are agreed on this issue. Similarly, 68 per cent OBC respondents also feel the same (table 6).

Table 6
Changes in the Priorities of BSP after it has Adopted *Sarva Samaj* Policy-II

Question	*Answer*	*Caste Affiliation of Respondents*				
		General	*OBCs*	*SCs*	*Muslims*	*Total*
What kinds of change have occurred in the priorities of the BSP Government on social welfare after it has adopted Sarva Samaj policy?	Attention on social welfare has reduced	1	13 (68)	42 (89)		55 (81)
	BSP is focusing more on social welfare than earlier		1 (5)	1 (2)		2 (3)
	Other	1	5 (26)	4 (9)	1	11 (16)
	Total	1	19 (100)	47 (100)	1	68 (100)

* Figures in parentheses are percentage of respondents to the respective caste total

The changes in BSP's fundamental positions like diverting attention from SCs and moving towards upper castes or reducing attention on social welfare are the results of the very need of the BSP to retain its political power in the state, and also its need of capturing power at the central level. In the view of one local BSP functionary- *"political tie with the upper castes (Under the Congress Regime in UP) which lasted till 40 years could not bring sweet breads to Dalits, and Dalits still remain at the same conditions of variability and deprivation where they were earlier. Now the BSP is doing same. We should not trust upper castes".*

Perceptions of local party men are not much different from the common people as we have seen in case of the beneficiaries' responses to the BSP government's preferences to social security. There is prevailing accord among the local BSP cadres that the BSP is not caring for the welfare of the poor, especially Dalits. The attention to welfare measures of the poor has reduced. Responses given in table 7 show that 26 percent party men say that the party is not giving attention towards the social welfare of the poor people. Remarkably, 61 percent people say, though a bit sympathetically, that the party is caring but attention has reduced than earlier BSP governments in the state. Therefore, total 87 percent party cadres accept that the party is going far from one of its basic principles and ideological standpoints, which is the social and economic upliftment of the poor and deprived people. This path breaking diversion in the functioning of the BSP Government has happened because of its recent political moves in terms of its inclusion of upper castes in the party strategy. Total 66 per cent party men say that the reduced attention of the BSP Government is because of its *Sarva Samaj* policy.

Table 7
BSP Government's Attention to Social Welfare

Responses	*Frequency*	*Percentage*
BSP is very keen towards social welfare of the poor	12	12
BSP is not taking care of the social welfare of the poor and deprived people	26	26
BSP is caring but attention has reduced than earlier BSP governments	61	61
Other	1	1
Total	100	100

Local party men assume that keeping upper castes in the basket of the party is very tough and nearly impossible. Therefore, it requires continuous attention to make them happy by offering them incentives and influential positions in the party and government. Therefore it becomes essential to the BSP to cut down the benefits of Dalits and drain them to others. A majority of 77 per cent party men say that Dalits are less benefited because of this policy. These are only Brahmins and Upper castes who are taking the benefits of this policy. Table 8 indicates the perception of local leaders who can judge well as to who are getting what at the local level. A sum of 78 per cent (36.4 + 41.6) party men agreed that either Brahmins or upper castes are reaping the benefits. Since, the *Sarva Samaj* Policy is the only guiding policy of the present BSP government, there are no other channels or policy to provide exclusive benefits to the poor and deprived in general and Dalits in particular.

Table 8
Benefits under Sarva Samaj Policy

Question 1	*Responses*	*Frequency*	*Percentage*
Are Dalits less benefited by the BSP because of the Sarva Samaj policy?	Yes	77	77
	No	21	21
	Don't Know	2	2
	Total	100	100
Question 2			
If Dalits are less benefited by the BSP because of the Sarva Samaj policy, then which section of society is most benefited?	Brahmins	28	36.4
	Thakurs	3	3.9
	Upper castes as whole	32	41.6
	None of these	7	9.1
	Other	7	9.1
	Total	77	100

CONCLUSION

Analysis of the BSP's priorities of social security schemes to the Dalits and the feelings of Dalit beneficiaries and party cadres about the BSP and its empowerment agenda in terms of implementation of these schemes reveals that BSP's attention on Dalits has reduced and has turned towards upper castes significantly. This result opens up two different dimensions to analyze BSP's politics for the Dalits. The one dimension which is often discussed in academia is that BSP has not been a party of Dalits as a whole. Christophe Jaffrelot (1998) has come up with extensive analysis of the BSP's politics, since its beginning to till 1998. He has suggested that the BSP has never been a party of neither Dalits nor lower castes like OBCs, as Kanshi Ram tried hard to forge a *bahujan* front combining STs, SCs and OBCs. On the other hand, it has also been witnessed that the BSP in Uttar Pradesh has benefited only few elite Dalits castes like *Chamars*, *Paasis* and *Balmiki* among about 66 Dalit sub-castes (Kumar, 1999). Therefore, by taking this aspect it can be concluded, though it can also be debated, that BSP's less attention on Dalits which has further reduced after its *Sarva Samaj* Policy is an inherent nature of the historical setting under which the party has grown up.

But this aspect loses its impression when it comes to the cultural policy of the BSP which is on the top of the BSP's public agenda, and has become most prioritized political agenda and public policy for the present BSP Government in UP. Therefore, second dimension comes into the picture which is about the growing attention of the BSP on Dalits in terms of its cultural policy. BSP is looking for an alternative of the empowerment of the Dalits. A long period of more than 60 years could not empower the Dalits, as they have been given protective measures in the constitutions and on the basis that they have been given special attention in terms of exclusive social welfare policies and reservation in public sector jobs. Therefore, empowerment is not about giving money or jobs to Dalits and other deprived sections of society but is about how and when they feel that they are empowered. Therefore, whole efforts of the BSP about giving attention on the building memorials and monuments in UP is becoming more important than the social welfare of the Dalits. Idea behind this policy is that Dalits would feel pride when they see the contribution of their own icons in the history of hierarchical domination.

But, the important question is whether the Dalits support BSP's idea of reducing social welfare measures and replacing them by the cultural policy. Field experiences suggest that even though Dalits do not have problems with the cultural and symbolic policy of the BSP as they receive it with pride that the party is sketching their history that was denied by the upper castes people; but, Dalits are very critical when it comes to lesser attention from the BSP for their upliftment. Things become more critical when these benefits are being shared by the upper castes and OBCs. Upper castes have always been posed as a potential enemy by the Dalit Movement and OBCs have emerged as a new threat in UP especially after the failure of Dalit-OBC coalition in 1993 when BSP and SP came together and formed the government. Therefore, Dalits are less satisfied with BSP's approach of overlooking key needs of Dalits which can be fulfilled only by the giving attention on their welfare and security not on monuments and memorials only. Hence, the agenda of Dalit empowerment becomes crucial for both – Dalits and the BSP which is projecting itself as a party of all but trying to be recognized as a party of only Dalits.

Notes

1. 'Uttar Pradesh Spends more on Elephant Statues than Lives One', e-article, available on *http://www.thaindian.com/newsportal/enviornment/uttar-pradesh-spends-more-on-elephants-statues-than-live-ones_100246947.html*, accessed on April 19, 2010.
2. Information about the constructions and their costs has been taken from the website: *www.sarvajan.ambedkar.org* accessed on 19 April, 2010.

3. Information about the estimated cost of a special security force to protect memorials is available on the website: *www.allvoice.com* accessed on 19 April, 2010.
4. Badri Narayan's analysis has been quoted in Darshan Desai's article-"Putting up Statues Part of BSP's Dalit Assertion", available on *http://www.thaindian.com/newsportal/politics/putting-up-statues-part-of-bsps-dalit-assertion_10039612.html*, accessed on April 19, 2010.

References

Dainik Jagran (Hindi news paper), Meerut, 4rth and 6th October, 1995 quoted in Pai (2003).

Hasan, Zoya (2002), 'Representation and Redistribution: The New Lower Caste Politics of North India' in Zoya Hasan (ed), *Parties and Party Politics in India.* (New Delhi: Oxford University Press). pp. 370-396.

Human Development Report for Uttar Pradesh (HDRUP) (2003), Planning Department, Government of Uttar Pradesh (New Delhi: Oxford).

Indian Express, *Maya Spent Rs, 4,500 cr on Memorials,* Internet edition, March 24, 2010, available at *http://www.indianexpress.com/news/maya-spent-rs-4-500-cr-on-memorials/594865/*, accessed on April 19, 2010.

Jaffrelot, Christophe (1998), 'The Bahujan Samaj Party in North India: No Longer Just a Dalit Party', *Comparative Studies of South Asia, Africa and Middle East,* Vol. 18:1, p. 50.

Kumar, Vivek (1999), 'Dalits and the BSP in Uttar Pradesh: Issues and Challenges', *Economic and Political Weekly,* Vol. 34:14 (April 3-9), p. 826.

NSSO, (2002), Household Situation in India, 58th round, Report No. 488.

Pai, Sudha (2003), 'Deprivation and Development in UP: The Economic Agenda of the BSP', *Man and Development,* 35(1), 35-54.

Singh, Shyam and V. Anil Kumar (2009), 'Politics and Public Policies: Politics of Human Development in Uttar Pradesh State of India', paper presented in the Fourth International Conference on The Public Policy and Management, organized by the Indian Institute of Management, Bangalore on 9-12 August.

Singh, Shyam (2010), 'Dalit Movement and Emergence of the BSP in Uttar Pradesh: Politics and Priorities', *ISEC Working Paper Series,* No: 242, April. p- 11.

Times of India (2010a), 'Maya to Centre: RTE Funding Difficult', internet edition, April 4, available on *http://timesofindia.indiatimes.com/city/lucknow/Maya-to-Centre-RTE-funding-difficult/articleshow/5758885.cms,* accessed on 23 April, 2010.

Times of India (2010b), 'After RTE UP does not have Funds to Light Villages', internet edition, April 9, available on *http://timesofindia.indiatimes.com/city/lucknow/After-RTE-UP-doesnt-have-funds-to-light-villages/articleshow/5776036.cms, accessed on April* 23, 2010.

Verma, A. K. (2005), 'BSP's Strategy for Uttar Pradesh: Wooing the *Brahmins* for a New Alliance', *EPW,* June 25, pp. 2647-2648.

ISSUES CONCERNING MUSLIM WOMEN - WITH SPECIAL REFERENCE TO THE OLD CITY OF HYDERABAD

YASMIN AND KANEEZ ZEHRA

INTRODUCTION

Empowerment is a multifaceted, multidimensional and multi-layered concept. Women's empowerment is a process in which women gain greater share of control over decision making in the home, community, society and nation, and to gain 'power'. According to the country report of Government of India, 'Empowerment means moving from a position of enforced powerlessness to one of power.[1]

Accordingly to Helen clark, UNDP Administration 'Gender equality and women's empowerment are human rights that lie at the heart of development and the achievement of the millennium development goals'.

Despite the progress that has been made, 6 out of 10 world poorest people are still women and girls. Less than 16 per cent of the world's parliamentarians are women, 2/3 of all children shut outside the school gates are girls and both in times of armed conflict and behind closed doors at home, women are still systematically subjected to violence. Development cannot be achieved if 50 per cent of the population is excluded from the opportunities it brings.[2]

The empowerment of women is one of the central issues in the process of development of countries all over the world. The contribution of writers and social reformers has been well documented. The government of India has made empowerment of women as one of the principal objectives of the Ninth Five Year Plan (1997-2002) and also declared 2001 as the year of 'Women's Empowerment'. These issues of gender equality are discussed is world conferences, etc. our constitution has conferred and guaranteed equality before law, universal adult franchise and equal opportunities for men and women as fundamental rights[3].

Within the framework of a democratic polity, our laws, development policies, plans and programmes have aimed at women's advancement in different spheres. From the Fifth Five Year Plan (1974-78) onwards has been a marked shift in the approach to women's issues from welfare to development. In recent years, the empowerment of women has been recognized as the central issue in determining the status of women. The National Commission for women was setup by an Act of Parliament in 1990 to safeguard the rights and legal entitlements of women. The 73rd and 74th Amendments (1993) to the constitution of India have provided for reservation of seats in the local bodies of panchayats and municipalities for women, laying a strong foundation for their participation in decision making at the local levels.[4]

Right from the beginning i.e. the 50's onwards, a number of welfare measures were adopted for women. The most important ones were the establishment of the central social welfare board, Mahila Mandals and the community Development programmes. There is no doubt about the fact that development of women has always been the central focus of planning since independence.[5]

PERUSAL OF THE FIVE YEAR PLANS

The second five year plan gave an impetus to the welfare approach. It was the third five year plan that promoted women's decade and the submission of the report on the committee on the status of women in India. A new thought process emerged to recognized women as critical inputs for National development rather than as targets for Welfare policies.

The plan identified areas of health, nutrition, education, legislation and social welfare for formulating and implementing action programmes for women. The outcome was the setting up of a women's welfare and development Bureau in 1976 to coordinate policies and programmes and initiate measures for women's development.

The Sixth Five Year Plan shifted its found from welfare to development. It was the seventh five year which operationalised the concern for equity and empowerment (1985-900. Women were to be perceived as a crucial resource for the development of the country. The eighth five year plan (1990-95) focused on empowering women, especially at the grass root level through panchyat raj institution.

Focus of the Ninth Plan was to encourage social issues like women empowerment, conservation of certain benefits for the special group of the society. The tenth plan aimed at all children in India in school by 2003 and all children to complete 5 years of schooling by 2007.

The eleventh plan's objective was to reduce the dropout rate of the children from elementary school from 52.2 of in 2003-04 to 20% by 2011-12, and also to raise the sex ratio from 935 to 950 by 2016-2017.[6]

To ensure that 33% of direct and indirect beneficiaries of all government schemes are women and girl child. An insight into the objectives of these plans clearly show that a lot of focus has been given to women and their development.

The census of India 2001 shows that the female population is 921:1000 which speaks about the later alarming decrease in the women's population. This shows that our society still prefers a male child when compared to a girl child. In order to save the girl child sex determination tests have been.

Apart from the five year plans and the National policy various states have also focused on women and their development through their respective policies.

NATIONAL POLICY FOR EMPOWERMENT OF WOMEN

The National policy for the empowerment of women was passed in 2001. The goals and objectives of the policy are:-

(1) Creating an environment through positive economic and social policies for full development of women to enable them to realize their full potential.

(2) The dejure and all fact enjoyment of all human rights & fundamental freedom by women on equal basis with men in all spheres – political, economic, social, cultural and civil.

(3) Equal access to participation and decision making of women in social, political and economic life of the nation.

(4) Equal access to women to health case, quality education at all levels, career and vocational guidance, employment, equal remuneration, occupational health and safety social security and public office etc.

(5) Strengthening legal systems aimed at elimination of all forms of discrimination against women.

(6) Changing societal attitudes and community practices by active participation and involvement of both men & women.

(7) Mainstreaming a gender perspective in the development process.

(8) Elimination of discrimination and all forms of violence against women and the girl child.

(9) Building and strengthening partnerships with civil society, particularly women's organizations. [7]

Besides the above mentioned objectives and goals the national policy focused on the overall development of women. The policy aims at bringing about changes in the personal laws with the initiative and the participation of all stake holders including community and religious leaders in matters pertaining to marriage, divorce, maintenance and guardianship and guardianship so as to eliminate discrimination against women.

In order to ensure easy access to credit facilities suppertive measurers would be taken to ensure adequate flow of credit through financial institutions and banks so that it helps women below the poverty line to have easy access to it.

Women's perspectives would also be included while designing and implementing macro-financial and social policies. Thus contribution in formal and informal sectors would be recognized appropriate policies would be framed regarding employment and working conditions. Measures would include "Reinterpretation and redefinition of conventional concepts of work, wherever necessary eg in census records, to reflect women's contribution as producers and workers, preparation of satellite and national accounts.[8]

The global economy has led to uneven economic disparities, gender inequality unsafe working conditions in the formed sectors as well as rural areas, strategies should be designed to empower women to meet unforeseen situation and negative impact of economy arising from the process of globalization.

In addition to this support services like child care facilities, including crèches, at the work place and educational institutions, home for the aged and disabled would be expanded women friendly personnel policies would be drawn up to encourage women to participate in the developmental process.

As far as education is concerned the policy ensures equal access to education of women and girls special measures would be undertaken to eliminate discrimination and create a gender-sensitive system, aiming at increase in enrolment and retention of girls as well develop vocational / technical skills. Special focus is to be on women belonging to weaker sections like SC, ST OBCs and minorities Gender sensitive curricula would also be undertaken.

Efforts would be geared for improving women's health. A holistic approach which aims at both nutrition and health services aims at both nutrition and health services and maternal mortality have been sensitive indicators of human development and is of grave concern.

To effectively deal with the problem of infant mortality and maternal mortality the availability of data is required. In order to ensure this there has been strict implementation of registration of birth and deaths and registration of marriage has been made compulsory. Efforts are being made to eliminate child marriages by 2010.

A lot of attention would be paid to meeting the nutritional requirements of women at all stages like infancy, childhood, adolescent and reproductive stage so that the problem can be dealt at the macro as micro-nutrient deficiencies especially in pregnant and locating women.

The policy also highlights elimination of discrimination against the girl child to prevent violation of her rights. It would focus strict implementation of the laws pertaining to the practice of female foeticide, infanticide, child marriage & child would also be undertaken by the government. (See Appendix for detail policy).

STATE POLICY OF ANDHRA PRADESH TOWARDS WOMEN EMPOWERMENT AND PROTECTION

The Andhra Pradesh government on May 5, 2010 launched a programme to facilitate effective protection of women and children by synergizing the service of government, NGOs and private sector.

The society for protection and empowerment of women and children (SPEWC) was set up for this purpose. Besides, the government also started an 'Integrated Child Protection' scheme. It also released a protocol on minimum standards of care in homes for victims of sex trafficking to effectively combat trafficking of women and provide all care and support to the victim.

Andhra Pradesh in the first state in the country to set up the society for women empowerment as well as frame the protocol against trafficking. As many as 10,000 cases of dowry harassment (domestic violence) are being registered in Andhra Pradesh every year while there is an increase in incidence of women and children being trafficked. It was noted that every year, an estimated 20,000 women and children are being trafficked from A.P. alone.

The Women Development and Child Welfare Department in collaborating with Prajwala, an anti trafficking organization for implementing the protocol on minimum standards of case.

The SPEWC would have a state level steering committee comprising ministers of different departments and a general body consisting of secretaries of departments and others. At the district level the society would be headed by the respective district collectors[10]. In Andhra Pradesh the sex ratio is 978:1000 make.

The scenario in the old city of Hyderabad for the lower middle class remains logged down by certain issues like lack of education, poverty and social inequality which acts as an impediment to the empowerment of women.

In Andhra Pradesh as far as the minority institutions are concerned they are reeling under a severe financial crunch. The State Minority Finance Corporation is yet to 80 crores towards scholarships and fee reimbursement for the year 2009-2010.

The position in the Urdu Academy is so bad that it had to scrap several schemes for want of funds, projects like open schools, infrastructure to urdu medium schools and computers to Deeni Madarasas are wound up[9].

The State Minorities Finance Corporation gets an annual grant of Rs. Ten Lakhs for monthly maintenance to poor divorced Muslim Women. The funds have not been released yet. Close to 200 applications are still awaiting sanction and the number keeps increasing by the day[10].

The Hyderabad City's population according to 2001 census was, total population 39 Lakhs, 29 thousand and 753 and the Muslim population was 15 Lakhs 76 Thousand and 583 making Hyderabad Muslim Community the largest in A.P. Muslim have substantial presence across the city and are predominant in and around the old city[11].

The lower middle class Muslim girls/women suffer from lack of education, there are different factors that are responsible for it.

1. Gender based inequality
2. Social discrimination and economic exploitation
3. Occupation of girl child in domestic chores
4. Low enrolment of girls in schools
5. Low retention rate and high dropout rate.

While writing this paper, we were greatly assisted by two voluntary organizations namely Shaheen Welfare Association and Haya which are both located in the old city. They made it possible form to interact with the girls/women who come to this organization.

According to a survey conducted in the old city comprising of 1000 households by a Welfare Association (Shaheen) it was found out that 33 persent had no education, 28 per cent were school dropouts, 24 per cent did not report and 15 per cent passed school board exams. The reasons for this were object poverty and poor economic conditions at home. One of the important reasons was lack of toilet facilities and no provision of Ayahs. In many schools many was contributed by teachers to arrange for Ayahs, speciality for the girls in the age group of 12-14 years. Lack of education and poverty lead children to take up employment in different areas in order to support their families. Some of them were married early and could not pursue their education, confining themselves to household duties. At the same time, these women had ambition to see that their children were educated as they believe that education would lead to progress and self reliance.

According to another voluntary organization Haya, parents attach more importance to the education of the male child that leaves the girls unattended as far as their education is concerned. Majority of the girls who come to this organization were to equip themselves with some skills are mostly high school dropouts.

As far as the economic scenario of Muslim women in Hyderabad is concerned, it is not very encouraging as most of them are engaged in semi-skilled occupations like embroidery, cap making, pin making, beedi making, kite making, domestic help, sweet boxes making etc. This goes to show that they engaged in semi skilled labour and their employment is not permanent. Some of them are seasonally employed (eg. Kite making). Women mostly prefer vocational training for their children.

Inspite of the constitutional guarantee and specific legislation which protect the interest of women, they continue to suffer because of ignorance of their legal rights. The menace of dowry continues unabated despite legislation prohibiting dowry and prescribing stringent measures for violating the law, violence against women, including that in the domestic sphere, continues even today[12].

The Domestic Violence Act was passed in the year 2005 and came in to effect from 2006. The survey showed that most women suffer violence in the marital home. 13 per cent of them showed that reasons for violence were varied, ranging from dowry harassment to sexual domination, harassment by in laws also takes place.

The survey (Shaheen) showed that 41.2 per cent of the women who were interviewed were subjected to physical violence on a daily basis. 34.4 per cent of the women reported that they faced abuse or violence of a sexual nature. About 5 per cent reported instances of emotional abuse in their daily lives. 26 per cent of the women who responded felt that they were deprived of finances. Men emerged as decision makers on all matters in the household. The women belonging to lower middle class are yet to find a foothold in the society and to realize their individuality.

When we interacted with the members of the organizations and the girls/women they were more interested in learning tailoring and beautician courses rather than studies. Lack of education has lead to economic problems and economic dependence of these women which comes in the way of this empowerment. Some women were forthcoming in sharing their experiences. A number of case studies were being undertaken few of them have been mentioned below:

Few Case Studies

(1) **Sultana** (name changed), we learnt was married at the age of 13 of a sheikh who left her after 15 days of marriage. Now she has a 13 year old daughter whom she wants to marry off as soon as possible as she is financially dependent on her father, and when asked will she marry her daughter to a sheikh the answer was in the affirmative.

(2) **Zaitun:** She works as a domestic help and works in five different houses, her husband is in alcoholic who does not support her financially, because of financial constraints, she got her son educated but her daughters accompany her to the work place hence lack education. She is also a victim of domestic violence. There is a clear gender discrimination in this case.

(3) **Zulekha Bi**: She is a widow, who has 4 daughters and 1 son. Lack of education made her to work as domestic help and to make both ends meet her daughters have

never been to school but sent her son to school but after 9th standard he gave up school and right now he is undertaking training for refrigerator repair work.

(4) **Asifa:** She is about 25 years old, has no education, works in a tailoring shop and her mother is not able to get her married because of dowry demands and as she said for her marriage is a distant dream. Now she is working overtime to save money for her marriage. This is a clear case of dowry menace that is prevalent among the lower meddle classes.

(5) **Maleka:** She was married 2 years back never had any formal education nor any vocational training after 2 years of marriage. She was divorced and is now not in a position to earn her livelihood in a dignified. She gets no maintenance form he former husband which has lead her to economic dependency on her parents who are already economically backward.

Observations

(1) Education is a prerequisite for the overall development of women. To create on awareness to educate women, so that it is possible for her to be economically independent.
(2) A sense of confidence has to be instilled in women so that if women work collectively it is possible to bring positive charge about in their lives and fight against all odds.
(3) Lot of effort has to be made by the Government to bring about an awareness of the govt. policies so that women are aware of these policies.
(4) Lack of knowledge and awareness is responsible for their backwardness.

CONCLUSION

No doubt a lot of efforts that have been put in by both Central and State Governments for the upliftment of women. Our interaction with these women has led us to the conclusion that lack of education in the root cause of lack of awareness of government policies and programmes with a little help from the government agencies and from the NGO's who are tirelessly working for their upliftment, certainly there can be positive development and certainly they would not lag behind either in education or economic independence.

Notes & References

1. *http://health.eguidex.com*
2. *www.undp.org.in*
3. National Policy *wcd.nic.in/empwomen.htm*
4. giri, Dr.Mohini, Emancipation and empowerment of women, (Gyan Pub. 2005), p. 39.
5. Aleem, Dr. Shameem, women's development problems and prospects (edited APH Publishing Corporation, New Delhi, 1996).
6. *Ibid*; pp. 20-22.
7. *wcd.nic.in/empwomen.htm* -
8. *Ibid*
9. *www.zeenews.com*
10. The Hindu, April 21, 2000.
11. *Ibid*
12. *Ibid*
13. Sapru, R.K. Indian Administration (Kalyani Publications, New Delhi, 2001), pp. 469-470.

APPENDIX

NATIONAL POLICY FOR THE EMPOWERMENT OF WOMEN(2001)

INTRODUCTION

The principle of gender equality is enshrined in the Indian Constitution in its Preamble, Fundamental Rights, Fundamental Duties and Directive Principles. The Constitution not only grants equality to women, but also empowers the State to adopt measures of positive discrimination in favour of women.

Within the framework of a democratic polity, our laws, development policies, Plans and programmes have aimed at women's advancement in different spheres. From the Fifth Five Year Plan (1974-78) onwards has been a marked shift in the approach to women's issues from welfare to development. In recent years, the empowerment of women has been recognized as the central issue in determining the status of women. The National Commission for Women was set up by an Act of Parliament in 1990 to safeguard the rights and legal entitlements of women. The 73rd and 74th Amendments (1993) to the Constitution of India have provided for reservation of seats in the local bodies of Panchayats and Municipalities for women, laying a strong foundation for their participation in decision making at the local levels.

1.3 India has also ratified various international conventions and human rights instruments committing to secure equal rights of women. Key among them is the ratification of the Convention on Elimination of All Forms of Discrimination Against Women (CEDAW) in 1993.

1.4 The Mexico Plan of Action (1975), the Nairobi Forward Looking Strategies (1985), the Beijing Declaration as well as the Platform for Action (1995) and the Outcome Document adopted by the UNGA Session on Gender Equality and Development & Peace for the 21st century, titled "Further actions and initiatives to implement the Beijing Declaration and the Platform for Action" have been unreservedly endorsed by India for appropriate follow up.

1.5 The Policy also takes note of the commitments of the Ninth Five Year Plan and the other Sectoral Policies relating to empowerment of Women.

1.6 The women's movement and a wide-spread network of non-Government Organisations which have strong grass-roots presence and deep insight into women's concerns have contributed in inspiring initiatives for the empowerment of women.

1.7 However, there still exists a wide gap between the goals enunciated in the Constitution, legislation, policies, plans, programmes, and related mechanisms on the one hand and the situational reality of the status of women in India, on the other. This has been analyzed extensively in the Report of the Committee on the Status of Women in India, "Towards Equality", 1974 and highlighted in the National Perspective Plan for Women, 1988-2000, the Shramshakti Report, 1988 and the Platform for Action, Five Years After- An assessment"

1.8 Gender disparity manifests itself in various forms, the most obvious being the trend of continuously declining female ratio in the population in the last few decades. Social stereotyping and violence at the domestic and societal levels are some of the other manifestations. Discrimination against girl children, adolescent girls and women persists in parts of the country.

1.9 The underlying causes of gender inequality are related to social and economic structure, which is based on informal and formal norms, and practices.

1.10 Consequently, the access of women particularly those belonging to weaker sections including Scheduled Castes/ Scheduled Tribes/ Other backward Classes and minorities, majority of whom are in the rural areas and in the informal, unorganized sector - to education, health and productive resources, among others, is inadequate. Therefore, they remain largely marginalized, poor and socially excluded.

Goal and Objectives

1.11 The goal of this Policy is to bring about the advancement, development and empowerment of women. The Policy will be widely disseminated so as to encourage active participation of all stakeholders for achieving its goals. Specifically, the objectives of this Policy include

(i) Creating an environment through positive economic and social policies for full development of women to enable them to realize their full potential

(ii) The de-jure and de-facto enjoyment of all human rights and fundamental freedom by women on equal basis with men in all spheres - political, economic, social, cultural and civil

(iii) Equal access to participation and decision making of women in social, political and economic life of the nation

(iv) Equal access to women to health care, quality education at all levels, career and vocational guidance, employment, equal remuneration, occupational health and safety, social security and public office etc.

(v) Strengthening legal systems aimed at elimination of all forms of discrimination against women

(vi) Changing societal attitudes and community practices by active participation and involvement of both men and women.

(vii) Mainstreaming a gender perspective in the development process.

(viii) Elimination of discrimination and all forms of violence against women and the girl child; and

(ix) Building and strengthening partnerships with civil society, particularly women's organizations.

Policy Prescriptions

Judicial Legal Systems

Legal-judicial system will be made more responsive and gender sensitive to women's needs, especially in cases of domestic violence and personal assault. New laws will be enacted and existing laws reviewed to ensure that justice is quick and the punishment meted out to the culprits is commensurate with the severity of the offence.

2.2 At the initiative of and with the full participation of all stakeholders including community and religious leaders, the Policy would aim to encourage changes in personal laws such as those related to marriage, divorce, maintenance and guardianship so as to eliminate discrimination against women.

2.3 The evolution of property rights in a patriarchal system has contributed to the subordinate status of women. The Policy would aim to encourage changes in laws relating to ownership of property and inheritance by evolving consensus in order to make them gender just.

Decision Making

3.1 Women's equality in power sharing and active participation in decision making, including decision making in political process at all levels will be ensured for the achievement of the goals of empowerment. All measures will be taken to guarantee women equal access to and full participation in decision making bodies at every level, including the legislative, executive, judicial, corporate, statutory bodies, as also the advisory Commissions, Committees, Boards, Trusts etc. Affirmative action such as reservations/quotas, including in higher legislative bodies, will be considered whenever necessary on a time bound basis. Women-friendly personnel policies will also be drawn up to encourage women to participate effectively in the developmental process.

Mainstreaming a Gender Perspective in the Development Process

4.1 Policies, programmes and systems will be established to ensure mainstreaming of women's perspectives in all developmental processes, as catalysts, participants and recipients. Wherever there are gaps in policies and programmes, women specific interventions would be undertaken to bridge these. Coordinating and monitoring mechanisms will also be devised to assess from time to time the progress of such mainstreaming mechanisms. Women's issues and concerns as a result will specially be addressed and reflected in all concerned laws, sectoral policies, plans and programmes of action.

Economic Empowerment of Women

Poverty Eradication

5.1 Since women comprise the majority of the population below the poverty line and are very often in situations of extreme poverty, given the harsh realities of intra-household and social discrimination, macro economic policies and poverty eradication programmes will specifically address the needs and problems of such women. There will be improved implementation of programmes which are already women oriented with special targets for women. Steps will be taken for mobilization of poor women and convergence of services, by offering them a range of economic and social options, along with necessary support measures to enhance their capabilities

Micro Credit

5.2 In order to enhance women's access to credit for consumption and production, the establishment of new, and strengthening of existing micro-credit mechanisms and micro-finance institution will be undertaken so that the outreach of credit is enhanced. Other supportive measures would be taken to ensure adequate flow of credit through extant financial institutions and banks, so that all women below poverty line have easy access to credit.

Women and Economy

5.3 Women's perspectives will be included in designing and implementing macro-economic and social policies by institutionalizing their participation in such processes. Their contribution to socio-economic development as producers and workers will be recognized in the formal and informal sectors (including home based workers) and appropriate policies relating to employment and to her working conditions will be drawn up. Such measures could include:

Reinterpretation and redefinition of conventional concepts of work wherever necessary e.g. in the Census records, to reflect women's contribution as producers and workers.

Preparation of satellite and national accounts.

Development of appropriate methodologies for undertaking (i) and (ii) above.

Globalization

Globalization has presented new challenges for the realization of the goal of women's equality, the gender impact of which has not been systematically evaluated fully. However, from the micro-level studies that were commissioned by the Department of Women & Child Development, it is evident that there is a need for re-framing policies for access to employment and quality of employment. Benefits of the growing global economy have been unevenly distributed leading to wider economic disparities, the feminization of poverty, increased gender inequality through often deteriorating working conditions and unsafe working environment especially in the informal economy and rural areas. Strategies will be designed to enhance the capacity of women and empower them to meet the negative social and economic impacts, which may flow from the globalization process.

Women and Agriculture

5.5 In view of the critical role of women in the agriculture and allied sectors, as producers, concentrated efforts will be made to ensure that benefits of training, extension and various programmes will reach them in proportion to their numbers. The programmes for training women in soil conservation, social forestry, dairy development and other occupations allied to agriculture like horticulture, livestock including small animal husbandry, poultry, fisheries etc. will be expanded to benefit women workers in the agriculture sector.

Women and Industry

5.6 The important role played by women in electronics, information technology and food processing and agro industry and textiles has been crucial to the development of these sectors. They would be given comprehensive support in terms of labour legislation, social security and other support services to participate in various industrial sectors.

5.7 Women at present cannot work in night shift in factories even if they wish to. Suitable measures will be taken to enable women to work on the night shift in factories. This will be accompanied with support services for security, transportation etc.

Support Services

5.8 The provision of support services for women, like child care facilities, including crèches at work places and educational institutions, homes for the aged and the disabled will be expanded and improved to create an enabling environment and to ensure their full cooperation in social, political and economic life. Women-friendly personnel policies will also be drawn up to encourage women to participate effectively in the developmental process.

Social Empowerment of Women

Education

6.1 Equal access to education for women and girls will be ensured. Special measures will be taken to eliminate discrimination, universalize education, eradicate illiteracy, create a gender-sensitive educational system, increase enrolment and retention rates of girls and improve the quality of education to facilitate life-long learning as well as development of occupation/vocation/technical skills by women. Reducing the gender gap in secondary and higher education would be a focus area. Sectoral time targets in existing policies will be achieved, with a special focus on girls and women, particularly those belonging to weaker sections including the Scheduled Castes/Scheduled Tribes/Other Backward Classes/Minorities. Gender sensitive curricula would be developed at all levels of educational system in order to address sex stereotyping as one of the causes of gender discrimination.

Health

6.2 A holistic approach to women's health which includes both nutrition and health services will be adopted and special attention will be given to the needs of women and the girl at all stages of the life cycle. The reduction of infant mortality and maternal mortality, which are sensitive indicators of human development, is a priority concern. This policy reiterates the national demographic goals for Infant Mortality Rate (IMR), Maternal Mortality Rate (MMR) set out in the National Population Policy 2000. Women should have access to comprehensive, affordable and quality health care. Measures will be adopted that take into account the reproductive rights of women to enable them to exercise informed choices, their vulnerability to sexual and health problems together with endemic, infectious and communicable diseases such as malaria, TB, and water borne diseases as well as hypertension and cardio-pulmonary diseases. The social, developmental and health consequences of

HIV/AIDS and other sexually transmitted diseases will be tackled from a gender perspective.

6.3 To effectively meet problems of infant and maternal mortality, and early marriage the availability of good and accurate data at micro level on deaths, birth and marriages is required. Strict implementation of registration of births and deaths would be ensured and registration of marriages would be made compulsory.

6.4 In accordance with the commitment of the National Population Policy (2000) to population stabilization, this Policy recognizes the critical need of men and women to have access to safe, effective and affordable methods of family planning of their choice and the need to suitably address the issues of early marriages and spacing of children. Interventions such as spread of education, compulsory registration of marriage and special programmes like BSY should impact on delaying the age of marriage so that by 2010 child marriages are eliminated.

6.5 Women's traditional knowledge about health care and nutrition will be recognized through proper documentation and its use will be encouraged. The use of Indian and alternative systems of medicine will be enhanced within the framework of overall health infrastructure available for women.

Nutrition

6.6 In view of the high risk of malnutrition and disease that women face at all the three critical stages viz., infancy and childhood, adolescent and reproductive phase, focussed attention would be paid to meeting the nutritional needs of women at all stages of the life cycle. This is also important in view of the critical link between the health of adolescent girls, pregnant and lactating women with the health of infant and young children. Special efforts will be made to tackle the problem of macro and micro nutrient deficiencies especially amongst pregnant and lactating women as it leads to various diseases and disabilities.

6.7 Intra-household discrimination in nutritional matters vis-à-vis girls and women will be sought to be ended through appropriate strategies. Widespread use of nutrition education would be made to address the issues of intra-household imbalances in nutrition and the special needs of pregnant and lactating women. Women's participation will also be ensured in the planning, superintendence and delivery of the system.

Drinking Water and Sanitation

6.8 Special attention will be given to the needs of women in the provision of safe drinking water, sewage disposal, toilet facilities and sanitation within accessible reach of households, especially in rural areas and urban slums. Women's participation will be ensured in the planning, delivery and maintenance of such services.

Housing and Shelter

6.9 Women's perspectives will be included in housing policies, planning of housing colonies and provision of shelter both in rural and urban areas. Special attention will be given for providing adequate and safe housing and accommodation for women including single women, heads of households, working women, students, apprentices and trainees.

Environment

6.10 Women will be involved and their perspectives reflected in the policies and programmes for environment, conservation and restoration. Considering the impact of environmental factors on their livelihoods, women's participation will be ensured in the conservation of the environment and control of environmental degradation. The vast majority of rural women still depend on the locally available non-commercial sources of energy such as animal dung, crop waste and fuel wood. In order to ensure the efficient use of these energy resources in an environmental friendly manner, the Policy will aim at promoting the programmes of non-conventional energy resources. Women will be involved in spreading the use of solar energy, biogas, smokeless chulahs and other rural application so as to have a visible impact of these measures in influencing eco system and in changing the life styles of rural women.

Science and Technology

6.11 Programmes will be strengthened to bring about a greater involvement of women in science and technology. These will include measures to motivate girls to take up science and technology for higher education and also ensure that development projects with scientific and technical inputs involve women fully. Efforts to develop a scientific temper and awareness will also be stepped up. Special measures would be taken for their training in areas where they have special skills like communication and information technology. Efforts to develop appropriate technologies suited to women's needs as well as to reduce their drudgery will be given a special focus too.

Women in Difficult Circumstances

6.12 In recognition of the diversity of women's situations and in acknowledgement of the needs of specially disadvantaged groups, measures and programmes will be undertaken to provide them with special assistance. These groups include women in extreme poverty, destitute women, women in conflict situations, women affected by natural calamities, women in less developed regions, the disabled widows, elderly women, single women in difficult circumstances, women heading households, those displaced from employment, migrants, women who are victims of marital violence, deserted women and prostitutes etc.

Violence Against Women

7.1 All forms of violence against women, physical and mental, whether at domestic or societal levels, including those arising from customs, traditions or accepted practices shall be dealt with effectively with a view to eliminate its incidence. Institutions and mechanisms/schemes for assistance will be created and strengthened for prevention of such violence , including sexual harassment at work place and customs like dowry; for the rehabilitation of the victims of violence and for taking effective action against the perpetrators of such violence. A special emphasis will also be laid on programmes and measures to deal with trafficking in women and girls.

Rights of the Girl Child

8.1 All forms of discrimination against the girl child and violation of her rights shall be eliminated by undertaking strong measures both preventive and punitive within and outside the family. These would relate specifically to strict enforcement of laws against prenatal sex selection and the practices of female foeticide, female infanticide, child marriage, child abuse and child prostitution etc. Removal of discrimination in the treatment of the girl child within the family and outside and projection of a positive image of the girl child will be actively fostered. There will be special emphasis on the needs of the girl child and earmarking of substantial investments in the areas relating to food and nutrition, health and education, and in vocational education. In implementing programmes for eliminating child labour, there will be a special focus on girl children.

Mass Media

9.1 Media will be used to portray images consistent with human dignity of girls and women. The Policy will specifically strive to remove demeaning, degrading and negative conventional stereotypical images of women and violence against women. Private sector partners and media networks will be involved at all levels to ensure equal access for women particularly in the area of information and communication technologies. The media would be encouraged to develop codes of conduct, professional guidelines and other self regulatory mechanisms to remove gender stereotypes and promote balanced portrayals of women and men.

Operational Strategies

Action Plans

10.1 All Central and State Ministries will draw up time bound Action Plans for translating the Policy into a set of concrete actions, through a participatory process of consultation with Centre/State Departments of Women and Child Development and National / State Commissions for Women. The Plans will specifically including the following: -

(i) Measurable goals to be achieved by 2010.

(ii) Identification and commitment of resources.

(iii) Responsibilities for implementation of action points.

(iv) Structures and mechanisms to ensure efficient monitoring, review and gender impact assessment of action points and policies.

(v) Introduction of a gender perspective in the budgeting process.

10.2 In order to support better planning and programme formulation and adequate allocation of resources, Gender Development Indices (GDI) will be developed by networking with specialized agencies. These could be analyzed and studied in depth. Gender auditing and development of evaluation mechanisms will also be undertaken along side.

10.3 Collection of gender disaggregated data by all primary data collecting agencies of the Central and State Governments as well as Research and Academic Institutions in the Public and Private Sectors will be undertaken. Data and information gaps in vital areas reflecting the status of women will be sought to be filled in by these immediately. All Ministries/Corporations/Banks and financial institutions etc will be advised to collect, collate, disseminate and maintain/publish data related to programmes and benefits on a gender disaggregated basis. This will help in meaningful planning and evaluation of policies.

Institutional Mechanisms

11.1 Institutional mechanisms, to promote the advancement of women, which exist at the Central and State levels, will be strengthened. These will be through interventions as may be appropriate and will relate to, among others, provision of adequate resources, training and advocacy skills to effectively influence macro-policies, legislation, programmes etc. to achieve the empowerment of women.

11.2 National and State Councils will be formed to oversee the operationalisation of the Policy on a regular basis. The National Council will be headed by the Prime Minister and the State Councils by the Chief Ministers and be broad in composition having representatives from the concerned Departments/Ministries, National and State Commissions for Women, Social Welfare Boards, representatives of Non-Government Organizations, Women's Organisations, Corporate Sector, Trade Unions, financing institutions, academics, experts and social activists etc. These bodies will review the progress made in implementing the Policy twice a year. The National Development Council will also be informed of the progress of the programme undertaken under the policy from time to time for advice and comments.

11.3 National and State Resource Centres on women will be established with mandates for collection and dissemination of information, undertaking research work, conducting surveys, implementing training and awareness generation programmes, etc. These Centers will link up with Women's Studies Centres and other research and academic institutions through suitable information networking systems.

11.4 While institutions at the district level will be strengthened, at the grass-roots, women will be helped by Government through its programmes to organize and strengthen into Self-Help Groups (SHGs) at the Anganwadi/Village/Town level. The women's groups will be helped to institutionalize themselves into registered societies and to federate at the Panchyat/Municipal level. These societies will bring about synergistic implementation of all the social and economic development programmes by drawing resources made available through Government and Non-Government channels, including banks and financial institutions and by establishing a close Interface with the Panchayats/ Municipalities.

Resource Management

12.1 Availability of adequate financial, human and market resources to implement the Policy will be managed by concerned Departments, financial credit institutions and banks, private sector, civil society and other connected institutions. This process will include:

(a) Assessment of benefits flowing to women and resource allocation to the programmes relating to them through an exercise of gender budgeting. Appropriate changes in policies will be made to optimize benefits to women under these schemes;

(b) Adequate resource allocation to develop and promote the policy outlined earlier based on (a) above by concerned Departments.

(c) Developing synergy between personnel of Health, Rural Development, Education and Women & Child Development Department at field level and other village level functionaries'

(d) Meeting credit needs by banks and financial credit institutions through suitable policy initiatives and development of new institutions in coordination with the Department of Women & Child Development.

12.2 The strategy of Women's Component Plan adopted in the Ninth Plan of ensuring that not less than 30% of benefits/funds flow to women from all Ministries and Departments will be implemented effectively so that the needs and interests of women and girls are addressed by all concerned sectors. The Department of Women and Child Development being the nodal Ministry will monitor and review the progress of the implementation of the Component Plan from time to time, in terms of both quality and quantity in collaboration with the Planning Commission.

12.3 Efforts will be made to channelize private sector investments too, to support programmes and projects for advancement of women

Legislation

13.1 The existing legislative structure will be reviewed and additional legislative measures taken by identified departments to implement the Policy. This will also involve a review of all existing laws including personal, customary and tribal laws, subordinate legislation, related rules as well as executive and administrative regulations to eliminate all gender discriminatory references. The process will be planned over a time period 2000-2003. The specific measures required would be evolved through a consultation process involving civil society, National Commission for Women and Department of Women and Child Development. In appropriate cases the consultation process would be widened to include other stakeholders too.

13.2 Effective implementation of legislation would be promoted by involving civil society and community. Appropriate changes in legislation will be undertaken, if necessary.

13.3 In addition, following other specific measures will be taken to implement the legislation effectively.

(a) Strict enforcement of all relevant legal provisions and speedy redressal of grievances will be ensured, with a special focus on violence and gender related atrocities.

(b) Measures to prevent and punish sexual harassment at the place of work, protection for women workers in the organized/unorganized sector and strict enforcement of relevant laws such as Equal Remuneration Act and Minimum Wages Act will be undertaken,

(c) Crimes against women, their incidence, prevention, investigation, detection and prosecution will be regularly reviewed at all Crime Review fora and Conferences at the Central, State and District levels. Recognised, local, voluntary organizations will be authorized to lodge Complaints and facilitate registration, investigations and legal proceedings related to violence and atrocities against girls and women.

(d) Women's Cells in Police Stations, Encourage Women Police Stations Family Courts, Mahila Courts, Counselling Centers, Legal Aid Centers and Nyaya Panchayats will be strengthened and expanded to eliminate violence and atrocities against women.

(e) Widespread dissemination of information on all aspects of legal rights, human rights and other entitlements of women, through specially designed legal literacy programmes and rights information programmes will be done.

Gender Sensitization

14.1 Training of personnel of executive, legislative and judicial wings of the State, with a special focus on policy and programme framers, implementation and development agencies, law enforcement machinery and the judiciary, as well as non-governmental organizations will be undertaken. Other measures will include:

(a) Promoting societal awareness to gender issues and women's human rights.

(b) Review of curriculum and educational materials to include gender education and human rights issues.

(c) Removal of all references derogatory to the dignity of women from all public documents and legal instruments.

(d) Use of different forms of mass media to communicate social messages relating to women's equality and empowerment.

Panchayati Raj Institutions

15.1 The 73rd and 74th Amendments (1993) to the Indian Constitution have served as a breakthrough towards ensuring equal access and increased participation in political power structure for women. The PRIs will play a central role in the process of enhancing women's participation in public life. The PRIs and the local self Governments will be actively involved in the implementation and execution of the National Policy for Women at the grassroots level.

Partnership with the Voluntary Sector Organizations

16.1 The involvement of voluntary organizations, associations, federations, trade unions, non-governmental organizations, women's organizations, as well as institutions dealing with education, training and research will be ensured in the formulation, implementation, monitoring and review of all policies and programmes affecting women. Towards this end, they will be provided with appropriate support related to resources and capacity building and facilitated to participate actively in the process of the empowerment of women.

International Cooperation

17.1 The Policy will aim at implementation of international obligations/commitments in all sectors on empowerment of women such as the Convention on All Forms of Discrimination Against Women (CEDAW), Convention on the Rights of the Child (CRC), International Conference on Population and Development (ICPD+5) and other such instruments. International, regional and sub-regional cooperation towards the empowerment of women will continue to be encouraged through sharing of experiences, exchange of ideas and technology, networking with institutions and organizations and through bilateral and multi-lateral partnerships.

CHANGING NATURE OF INDIAN STATE AND OBSTACKLES TO ADIVASI EMPOWERMENT—A CASE STUDY OF BASTAR IN CHATHISGARH

Gunti Ravinder

The Liberal Democratic Political System in India is making efforts to empower different sections of civil society by adopting various development strategies. The Indian state, as such, is engaged in positive interventions to bring qualitative change in the living patterns of people. In the process, the nature of classical Indian state of early 1950s in drastically changed and it has acquired a new and unique nature of a technocratic state. This technocratic state is governed and guided mainly by technical advisors, commercial interests and mining magnets. Though the new form of its nature appeals for development and excessive use of technology for the social progress, at the operational stages it bewilders certain communities like adivasis with its policies of evacuation and expansionism.

Particularly, these policies have created a fear psychosis in the minds of adivasis of Chhattisgarh. The present paper analyses the opposition of adivasis of Dantewada in Chhattisgarh to the policies of Indian government in matters of mining, exploitation of natural resources and evacuation of Native Adivasis in the name of Green Hunt.

Indian State with its powerful apparatus is making all efforts to global and local commercial interests to exploit the mines and minerals. The Multi National Corporations like Vedanta, Posco, Tata, Jhindal, Laxmi Mittal and Essar are given freehand to penetrate in to reserved forest inhabitations of Adivasis and evacuate them to have free access over natural resources.

The governments both Centre and State are resorting to violence and large scale violation of human rights. For the last ten years or more, nearly sixteen lakhs people in Andhra, Chhattisgarh, Jharkhand and Orissa are displaced. Out of these displaced, eighty percent of are adivasis. In these four states around eighty special economic zones (SEZs) are contemplated and the chathigarh state has even offered a congenial mining policy for the benefit of multi-nationals and powerful commercial interests of domestic market. Between 2001-2009, its has undertaken 113 MOUs and declared concessions, tax holidays and other facilities. There are around 28 valuable minerals available on chathigarh soil ready for exploitation.

In the process of inviting the commercial interests, the state government compels the native adivasis to oblige for evacuation. This confrontation between the administrative machinery coupled with Para Military Forces and Adivasi population raises certain serious questions of adivasi survival, human rights violation and violence and counter violence against Adivasis.

In the attacks of Operation Green Hunt (it is more appropriate to call this as Operation Greed Hunt), at least 70 innocent adivasis were murdered in the districts of Dantewada and Bijapur in Chhattisgarh alone. The reports in *Tehelka magazine*, one of the few magazines that displays the courage to bring to light the facts—whatever be the magazine's actual views regarding the ongoing movements, the organizations leading them, and the ideologies subscribed by those leading those movements— have exposed some of the atrocities in Dantewada, Lalgarh, Orissa and elsewhere. These facts, which are glaringly evident even to the naked eye, have been blacked out by the entire mainstream media that is now addicted to the more remunerative "paidnews" culture with an occasional harmless exposure.

In Chhattisgarh, there have been at least 120 murders of innocent adivasis in the year 2009 by the central and state forces. Central Home Minister has been pushing aggressively to deploy more forces to carry out the state-organized mayhem and massacres. But the media hardly speaks against these crimes against humanity. Our direct enquiry into the murder, destruction of property and burning down of the houses of adivasis by the specially-trained elite CoBRA force when they began their Operation Greed Hunt in the middle of September brought several startling facts into light—facts that are irrefutable and glaring to the naked eye. An arms factory near Singanamadugu village in Kishtaram area of Dantewada district and gunning down 12 Maoists after losing six CoBRA personnel including two assistant commandants. The government claimed that it was the first major success against the Maoists. Innumerable stories and analyses appeared in the media. But what are the facts?

On September 17, 2009 hundreds of CoBRA, CRPF, Chhattisgarh police and SPOs raided six villages—Singanamadugu, Palachelima, Gattapadu, Gacchampalli, Ethrajpadu and Endapadu. A police raid means indiscriminate murders, cruel tortures, abductions, rape of women, burning down houses, stealing chicken, pigs and goats, looting money and property of adivasis, destruction of adivasi belongings and other atrocities. Ever since the state-sponsored salwa judum came into existence in June 2005 adivasis of Dantewada and Bijapur have understood from their own direct experience that a visit by the police only meant a virtual reign of terror on the hapless adivasis. That is why the adivasis generally flee their homes and take shelter in the forest whenever they come to know that police are coming to their villages. In the eyes of the adivasis policemen are not a breed of the human species. They are looked upon as some alien beasts of prey that know only murder, rape and torture. While the adivasis have been living in the forest for ages without any fear of the wild beasts of the jungle, they shudder at the very thought of the salwajudum and paramilitary forces who commit pre-meditated sadistic murders and other atrocities on everyone right from a child to a disabled old person. The hatred and wrath against the police is so intense among the adivasis that they would not hesitate a bit to hack a policeman to pieces if he falls into their hands. Those who let out shrill cries about the "cruelty", "inhumanity" and the "senseless killings" of the Maoists should realize why the peace-loving adivasis are driven to such a situation. One can only understand it if one were to experience the inhuman murders, rapes, tortures, abductions, destruction and looting of property, mental and physical harassment and endless police atrocities on almost a daily basis. It would not be an exaggeration to say that the adivasis had no proper sleep particularly since the state-sponsored Salwa Judum began its murderous campaign accompanied by the central and state police forces.

The fundamental rights guaranteed by the Indian Constitution have never been known to the millions of adivasis. All this is evident to anyone who visits the adivasi villages. But visiting the adivasi villages is not an easy thing. It requires great courage and preparedness to undertake the risk of even losing one's life. In the police state of Chhattisgarh where only the diktat of the police runs virtually everything from the civil administration to the media, where salwa judum goons and mercenary SPOs attack anyone who dares to investigate facts, beat up and lynch anyone from "outside" who dares to enter the adivasi villages, it indeed requires enormous guts to undertake such a venture. Chief

Minister has been inviting the civil rights activists and other outsiders to visit Dantewada and Bijapur districts to taste the state sponsored "adivasi wrath" against whoever spoke in favour of the Maoists (in actual terms it means speaking against police atrocities). And when the visits did take place, the CM had let loose his state-sponsored salwa judum on the fact finding teams and others. Thus the police state in Chhattisgarh has ensured that the countless crimes perpetrated by its various repressive wings do not get publicized and that only the police stories do the rounds in the media. That is how the 12 adivasis who were murdered by the CoBRAs on September 17 became Maoists in police jargon and the media had become an accomplice by propagated this white lie. Let us look at the gory happenings of September 17 to understand the truth behind the barrage of lies floated by the police and C.M. of Chhattisgarh. Basing on information that Maoists had gathered at a place near Singanamadugu village, the central forces, state police and SPOs led by CoBRA force surrounded the area on the night of September 16th itself. The people have been generally vigilant about the police attacks but this time the forces had managed to approach the area secretly with the help of a police agent and the people had no idea until the next morning when the attack began.

On the 17th morning the adivasis of Singanamadugu village commenced their daily chores. Suddenly they heard continuous firing and they knew that the guerrilla camp in the proximity of the village was attacked by the police forces. They fled the village on hearing the shots. The guerrillas too retreated safely from their camp after putting up resistance for some time. But Madivi Deval, a resident of the village had gone to the neighbouring village of Chinna Kedwal the previous day. When he was proceeding to his village in the morning the police abducted him, tortured him cruelly and murdered him. They even took away his dead body. Deval has left behind his wife and three children.

The youngest child is just 4 months old. The mother and wife of Deval were not aware of his fate for some days. They thought he might have been in Chinna Kedwal but when the people of Kedwal informed them that Deval had left for Singanamadugu on 17th early morning they were worried. They found the cycle and chappals of Deval at the place of his abduction and initially they thought he might have fled into the forest upon hearing the shots. They were eagerly waiting for his return. But by 21st it became clear to them that Deval was murdered by the police. Three villagers from Thummal village were forcibly brought to Singanamadugu by the police when they went for the raid on September 17th. Deval was shot dead in front of the three villagers and they were forced to carry the dead body to Chintagufa. Police buried Deval's dead body in Chintagufa. They did not even have the humanity to hand over the dead body to his family members. It was only after the Thummal villagers revealed this that the family members of Deval and other people came to know about the murder. They also showed the spot where Deval was shot dead by the police and the blood-marks were still there four days after the ghastly murder. The family members who were deprived of even having a last glimpse of the dead body of Deval by the inhuman killing by the police.

On the same day the numbering around 300 raided Gachampalli village. Those who could flee on sighting the police were saved. The few who could not make it due to old age and physical disabilities became victims of police atrocity. One of the unfortunate ones who fell into the hands of these khaki mercenaries was 70-year-old Dudi Muye. Both her legs were disabled due to some disease. Hence when everyone fled she could not do anything even as Cobras advanced towards her. When her house was set on fire she asked why they were burning her house a second time (the police had burnt down some time ago). The CoBRAs became furious and shot her thrice. Her dead body was left behind and there were bullets in her chest, thigh and leg. The brutal shooting down of Dudi Muye was witnessed by her neighbor who hid herself in the nearby maize field and thus saved herself. The second batch of Cobras found Adamal and his wife Jogi tilling their field. They first caught Adamal and then his wife whose attempts to flee did not succeed. Both were stripped naked by tearing down the clothes with a knife and they were taken into the village thrashing them all the way. Around the same time they also caught Chulal who was tilling his field along with his son Jogal. He managed to escape upon seeing the Cobras but Chulal fell into their hands. His wife Muke too was picked up by the police from another place. Kowasi Pojje and her 12-year-old daughter Bhime were arrested from their homes. Both Muke and Pojje were stripped naked.

All these arrested adivasi villagers were taken to the village community centre where they were made to squat. Adamal and Chulal were first shot dead; while doing this Cobras shouted at the wives of the two men to witness how their husbands were dying. After murdering the two men they cut off the penis of Adamal. The cruelty exhibited by these death squads is horrifying. Such is the "rule of law" without which the democracy would collapse like a pack of cards. Cries of death shattered the peace of the place where the adivasi boys and girls used to perform dances with great glee. After this atrocity the house of Adamal and Jogi was burnt down. Later the three women were dragged in to the bushes in the centre of the village and raped. Yet another batch of Cobras found a 60-year-old Madivi Jogal who stayed in his house hoping that the police may not do harm to old-aged men. His wife Gangi too stayed back with her husband dropping her instinctual urge to flee. But Jogal was mistaken about the element of humanity he though the invaders might have. These were poisonous Cobras sent all the way to Dantewada by the powers in Delhi. They do not discriminate between old and young, men and women. Their fangs can sting anyone. Both Jogal and his wife were thrown to the ground and beaten severely as a result of which all the teeth were broken. Later Jogal was shot dead and Gangi was stripped naked and raped. Old age too does not dissuade these rapists sent by the Centre. Their house was burnt down. Gangal was another old-aged man who became a victim of state terror in the village that day.

This 70-year-old had lost vision in both the eyes and hence had no other option than to stay back in his house when the Cobras arrived. He was caught and cruelly tortured: his hands were broken, stabbed several times with knives and peeled out parts of his flesh. Then they left him to die a slow and painful death. They burned down his house before leaving the village. After the tormentors left the village those who had fled returned. Gangal's children tried to make him drink some water. Gangal said he would not live and within a short while breathed his last. Thus in this village of about 70 houses five adivasis were murdered. The houses of four of them—Muye, Gangal, Adamal and Jogal—were burnt down. Besides these, the houses of Madivi Idumal, Kowasi Ungi, Kowasi Kosal, Muchhaki Bheema, Sodi Mangdu, Sodi Ita, Sodi Somal, Sodi Jogal, Madivi Madal were also burnt. The meager belongings of these poor adivasis like food grains, clothes, utensils, cycles and radios were reduced to ashes. Money was looted from these houses: Rs. 800 from Dudi Bheemal's house, 1000 from Madivi Jogi's house, 500 from Kowasi Kosa's house, 200 from Madivi Madal, 3300 from Sodi Mangu, 2000 from SodiSomal, 3500 from Sodi Ital. Gold valued at Rs. 7000 was burnt along with the house of Kowasi Rajal. These might seem trivial to outsiders but they are a treasure for the adivasis whose sweat and tears had gone to earn these sums of money. The police took into custody Adamal's wife Jogi, Chulal's wife Muke, Jogal's wife Gangi, Pojje and her daughter Bheeme, Sodi Kosi and her five-year-old daughter, and a deaf old man named Madivi Madal. Jogi, Muke, Pojje and Gangi were raped by the Cobras and other policemen accompanying them. Even 12-year-old Bheeme was sexually harassed by squeezing her breasts and hitting her private part with the rifle.

The police stayed only for 30 minutes in this village. They would not dare to stay longer fearing attacks by Maoist guerrillas. Their motto is: *"Kill all, Burn all and Destroy all"* In the 30 minutes they took the lives of five innocent adivasis. Raped four women. (*Many more would have suffered the same fate had they not escaped into the forest upon seeing the policemen.)* Set on fire 16 houses belonging to 14 families. Burnt property of the villagers. Looted thousands of rupees from the houses. Of the five people who were murdered by the police three are old-aged men and physically disabled. None of the dead or arrested no relation with Naxals. Then why did the police and central paramilitary forces indulge in such cruelty and murdered old harmless people?

The abducted villagers were taken up to Kollai village. These villagers had lost all hope that they would live to see their families again particularly after the horrors they had witnessed in the village committed by these beasts which knew no mercy. But as they approached the village of Kollai there was sudden firing from the people's militia which created panic among the Cobras and other police forces. Moreover, there was heavy downpour. Taking advantage of this condition all the abducted villagers managed to escape using the cover of the trees and bushes. The terror of September 17 still haunted them. Most of them stayed in temporary houses deep inside the forest.

From Gachampalli we went to Gattapadu. The police raided this village between 10 and 11 on the morning of September 17. The most of the people were staying outside their village during nights. In this village three adivasis—Paddam Deval, Sodi Masal and Dudi Pojjal—were shot dead by the police. Two other villagers—Dudi Kosal and Dudi Ungal—were let off after severe beating. Deval has a small child who has not even completed its first year. Then we went to Palachelima village. Here three adivasi villagers—Tuniki Sinnal (35), Sodi Sanesh (43) and Dudi Adamal (35) were brutally murdered by the police. The police went to the village between 10 and 11 on 17th morning. Immediately they picked up 16 people and beat them severely. They tried to take them away to enact another fake encounter to claim that 16 Maoists were eliminated by the forces to provide security to the exploiting rulers. However, they were prevented by the people of the entire village. Family members of the arrested people including children clung to them and did not let them be whisked away. The tussle between the police and the women and children of the village went on till 5 in the evening. The police threatened that they would shoot all of them dead but the people did not budge. At last, the had to let off the arrested people. They demolished the martyrs' column in the village built in memory of a Maoist leader comrade Sukhdev. When these police were leaving the village in the evening another batch of salwajudum and Para military forces arrived on the scene. As soon as they came they arrested Sinnal, Sanesh and Adamal. Sanesh was in the house of Adamal when the police arrived. Sinnal was in his house nearby. All the three were taken away as soon as they were arrested lest the others offer resistance. Tuniki Sinnal also known as Ramakrishna has a wife named Veere, father Ramulu and two children. Eldest is 8 years and the younger is less than a year old. Wife Veere was not in the village when her husband was taken away by the police. She had been to another village and came to know about the arrest of Sinnal only two days later. Sinnal has a brother who is studying in school. His sister Muthi married Sanesh who too was murdered by the police. Sanesh has two siblings: one is two-year-old and another is still suckling milk. Sanesh has a mother named Budri.

The family's tragedy after losing the two working men is indescribable. How would the old parents and four children and the women survive? How are Home Minister and CM of Chathisgarh going to achieve victory over the Maoists by murdering such innocent adivasi villagers and ruining entire families? Is this how Central Home Minister wants to reclaim territories held by Maoists and the type of development he and CM of Chhattisgarh want to achieve?

All these came to mind as I watched the unfortunate children of Sinnal and Sanesh who would never again see their fathers and, as they grow up, would never even know how they looked like. Adamal who was picked up in the house of Sanesh has a wife named Gangi, father Sukhram and mother Ite. He has no children. After the three were taken away that evening their family members went to the police station in Kishtaram in the early hours. But they were scared to enter the station and stayed at a distance hoping to see their loved ones. Some people who met them told them that three people were shot.

Dead and their dead bodies dressed in olive green uniforms were brought to the station. As the three who were picked up in Palachelima were in lungis their relatives though that the dead were some others. But when the reporters showed the photos they broke into tears. Their men had suddenly become dalam members wearing guerrilla uniforms.

Of the six who were taken away from Gattam and Palachelime villages five were shot dead near the road between Nallabelli and Gollapalli. Adamal was murdered near Pydagudem which was at a short distance from there. The family members went to the spot where their beloved ones were murdered. But what remained there was dried up blood and pieces of clothes worn by the dead. They took those pieces of clothes to preserve as the last symbols of their beloved ones. At the spot where Adamal was murdered his towel was found. All his clothes were torn into pieces. "Even his underwear was torn up. Nothing was left behind by the murderers" wailed his wife with deep agony.

"Why didn't they kill my son in the village itself? At least we would have had his dead body," cried out Adamal's mother. Her pain at not having performed the last rites for his son was evident in her words. In adivasi society the dead are buried and the personal belongings are kept over near the burial place. But the sent by Central Home Minister and CM of Chathisgarh did not even have the humanity to hand over the dead and their belongings to their families. *"Even if they had killed my husband they should have done it in the village. Why did they have to do it at an unknown place and prevent us from seeing their dead bodies?"* said Sinnal's wife Veere and Sanesh's wife Gangi. In those words is the ingrained understanding that the Indian state is not their state, that they had no fundamental rights and that the enemy state would kill people like them. But at least they felt, the dead bodies could be given. Their state of mind shows the pathetic situation in our democracy where a significant section of the population does not even know that they have some rights that are supposed to be inalienable and guaranteed by the Constitution.

Why can't Central Home Minister and CM of Chhattisgarh and implement the laws of the land that the dead body of anyone found dead should be handed over to their relatives? As per the law the police should publish the photographs of the dead body of even an unidentified person but in the tale of endless tragedy of Dantewada the police had not only committed heinous cold-blooded murders after picking up adivasi villagers right from their homes in the face of protests by their kith and kin, but had even refused to hand over the dead bodies. The DGP and his police tribe had deprived the adivasi families even the basic human right guaranteed by civilized societies the world over to bury their dead. This inhumanity is not just the characteristic feature of these uniformed police. It permeates the entire political establishment: our Rulers and all the vultures who rule this country watch this tragedy of citizens of their own country without any feeling of guilt at what their mercenaries are doing to poor adivasis. Why should they, when all these inhuman episodes are actually a part of their own hideous plan to evict the entire adivasi community from their homes and thereby pave way for the entry of the tiny corporate elite in whose class interests they were brought to power? Criminal silence is maintained by those ruling our country even as heart-rending stories of mass murders, rapes, abductions, tortures of innocent unarmed Adivasi villagers, gagging of the media and a virtual news blackout by the police at the point of gun, obstruction of fact-finding teams and protests, abound in a section of the media.

Who will assume responsibility for the tragic deaths of Madivi Deval of Singanamadugu; Dudi Muye, Adamal, Chulal, Madivi Jogal and Gangal of Gachampalli; Paddam Deval, Sodi Masal and Dudi Pojjal of Gattapadu; Tuniki Sinnal (35), Sodi Sanesh (43) and Dudi Adamal of Palachelima? And such "encounters" with the "Maoists" go on unabated: the protests by the kith and kin of the dead adivasis, by the civil rights activists and others of civil society have no affect at all on the thick-skinned lawless goons going in the name of security forces who are given complete immunity by the rulers whatever be the inhuman crimes committed by them. Goompad is another village that has been a witness to the murder of nine adivasis on October 1, 2009 who were again shown by The police as Maoists. Ever since then the eye-witness to the gruesome murders, Sodi Sambo, also injured by a police bullet in her leg, is being shadowed round-the-clock to make her into another Zahira, or bump her off. The state government of Chhattisgarh and the congress-led UPA government at the Centre are leaving no stone unturned to silence the eye-witness lest the secret of their encounters of Maoists becomes public. Even when Sodi Sambo is admitted for treatment in the AIIMS in Delhi, the police are "guarding" her. Then there are encounters of seven "Maoists" in Tetemadugu, Dokpad and Palodi near

Kistaram on December 10th. Another three Maoists were murdered in such encounter between Pamulvai and Pallewada in Bijapur district on December 23. Then there are adivasis who are abducted by the police and nothing more is heard of them until their photographs suddenly appear in papers as dead Maoists. 24 such adivasis are still "mysteriously missing" from Burkapal, Elma Gonda and Minpa villages falling under Chintagupha police station area between 7th-9th November 2009. These adivasis, abducted by the CoBRAs, CRPF and SPOs, might anytime reappear as dead bodies of "Maoists killed in encounters". One of the horrific methods used by DGP and his police thugs is to abduct villagers, keep them in illegal police custody as long as they need, and when they want some results to be shown in their war against Maoists, murder them and present them as "Maoists" killed in encounters. They imagine this would keep up the sagging morale of their men who are brought in from various parts of the country.

Our Democracy allows such abductions and murders by the state's forces without any questions ever being raised let alone punishing the culprits. The latest incident of encounter claimed by CM of Chhattisgarh government is the murder of 12 "Maoists" in Bijapur district. They, however, said they could not find a single body and that all the 12 bodies were taken away by the retreating Maoists. Every murder, rape, abduction, torture and atrocity creates anger and hatred generated by these atrocities would burst out like a volcano.

Conclusion: The changed nature of Indian State from a classical socialistic pattern of state to Technocratic State raises certain important questions with regard to the survival of marginalized communities.

(a) In the name of social progress and under the guise of development, the State facilitates ruthless exploitation of nature and natural resources. Any quarter that opposes this ruthless process in branded as anti-constitutional, Maoists and anti development.

(b) On the 'Modus Operandi' of development and development strategies, the Liberal Democratic System should allow political space for divergent views in any civil society. The view on alternative politics, opinion on development strategies need not be considered as anti-State.

(c) In the process of implementing its policies, the State compels the people to evacuate their traditional inhabitations. Opposition to such policies and protest against this process in ruthlessly crushed with negative intervention by using paramilitary and police forces. Besides these police and Para Military structures, atrocious and unconstitutional outfit like SALWA JUDUM are created to expedite the harassment and human rights violations. The whole programme of GREEN HUNT is meant to serve commercial interests and encourages violence and counter-violence between state and adivasis. Infact outfits of like salwa judum are being operated to perform the role of both violence and counter-violence. In a way the Indian State by itself violating the written guarantees on human rights enshrined in Part III of the constitution.

(d) The political executive and bureaucracy are over active and proactive to provide harmonious atmosphere for MNCs and other commercial interests and the interests of the grassroots and downtrodden are grossly neglected. In fact the violence perpetuated by police and Para military has also attracted stiff indictment from judiciary (Supreme Court) and other political structures like national human rights commission.

(e) The social movements of the anxious adivasis are met with ruthless crushing and the administration creates fear and insecurity in minds of outsiders who express their solidarity with the cause of adivasis. This is leading to a state of alienation and social exclusion in the minds of adivasis.

(f) In the initial years of independence, Pundit Nehru gave a call for a tribal panchasheel to provide autonomy with a slogan 'Live and Let Live the Tribal's alone' with due respect to their distinct cultural specificities. But the contemporary thinking negates the Nehruvian idea and enforce 'Absorb their lives and kill themselves alone' with its policies of ruthless oppression and exploitation without any outside solidarity pangs of alienation to adivasis.

Theoretically Indian state provides all the written safeguards for human survival and human rights. But in practice, the interests of the downtrodden and marginalized communities, particularly the adivasis are endangered with the changing nature of its policies. The governments both at centre and state are resorting to violence and counter-violence.

In this context, it is the compelling obligation of all the intelligential, scholars, researchers and others to show their solidarity and express sympathy towards their problems. The initiatives like the GREEN HUNT that creates liquidation, insecurity and displacement among adivasis should be dispersed with. The natural rights of adivasis over the forest and forest products should be acknowledged. They should have the rights on land, resources and culture.

References

Aravind Kumar: Tribal Development and Planning, Anmol Publications, New Delhi.

Prof. K. Seetha Rama Rao: Rights of Adivasis and the State in Indian *Journal of Human Rights*, Vol. II No. 1&2, 1998, University of Hyderabad, Hyderabad.

Sharma B. D., "Constitutional Provisions for the Scheduled Tribe : An Overview, *The Great Concern*, Vol. 20, No. 2, 1993, pp. 38-40.

Dr. B. Janardhan Rao :Forest Policies in India, Krushi Publications, Warangal, 1993.

Oommen, T. K. (ed.), (2010), Social Movements I & II, Oxford University Press, New Delhi.

Govind Prasad and Anil Dutta Mishra (Ed); Globlisation-Myth and Reality. Concept Publishing Company, New Delhi, 2004.

K. Venugopal : Evaridhee Ghathukam, Oct. 16th *Andhra Jyothi,* 2007.

Markendeya: Mad Gondulu - Jeevitham, July 22nd *Andhra Jyothi,* 2009.

Arundathi Roy: The Heart of India is Under Attack, Times of India.

Dr. Vara Vara Rao : Abivruddi Namoonapy Charcha, July 30th *Andhra Jyothi,* 2009.

Aravind Kumar: Tribal Development and Planning, Anmol Publications, New Delhi.

Arundathi Roy: Walking with the Comrades, Outlook, March, 2010.

Aman Sethi : Green Hunt: The Anatomy of an Operation, Feb. 6th Hindu, 2010.

Aman Sethi : Police Killed Villagers, say Goompadu Witnesses, Feb. 22nd Hindu, 2010.

DEBT AMONG NATIONS: A CASE OF DISEMPOWERMENT OF ENTIRE SOCIETIES AND COUNTRIES

G. Ram Reddy

The discourse around the notion of empowerment usually looks at problems that are internal to particular societies and particular countries. It is therefore common to hear about the problem of empowerment of lower caste groups in India or that of the Hispanics and African Americans in the United States of America and also that of women in traditional and conservative societies such as the Islamic societies. Not too much effort goes into the understanding of certain problems that can disempower whole nations. In the decades that preceded the 1990s it was common to hear analyses of debt traps and the whole range of problems associated with them. But with the latest round of globalization which has seen countries such as India and China come out of the ranks of the third world and with the disappearance of the Soviet Union which pledged support to societies that were post colonial and struggling under the weight to debt the vocabulary of debt related problems has taken a back seat. But that does not mean that the problem has disappeared. There are all the countries of the third world which are still in the same problem of not finding debt relief and therefore at the mercy of developed countries and global financial institutions such as the World Bank and the IMF. The original problem of dependency and the debt was in the Latin American region which was effectively the back yard of the United States of America. Despite varied attempts aimed at breaking the debt trap the Latin American countries, especially Argentina, have still to find an effective way out of debt. One of the more talked about and touted plans has been the "Washington Consensus"[1].

The expression "Washington Consensus" is only useful if interpreted as a short for "Washington support for the Latin American Consensus". By the mid 1980's a Consensus emerged among economists and democratic political leaders all across Latin America on the need to introduce "new rules of the game" for the national economies in order to defeat hyperinflation and renew growth. But these reforms could not be successfully implemented unless Washington would provide help to free Latin American nations from the Debt Trap. Washington support came with the Bush and Clinton Administrations. But seems to have "gone with the wind" of the Bush Administration. On the Latin American side the consensus started to disappear with Chavez in Venezuela and Duhalde in Argentina. It needs to be examined if the lack of Washington support for the disappearing Latin American Consensus will make room for better reforms or will simply consolidate the very discouraging current landscape in Latin America. Or, even worst, will recreate the situation of the 70's and 80's.

In the aftermath of the WWII, ideological discussions in the world focused on the dichotomy Socialism versus Capitalism. Naturally this dichotomy embodied the economic aspect of the East-West confrontation that characterized the Cold War. Latin American countries tried not to get involved in this confrontation adopting what Juan Domingo Perón, who was the Argentine President at the time, called "The Third Position". These ideas would be the seed of the Not Aligned Countries Movement, which in turn several developing countries joined. At the same time, in

Latin America economic academic thinking moved towards the so called "Structuralism" as opposed to the "Orthodoxy" that had prevailed in previous decades. "Structuralism" looked like the "Keynesianism" of the Developing World. A good account of the Structuralist School is offered by Rhys Jenkins in the book entitled Industrialization and Development edited by Hewitt, Johnson and Wield. "Structuralism" gave intellectual support to the Import Substitution Industrialization (ISI) growth strategy and the Populist Macroeconomic Policies that most Latin American governments implemented since the mid forties until the eighties with varied intensity. The economic organization and the economic policies suggested by "Structuralism "were functional to the political regimes that prevailed in most Latin American countries in those years: either civilian governments in corporate state democracies or military dictatorships. For them "Statism" was a way to accumulate and preserve political power.

The only case of a military dictatorship that implemented economic reforms departing from the Structuralist Policies was Chile under Pinochet. But the very fact that the Economic Liberal Reforms had been decided and implemented by a repressive regime had added more passion to an already heated debate. Even though very informative from the economic point of view, the Chilean Experience could not be easily digested by the political leaders of the emerging democratic regimes of Latin America during the 80's. In Mexico and Brazil, strong criticism to the Import Substitution Industrialization growth strategy began to be heard only after the eruption of the Debt Crisis in 1982. Indeed, economic discussions had started to take place prior to 1982 analyzing whether the development strategy based on the ISI model was exhausted. These discussions overlapped with a few, but not really frequent, episodes of Populist Macroeconomic Policies based on the Structuralist mindset. But, all in all, the ISI growth strategy had delivered rapid growth in both countries during the period 1945-1982. The good results had been undisputable until the first oil crisis in 1973, and the difficulties created by the commodity crisis of the 70's had been overcome by readily available foreign financing. By the mid 80's the criticism regarding the Import Substitution Industrialization growth strategy that had emerged at the time of the Debt Crisis became strong and convincing because the difference in economic performance between East Asia and Latin America during the period 1965-80 spoke by itself[2].

In Argentina the evidence against the policies recommended by Structuralism were even more eloquent and came from a different comparison. Until the WWII, Argentina had achieved a standard of living quite close to that enjoyed by the most advanced countries in the world. This was the outcome obtained from the combination of its vigorous international trade, its infrastructure and its education system. In turn, the implementation of the Import Substitution Industrialization strategy along with Populist Macroeconomic Policies produced a disappointing outcome instead. The disappointing consequence of implementing the last set of policies was a stagnant economy suffering high levels of inflation since the mid 1970s. The Argentine case when compared to countries with similar endowment of human and natural resources such as Canada and Australia shows that there was an obvious divergence among the economic performances of those countries from the WWII on. What then are the reasons of Argentina's backwardness? The disappointing performance of Argentina after the WWII was due to a certain institutional misplace, which had been a consequence of the trade and macroeconomic policies implemented thereafter. In a well-organized mixed economy, resources are efficiently allocated by means of the signals sent by relative prices. Relative prices, in turn, are determined in competitive markets. On the other hand, redistributive policies are explicitly included in the government's Budget.

In Argentina, on the contrary, those instruments of economic policy had switched roles. Instead of being instrumental in the efficient allocation of resources, relative prices were controlled by the government aiming at redistributing income. On the other hand, instead of playing a role in the redistribution of income, the government's Budget aimed at allocating investment and employment. This work along with the work of other authors laid the foundation of our position on the matter. We explained that Argentina's problem was not that it had too much Capitalism as Structuralists argued, nor was it that it had too much Socialism as the Orthodox Economists said. The real problem was that it has a poor combination of both Capitalism and Socialism. Its economy was a mix of "Capitalism without a Market and Socialism without a Plan." The New Rules Plan was never accepted by the United States Administration and therefore the debt trap was never broken. In fact, the 1990s saw spiraling inflation in Argentina that led to a huge economic and political crisis, out of which the country is only just limping[3].

THE AFRICAN DEBT TRAP

The Latin American region is not the only one caught in the debt trap. Most African countries are also caught in debt traps that they have not been able to break out of. The World Bank and IMF have been the agencies that have played a very key and pivotal role in the creation and perpetuation of debt traps. The IMF began to specialise in lending to the Third World, providing short term loans to poor countries in Africa and elsewhere that were experiencing trade deficits (ie an excess of imports over exports) and balance of payments crises in the wake of the 1974-75 recession.

The majority of sub-Saharan African countries were particularly vulnerable to downturns in the world economy because of their reliance on a narrow range of price sensitive primary commodity exports (like cocoa, coffee or copper) - a legacy of colonial rule. The slump of the 1970s saw most raw material prices collapse at a time when the cost of oil imports was shooting up. The IMF began to offer short term loans to 'stabilise' these countries' balance of payments. But harsh 'conditionalities' forced borrowers to implement an 'austerity programme' of slashing imports, reducing public expenditure and cutting wages in order to reduce their trade deficits and promptly repay the IMF. A second round of oil price rises and even deeper recession deepened the IMF's hold over the poorest African states. The nominal price of primary commodities fell a staggering 30 per cent between 1980 and 1982; in real terms, allowing for inflation, they hit their lowest level since the end of the Second World War. As one African economy after another effectively collapsed, the fund devoted more of its financing facilities to the region. In 1970-78 only 3 per cent of the IMF's new conditional credit went to Africa, but by 1979-80 this figure reached a very big figure of more than thirty per cent.

Both the IMF and the World Bank were able to consolidate their hold over Africa as a direct consequence of the debt crisis. They now assumed a dual role. They ensured that the commercial banks were repaid by lending African states more money to service their private debts. And they acted as debt collection agencies for the Western powers and themselves, working with the creditor governments through the Paris Club. This is an informal grouping of 19 states (Western Europe, Canada, the US, Japan, Australia, Russia) that aims to squeeze the maximum repayments out of the Third World debtors and ensure they don't default. It divides and rules by insisting all bilateral debts are rescheduled on an individual basis and will only agree to negotiate with a country if it has already signed a debt management agreement with the IMF[4].

The International Financial Institutions also insisted on the repayment of their own multilateral loans on even harsher terms. The charters of the IMF and World Bank specifically forbid debts that they hold to be rescheduled or written off. Moreover, most of this debt is charged at market rates. This is one of the main reasons why Africa's total debt has continued to grow while an ever greater volume of resources has flowed out of the continent.

When the Latin American states came to the brink of default in the early 1980s, the concentration of private bank loans in just three countries threatened to destabilise the entire international financial system by wiping out some of the world's largest banks. The major powers had no choice but to rush in and attempt to rescue the banks through massive bailouts and schemes designed to shift the burden of repayment onto the shoulders of the workers & peasants.

The African debt was quite different. Not only was it small to the point of insignificance in world terms, but it was also spread over a large number of poor countries which had become increasingly dependent on Western aid as well as loans. As such, individual defaults did not present much of a threat to the system. This gave the International Financial Institutions extraordinary leverage over sub-Saharan Africa and, through this, unparalleled capacity to launch the neo-liberal assault[5].

The principal levers of the neo-liberal offensive were the new Structural Adjustment loans of the World Bank and the IMF. Their overarching aim was, in the words of then US Secretary of State, James Baker, 'encouraging the private sector and allowing market forces a larger role in the allocation of resources'.40 This would be achieved through a radical programme of privatisation, liberalisation and reduced public spending that would 'roll back' the state and subject the indebted economies to the full rigours of global competition. Structural Adjustment Programmes (SAPs) had effects in Africa over the course of the 1980s and 1990s which significantly shaped the form and content of the debt relief schemes that followed.

They systematically undermined the formal independence of the African states. The new and powerful conditions attached to the loans enabled the International Financial Institutions to dictate the economic policy of almost the entire continent. Regardless of whether an African country carried the trappings of formal democracy or was the most authoritarian of states, its key ministries were now answerable to the IMF and the World Bank. Their remit was further extended in the 1990s when the World Bank adopted its 'good governance' agenda. Now African states would themselves be re-engineered to complement the market economies forcibly constructed by the earlier wave of reforms.

They significantly boosted the power and profits of the Western multinational corporations operating in Africa. Successive rounds of deregulation stripped the African states of what little control they had previously exercised over the activities of foreign firms. The wholesale privatisation of state-owned industries and utilities simultaneously provided the multinationals with 'public goods' in the form of bargain basement assets that could be stripped, squeezed and sold on. Between 1985 and 1995 the profits repatriated by the multinationals from sub-Saharan Africa rose from $4 billion to $4.5 billion; and by 1997 the rates of return on US direct investments in the continent were, at 25.3 per cent, the highest of any region in the world.

They spectacularly failed in their own terms. The stated aim of 'macroeconomic shock treatment', as the World Bank called it, was to jumpstart growth and get Africa back on its feet. The indebted economies would be reoriented on the world market by shifting them away from industrialisation strategies of the early decades after independence from colonialism. They were to be (re)specialised in a narrow range of raw material and cash-crop exports. As a consequence, sub-Saharan Africa was effectively deindustrialised. But the new surge in primary commodity exports only flooded already saturated markets and forced world prices further down[6].

Africa's fragile and marginalised economies went deeper into crisis. Annual average growth rates fell from a respectable 4 per cent in 1970-79 to 1.7 per cent in 1980-89 and 0.4 per cent in 1990-94. Even the World Bank was forced to admit in 1989 that 'overall Africans are as poor today as they were 30 years ago' and per capita income in sub-Saharan Africa in 2000 was 10 per cent below the level reached in 1980.

They relentlessly assaulted the livelihoods and welfare of Africa's workers, peasants and poor. To take the example of Zambia, there were 140 textile manufacturers employing 34,000 people in 1991; just eight remained by 2000. Formal manufacturing employment fell from 75,400 to 43,320 between 1991 and 1998; and paid employment in agriculture from 78,000 to 50,000 in that decade. Real wages in nearly every African country were estimated to have fallen between 50 and 60 per cent since the imposition of the Structural Adjustment Programmes. Food prices rocketed following the removal of subsidies on staples like maize, while the collapsing health and education sectors fell out of reach of most people thanks to the imposition of user fees.

But there was immense resistance to the SAPs. Anti-IMF strikes and riots broke out across the continent in the 1980s and gathered momentum towards the end of the decade. Protests against the SAPs turned into struggles against the states that were implementing them. Between 1989 and 1992 some 20 African countries were rocked by mass democratisation movements which brought down one government after another. It is against this background that the debt relief schemes now hailed by Brown began to emerge.

On Saturday 11 June 2005 a meeting of the G7 finance ministers in London reached agreement on multilateral debt relief ahead of the July Gleneagles summit. The proposed scheme is a compromise between the rival British and US positions and a third plan put forward by Germany, Japan and France at the last minute. Gordon Brown and his press have hailed the deal as a "historic breakthrough" and the "largest debt write-off ever"[7]. But this is not true.

Multilateral debt relief will apply to an outrageously small number of countries. Only those that have gone through the entire HIPC process will qualify. A mere 18 countries have reached 'completion point' so far; together, they represent just 5% of the total population of the Global South. Poor and indebted countries like Angola, Kenya and Nigeria will continue to be excluded. The colossal debts of 'middle income' countries like Brazil are completely off the G8 radar. The ability of countries to take advantage of multilateral debt relief is entirely dependent on their ability to fulfill their neo-liberal reform programmes to the World Bank and IMF's satisfaction. In the meantime, tens of thousands will continue to die from lack of basic healthcare.

A portion of the multilateral debt of the qualifying countries will be written off, but the amounts involved are small and will lead to reduced aid disbursements for the 'beneficiaries'. At one level, anti-debt campaigners have achieved a small but significant victory by forcing the G8 to establish the principle of 'full' multilateral debt cancellation in the new scheme. Brown was proposing no more than a ten year moratorium on debt service payments and Germany, France and Japan were opposed to even this. Likewise, the inclusion of IMF debt represents a partial retreat on the part of the US, which was adamant that the Fund's debt should remain untouched. However, pressure from below was not the only factor at work in the London deal. Imperialist rivalry also significantly shaped the debt compromise the outcome of which is reflected in both the scope and means of the write-off. To make sense of this, it is useful to briefly outline the different strategic relationships between the G7 states and the International Financial Institutions, and how these manifested in the debt negotiations.

The World Bank, IMF and other multilateral institutions should of course be understood as instruments of the West's collective domination over the Global South. But they are also arenas of the competitive struggle between the major powers as they pursue their distinctive economic and geo-political interests. The broad shift towards US unilateralism under Bush has in part been expressed through a strategy of reducing the role of the World Bank while reinforcing that of the IMF and establishing more bilateral aid and trade agreements with key regions in the Third World. In particular, the Bush administration has increasingly pushed for the World Bank to phase out loans in favour of making grants (aid) and devolve its lending responsibility to regional multilateral banks, like the Inter-American Development Bank, in line with the recommendations of a Congress Commission headed by the conservative academic, Alan Meltzer, which reported in February 2000. The aim is to erode the Bank's centralised creditor power over the Third World and, with it, the leverage of its other major shareholders – like Japan, Germany and to a lesser extent Britain – who are at once America's major competitors.

The appointment of arch-neoconservative Paul Wolfowitz to the World Bank was the most obvious expression of the drive to transform the Bank from the general representative of the advanced capitalist states into a narrower tool of US imperialism. At the same time, America has been strongly opposed to any attempt to weaken both the creditor status of IMF through the sale of its gold, or its bilateral and heavily conditional aid scheme, the Millennium Challenge Account, through Brown's proposal for the multilateral International Finance Facility. By the same token, the other advanced capitalist states have to varying degrees resisted the downgrading of the World Bank, which remains their favoured vehicle for opening up the Global South to their multinationals and retaining a check on US power. This is the main reason why Japan, France and Germany on the one hand, and Britain on the other, formulated debt relief proposals that would keep some, if not most, of the World Bank's multilateral debt stock intact, contra the US position of writing off debts.

The debt deal has been designed to retain World Bank and IMF control, and hence deepen neo-liberal conditionality, in three mutually reinforcing ways. First, and most obviously, the new debt scheme will strengthen and expand the discredited HIPC (Heavily Indebted Poor Countries) approach. At present, the G7's proposal only applies to the countries that were arbitrarily identified for the HIPC initiative by the World Bank in the 1990s and by the same token continues to exclude those that were left out of the original selection. It also significantly increases the incentive for struggling participants to see the whole HIPC process through – and thus the heavy programs of neo-liberal reform that accompany it – as completion is now the only way to become eligible for multilateral, as well as bilateral, debt relief[8]. With this new lease of life, the HIPC scheme will be widened to include a new tranche of 'worthy' poor and indebted countries. The World Bank is said to be drawing up a new list. The International Financial Institutions, and through them the Western powers, will thus not only continue to be the arbiters of who is 'fit' to be relieved of their debt burden, but will also be able to extend this form of neo-liberal control. The Committee for the Cancellation of Third World Debt has summarised the horrors that will be entailed:

"Privatisation of natural resources and of strategic economic sectors to the benefit of transnational corporations; higher cost of health care and education; a rise in VAT; free flow of capital, which leads to capital leaving the country as shown by UNCTAD reports; lower tariff protection, which leads to thousands of small and middle producers losing their livelihoods because they cannot compete with imported goods"[9].

Second, those countries that have passed through HIPC and received multilateral debt relief will be forced to maintain the momentum of neo-liberal reform in order to meet the criteria of the World Bank's Performance Based Allocation (PBA) system – the new prerequisite for clawing back some of their lost aid. Moreover, the PBA system will itself be enhanced to maintain control over these 'beneficiaries'. During the G7 negotiations, Germany, France and Japan argued that full-scale debt relief would "encourage corruption", condone "reckless borrowing" and, above all, "leave the west with few tools to reward countries for good governance". This, of course, was code for their fear that the World Bank would lose its principle means of opening up the economies of the Global South and see a steady erosion of its creditor power in line with US strategic interests. The compromise reached will see the International Financial Institutions report on ways to ensure that the additional finance to the IDA is used for "poverty reduction and does not lead to corruption". The PBA system will also include new "governance and transparency" conditionalities. If 'corruption' in a recipient country is deemed to have increased after debt relief, it will be penalised with reduced aid flows.

Finally, a new mechanism is being devised to ensure that the IMF does not lose control over countries freed of its debts. The US, as we have seen, was strongly opposed to any weakening of the IMF's creditor power and only conceded to a small, internally funded write-off to bury Brown's gold sale plan. But this does not mean that America wants to see the IMF's role reduced after debt relief. On the contrary, US Treasury Secretary John Snow has been working on a new IMF 'facility' – the Policy Support Agreement (PSA) – which will allow conditions to be imposed on developing countries even if they are no longer officially indebted to the IMF or taking loans from it[10].

The net effect of the new multilateral debt initiative will, then, be to entangle developing countries in new and refined forms of neo-liberal conditionality. This in turn ensures that they will remain trapped in perpetual debt. All ready crippled after decades of structural adjustment and confronted with forms of 'debt relief' which effectively reduce resource inflows, the Global South is kept on its knees. Ceaseless neo-liberal restructuring means that as soon as poor countries have one set of debts reduced or cancelled, they are forced to borrow more. Tanzania, which had $2 billion in bilateral debt written off in exchange for years of wrenching HIPC conditionality, has had to continue borrowing. It now has debts of $8.2 million the service on which accounts for 12% of its tiny $3.7 billion national budget. And herein lays the ultimate genius of the G8's debt trap. It provides the illusion of escape, but only through a route which strengthens its grip. It cannot be reformed, only smashed.

The net result is nations and countries that are caught in debt traps find themselves disadvantaged and disempowered. When a country is disempowered it automatically follows that the people of that country are all disempowered. The globalised world in order to be equalitarian will have to find more truthful and sincere ways of writing the debt of the struggling nations off. Chicanery in the creation of relief schemes will ultimately only serve the purpose of postponing a crisis that will ultimately don global proportions and affect even those who may think that they will never be affected.

Notes

1. D. Millet and E. Toussaint. Who Owes Who? Fifty Questions About World Debt (London, 2004), p. 87.
2. A Callinicos, Imperialism Todav , in A Callincos *et al.* Marxism and the New Imperialism (London, 1994), p.35.
3. *ibid.*

4. E. Toussaint. Your Money or Your Life! The Tyranny of Global Finance (London, 1999), p. 198.
5. J. Boyce and L. NTdikumana, 'Africa's Debt: Who Owes Whom?', Political Economy Research Institute Working Paper Series. 48 (2002).
6. L. Harris, The Bretton Woods System and Africa', in B Onimode (ed), The IMF, the World Bank and the African Debt: The Economic Impact (London, 1989).
7. W. Bello, Deglobalization: Ideas for a New World Economy (London, 2004).
8. S. Riley, Debt, Democracy and the Environment in Africa', in S Riley (ed) The Politics of Global Debt (Basingstoke, 1993).
9. *ibid*
10. K. Owusu *et al.*, Through the Eye of a Needle: The Africa Debt Report , Jubilee 2000 Coalition Reports, (London 2000).